THE AMERICAN STORY

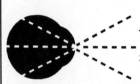

THE AMERICAN STORY

CONVERSATIONS WITH
MASTER HISTORIANS

DAVID M. RUBENSTEIN

THORNDIKE PRESS
A part of Gale, a Cengage Company

LIBRARY OF CONGRESS CIP DATA ON FILE.
CATALOGUING IN PUBLICATION FOR THIS BOOK
IS AVAILABLE FROM THE LIBRARY OF CONGRESS

ISBN-13: 978-1-4328-7618-0 (hardcover alk. paper)

Published in 2020 by arrangement with Simon and Schuster, Inc.

Printed in Mexico
Print Number: 01   Print Year: 2020

*To Alexa, Ellie, and Andrew,
and the teachers of American
history and civics*

CONTENTS

FOREWORD
BY LIBRARIAN OF CONGRESS
CARLA HAYDEN. 13
INTRODUCTION
BY DAVID M. RUBENSTEIN . . 17

1. Jack D. Warren Jr.
   on George Washington 31
2. David McCullough
   on John Adams 75
3. Jon Meacham
   on Thomas Jefferson 107
4. Ron Chernow
   on Alexander Hamilton. 146
5. Walter Isaacson
   on Benjamin Franklin 189
6. Cokie Roberts
   on Founding Mothers 233
7. Doris Kearns Goodwin
   on Abraham Lincoln. 272

7

8. A. Scott Berg
   on Charles Lindbergh 314
9. Jay Winik
   on Franklin Delano Roosevelt . . 357
10. Jean Edward Smith
    on Dwight D. Eisenhower. . . . 393
11. Richard Reeves
    on John F. Kennedy 432
12. Taylor Branch
    on Martin Luther King Jr. and
    the Civil Rights Movement . . . 467
13. Robert A. Caro
    on Lyndon B. Johnson 507
14. Bob Woodward
    on Richard M. Nixon and
    Executive Power 548
15. H. W. Brands
    on Ronald Reagan. 582
16. Chief Justice John G. Roberts Jr.
    on the U.S. Supreme Court . . . 625

ACKNOWLEDGMENTS 663
ABOUT THE
   CONTRIBUTORS 669
IMAGE CREDITS 681

President Abraham Lincoln delivering his second inaugural address, March 4, 1865.

FOREWORD

As Librarian of Congress, I am frequently asked two questions that are similar but come from diametrically opposed assumptions. First, "Is the Library of Congress only for members of Congress?" And second, "Do members of Congress actually use the Library?"

The answer to the first is, no, the Library of Congress is for everyone — and I hope everyone reading this will visit (there is plenty to visit online, even if you can't come to Washington). The answer to the second is a resounding yes, members of Congress use the Library, and they use it all the time and in many different ways.

Members have access to a unit of dedicated experts who provide nonpartisan research and analysis, fielding thousands of queries every year. Members check out books by the thousands. And members use the Library's physical spaces for all kinds of activities. As well, the Library hosts many programs throughout the year — some for broader audiences and some just for members of Congress.

It is in support of our mission to provide information to Congress that the Library has hosted the Congressional Dialogues series. These events are an opportunity for members to come to the Library for an evening built around the study of individuals who have been significant in American history. They feature treasures from the Library collections related to the individuals and topic, illuminated by our historians and curators — and, of course, the main event, a conversation with biographers and historians who have studied and written acclaimed works about these figures. Members have the opportunity to listen, ask questions, and dialogue with the guest author and with each other — a rare opportunity for bipartisan gathering and learning.

I have learned something too, on every one of these occasions. In part that is due to the exceptional interviewer who moderates and asks questions of each guest author, David M. Rubenstein. David is a remarkable person for many reasons. He describes his approach to charitable giving as "patriotic philanthropy." But don't think he has simply coined a phrase. His actions bear this out, in extraordinary ways. In addition to his support of the Library of Congress and its programs, including the National Book Festival, he has made historic contributions to the National Archives, restored the Washington Monument, mounted the panda program at the National Zoo, and too many other endeavors to fully chronicle here. In addition to all this, David and I share a voracious love of reading. It is his reading and preparation that help make these conversations insightful, spirited, and memorable.

Which brings me back to the first question about whether the Library is only for members of Congress. While these sessions are, in fact, for Congress, I am grateful to David for his vision in sharing the portion of these programs devoted to his discussion with the authors. In these pages you will find thoughtful exchanges about some of the giants in history — what motivated them, what scared them, what inspired them? It is my hope you will be inspired as well, to read some of these books in their entirety and expand your understanding of the shared history of our nation.

Carla Hayden
14th Librarian of Congress

INTRODUCTION

The American story is one that surely could not have been foreseen by those who helped to create the United States in 1776, when the Declaration of Independence was adopted, or in 1787, when the Constitution was created.

Who then could have predicted that thirteen colonies would evolve, with many starts and fits, into the world's largest economy, most powerful military force, leading political power, and also — for so many — a leading symbol of liberty, freedom, and justice?

Who then could have predicted that so many extraordinary leaders — men and women, from all kinds of backgrounds, with so many different types of skills and talents — would emerge to create the American story? Who then could have predicted how hard it would be, more than two hundred years later, to convey the depth and breadth of that story to those interested in learning how the United States evolved?

This book is designed, through interviews with leading American historians, to provide a glimpse into the American story.

Why is it so important to know about history?

George Santayana, a Spanish-born Harvard professor of philosophy (among many other subjects), may have said it best: "Those who cannot remember the past are condemned to repeat it." In other words, a knowledge of history is likely to help individuals, and perhaps especially policymakers, to avoid the mistakes of the past, and thereby, one hopes, make better decisions about the future.

To be sure, life (and policymaking) is more complicated than that. Those steeped in a knowledge of history do not always make perfect decisions.

Still, having such knowledge improves the chances of avoiding the mistakes of the past. One of the best ways to acquire it is to read and learn from the painstaking, laborious, read-the-original-documents work of historians. Alfred Nobel did not create a history prize, but that oversight should not be taken to mean that the work of historians in educating us about the past (and, in effect, about the future) is less significant than the work of those who do win Nobel Prizes.

My lifelong interest in history may stem from several factors. Perhaps it came about because my grades in history were better than my other grades, or perhaps because I was fortunate at a young age to work on Capitol Hill and in the White House — two places at the center of American history. Or perhaps because I became involved with trying to preserve historic documents and historic buildings.

After college at Duke University and law school at the University of Chicago, I practiced law in New York, worked for the late Senator Birch Bayh of Indiana and President Jimmy Carter, and then practiced law in Washington, D.C. My career did not lead anyone to think that I had the skill set or background to enter the investment world. Most especially was that true of my mother, who thought I should always keep my law license in case my investment efforts went south. And, to please her, I have remained to this day a member of the D.C. Bar.

In 1987, I started the first buyout firm in Washington with three others, each of whom, fortunately, had a background in finance. The firm — the Carlyle Group — became one of the world's largest private-equity firms. And its success enabled me to indulge a bit more my love of reading, books, and history.

In 2007, I heard that the only privately owned copy of Magna Carta was going to be sold at Sotheby's. I was invited to view this historic document a day before the sale. I was told that this copy, also the only one in the U.S., would likely be sold to a buyer from outside the country.

I knew enough about American history to know that Magna Carta was the inspiration for the Declaration of Independence, and that the American colonies had generally been created with charters that guaranteed the colonists the rights of Englishmen. The colonists believed that included the Magna Carta principle of no taxation without representation.

To ensure that at least one copy of Magna Carta stayed in the U.S., I decided to try to buy the document the next night. I succeeded, and immediately placed it on permanent loan to the National Archives, so that all visitors could see this unique charter of Western democracy.

Subsequently, I bought other rare copies of historic documents — the Declaration of Independence, the Emancipation Proclamation, the Constitution, the Bill of Rights, the Thirteenth Amendment — and placed them on public display at places like the Smithsonian Institution, the National Constitution Center, Mount Vernon, the Library of Congress, and the National Archives. My hope was that as more visitors saw these historic documents, they would be inspired to learn about the history surrounding them.

I had a similar perspective when I began

helping to restore a number of historic monuments, memorials, and homes. That undertaking began in 2011, when I helped finance the restoration of the earthquake-damaged Washington Monument. Later, I agreed to provide the lead funding to restore or rehabilitate Monticello, Montpelier, the Arlington House at Arlington National Cemetery, the Iwo Jima Memorial, the Lincoln Memorial, the Belmont-Paul Women's Equality National Monument, and the Kennedy Center for the Performing Arts, the living memorial to President John F. Kennedy in Washington, D.C.

Here too my hope was that if we made these buildings more appealing to visit, more Americans would do so. And the result might be an enhanced interest in learning more about American history.

I called the effort to preserve historic documents and buildings "patriotic philanthropy." By that I mean philanthropy designed to educate Americans about their history and heritage — the good and the bad.

Toward that end, on the spur of the moment in early 2013, I had a thought that it might be a worthwhile exercise to do a series of interviews with accomplished American historians about their books, in front of an audience principally comprising members of Congress.

Like many ideas that seem to click from the start, the inspiration for what we called the Congressional Dialogues series was not the result of a committee report, or a strategic planning exercise, or a long-thought-out intention. It was simpler and quicker than that.

The idea was simply to provide the members with more information about the great leaders and events in our country's past, with the hope that, in exercising their various responsibilities, our senators and representatives would be more knowledgeable about history and what it can teach us about future challenges. I also felt that bringing the members together in a neutral, nonpartisan setting might modestly contribute toward reducing the partisan rancor that has become so commonplace in Washington. I was encouraged in this idea by Debbie Dingell, a friend who is now serving in Congress, succeeding her husband, John Dingell.

I brought the idea to the then Librarian of Congress, the late Dr. James Billington. I believed that Jim, who had been the Librarian for nearly a quarter century (and previously a well-recognized historian and professor), would recognize the potential benefit of such a program for members of Congress.

I also thought the Library of Congress would be a natural host for this kind of session, since its mission is to provide Congress with objective, authoritative, and nonpartisan research and analysis to help inform the legislative debate.

I had known Jim for many years but had begun working with him more closely in 2010 when I became the principal supporter of the National Book Festival, an extraordinary event the Library organizes annually to bring together tens of thousands of book lovers of all ages with hundreds of authors. The event was inspired by then first lady Laura Bush, who asked Jim Billington, at the inaugural events for President George W. Bush, if there was a book festival in Washington similar to the Texas Book Festival she had started. He said there was not, but there would be.

Jim organized the first National Book Festival on the Mall in 2001. I have had the privilege to be the co-chair of the festival for the past decade, and to conduct interviews with noted historians and other authors who have appeared there.

To my delight, Dr. Billington agreed immediately that the Library would be the ideal host for the proposed congressional gatherings. And to enrich the experience, he suggested that the Library could supplement the discussions by sharing related treasures from its unmatched collections. Jim also asked that I serve as the interviewer of the invited historians, and I said that I would be honored to do so.

The first Congressional Dialogue occurred on June 18, 2013, with Jon Meacham discussing his recently released book *Thomas Jefferson: The Art of Power.*

Six years later, the Era of Good Feelings has not really taken over the Capitol, but — without overstating the value of the Dialogues — a modicum of progress has been made. Thirty-eight Congressional Dialogues have now taken place. As of this writing, the interviewees have included A. Scott Berg, Taylor Branch, Robert Caro, Ron Chernow, Doris Kearns Goodwin, Walter Isaacson, David McCullough, Cokie Roberts, and Bob Woodward, among many other distinguished and award-winning authors. And there was one special interview with someone who once thought about being a historian: U.S. Supreme Court Chief Justice John Roberts.

The many members who have attended have told me that in fact they have learned a great deal about American history from these events. Members have also told me that they look forward to what they see as a unique opportunity to spend time in a nonpolitical social and intellectual setting with their colleagues from across the aisle and from the other chamber (for this rarely occurs anymore). Some members have actually said that the Dialogues are the most enjoyable events on their congressional schedules.

Jim Billington's enthusiasm for the series

continued until his term ended on September 30, 2015. He hosted and attended every single Dialogue.

Fortunately, Jim's support has been matched by his successor, Dr. Carla Hayden, who was appointed by President Barack Obama in 2016, after having served for twenty-three years as the director of the Enoch Pratt Free Library in Baltimore (my hometown). Carla, the first woman and first African American to serve as Librarian of Congress, has also hosted and attended every Dialogue. And she has become its most ardent supporter.

This book is my attempt to share with readers some of the wealth of historical knowledge that members of Congress have learned over the past six years. I have selected, edited (with the help of Jennifer Howard), and introduced some of the most intriguing conversations in the series. Taken together, these interviews with some of our country's most eminent historians give an interesting look at America over more than two hundred years.

To be sure, this book is just a snapshot. It is not a comprehensive look at the American story. That is beyond its scope. But I hope this snapshot will whet the appetite of the reader to learn more about American history, and will make the reader feel that, at a minimum, reading the entirety of the book discussed by each author would be a worth-while exercise.

The American Story begins with an interview about the man who set an enduring model for future American leaders — George Washington — and moves chronologically through the lives, careers, and lessons imparted by some of the notable figures who both followed him and shaped the course of national events from the Founding Era to the late twentieth century. In these pages, you will read about many of the pivotal moments in American history and likely learn facts you never knew about Alexander Hamilton, Benjamin Franklin, Abigail Adams, Martha Washington, Abraham Lincoln, Franklin Delano Roosevelt, Martin Luther King Jr., John F. Kennedy, and other leaders who changed the course of the nation. And you will also see images of original materials from the Library's historic collections.

I hope that the readers of this book will get a sense of the sweep of American history, as seen through the lives of some of the country's most significant leaders. I also hope that the book will prompt the book's readers to read not only the books discussed in the interviews, but other books relating to American history as well.

The historian's trade depends on asking questions and digging into primary and secondary sources in search of answers. The authors featured here typically spent five to ten years researching their books. In the Dialogues, they addressed some of the most essential questions relating to their subjects. For instance:

- Was George Washington indispensable to winning the Revolutionary War, to drafting the Constitution, and to creating the U.S. presidency as we know it today?
- How could Thomas Jefferson have written "all men are created equal . . ." in the Declaration of Independence when he was a lifelong slaveholder?
- How did a penniless West Indies orphan, Alexander Hamilton, manage to become such an important advisor to George Washington as well as the key creator of the American financial system?
- How did women in the eighteenth and nineteenth centuries, with no right to vote or to hold office, make their influence felt in public life?
- Did Lincoln issue the Emancipation Proclamation principally to help the Union win the Civil War, or did he really believe that slavery had to be ended and that the moment to end it had arrived?
- How close did the world come to its first nuclear war during the Cuban Missile Crisis, and how did John F. Ken-

nedy devise a successful solution to this crisis?

- Why did it take a hundred years after the Thirteenth, Fourteenth, and Fifteenth Amendments for the U.S. to really address the civil rights of African Americans, and was Martin Luther King Jr. the indispensable leader of this effort?

- Why did LBJ — a Texas native and close friend of the Senate's leading segregationists — decide to push through Congress the 1964 Civil Rights Act when he knew that it could impair the Democrats' electoral prospects in the South for generations to come?

The interviews included here have been updated as needed and edited for clarity and length, with the approval of the authors.

All royalty revenues from sales of this book will be donated to the Library of Congress's Literacy Awards, a program I worked with the Library to create and fund in 2013.

Enough about the background. Now on to the interviews. I hope that you will enjoy reading this book as much as I have enjoyed doing the interviews on which it is based; that you will find the conversations to be enjoyable and memorable; and that you will be spurred to learn more about American history.

David M. Rubenstein
April 2019

1
JACK D. WARREN JR.
ON GEORGE WASHINGTON

"Our national independence is
Washington's legacy."

BOOK DISCUSSED:
The Presidency of George Washington
(U. of Virginia Press, 2002)

We don't lack for George Washington scholars. The United States has an abundance of
them, and their books have together given a

relatively full rendering of the Revolution's indispensable man — the man of whom it was said at his funeral that he "was first in war, first in peace, and first in the hearts of his countrymen."

Like many Americans, as a youth I was taken by my parents to Mount Vernon. That began my own lifelong admiration for our first president, the only Founding Father to free his slaves at his death.

When I took my own son, then about eight years old, to visit Mount Vernon, he saw a large twig on the ground and asked if that was a part of the cherry tree that Washington had cut down as a young boy. Although the cherry-tree story is a myth, I could not destroy the illusion for an eight-year-old. I replied that I could not tell a lie and that it indeed had been a part of the cherry tree.

I asked Jack Warren to do the interview on George Washington because Jack has an encyclopedic knowledge of our first president, having devoted much of his adult life to studying him. His book on Washington's conduct as president is an excellent look at how Washington essentially invented the office and established traditions and practices still in use more than two hundred years later.

Jack has devoted his career to promoting the memory of Washington and the American Revolution. For a good number of years, Jack served as an editor for *The Washington Pa-*

pers, a project still ongoing under the auspices of the University of Virginia. He fought successfully to save the site of Washington's childhood home. Today, Jack leads the American Revolution Institute, a public nonprofit created to ensure that all Americans understand and appreciate the achievements of the American Revolution. He is also the executive director of the Society of the Cincinnati. (The modern members of the society are descendants of Washington's officers.)

Although there were no Rubensteins who served as officers in the Revolutionary War, a few years ago I was made an honorary member of the Delaware chapter of the society. Through the society, and through events at its headquarters (Anderson House in Washington, D.C.), I have interviewed Jack more than a few times. His affection and respect for Washington and his knowledge of Washington's life are unmatched, as is apparent in the interview.

In our conversation, Jack Warren makes clear why George Washington was easily the first among equals of the Founding Fathers. On three occasions, he left the tranquility and comfort of Mount Vernon to help his fellow citizens, fulfilling a role that no one else in the colonies (and later the country) could have done as well, if at all.

First, he led the American troops in battle against the seemingly invincible British. (Few

Americans had Washington's military experience.) Second, he presided over the Constitutional Convention, an assemblage unlikely to have even occurred, much less succeeded, without his presence. Third, as the first U.S. president, he ensured the new American government would work, and set the precedents that have helped guide his forty-four successors so far.

As Jack recounts, Washington was able to achieve these three feats not because of an engaging, back-slapping, hail-fellow-well-met personality. Standoffish, if not regal, in bearing and demeanor, he was more than a bit distant from his colleagues and even his fellow Founding Fathers. He led not through a dynamic, engaging personality but through example. He set a high bar for himself and met or exceeded it. Others saw this and followed his lead.

But Washington's greatest legacy was his willingness to give up power. Generals who led military victories typically became rulers for life if they could. Washington returned to Mount Vernon at the end of the Revolutionary War, content to resume the life of a gentleman farmer and plantation owner. He could readily have had a third term and presumably served as president until his death, but he chose the opposite course. He retired to his home and gave up all his government power.

Back at Mount Vernon, Washington lived only two and a half more years. He could have lived longer had he been less hospitable: after riding several hours through a rainstorm, he arrived home drenched and cold, but refused to change clothes and keep his dinner guests waiting. The result was a swollen epiglottis, difficulty in breathing, and a failed effort to address the problem by bloodletting (i.e., cutting veins to let the "bad blood" out of the body). That shortly produced shock, and ultimately death. Jack relates the unfortunate outcome in the interview.

Interestingly, Jack notes, Washington had two uncommon provisions in his will. First, he arranged for his slaves to be emancipated after his death (the only Founding Father to do so). Second, he asked not to be buried for two days. In those days, doctors left something to be desired, and they sometimes authorized patients to be put in coffins before death had actually occurred. Washington was, in fact, dead before being placed in his coffin.

MR. DAVID M. RUBENSTEIN (DR): Of all the Founding Fathers, the one who still commands the most admiration and respect is probably George Washington. Why is that?

MR. JACK D. WARREN JR. (JW): George Washington led the Revolution for our independence. Without him, our revolution would have failed. Our national independence is Washington's legacy. We are sitting in this city in the greatest country in the history of the world, in the greatest republic since the fall of the Roman Republic, as a consequence of Washington's actions.

DR: George Washington grew up in what's now called Mount Vernon — named, ironically, after a British admiral. Washington's older half brother was an officer in the British navy, is that right?

JW: Washington moved around as a child, but when he was a teenager, he spent a lot of time at Mount Vernon, which was the home of his half brother Lawrence Washington. Lawrence was an officer in the Virginia colonial militia and served as a volunteer officer under Admiral Edward Vernon in an attack on Cartagena in a brief naval war between Britain and Spain, oddly named the War of Jenkins' Ear.

DR: So his brother named Mount Vernon.

JW: He did. He had admired Admiral Vernon. George Washington later inherited Mount Vernon, but he never changed the name, and so lived in a house named for a hero of the British Empire.

DR: George Washington wanted to be an officer in the British military at one point?

JW: Lawrence thought George might become an officer in the Royal Navy, but there is no evidence George ever warmed to the idea. When he was in his twenties, George Washington wanted to secure an appointment as an officer in the regular British army.

DR: And he was rejected?

JW: He played an important role as a Virginia militia officer in the French and Indian War and came to the notice of regular British army officers — including men he would later fight during the Revolutionary War. He realized then that the British army offered no real opportunities for a colonial and that his ambition was never going to be realized.

DR: Washington does do some fighting in the French and Indian War of 1754 to 1763 and gets a reputation. Then he's elected to the

Continental Congress — the governing assembly in Philadelphia, made up of delegates from the thirteen colonies — and serves as leader of the American forces during the Revolution. Why did they pick George Washington, who wasn't that famous a military tactician or general? Why did the Continental Congress say, "We want you to lead the troops in the American Revolutionary War"?

JW: He was the best man available. He was a Virginian. The Revolution had begun in Massachusetts, and most of the early fighting was in New England. Congress realized it needed somebody from outside New England to lead the army. Although George Washington had never led more than a couple of hundred men, he was the most experienced military leader in Virginia, the largest of the colonies. Moreover, Washington had the bearing of a soldier. He stood out.

DR: Because he was six foot two?

JW: Yes, but much more than that. Because he commanded respect. In the weeks after the fighting at Lexington and Concord, Congress debated how to respond. George Washington said very little in those debates. He was never much of a public speaker. But he appeared each day in his Virginia regimental uniform, as if to say, "A war for the liberty of America has begun. We must fight, and I am prepared to do it."

DR: People say that when they asked him, "Why don't you be the leader of our troops in the Revolutionary War?" he said, "No, I don't want to do it." Finally he said okay, and it turned out he had already brought all of his uniforms up from Mount Vernon. Is that true?

JW: He was modest, which is one of the things people admired about him. In accepting the command, he said, "I beg it may be remembered by every gentleman in the room that I this day declare with the utmost sincerity, I do not think myself equal to the command I am honored with."

But if I could be a fly on the wall, one of the scenes I would like to see is Washington packing his military uniform for the trip to Philadelphia. Surely Martha knew he was taking his uniform, and what this might mean.

After he had accepted command of the Continental Army, he wrote a letter to her, one of the only letters he wrote to her that survives. "You may believe me, my dear Patsy," he began, "when I assure you, in the most solemn manner, that so far from seeking this appointment, I have used every endeavor in my power to avoid it, not only from my unwillingness to part with you and the family, but from a consciousness of its being a trust too great for my capacity. . . . But as it has been a kind of destiny, that has thrown me upon this service, I shall hope that my undertaking of it, is designed to answer some good purpose."

It's a charming letter, but the idea that he had tried to avoid the appointment is not true. He wanted it. He just didn't imagine that the war would last for eight years, and that in those eight years he would see Mount Vernon only once, for a single night, when he was on his way to Yorktown.

DR: How old was he when he became the general of the American forces in the Revolutionary War?

JW: He was just forty-three.

DR: The same age as John Kennedy was elected president.

JW: We are used to thinking of Washington as a mature man — a man in his late fifties or sixties, as he was when the most familiar portraits were painted. But in 1775 he was a robust young man in the prime of his life. He was a great horseman, a fine dancer, and a gifted athlete.

DR: He was robust and athletic, but he had not been educated, right? No college, no high school, no grade school.

JW: Washington had had as much education as a typical planter in his station. His formal education ended when he was about fourteen. Our thinking about his education is skewed, because some of the other leaders of the Revolution benefited from a fine formal education. Thomas Jefferson graduated from the College of William and Mary, James Madison from Princeton, and Alexander Hamilton from Columbia.

But some of the greatest minds of that century, and certainly the greatest Americans of that generation, were more simply educated. Franklin had little formal education. Patrick Henry was the most eloquent American of the eighteenth century, if not of all time, and he had no more formal education than Washington.

DR: So Washington took the job and said, "I'll do it, but I don't want to be paid. Just cover my expenses." Is that what almost broke the Continental Congress? Because his expenses were pretty significant.

JW: Washington's expenses were significant. Some revisionist historians try to poke holes in Washington's reputation by pointing out

After leading American troops to victory in the Revolution, George Washington served as president of the Constitutional Convention in 1787 that oversaw the creation of the U.S. Constitution, establishing a federal system for the newly independent country.

that this was really a good deal. But keep in mind that Washington's expenses as commander in chief included all the expenses of his military staff. He also had to pay the costs of espionage. There was no NSA, CIA, or military intelligence apparatus, and no congressional appropriation for intelligence. Washington managed much of that himself, and the costs show up in his expense accounts.

DR: That's a fair point. How many troops did he actually command in the Revolutionary War? Was it more than twenty thousand at any point?

JW: At its peak, when the army was gathered around New York City in the summer of 1776, Washington had about thirty-five thousand men to defend America from the greatest military expedition any European power had ever sent overseas. Those thirty-five thousand included the Continental Army — the regular army upon which Washington relied — and short-term militia.

DR: And many of those men were not well armed or well equipped. At Valley Forge, for example, one-third had no shoes. Was he always fighting with Congress to get them paid? How did he actually hold them together?

JW: Washington was continuously struggling to keep the army together. The army was always underpaid. It was always underfed. It was always poorly shod. It was always short of arms.

When the war began, we didn't have a single factory for making muskets or a gunpowder mill capable of supplying an army. We didn't have bronze for making cannon barrels or sufficient lead for musket balls. We had no workshops to produce tents, uniforms, knapsacks, and all the other things consumed in war. We never had enough money. Congress issued paper money unsupported by gold or silver, and it soon became worthless.

Washington appealed continuously for support from Congress and from the states. He appealed to the patriotism of his men. He shared their suffering. He held the army together through the force of personality. People believed in Washington. The men who fought with him believed that he would lead them to victory.

DR: He camped in Valley Forge during the winter. Why was it that when winter arrived, the troops just stopped fighting? In other words, the British said, "We're not going to fight in the winter." And the Americans didn't fight then either. Why did they not think they could fight in the winter? It was too cold?

JW: Fighting slowed dramatically in winter, but it rarely stopped. Washington kept patrols on the roads around the British army to prevent them from collecting supplies from American farms. Skirmishing went on all the time.

The British were in an unusual situation, conducting a war of conquest thousands of miles from Britain. They were able to take American cities, including New York, Philadelphia, Charleston, and Savannah, but they were never able to establish control of the interior. They were never able to live off the land. They had to depend on supplies brought from overseas. Moving supplies overland in winter was simply too arduous, so the British went into winter quarters and waited for spring. Every year the British hoped that this would be the year they would bring Washington to bay.

DR: In November 1776 there was a battle at Fort Washington, on the island of Manhattan, and almost three thousand American troops were captured. As general, Washington himself you could say was responsible for that. We lost several thousand men. There was a movement afoot to replace him as the general of the American army. Did that get very far? Did Congress lose confidence in him?

JW: This was the darkest moment in the war. The British attacked New York in the summer of 1776 with some thirty-six thousand men, including German mercenaries, and a fleet of warships. Their goal was to take the city, crush Washington's army, and end the rebellion in one swift campaign. Congress expected Washington to defend the city, but the task was nearly impossible. New York is an island city, surrounded by a maze of navigable waterways that favor an attacker who enjoys naval superiority. The British could move their army at will. They took the city without much difficulty, and they beat Washington's army in a series of battles.

Fort Washington, which is at the north end of Manhattan, was the last American stronghold on the island. Washington's officers assured him they could hold it against a British attack for months. When the British attacked, the fort fell in a matter of hours. The German mercenaries, the Hessians, led the attack, and when they took the fort, they began slaughtering American prisoners. Washington watched through a spyglass from the other side of the Hudson. He knew that he had made a tragic mistake, and he quietly wept as he watched. Washington retreated with what was left of the army, fewer than six thousand men, across New Jersey, hoping to get across the Delaware into Pennsylvania. Congress fled Philadelphia, expecting the British to take that city as well. It looked at that moment like the war was coming to an end.

DR: Did he not write, "I think this is the end. We're not going to make it"?

JW: The crisis led Washington to draw on his innermost strength. He refused to accept defeat. He worked to keep what was left of his army intact, and he assured his men that they could still prevail. He told them to hold firm and that victory could be achieved.

Thomas Paine, who was with the army, caught that spirit of defiant determination, and wrote a pamphlet called *The Crisis* that Washington had read to the army. "I call not upon a few," it said, "but upon all: not on this state or that state, but on every state: up and help us; lay your shoulders to the wheel; better have too much force than too little, when so great an object is at stake. Let it be told to the future world, that in the depth of winter, when nothing but hope and virtue could survive, that the city and the country, alarmed at one common danger, came forth to meet and to repulse it."

Washington understood that the British needed to win the war quickly. The longer it went on, the more likely the French, Britain's historic foe, would join the war on America's side. Washington was determined to hang on. His battered army believed in him and followed him back across the icy Delaware to victories at Trenton and Princeton — victories that shocked the British and inspired Americans to keep fighting. This was his greatest moment.

DR: Eventually we won the war at Yorktown. On October 19, 1781, the British general Lord Cornwallis surrendered to the American forces, led by Washington, and their French

47

allies led by General Rochambeau. The war dragged on for another eighteen months, but the British finally accepted American independence and signed a treaty of peace in 1783. At that moment, Washington resigned his commission and went home to Mount Vernon. When he heard this, King George III said, "If George Washington gives up power, as I hear he's going to, he's the greatest man in the world." Why did he say that?

JW: Because it had never happened before and has scarcely happened since. Whether we're talking about revolutions we like or revolutions we don't, revolutions of the far right or the far left, they have a defining feature. The men who led them hold on to power. They convince themselves that they are the revolution. And they behave as Cuba's Fidel Castro behaved, and hold on to power as long as they can. And more often than not, they become ruthless tyrants.

Washington believed the revolution he had led was our revolution. When it was over, he surrendered the authority he had been given and entrusted the fate of the nation to its people. He knew that it was a critical moment. He wrote a letter to the states, which was immediately published all over the country, in which he asked Americans to dedicate themselves to the high ideals of the Revolution. "It is yet to be decided," he

48

wrote, "whether the Revolution must ultimately be considered as a blessing or a curse: a blessing or a curse, not to the present age alone, for with our fate will the destiny of unborn millions be involved."

DR: So, for example, Cromwell, Napoleon, Mao, Lenin, Castro — when they led revolutions, they stayed in power. The fact that Washington went back to Mount Vernon was unusual. When he went back to Mount Vernon, what did he do? He just went back to being a planter?

JW: He did, although it was difficult for him. Washington enjoyed farming, at least as an intellectual exercise. He enjoyed experimenting with new crops and improving his plantation. But he was, even in retirement, the most important figure in the country. People came to see him and wrote to him about public affairs almost continuously. He knew almost everyone in public life and was universally respected. Mount Vernon, he quietly grumbled, was "like a well-resorted tavern," always filled with visitors, and they invariably wanted to talk with Washington about political issues.

DR: The country was then being governed under the Articles of Confederation, which brought the original thirteen states together

Washington's roles of general and gentleman farmer combine in this mid-1800s image showing the general and his family at Mount Vernon in 1784, bidding farewell to General Lafayette, Washington's staunch French ally.

in a loose confederation that gave little power to the federal government. James Madison says it's probably not working. He goes to George Washington and says, "Would you be willing to chair a convention to figure out how to amend the Articles of Confederation so as not to completely get rid of them?" Why did George Washington agree to do that?

JW: Madison persuaded him by reminding Washington of what mattered most to him. He predicted that the republic would fail, and Washington's legacy would be forgotten, if Washington refused to act.

Washington — like Benjamin Franklin and some of the other leaders of that generation

— had conceived a vast ambition. He wanted to be remembered, like the heroes of classical antiquity that he'd been taught to admire since boyhood, as the founder of a great republic. He wanted us to have this conversation about him this evening. That was his private ambition. He wanted us to remember him.

Madison warned him that the republic would crumble if Washington did not lead the effort to reform the Articles of Confederation. Washington didn't want to be remembered as the virtuous founder of a failed republic. He was willing to risk his reputation by coming out of retirement to save the republic he had spent so many anxious days and sleepless nights to establish.

DR: The Declaration of Independence was adopted in Independence Hall in Philadelphia. In 1787, the Constitutional Convention is convened in the same place, Independence Hall, and George Washington is elected the head of it. The entire time the new Constitution is being debated, he doesn't say one word, except at the very end. Why was that?

JW: Washington was one of the most skilled politicians of all time and lived by the general principle that what it's not necessary to say, it's necessary not to say. He knew that he didn't have to say much in the convention.

51

James Madison had arrived with a plan for a new constitution, and the men who could be counted on to support discarding the Articles of Confederation and adopt a new and more effective form of government included some of the most gifted minds of the early modern world.

Washington also understood that one of the main tasks of the convention would be to provide for an effective federal executive. Nearly everyone present agreed that the convention should propose a single executive with considerable authority. There was only one person anyone could imagine entrusting with that authority, and he was sitting quietly in the front of the room. Washington was destined to lead the new government, and he made sure that it was a government designed by others, so that no one would suggest he had fashioned its powers for himself.

DR: When the convention concluded and the Federal Constitution was submitted to the states for ratification, Washington didn't get involved. He didn't urge anybody to ratify the document. Why?

JW: He had, in fact, endorsed the Constitution by signing it. He had associated his own prestige with the Constitution, and no argument offered in favor of it was as powerful as Washington's endorsement. He fully expected

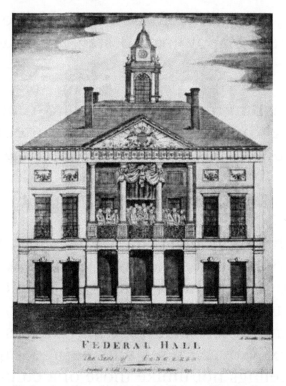

Reluctantly elected as the nation's first president, Washington was inaugurated on April 30, 1789, at Federal Hall in New York City, then the seat of the U.S. government.

the document would be ratified, and that he would be called upon to lead the new government. He saw no reason to spend his political capital in debate. He didn't believe he needed to, and events proved him right.

DR: So the Constitution was ratified, and George Washington was elected president by the unanimous vote of the electors. Did he really want to be president of the United

States, or was he forced into it? Would he have been happy just to stay at Mount Vernon?

JW: Washington wrote and said repeatedly that he didn't want to be president. And when politicians say that kind of thing —

DR: Remember who you're talking to here.

JW: When politicians say, "You know, I don't want to be elected, don't do this" — we don't believe them. But Washington meant it. He wrote to Henry Knox, his intimate friend, in a private letter, that "my movements to the chair of Government will be accompanied with feelings not unlike those of a culprit who is going to the place of his execution: so unwilling am I, in the evening of a life nearly consumed in public cares, to quit a peaceful abode for an Ocean of difficulties. . . . Integrity & firmness is all I can promise."

DR: He was elected unanimously. And under the Constitution, whoever got the most votes from the electors was president and whoever got the second most was vice president. So the vice president was John Adams. At the beginning of their administration, Washington thought he would involve Adams in governing, but he got mad at him. He never talked to him for eight years. Is that right?

JW: At the outset, Washington didn't know Adams very well, and neither man had a very clear idea what the vice president ought to do. In the early weeks of the administration, Washington called on Adams for advice, and if things had happened differently, the vice presidency might have emerged as a much more important role.

But early in the Washington administration, Adams pressed the Senate to adopt a title for the president similar to those associated with kings. A committee finally suggested "His Highness, the President of the United States, and the Protector of Their Liberties," which Adams endorsed. This proposal did not go over well in Washington's own Virginia, where critics continued to warn that the new government would deprive the people of their liberties. Thereafter Washington kept his distance from Adams. He treated Adams cordially but gave him no responsibilities, which led Adams to call the vice presidency "the most insignificant office that ever the invention of man contrived or his imagination conceived."

DR: George Washington wanted to be called "Your Excellency"?

JW: Washington actually shared Adams's concern about establishing public respect for the presidency and the new government in general. "Your Excellency" was a common way of addressing a state governor, and not consistent with the dignity of the presidency Washington worked to establish. James Madison proposed "Mr. President," which has endured.

Washington understood, better than others, that respect for the presidency would ultimately have little to do with titles and other formalities. He knew that public regard for the office would depend upon the conduct of the men who held it. He recognized that the eyes of the world were on him, and he worked constantly to promote the public interest, discourage partisanship, and avoid the slightest appearance of using his office for his private benefit or the benefit of friends or relatives.

In this regard, as in many others, he was a revolutionary, though we don't always recognize it. Consider the familiar Gilbert Stuart portrait of Washington, in which Washington wears a simple black suit. Today that kind of suit — or some variant — is the daily attire of most heads of state. But in 1789, when the world was ruled by kings and emperors wearing crowns and purple robes edged with ermine, Washington's dress was a revolutionary political statement. Washington's revolution is now so complete that we no longer see how revolutionary it was.

DR: The new government met first in New York and then moved to Philadelphia, but quickly passed the Residence Act, saying that we're going to have an entirely new capital and that the man in charge of figuring out where it's going to be is the president of the United States. And the president of the United States decides he wants to build it somewhere on the Potomac River. How did he decide? Did he come down and actually look at the sites himself? Did he have other things he had to worry about, or did he have time to go find a site?

JW: The Residence Act called for the establishment of the federal seat on the Potomac River, somewhere between the mouth of the Anacostia River and a stream called Conococheague Creek, which is up in Washington County, Maryland, near Hagerstown. Washington had lived on the Potomac River all of his life, and he knew exactly where he wanted to put this city, but he didn't want to appear impulsive or biased in any way, so he rode up the river and visited all the potential sites. In fact, he'd already made up his mind, and the tour was political theater. He had chosen the area between the mouth of the Anacostia and Rock Creek. He believed that this could become the site of the greatest city on earth.

DR: And the city was built by slave labor?

JW: Slave labor was involved in the construction of most buildings and other improvements in Washington through the Civil War. The site of the federal city was a mix of undeveloped woods interspersed with small farms. In the early years there was never enough labor to clear the land, construct the unpaved streets, and build the essential buildings. The managers had to hire slaves from local plantation owners.

DR: It was hard to get the money, so Washington came up with a lottery system to try to raise money. In the end, it almost didn't happen. How close did it come to not actually getting built?

JW: Very close. The Residence Act of 1790 was the mother of all unfunded mandates. Congress authorized Washington to choose the site for a federal city but neglected to appropriate any funds to acquire the land or build the public buildings.

DR: That would not happen now.

JW: No. Nothing like that happens anymore.

Actually, the whole business was as politically charged as anything in our history. Congressmen from Pennsylvania didn't want to see the government leave Philadelphia, and congressmen from other northern states hoped the city would never be built and that the government would remain in Philadelphia or return to New York. So they refused to appropriate money for the project. They didn't understand Washington's determination. The president came down to Georgetown, which was then a little port town, and met with all the local landowners.

I picture this scene — forgive me, this is a little bit irreverent — like one of those late-night infomercials about buying real estate with no money down. In effect, Washington said, "Look, here's the plan. All of you are going to deed over the rural land you own to a neutral trustee. And the neutral trustee is going to divide it up into building lots and city streets. And you're going to get back two-thirds of the land that you gave us in city lots. That means you are going to give away a third of your land to us, some of which is going to be used for city streets, and some as lots for public buildings. The government won't pay you for your land, but your city lots will be worth a lot more than your rural real estate. The federal government is going to sell off most of its lots and with the proceeds we will pave all the streets, which is going raise the value of your real estate. What do you say?"

And, of course, this is George Washington making the pitch, and everybody signs on. With that the city was born, despite the fact that Congress didn't appropriate any money.

Washington watches every detail of the development of the city. He's determined to see it rise. He thinks that it can be a combination of contemporary London and Paris. It can imitate the glories of ancient Rome and Athens. He thinks it can be the greatest city on earth.

DR: Did he say, "Let's name it Washington"?

JW: No. George Washington was far too modest for that. He referred to it for the longest time as the Great Columbian Federal City. Considering the fact that it was undeveloped woods and farmland, this was a bit of real estate development hyperbole.

DR: Where did the idea of naming the city after Washington come from?

JW: The idea of naming the city after George Washington was tossed around in the press and in private correspondence from the time the Residence Act was passed. Washingtonople and Washingtonopolis were both suggested. So was Columbia. Congress decided to name the entire one-hundred-square-mile federal enclave the District of Columbia and authorized the president to appoint commissioners to oversee the construction of the city inside the district. The commissioners voted to name the city Washington.

DR: In his lifetime it was called Washington?

JW: Yes, in his lifetime.

DR: As president of the United States, George Washington only had three people in the cabinet?

JW: Four, if you include the attorney general. Congress authorized the departments of state, treasury, and war, with secretaries to run each department. The attorney general — Edmund Randolph — didn't have much public business to do and was admitted in the courts of Pennsylvania.

DR: Washington's secretary of state was Thomas Jefferson, and his secretary of the treasury was Alexander Hamilton. And they didn't get along too well?

JW: They were two of the most brilliant men of their time, but they had little in common. Jefferson was a Virginia planter and well connected socially. Hamilton — some ten years younger — was a West Indian immigrant who had pulled himself up from obscurity. Jefferson had spent the Revolutionary War as a legislator, governor, and diplomat. Hamilton had been a soldier — an artillery officer and

61

then aide-de-camp to Washington. They were barely acquainted before they met in Washington's cabinet and they almost immediately developed a dislike for one another.

DR: Hamilton was in favor of a stronger federal government and Jefferson was in favor of a weaker federal government. Is that a fair characterization?

JW: I see it a little differently. Both men wanted to ensure the survival of the republic and wanted the federal government to be a success.

Jefferson was in Europe, serving as our ambassador to France, when the Federal Constitution was framed and ratified, and he was a rather remote spectator to the process. He supported revision of the Articles of Confederation, but his friend James Madison had to convince him of the wisdom of adopting the new Federal Constitution. When he arrived home to take up his duties as secretary of state, he was in favor of a small federal government empowered to conduct the diplomatic affairs of the new nation and provide for the common defense, but otherwise limited in scope.

The problem with Jefferson's vision is that it did not provide for dealing with the crippling debts left over from the Revolutionary War. Brilliant as he was — and this great

Library of Congress is a monument to the energy and scope of his imagination — Jefferson was obtuse about economics. He never understood banking and finance and was deeply concerned that Hamilton's solutions for the nation's debt crisis would destroy the republic by placing inordinate power in the hands of financiers.

Hamilton's experience as a soldier had convinced him that only a robust federal government could protect the republic from impotence and insolvency. Hamilton was in favor of a *solvent* federal government.

When Washington became president of the United States — you all may laugh at this — the United States was about $85 million in debt. I realize the national debt of the United States has increased $85 million while David and I have been talking. But $85 million was an enormous amount of money in 1789. It was so much money that few Americans imagined that the United States could get out of debt within fifty years even if all of the revenue that the government could expect to raise through customs duties, the chief source of federal revenue, was dedicated exclusively to retiring the debt without doing anything else.

Hamilton created a plan to save the United States from indebtedness by creating a reliable system for funding the debt. This stabilized the value of federal securities and increased market liquidity by making it possible for debt instruments to circulate like money. This in turn encouraged investment and entrepreneurship and helped to release the creative energy of the American economy. Jefferson never understood any of this. He saw it as a system that would fasten debt and taxes on the American people and deprive them of personal independence.

DR: Did Jefferson anonymously write articles or have them written criticizing Hamilton while he was secretary of state?

JW: Yes, and Washington knew it very well. I marvel when people say we live in a time of unprecedented political partisanship. In the Washington administration, the secretary of state put a man on the public payroll, ostensibly as a translator, whose actual role was to edit a newspaper critical of the Washington administration.

DR: Of which Jefferson was the secretary of state.

JW: Right.

DR: Ultimately Jefferson resigned, went back to Monticello, and said some things that are not so favorable about the intellect of George Washington. And I gather Washington never talked to him again. Is that true?

JW: Jefferson returned to Philadelphia in 1797 when he was elected vice president. They went in together to the hall where Adams and Jefferson would take their respective oaths of office — a fascinating scene, because Washington arrived at the door first but then stepped aside so Adams could walk through, leaving Washington and Jefferson in the doorway. Jefferson waved his hand, deferring to Washington, but Washington shook his head, insisting that the new vice president precede him. They shook hands, exchanged pleasantries, and never spoke again as long as they lived.

DR: All right. So Jefferson's back in Monticello. Washington doesn't really want to run for a second term, but people come to him and say, "You're the only person, run again," and he decides to run again. Is that correct?

JW: Washington had been reluctant to serve as president. He wanted to get out of the presidency as quickly as possible. In 1792, at the end of his first term, he sat down to write a farewell address. It's not as eloquent as the one Hamilton helped him write later. It actually has a little Nixonian ring to it, a kind of "You're not going to have George Washington to kick around anymore" tone. He was our first president, and he was the first person to get a real taste of what being president was like. Washington never got used to being criticized in the press, and by 1792 he was ready to retire.

His advisors, including Jefferson and Hamilton, talked him out of it. The last thing that I think Thomas Jefferson and Alexander Hamilton ever agreed on was that Washington had to accept a second term or the Union would fragment. Washington relented. He accepted a second term and came to regret it.

DR: At the end of that second term, when he leaves, he writes what's called a farewell address that Hamilton helped write. But it wasn't an address. He didn't deliver it to anybody. He sent it out as a letter and left for Mount Vernon and just went home.

JW: He didn't intend to give it as a speech. He issued it to the newspapers, explaining that he would not accept another term as president of the United States, and offering some parting advice. He left us to manage our own affairs. Hamilton helped Washington write it, but the sentiments are very much Washington's own. And like our greatest state papers, it still has much to teach us.

DR: So he just went home to Mount Vernon and said, "You go elect somebody else"?

Washington's example, and his exploits, continue to resonate in American culture. This 1940s pie advertisement invokes the general's famous crossing of the Delaware River.

JW: He remained in Philadelphia through the election and inauguration of his successor, and then he packed up and went home. We are now so used to this ritual transfer of power that we no longer see how truly revolutionary it once was. In a world ruled by kings, there were no former heads of state.

DR: When he gets back to Mount Vernon, he becomes a country squire again. But at one point, when Adams was president and we were afraid that France might invade the United States, Adams went to Washington and said, "Would you lead the army again?"

JW: Washington agreed to command a provisional army organized to defend the nation in the event of invasion. He makes a couple of trips to Philadelphia to confer about the business and entrusted the organization of the army to Alexander Hamilton, who was made second in command at Washington's request. Washington didn't expect a French invasion, but he was willing to lend his prestige to the administration to calm public fears, which were soon dispelled.

DR: So Washington was back at Mount Vernon, and then one day it begins to sleet while he's out riding around his estate. He comes back completely wet. He has guests for dinner. (I think I read that he and his wife had not had dinner alone together for twenty years because they always had guests.) Rather than go up and change out of those wet clothes — he didn't want to be impolite and hold his guests up any longer — he sits down and has dinner with them. And then what happens?

JW: He had been out riding in sleet and rain for several hours, and by night he was very sick. Whether he would have avoided it by changing out of his wet clothes and warming up, we'll never know. For a long time, historians thought he had developed pneumonia, but the current view is that he contracted epiglottitis, an infection of the cartilage covering the windpipe — something that can be cured very quickly with antibiotics today. When it is badly infected and swells, the epiglottis blocks the flow of air into the lungs. Every breath is agonizing, and the sufferer gradually suffocates.

DR: Three doctors came. They looked at him and said, "The treatment that you need is to get rid of your blood. You have too much blood." So they let one quart of his blood out of his system.

JW: In their defense, therapeutic bleeding was a common early modern treatment, particularly for fevers. Washington was a big believer in therapeutic bleeding. He'd actually instructed one of his farm managers to come and bleed him before the doctors arrived. So it was his idea. The bleeding undoubtedly weakened him, but it probably didn't cause his death.

DR: He was sixty-seven when he died. He said, "Do not bury me for two days." What is the reason for that?

JW: There had been a great deal of literature in the latter part of the eighteenth century about people being buried prematurely — often people who were in shock, which is a medical condition doctors were only beginning to understand. Washington had read some of this literature and was worried about that.

DR: After he died, there was a debate about whether he should be buried up at the Capitol or at Mount Vernon. Where is he buried?

JW: Washington had directed that his body should be placed in a simple tomb at Mount Vernon. Many public officials thought that Washington should be entombed in the Capitol, and Mrs. Washington, with considerable reluctance, agreed, but it took many years for the proposed crypt beneath the Rotunda to be finished. When it was finished, the new owner of Mount Vernon refused to allow Washington's remains to be disturbed. The crypt in the Capitol is empty, and we have been spared a spectacle like Lenin's Tomb. I think Washington would be pleased.

DR: Now, in his will, he did something that no other Founding Father, I believe — certainly none from Virginia — did, which is he freed his slaves. He had about 130 or so slaves, but he actually directed that they should be free upon the death of his wife. If you were Martha Washington and you were told that the slaves will be free as soon as you're dead, is that a good thing for you to know? How did they resolve that?

JW: With great difficulty. George Washington had been born into a world in which slavery, as abhorrent as it is to us, was a part of every-

70

day life. He benefited all of his life from the labor of people he deliberately enslaved. But during the Revolution and the years that followed, he came to the conclusion that slavery was both inefficient and unjust, and made plans to free his slaves.

The situation was complicated. Half of the roughly three hundred slaves at Mount Vernon in 1799 were so-called dower slaves. They, or their mothers or grandmothers, had once belonged to Martha Washington's first husband, and George Washington did not own them. He benefited from their labor, but they were the legal property of the Custis heirs and would eventually go to Martha Washington's grandchildren. George Washington could not free them. His own slaves had intermarried and mixed with the dower slaves, and freeing his own slaves while leaving the dower slaves in bondage would break up families.

The law, moreover, discouraged freeing slaves. Legislators were reluctant to facilitate the growth of the free black population, into which runaways might disappear. The market for the labor of freed slaves was limited. And while legislators rarely considered the interests of enslaved people, they discouraged slave owners from evading their responsibility to care, in a minimal way, for elderly, infirm, or chronically ill slaves by making it hard to free them. In anticipation of freeing them at

Washington included a provision in his will to emancipate the enslaved people he owned. In this portrait of George and Martha with her grandchildren, the unidentified man in the background may be William Lee, an enslaved African American who served with the general during the Revolution.

his death, Washington worked to ensure that many of his slaves learned crafts that would provide them with marketable skills, and he provided funds to care for the elderly and infirm for the rest of their lives.

When the terms of Washington's will became public, Washington's slaves learned that they would be free when Mrs. Washington died. She decided not to wait and freed them herself.

DR: Washington's most famous eulogy was

given by Henry Lee, who said that George Washington was "first in war, first in peace, and first in the hearts of his countrymen." As a scholar, you have spent your entire life studying George Washington. Do you admire him more now, or do you see his flaws and admire him less than when you started your studies?

JW: It has been the greatest privilege of my life to spend it in the study of this person. He's the only historical character I've studied who rises in my estimation every year that I study him. Washington was an extraordinary person.

He had flaws and he made plenty of mistakes. But he learned from his mistakes, and rarely made the same one twice. He was an immensely prudent person. He was a man of great character. He was also an idealist — even a visionary. We don't usually think of him that way, but we should. Here we are, in a city he imagined, in a nation he devoted his life to creating, living under a form of government he did more than anyone else to vindicate — a government dedicated not to the interests of kings and aristocrats, but to the interests of ordinary people. Nothing like it had ever been seen in the world.

There is another characteristic of George Washington I particularly admire. He thought in the long term. His correspondence is laced with the phrase "a century hence." He thought about what our country would be like in a hundred or even two hundred years. And he did so in the crush of everyday political life, in which decisions had to be every day made under the pressure of events, in a hectic world like our own. He thought about us. He thought about the twenty-first century. He challenges us to think about a distant posterity — about the world we are making for generations yet unborn.

2
DAVID MCCULLOUGH
ON JOHN ADAMS

"There's present-day time and then there's the time of history. And the best and most effective people in public life, without exception, have been the people who had a profound and very often lifelong interest in history."

BOOKS DISCUSSED:
John Adams (Simon & Schuster, 2001)
Truman (Simon & Schuster, 1992)

David McCullough has devoted his life to telling the American story in eloquent and riveting prose. His books have won Pulitzer Prizes and regularly achieve *New York Times* number-one-best seller status, and he has garnered virtually every other honor possible for an author, including the National Humanities Medal, the Presidential Medal of Freedom, and more than fifty honorary degrees from the country's leading universities.

David's personal recounting of the stories and the individuals he has written about shows a love and enthusiasm for American history that is infectious. Listening to him talk about American history is even more compelling — if that is possible — than reading his words.

In this interview, David and I discuss John Adams, probably the least honored of the Founding Fathers until David's book on him was published in 2001. That book, which won a Pulitzer Prize, reopened the eyes of Americans to our first vice president and second president, an individual who was perhaps most responsible for the resolution in the Second Continental Congress in 1776 that called for the dissolution of ties with England, leading to the American Revolution.

I have known and greatly admired David for a good many years and have interviewed him on numerous occasions. He really needs little prompting from an interviewer, for he is the consummate storyteller, raconteur, and spokesman for America's history.

If there is today a living Mr. American History and Mr. American Spirit, it is David McCullough, not just because of what he has written and said or what he represents but also because of his great many human qualities.

One of these was evident to me at a recent award ceremony where David was being honored. Rather than just accept the award for his many accomplishments, he talked instead about how his wife, Rosalee McCullough, was his indispensable partner. She has read out loud to him every word he has written and is his best editor and critic. He actually seemed to be giving her the award — and it was clear from his talk how vital she was to his work. Few others would have shared the credit so convincingly and so lovingly.

In the interview, David points out that he originally intended to write a book about the relationship between Thomas Jefferson and John Adams. But in doing the early research, he realized how compelling (and relatively unknown) Adams was, and how a book on him — there had been few — would enable Americans to realize that the second president, while not as celebrated or as glamorous as the first and third, deserved real praise for his unheralded intellect, principles, scholarship, passion, and patriotism.

McCullough's work did the trick. His book is in its forty-eighth printing and helped to move Congress to correct a major lapse in Washington. There is, after all these years, authorization for a monument to Adams in Washington, though no funding at this point.

David also won a Pulitzer Prize for his book on Harry Truman, and in the interview noted the similarities between his subjects: both men held firm to their core principles, were relatively simple in their interests, were not popular while in office, and reemerged in public acclaim only many years after they left office.

After listening to David McCullough, it would be difficult to not really like and admire both Adams and Truman. But it would also be difficult to not really like and admire McCullough himself, in part for his writing skills and in part for his peerless description of what makes America so unique.

MR. DAVID M. RUBENSTEIN (DR): David, thank you very much for doing this. Before we start, how many people here would rather hear David McCullough than be at the White House for the state dinner? Raise your hands. Okay.

So, David, you have written several books that have won Pulitzer Prizes, and we're going to talk about one of them tonight. I would like to start by asking you this question. After your book came out, people were amazed that John Adams had this incredible life, and said, "How can it be the case that we have a monument to George Washington, we have a monument to Thomas Jefferson, but for the second president of the United States there's no monument in Washington?"

Ten years after your book came out, there's still no monument. So here are the people who can do something about that. Why should there be a monument to John Adams?

MR. DAVID MCCULLOUGH (DM): In 2001, Congress voted to provide a place for a John Adams memorial within the District of Columbia, and it was signed by President George W. Bush, so that all the legal aspects of the idea have been covered. The real problem is to organize enough support for it, because John Adams doesn't have a constituency, say, the way American nurses or teachers do.

And it's a shame. He's the only one that isn't represented. I would be all for it, but I wouldn't want it to be tucked off someplace where it was not part of the experience of people coming to see our capital and to appreciate it.

I love what he said about this subject in my notebook here, and it was a tribute he wrote to the capital, his benediction. Some of you may know it. It's a simply marvelous message that I hope will be remembered for generations: "Here may the youth of this extensive country forever look up without disappointment, not only to the monuments and memorials of the dead, but to the examples of the living."

Adams was a great optimist, and I think that's part of why he's so American. We are by nature optimists, and we know that the hard times and troubles and periods where nothing seems to be happening very effectively come and go. And that we can do it if we work together.

America is a joint effort in everything. If you read history, you know that nothing of any real consequence, or very rarely, has ever been accomplished alone. And he knew that.

I think he's one of the most remarkable human beings in our story as a nation. I also think his wife, Abigail Adams, was one of the greatest of Americans. They led extraordinary lives. Theirs is an amazing story.

There's an old adage about writing novels: keep your hero in trouble. Both John Adams and Harry Truman were constantly in trouble, so I didn't have to worry about that.

DR: Now, when you started to write your book on John Adams, you were actually going to write a different book. You were going to write a book about Revolutionary heroes, including Jefferson. Why did you decide to just write a book on Adams?

DM: I had the idea of doing a dual biography. It was going to be Jefferson and Adams. I thought that having both onstage, as it were, I could see them in a different way from how they have been seen before, or even how they were seen in their own time.

I was a little worried how I could keep the glamorous, famous, handsome Thomas Jefferson from upstaging this short, cranky Yankee. Once I got into reading what Adams wrote — the way he poured out his heart and soul in his letters and diaries — I realized what a human being he was.

History is human. That's what it's about — "When in the course of human events . . ." History is about people, and it's the people of history that we need to know and understand. Why they did what they did, why they were the way they were. What were they up against, what were their advantages, and so forth? Who were their friends? To whom were they married? All of that.

Jefferson tells you nothing about his wife. We don't even know what she looked like. He called in every letter that she may have written to friends of theirs and destroyed them. Destroyed every letter that he wrote to her and she wrote to him. How can you portray this man very effectively? He built a wall around his personal life. He didn't want people intruding on that. And you go where the material is.

If I may just sidestep a little bit, I was giving a talk at a university in California, and during the question-and-answer period one of the questions was, "Aside from Harry Truman and John Adams, how many other presidents have you interviewed?" And I said, "Appearances notwithstanding, I did not know President Truman or President Adams."

But if you get to read their letters, if you're surrounding yourself with what they said privately, publicly, what they said to someone they love, what they said to their children, what they said to themselves in their diaries, you get to know them, in many ways, better than you know people in real life. In real life you don't get to read other people's mail.

The unfortunate thing about all of us is that none of us write letters anymore, and no one in public life dares to keep a diary anymore.

It can be subpoenaed against you in court. And here were these people pouring their selves out on paper because of the old sense of working your thoughts out on paper.

Adams writes about this. He says, "It's only when I sit down at the desk with a piece of paper and my pen that I can really start to think." And again and again in his diary you'll read, "At home thinking." Imagine. Taking time to think! And what a mind. What an incredible brain.

So I thought, "No, I'm going to write about Adams. And that's more than enough, right there. That's one of the greatest American lives I know about."

DR: Maybe we can convince people that there should be a great memorial. Let's go through his life a bit. John Adams was from a not wealthy family but a family that had been around Massachusetts for a while. His father was a farmer and a preacher. John Adams went to Harvard and then became a lawyer. He was well respected, and ultimately he was elected to the First Continental Congress. When he got there, it turned out that he was more articulate and a stronger believer in independence than other people. How did he become such a leader from the beginning?

DM: I'd like to recast what you said a little bit. John Adams came from very humble origins. His mother was illiterate. They had maybe one book in the house, which was the Bible. And they had no money.

The father did something he'd never done, to help pay for him to go to Harvard. He sold some land. The father was a farmer, as you say. And John went to Harvard on a scholarship, and when he got there, he said, "I discovered books and I read forever."

You have to keep in mind this is not the Harvard that we know today. This is a small school with a small faculty, six or seven professors, several hundred students. And he did get a law degree. He taught school for a while. And he stood for practicing what you preach.

One of the bravest and most important acts of his life took place when no one would defend the British soldiers after the Boston Massacre. No one would dare do that because it would have been so infinitely unpopular. He said, "Well, if we believe in what we say, somebody's got to represent them. If you all won't, I will" — knowing in his heart at least that it would probably destroy any ambitions he had for a leadership life in Boston or Massachusetts or national politics.

But instead, it made him more popular. Because they saw what backbone this man had. That he wasn't just doing this to follow the crowd. He was doing what he felt was right. And he did that again and again and again in offices he held right up to and including the presidency.

DR: After he defended the British soldiers who took part in the Boston Massacre, he was elected to the legislature in Massachusetts, and then they sent him to the First Continental Congress. And there he became a leader from the beginning?

DM: Yes. Because he was a man who was willing to get into the arena. He would stand up on the floor of the Congress and battle articulately, and never with personal invective, for what he stood for. He's the one that really put the Declaration of Independence over, on the floor of the Congress. If he'd only done that, he would be someone of infinite importance in the story of our country.

Remember, everybody that signed that document was signing his death warrant. All the odds were against us. Only about a third of the country was for independence. A third of the country was against it. And the remaining third, in the good old human way, was waiting to see how it came out. We had no military strength, we had no money, we had very little in the way of military experience, and we were up against the most powerful nation in the world, with the most powerful navy, most powerful army, and we thought we could do it.

The other thing people don't realize, or unfortunately don't know enough about, particularly students, is that the Revolutionary War wasn't a quick little thing. It was eight and a half years. It was the longest war in our history except for Vietnam. And very bloody, proportionate to the size of the population.

DR: In addition to being the most ardent advocate for independence, Adams made two decisions. He recommended somebody to be the general of the army for the American colonies and somebody to write the Declaration of Independence. Why did he pick George Washington and why did he pick Thomas Jefferson?

DM: He picked Jefferson because he felt he was the best writer. And he liked him very much and admired him very much.

Washington was a clear choice. There wasn't really much mystery about that. There were so very few to choose from, and they were all young, in their thirties or early forties, with no experience. They'd never done this before; none of them had. And it's just miraculous, out of this tiny population — 2,500,000 people, and 500,000 of them were slaves held in bondage. Couldn't vote, had no say.

One of the most important virtues or admirable qualities that we all should know and understand about John Adams is he's the only Founding Father to become president who never owned a slave. As a matter of principle. And Abigail was staunchly of that same point of view. The slaves weren't all in the South. They were sort of a status symbol in Boston, and you had servants who were slaves. That was the thing to have.

DR: He was not an abolitionist, though?

DM: No, he wasn't. Nobody was making an issue of that at the time because they had determined that "we can't solve this one now — we've got to sidestep that." They were really putting in the closet an issue they knew eventually had to be solved.

DR: The Continental Congress vote to separate from England takes place on July 2, 1776. John Adams then writes to Abigail, "This will be the most important day in the history of our country, July the 2nd." Why do we celebrate Independence Day on July 4 instead of July 2?

DM: This is something that he wrote on July 2, 1776. That was the day they voted. Your wonderful Rotunda of the U.S. Capitol has the painting of the signing of the Declaration of Independence by John Trumbull, and almost everything about it is wrong.

Nothing happened on July 4. That's the date on the document. And all those people weren't assembled to sign it. They signed it when they were in town, as it were. Some of them signed in the fall, some were signing all the way up to Christmas. And the furniture in the painting is wrong. The room, the decorations of the room are wrong.

The only thing that's right, and it's what's most important, are the faces. They were all representative of individual Americans — free, independent Americans — who are stating their political faith and who are accountable. In other words, they can't hide anymore. There they are. Proudly, but not without courage to do that.

Adams wrote that day or the next day: "The 2nd day of July, 1776, will be the most memorable epoch in the history of America. I am apt to believe that it will be celebrated, by succeeding generations, as the great anniversary festival. It ought to be commemorated as a day of deliverance by solemn acts of devotion to God almighty. It ought to be solemnized with pomp and parade, with shows, games, sports, guns, bells, bonfires, and illuminations from one end of this continent to the other, from this time forward forevermore."

Think about it for a minute. He's saying,

"*Just the thing for a Child to have!*" *Commemorative 1850s broadside of Adams's passionate letter, July 5, 1776, about the importance of the Declaration of Independence.*

"From one end of the continent to the other." The country at that point didn't even reach the Allegheny Mountains. And he's seeing this dream, this ambition. Like John F. Kennedy saying, "We will go to the moon." This is an American moment, and it is more than just legally interesting or legally important, profound, and unprecedented, which it was. And Adams had that capacity.

Adams was short, and he was not very handsome, and he comes right after the presidency of the tallest, most glamorous, important figure in the world then, George Washington, and before the glamorous Thomas Jefferson. And to me, it's very interesting that it's the same situation with Harry Truman. He comes after Franklin Roosevelt and is succeeded by Dwight Eisenhower, two of the most luminous figures of that day. But you have to wait for the dust to settle, and you begin to see who really did matter.

Right here, across the way here, over at the National Statuary Hall in the U.S. Capitol, there's a piece of sculpture commemorating the goddess of history, Clio. She's riding in her chariot, and there's a clock on the side of the chariot, and she's writing in her book.

The idea behind putting the statue there was that the members of Congress would look up to see what time it is. That clock still keeps perfect time. That's a Simon Willard clock, made in Massachusetts about 1850. They would look up to see what time it is, and they would be reminded that there was another time — history — and that what you're saying today, what you're doing today, here on the floor of this legislative assembly, is going to be judged in time to come, in the long run.

There's present-day time and then there's

the time of history. And the best and most effective people in public life, without exception, have been the people who had a profound and very often lifelong interest in history. You have to understand history in order to understand who we were, how we got to where we are, why we are the way we are, and where we might be going. And that you are going to be judged by history, not just by tomorrow morning's headlines. And they were worried about this back at the very beginning.

DR: Was Adams upset that later on we didn't celebrate July 2, we celebrated July 4? And why do we celebrate the Fourth?

DM: Because that's the date that's on the document. "When, in the course of human events . . ." July 4, 1776. But no, he didn't mind.

So often in history, what really happens, you couldn't put it in a novel. Nobody would believe it. The truth is stranger and more wondrous, very often, than fiction.

The idea that Thomas Jefferson and John Adams, the two men who put the Declaration of Independence over and changed history, changed the world, then died fifty years later on the same day, July 4, 1826 — unbelievable. And yet it really happened.

They came to Adams right before he died.

It was about two or three days before. The newspaper reporters came to him and they said, "Mr. Adams" — he was sitting up in a chair that's still there in the Adams house in Quincy, Massachusetts — "we're going to be celebrating the fiftieth anniversary of the Declaration of Independence. Do you have anything to say?"

He said, "Yes. Independence forever."

"Would you like to say a little more, Mr. Adams?"

"Not a word."

DR: After the Declaration of Independence is signed, the Revolutionary War goes forward; Adams is asked to go to France and see if he can get the French in as allies to help America in the Revolutionary War. How did he get to France? He couldn't fly over, so describe the boat ride and how he went and whom he took with him.

DM: He went over by sailing ship, which was the only way you could go anywhere. And he took his little boy with him, John Quincy Adams. So you had two future presidents riding in the same ship.

It was dangerous just to go to sea in those days, but very dangerous to be going to sea when the sea happened to be controlled by the British navy. And if they were captured, he would be taken and hanged.

And he didn't speak a word of French. He began scurrying around and buying all the books he could get on France and managed to teach himself French pretty effectively on the voyage over. It was a very difficult voyage, and he did it several more times before he was finished. Going, coming back, and going back to Europe a second time. He was a very brave man.

It was a very courageous time. You have to understand what they were reading at the time. For example, they had no rules of punctuation. Never used quotation marks — nobody did. When you're reading their letters, you'll come across a wonderful line or two. You think, "Oh, isn't that great?" And then you find out that, no, they're quoting a line from some poet or Shakespeare. It happens all the time.

They all did it, because they knew that the person they were writing to knew the line. It would be as if in a letter you would say, "Well, I guess we'll just have to follow the Yellow Brick Road." You probably wouldn't put quotation marks around that.

One of the lines that appears again and again in the Founding Fathers' writings is a line from Alexander Pope's "Essay on Man": "Act well your part, there all the honor lies." In other words, history has cast you in these roles and you better damn well play that role to the best of your ability. And why? "There all the honor lies."

Nobody talks about honor anymore. Not money, not fame, not power — *honor.* And they really believed that. Of course, they didn't always live up to it, but they believed it.

So there's a certain creed, a certain faith that we need to know more about, because it was the fuel of their courage and their persistence in the cause of equality and freedom and the freedom to use our minds to think for ourselves. This great institution [the Library of Congress] was signed into existence by John Adams, a man who never stopped reading.

When he was in his eighties, he embarked on a sixteen-volume history of France in French, which he taught himself. And he told his son, little John Quincy — one of my favorite of all lines — "You'll never be alone with a poet in your pocket." Take a book, carry a book. Don't go anywhere without a book. And he would urge poetry.

There's so much about this man that needs greater appreciation, but I feel immensely gratified that my book has reached such an audience as it has. The book is now in its forty-eighth edition.

Nothing can please me more than that the story of that amazing American is out there for people to know him and be enlarged by him. Adams et al. set such an example, and that's why it's so imperative that we teach history — the example of those who preceded us.

DR: When Adams finally gets over to France, he finds out he's got two colleagues he's got to negotiate alongside: Thomas Jefferson and Benjamin Franklin. They're in France as well. What was it like for the three of them representing the United States? Was it easy for the three of them to get along?

DM: Well, I say this not to put Jefferson down, but Jefferson didn't arrive until the war was over. So all the tough stuff was over. He came in when it was easy. Franklin was there before Adams.

Jefferson was not one to get in the arena. He would not get up on the floor of the Continental Congress and say what he really thought. He wasn't that kind of man. That's in keeping with when he goes to France. It was all safe. The war was over.

Adams gets there and discovers that Franklin is loved by everybody. Anything the French want, he's all for it. His way of dealing with them was to just be as nice as he could and try to be as much like them as they were and enjoy some of the privileges of life that weren't always approved of at home.

And he was not well, so he couldn't get around very well. He really didn't swing into action until about eleven-thirty in the morning.

DR: He seemed to have a lot of girlfriends. He was very popular?

DM: He was very popular with the people out in the street. I hate to use this analogy, but it really was a good cop / bad cop situation. Franklin was the one the French all loved; Adams was the one who kept saying, "You gotta do something. We could lose this war any day now."

Keep in mind — this is so important to understand — how different that time was. We think of transportation and communication as two different things. In that day they were the same. You couldn't communicate anything across the ocean any faster than it would take you to go across the ocean on a boat.

So when a diplomat arrived in a foreign country, the decisions that that person made, the actions that he took or things that he said, were his decisions. He wasn't getting orders from back home. If he did get orders from back home, they might be two, three months late getting there. The war could have been over back here, and John Adams and Benjamin Franklin might not have known until three or four weeks or more after it had ended.

The responsibility they felt — it's the same thing with women at the time. When Abigail had to decide whether to inoculate their children for smallpox, knowing that the very process of the inoculation could cause the death of one of her children, she couldn't call up John down in Philadelphia and get advice over the phone or tell him: "You get on the next plane and come back here. I want you to be here for this decision." She had to make that decision herself. And right or wrong, it would always be her decision.

We spread responsibility. We divide it up. They had to make decisions themselves, on their own, and right or wrong, it was their responsibility.

DR: The Americans win the war, and Adams is appointed to be our ambassador to, of all countries, England. What was it like for him to go over to England and meet King George III, who was the terrible hated figure? How did that work out?

DM: It worked out quite well. They really admired each other. George III was a much more interesting and appealing man than I ever understood before. Yes, he made very unfortunate decisions. And yes, he could be stubborn in the extreme. But he was interesting and not without feeling. He had a good heart.

Once they got over the stagy difficulties of the first presentation, when they first met each other in the ceremony where the new ambassador goes to present himself, both of them were so emotionally moved by that moment they couldn't speak. A very powerful scene.

I must say that the rendition of it by Paul Giamatti in the HBO miniseries *John Adams* was superb. The whole series was superb. That's the finest rendition, the most accurate portrayal of life in the eighteenth century that's ever been on the screen.

It's really due to the integrity of executive producer Tom Hanks. When we first met to talk about it, I said, "I don't want it to be a costume pageant. I want you to show what life was like — dirt under the fingernails, bad teeth, suffering, smallpox." When the British representative was tarred and feathered — tar and feathering was cruel punishment, it was torture, it wasn't some adolescent prank — that's all in that film, which is sometimes very hard to watch.

And the other thing I said was: "Don't violate the vocabulary. Keep it in the language of the time. Let's hear that beautiful use of the English language." And because both Paul and Laura Linney, who played Abigail Adams, were trained as classical actors, they could handle those lines. To my knowledge, there was never any complaint from viewers that they couldn't understand what the characters were saying.

DR: When Adams is finished as ambassador and comes back to the United States, we have a new Constitution. After spending a little time on the side writing the Massachusetts state constitution by himself, he's elected vice president. Was it a foregone conclusion he would be vice president? And how did he get along with President George Washington?

DM: He was elected vice president by popular vote, and he took his job very seriously in that he officiated over the Senate every day. I'm sure there were days he wasn't there, but very few. Probably no one who's ever had the job was more conscientious about showing up for work.

And you think the Congress has its difficulties today? They went at each other one day on the floor of the Congress with fire tongs. It was rough and tough, lots of contention. Washington stayed away from it. He didn't want anything to do with Congress. He wanted to play the role of the chief executive, and he played it superbly.

One of the greatest, luckiest breaks in our whole history as a nation is that George Washington was our first president, because he set the example of integrity, strength of purpose, and devotion to the country. Patriotism — not just the flag-waving kind, but real love of country. Keep in mind too that he was our chief executive, he was our commander in chief, for sixteen years, because we had no president during the war, and he was the commander.

As you know, when George III heard that he was going to retire and not take power after winning the war, the king said, "If he does that, he will be the greatest man on earth." And, again, there was the example. And Washington retired in 1783, when the Treaty of Paris was signed ending the war. He was elected president in 1789, after the U.S. Constitution was ratified. He really did nothing wrong or embarrassing or corrupt or self-serving as president.

DR: But Adams thought that the title "Mr. President" wasn't appropriate. The president should be called something better?

DM: Yes.

DR: There was a little fight over that, and George Washington and Adams for eight years barely talked. Is that true?

DM: No. Not true.

DR: How much did they talk?

DM: They didn't talk the way we do today. Well, yes, maybe they did. Not too much talking seems to be going on today.

No, I think it had more to do with the interpretation they each had of the role they were playing. But there was no animosity between them. It was difficult sometimes. They were two very different human beings. But Adams hugely admired Washington, and so did Abigail. Abigail just thought he was "it." And he was "it."

DR: When Washington says, "After eight years, I'm going to retire," was it a foregone conclusion that Adams would become president?

DM: Yes. But of course he had to get elected. And he would have been reelected.

This is something that isn't taught, and we don't know it — he kept us out of a war with France. And he knew that if he did that, it would probably cost him reelection.

He did it because he had common sense. We were up against this very powerful nation. In that day, if you went to war with France, you were going to war with Napoleon, and you didn't mess with that guy. We had no money, we had no army, we had no navy to speak of.

Adams and John Marshall, who became chief justice, figured out, "We can get out of this and we don't have to go to war" — and they didn't, and thank heaven they didn't. Adams said, "If I have anything on my gravestone that I should be remembered for, it's 'I kept us out of an unnecessary war.' " And it was true, and of course he did lose the election of 1800.

DR: He lost to his own vice president, Thomas Jefferson?

DM: Yes, he did. And he lost in a very major way because of what he did.

I wanted to tell you a little story about Adams. His son died of alcoholism and his mother died, all right around the change of the new year into 1801. He'd lost the election. He had every reason in the world to be the bluest, most depressed creature imaginable — and he was, to a very large degree.

One night in the White House, before he had to leave — with newly elected Jefferson coming in — he looked out and saw that the Treasury was on fire. There was snow on the ground. He immediately jumped up — the president of the United States — grabbed his coat and hat, ran across the lawn over to the Treasury building to help the bucket brigade put out the fire. And they succeeded. The next day there was an article in the paper saying that citizens all gathered and got the bucket brigade going and, inspired by the

When Adams lived in Washington, D.C., as president, much of the nation's new capital was still semirural.

example of their leader, put the fire out.

Now, the question is, why did he do that? He didn't have to do that. He was the president. There'd be other people doing that. It was instinctive. You're a good citizen; you pitch in. Very New England, very rural, very understanding of how we make civilization work.

DR: If you had the chance to have dinner with John Adams, what would you want to ask him?

DM: I'd want to ask him: "What can we do to increase the love of learning? What can we

Late-eighteenth-century plan of the city of Washington.

do to bring back the attitude toward reading and books and knowledge and thinking that was such a part of the adrenaline of your time?"

I'd like to read you a clause in the Constitution of Massachusetts, which John Adams wrote. Wrote the whole thing. It's a clause that was never in any constitution up till then and is still not in any other constitution except New Hampshire's. I think it's a reminder to all of us of what our obligations are, not just to these oncoming generations, but to our country and its future.

He says, "Wisdom and knowledge, as well as virtue, diffused generally among the body of the people, being necessary for the preservation of their rights and liberties; and as these depend on spreading the opportunities and advantages of education in the various parts of the country, and among the different orders of people" — in other words, everybody — "it shall be the duty of legislatures and magistrates, in all future periods of this Commonwealth, to cherish" — wonderful word — "cherish the interests of literature and the sciences, and all seminaries of them in public schools and grammar schools in the towns; to encourage private societies and public institutions, rewards and immunities, for the promotion of agriculture, arts, sciences, commerce, trades, manufacturers, and the natural history of the country; to countenance and inculcate the principles of humanity and general benevolence, public and private charity, industry and frugality, honesty and punctuality in their dealings; sincerity, good humor, and all social affections, and generous sentiments among the people."

How about that?

DR: If you had a choice to have dinner with John Adams or Harry Truman, who would you have dinner with?

DM: John Adams, because I want to know more about that very distant and different time.

I didn't know Harry Truman. I saw him once. But I really understood a lot about Harry Truman. I would love to have talked to Harry Truman. There's so much about him that people of the time didn't know. People of the time didn't know that Truman sat at home at night and read Latin for pleasure. This was the failed haberdasher. He knew nothing.

Truman had many qualities that are similar to John Adams. They both had great courage. Backbone. They were willing to say what they felt. They knew how to make decisions.

And they also understood that they were a link in a long chain, that the sun didn't rise and set on them; they weren't the greatest thing that ever happened in the history of the country, and they better act well their part and play their part. "There all the honor lies."

Harry Truman made some very difficult, very unpopular decisions, but he knew they were right, best for the country in the long run. They were willing to lose in order to do what was right. And to hell with what the public ratings and tomorrow's headlines could say.

3
JON MEACHAM
ON THOMAS JEFFERSON

"No one ever said it better and no one ever really fell so short, and I think in that tragic distance lies an extraordinary American life."

BOOK DISCUSSED:
Thomas Jefferson: The Art of Power
(Random House, 2012)

The first of the Congressional Dialogues was

the interview I had in 2013 with Jon Meacham about his new book on Thomas Jefferson. Had that not gone well, I guess the series might not have had a second interview.

But Meacham did an extraordinary job of describing his take on our third president: Jefferson, for all of his considerable intellect and intellectual interests, was actually a skilled acquirer and user of power, and was much more politically skilled than is commonly thought.

In focusing on Jefferson's political instincts and capabilities, Meacham wrote about a subject that has not been heavily commented upon. And he brought to the task both a journalist's easy-to-read style and a historian's commitment to accuracy and detail. Meacham's insights on Jefferson were so well respected by the Thomas Jefferson Foundation, which operates Monticello, Jefferson's iconic home, that he was recently elected its president.

Given Meacham's background, this should not have been a surprise. He had been a newspaper journalist in his native Tennessee as well as the editor in chief of *Newsweek* and the Pulitzer Prize–winning author of a biography on Andrew Jackson. He also wrote award-winning biographies on Churchill and Franklin Roosevelt, and on George H. W. Bush, and will soon complete his biography of James and Dolley Madison.

Meacham brought to this interview another helpful attribute: he is an engaging and witty conversationalist and storyteller. That is clear to anyone who watches him on the various television news shows (such as *Morning Joe*) on which he appears. I have interviewed Jon on a good many occasions, and he is always able to capture the audience's attention with his rare combination of knowledge, enthusiasm, and humor, not to mention an appealing southern drawl.

I should note my own interest in and involvement with Jefferson. Perhaps this stemmed from my parents taking me as a young boy to Monticello and to the Jefferson Memorial in Washington. In recent years, I have worked with the foundation to rehabilitate and restore Monticello, including a re-creation of Mulberry Row, the area where the enslaved people owned by Jefferson — including Sally Hemings — worked.

There has been considerable discussion about Jefferson's relationship with Hemings. The Jefferson Foundation has adopted the position that the relationship did occur and likely produced six children.

Sally Hemings was sixteen when the relationship with Jefferson apparently began in Paris. Jefferson's wife had died several years earlier, and had asked him, on her deathbed, never to remarry.

Was this a consensual relationship? Can an

enslaved person and a slave owner ever have a consensual relationship? What was Hemings's special appeal to Jefferson? Does this relationship of several decades change the generally high regard that historians and Americans have for their third and perhaps most intellectual president? Should it? These are some of the questions Meacham addresses in the interview.

Also addressed is the other great Jefferson mystery: How could he write, in the Declaration of Independence, that all men are created equal, when he was a lifelong slave owner? In the interview, Meacham indicates that Jefferson was referring only to white men. According to Meacham, Jefferson had earlier spoken and written against slavery, but eventually realized such views would end his political career and sublimated them for the remainder of his public life.

That sentence about all men being equal forms part of the preamble to the Declaration of Independence. When Jefferson wrote that sentence, with editing by Benjamin Franklin, it was not considered all that important. The significant part of the Declaration was considered to be the list of offenses committed by King George III against the colonies.

But as history has unfolded, that sentence has become perhaps the best-known sentence in the English language. It has served as the creed not only for the United States but also for so many other English-speaking and Western societies: "We hold these truths to be self-evident, that all men are created equal, that they are endowed by their Creator with certain unalienable Rights, that among these are Life, Liberty and the pursuit of Happiness."

Jefferson did not realize, when he was writing the Declaration and in the years immediately following its dissemination, how significant that sentence — and the entire document — would become.

It was nine years before Jefferson first publicly admitted to being the Declaration's author. He earlier felt that his initial version was much better than the "mutilated" version the Second Continental Congress actually adopted. Much later, toward the end of his life, it was "Author of the Declaration of Independence" that Jefferson wanted listed as the first accomplishment on his tombstone. And it was.

MR. DAVID M. RUBENSTEIN (DR): Many people in this city, and people around the country, would say the highest calling in political life is being president of the United States. Maybe you would say being vice president isn't too bad or being secretary of state isn't too bad. Yet when Thomas Jefferson was asked what he would like to have on his tombstone, he didn't say president of the United States, secretary of state, or vice president. He said, "Author of the Declaration of American Independence, Author of the Virginia Statute for religious freedom, and Father of the University of Virginia." Was he not happy with his tenure as president of the United States? Why did he not put his government positions on his tombstone?

MR. JON MEACHAM (JM): I think the epitaph that he designed — he drew the tombstone, and we still have that document — is one of the great acts of misdirection in American history. As Freud will tell you, often what you do not say is as important as what you say. I think Jefferson realized that his political career would be forever controversial, because political careers by their very nature are controversial. When you are elected, if you're doing really well, you get 55 or 60 percent of the vote, and that's not all that common. On your best day, 40 to 50 percent or more of the people you see are against you. I often

Jefferson sketched out his own epitaph and grave marker, probably in March 1826, not long before he died.

wonder how presidents get up in the morning realizing that almost every other person they see doesn't want them to be doing what they're doing.

Jefferson disliked controversy, yet he was irresistibly drawn to it. That's one of the contradictions of his life. He loved politics, he loved the arena, but he believed that being seen as the author of the document about human equality, about liberty of conscience and enlightened education, would be an achievement about which there would be less debate going forward than whether the embargo should have gone in in 1808 or what he did during his vice presidency or as secretary of state. [The Embargo Act of 1807, which took effect in 1808, embargoed British and French trade during the Napoleonic Wars, with serious negative consequences for the U.S. economy.]

DR: You've now spent five years of your life studying Thomas Jefferson. You've spent almost every waking hour learning about him, reading everything about him, and you've produced a best-selling book. After five years of studying him, do you admire him more than you did before, or do you see so many flaws that you say, "This is not the man I thought he was"?

JM: I admire him more because I see more flaws. Let me explain that.

You can tell I'm a southerner and a Christian, so I believe in forgiveness. I do what I do in part because for a long time I was a working journalist — for twenty years — and I started looking back at Franklin D. Roosevelt and Winston Churchill, Andrew Jackson and Jefferson, in part to see whether the world seemed as complicated and confounding and difficult in their time as our world does now. And the answer is yes, for in real time we never know how the American story is going to turn out. We now know how the founding of the United States turned out, we now know how the Civil War turned out, we know how the civil rights movement turned out, we know what happened at Normandy on D-Day in World War II and beyond, but they didn't.

The reason I find biography so compelling is that when you look at great American figures, whether it's Jefferson or, Lord knows, Jackson — Andrew Jackson's life was sort of a combination of *Advise & Consent* meets *Bonanza;* you didn't want to cross him because he would shoot you — Lincoln, Roosevelt, Kennedy, when you look at the great figures, their vices are almost as large as their virtues.

To me, the whole world turns on the word *almost.* To me, it's remarkably inspirational that flawed, sinful human beings were able to, at moments of great crisis, transcend those limitations and leave the country a little better off than it was before. And Thomas Jefferson did that. For all his contradictions, for all his derelictions, which I'm sure we'll talk about, the country was a better place, the world was a better place on the Fourth of July 1826, when he died, than it had been in

115

April of 1743 when he was born.

DR: On July 4, 1826, Thomas Jefferson was eighty-three years old. It was fifty years to the day after the Declaration of Independence was approved by the Continental Congress in 1776. What happened on that day in 1826 elsewhere?

JM: Well, in Massachusetts, John Adams once again got his headline stepped on by Thomas Jefferson. Poor Adams could never get one clean news cycle. He died on the same day. One of the last things he said was, "Jefferson lives." He was wrong in that particular moment, because Jefferson had died earlier in the day, but Adams was right on the bigger point, because Jefferson does live. He does continue to resonate. Of the early founders, he is the one who resonates the most for us.

I'd be bold enough to say I think that might be particularly true for members of Congress, because he did what you do. From 1769 until 1809, he was almost constantly holding or seeking public office. He left George Washington's cabinet in order to do that. As John Adams put it, it's remarkable how political plants tend to grow in the shade.

I believe that on that day in 1826, Jefferson, revered as the author of the best of the American promise in the Declaration of Independence, knew that his epitaph would stir up a deep interest. He also knew, I think we know now, and people in his own time knew, that very few people had failed so clearly in their own personal lives to realize that promise. No one ever said it better and no one ever really fell so short, and I think in that tragic distance lies an extraordinary American life.

DR: The Declaration of Independence contains a sentence that Jefferson wrote — with some editing we'll talk about — and that some people would say is the most famous sentence in the English language. I think you all know it by heart: "We hold these truths to be self-evident, that all men are created equal, that they are endowed by their Creator with certain unalienable Rights, that among these are Life, Liberty and the pursuit of Happiness." How could a man write that all men are created equal when he had two slaves with him in Philadelphia, owned sixty slaves at the time, and owned six hundred slaves during his lifetime, and there's no evidence that he freed very many slaves when he died? How could he have said all men are created equal?

JM: He meant all white men at the time. The contradiction you point out is that tragic failing to see how the promise he articulated could apply to those other than his own kind. Remember what was going on when he wrote that sentence. It's a civilizational shift. This is not just American exceptionalism, it's really remarkable. The political tradition of which you are the heirs, the operative heirs, was the clearest Western manifestation of the greatest shift in a thousand years or more.

What had happened in the century or so before the American Revolution? The Protestant Reformation, the translation of sacred Scripture into the vernacular, the European Enlightenment, the Scottish moral enlightenment, John Locke and the idea of self-government. The world was going from being vertical to being horizontal. It was vertical for a long time — with the divine right of kings, your entire destiny was shaped by the station to which you were born, and you had no other alternative. Everything came from above.

What did Jefferson do? He gave political manifestation to this shift from a hierarchy to a democratic — lowercase *d* — ethos, in which suddenly human rights, or the rights of all men being created equal, came from the Creator. What did that mean? If they came from the Creator, that meant neither the hand of the king nor the hands of a mob could take them away. It was an incredibly important intellectual and political shift.

DR: As a young man, Jefferson said some things that were not favorable about slavery, but he realized he wasn't going to get anywhere in Virginia politics if he was in favor of abolition. Was his view really that we had to tolerate slavery? What was his solution to that problem?

JM: In a very un-Jeffersonian way, he had no solution. The slavery issue is one of our central original sins. The other is the forced removal of Native Americans.

The Constitution codified our compromises on slavery. Everyone here knows that. Thomas Jefferson would not have been president of the United States — the Virginian presidential dynasty of Washington, Jefferson, Madison, and Monroe would not have been possible — without the Three-Fifths Compromise. [At the Constitutional Convention in 1787, delegates agreed that three-fifths of each state's enslaved population would count toward that state's total population, an important number for determining how many representatives each state would get in Congress. The compromise increased the political power of the southern states.]

The purchase of Louisiana in 1803 led to the first great secessionist movement in the country, which was not in the American South but in New England, because New England saw the country moving south and west and slave states being added that would dilute the power of New England. When I

119

was working on the book and I was thinking about the psychology of that moment, I was reminded of when my wife and I had two children, a boy and a girl, and my wife became pregnant and we found out it was going to be a girl. My son came to me and said, "Daddy, we're going to be outnumbered, and I don't like our chances."

That's what Timothy Pickering was doing in Massachusetts. He was going to be outnumbered, and it wasn't going to work out very well, and in fact it didn't, because the political power of New England was diluted. [Pickering, a Massachusetts politician who served as secretary of state and in the U.S. Congress, opposed the Louisiana Purchase because he worried that New England would lose its influence if the country expanded westward.]

The reality of slavery in that era was that there were some plans for emancipation, there was some talk about expatriation [i.e., sending African Americans to Africa], but William Lloyd Garrison [the famous abolitionist crusader] was not a force in the early part of the nineteenth century. If Thomas Jefferson had fallen off a horse in 1783, he would have been a source of great tags of rhetorical flourishes for the abolitionists, because on four or five occasions as a young man — as a trial lawyer, a young legislator — he did try to take steps to reform the institution of slavery, and he lost each time.

We're here in a room of political folks. What do political folks dislike a great deal? Losing.

So when, in the Confederation Congress in 1783–84, he had written a provision that would have banned the expansion of slavery to the west, he lost by a single vote. [The Confederation Congress ran the new country from 1781 to 1789.] A delegate from New Jersey hadn't shown up, and Jefferson later wrote, "In that moment the voice of heaven itself was silent and the fate of millions still unborn hung in the balance."

It's a wonderful phrase. No president ever spoke in needlepoint-pillow terms better than Thomas Jefferson. It's a goose-bump kind of line, but it was, in fact, simply rhetoric. At that point, he realized his political power would be diluted in direct proportion to his opposition to slavery.

He also could not imagine his own life without it. One of the first things we know about Jefferson, his first memory, is of his being handed up on a pillow to a slave on horseback to be taken on a family journey in Virginia.

One of the last things we know that happened in that summer of 1826 is that he's lying in that alcove bed in his home at Monticello, which I'm sure many of you have seen, and he's uncomfortable, and he's trying to signal to his family what's wrong, his white family, and no one gets it except an enslaved butler who reaches over and fixes the pillow and all is well again. His life was suffused and made possible and supported by slavery, and he simply could not make the imaginative leap to emancipation.

The final thing I'll say on this is that we can put a lot of freight on Thomas Jefferson. I just gave him credit for being the great articulator of the manifestation of the Enlightenment that shaped the modern world, so you can't let him off the hook for what he didn't do.

But it did take a civil war and forty years after he died and six hundred thousand American casualties to abolish slavery. Those of you who come from my native region in the South know that in the lifetime of most of the people in this room, we had to have federal legislation so that poll watchers would not put a box of Tide on a voting table and say to an African American, "You can have a ballot if you can tell us how many flakes of soap are in this box." So before we're self-righteous about Thomas Jefferson, I think we should take a moral accounting of ourselves.

DR: One last thing relating to slavery. In recent years, a lot of discussion has occurred about his relationship with a slave, Sally Hemings. He fathered six children with her, and he appears to have been an attentive father to those children, and he more or less stayed with her until he died. How do you explain a slave owner like that having a relationship with an enslaved person? Was that common or not common, and how did he hide it? When it was made public in those days, he never denied it, really, and he never affirmed it. Lastly, based on DNA evidence or anything else, do you have any doubt that the Sally Hemings–Thomas Jefferson relationship was true?

JM: To take them in reverse order, I do not have any doubt. Even in the absence of the DNA evidence, which is 99.9 percent convincing, I do not believe that a man so driven by appetite for power, for books, for food, for wine, for art, for knowledge, could at the age of forty, after his wife died, simply stop short of indulging the most sensuous appetite of all.

If you disbelieve the Sally Hemings story, then you are disbelieving a perennially coherent, oral history tradition from the African American community, and you are ascribing to Jefferson a kind of discipline that is almost superhuman. I do believe that it happened. It was common.

There was an old line of Mary Boykin Chesnut [a South Carolina writer and the wife of a plantation owner], who wrote a diary of a trip through the Carolinas a few years after Jefferson's death. She pointed out that white women on plantations could tell you with great precision the parentage of any mixed-race children on every plantation in the county except their own, where apparently the children simply descended like manna from heaven. So there was a culture of desire and denial in my native region that was extraordinary. It was extraordinarily pervasive. It's very hard to put ourselves back there.

It is one of the many hypocrisies of Jefferson's life. His children by Sally Hemings were the only slaves he freed. Let me just take a second about how the Jefferson-Hemings relationship began.

It began in Paris. Sally Hemings was his wife's half sister. Let me say that again. Sally Hemings was his wife's half sister, so the Hemings family itself, in the odd world of slavery, was — and a white southerner really hesitates to use this word — but they were a privileged slave family, as horribly ironic as that statement is. They were to be taken very good care of and overseers were not to give them orders. If I may, they were family. And so when Sally Hemings arrives in Paris, when Jefferson is the American minister there from 1785 to 1789, the relationship begins.

DR: She was fourteen?

A study in contradictions: the author of the Declaration of Independence was also a lifelong slave owner.

JM: No, she was sixteen. Before we go into that, we should point out quickly that James Madison wooed a fifteen-year-old daughter of a congressman from New York. Lock up your daughters. John Marshall married a girl when she was fifteen or sixteen. The age of consent in Virginia in 1800 or so was twelve. Let's not be anachronistic. We have to put ourselves back in that world, in that time.

In what I find one of the most moving and courageous moments in the whole Jefferson saga, here's this woman — this girl, as you

125

say — Sally Hemings. She is in Paris, she has become pregnant by the man who owns her, who totally controls her fate, and he wants her to go back with him when he returns home to become the first secretary of state.

If she stays in France, all she has to do is go down to the Paris City Hall and declare that she is a slave being held in France, and she will be free. Her brother is there, he can help her with it.

In what I find to be one of the most compelling moments, she negotiates with one of the most powerful men in the world, and she bends him to her will. She says, "I will go back with you if any children we have are freed at the age of their majority."

I have friends who are lawyers who say they could have gotten her a much better deal, but I think, in context, her courage, her savvy in some ways, to make the best of what was, I think for everyone in this room, a virtually unimaginably difficult and tragic situation, is a testament to her courage and a remarkable character about which we know almost nothing. But that relationship did last until the day Jefferson died forty years later.

Let me quickly say something about the press — I know, a big favorite of everyone here. Jefferson dealt with this regarding the story of Hemings, beginning in September 1801. He had not been president for a year when the story — almost entirely accurate, with just two little mistakes — appeared in a Richmond newspaper, written by an alienated former ally of his. He denied it. It's a little unclear what he was denying, but this was very much part of his political life.

There were political cartoons in the newspapers during his presidency with his head on a rooster's body that called him a philosophic cock, with "dusky Sally," as she was known, in the background as a hen. I know a lot of you all want to think that cable TV just made this a lot worse, but it's been a perennial problem.

DR: When Jefferson was at the White House, did Sally Hemings ever visit?

JM: No, no. He was very much embarrassed by his slave-owner status whenever he left Albemarle County. He took slaves to Philadelphia for the Continental Congress, but with the Adamses, who were opposed to slavery, he was very careful about it. He did not want the people in Washington to see him as a southern politician. He wanted them to see him as a national politician.

DR: Let's move on to the Declaration of Independence. Thomas Jefferson writes it in more or less four days. He had seventeen days, but like many people he said, "I'm busy, I waited until the last moment," and so he spends four days on it. Why was he picked to write this important document? He was only thirty-three years old, relatively young. Who edited it, who else was on the committee with him, and how did that get to be so important?

JM: Well, thirty-three is a good age. Jesus did a lot that year. I don't think that joke violates the wall of separation between church and state, does it?

Jefferson showed up in Philadelphia in 1775 with, as John Adams put it, "the Reputation of a masterly Pen." He had written *A Summary View of the Rights of British America* in 1774. It had gotten wide circulation in the colonies. Nothing like Thomas Paine's famous pamphlet *Common Sense* later in 1776, but it was a document that showed, as Adams again put it, a certain "felicity of expression," and we have to put ourselves back in June 1776.

Everything in the world was going on. They were trying to make a whole new world. Jefferson was on something like six committees, he was in charge of creating a plan for Canadian defense, every kind of legislative question was coming up.

John Adams believed, being a lawyer, that the resolution to reorganize state governments that had passed a few days before had been the real break with Britain that would be celebrated. Only a lawyer could think that way. The Declaration of Independence was kind of an afterthought. It was something they wanted to do, they thought they should do it, so one of the world's great subcommittees was formed.

DR: With John Adams, Benjamin Franklin, Thomas Jefferson, and Robert R. Livingston from New York.

JM: And Roger Sherman of Connecticut.

DR: Five people. But as I understand it, what they said to John Adams was, "We really would prefer Jefferson to write it," because Jefferson was from Virginia and the Massachusetts people were seen as being in favor of breaking away, so having this man from Virginia write this declaration might bring the southerners into the fold.

Jefferson sits down, he writes for four days, he brings the draft back to Congress, it's edited mildly by the committee. Benjamin Franklin made a couple of changes. They decide on July 2, 1776, that we're going to break away from England. What does the Congress do with the Declaration on July 3 and July 4?

JM: They applied the wisdom of a great legislative body. That was their view. In Thomas Jefferson's view, they mutilated it.

Those of you who are writers will know that being edited is a great and important and wonderful thing to go through, akin to colonoscopies and other things like that. Jefferson hated it so much, he was sitting next to Franklin on the floor there in Carpenters' Hall in Philadelphia, and his leg started doing this jiggling. Franklin had to reach over and put his hand on his leg to calm him down, because Jefferson thought the document was being torn apart.

The one great edit, I think, which came in the subcommittee process, was made by Franklin, who was suffering from gout at that point — the wages of a well-lived life. He changed the word *sacred* to *self-evident* — "that these truths are self-evident" — in order to ground the notion of human rights more in the ethos of reason than in the ethos of religion. He thought that would work better over time. It was a critical change that Jefferson enjoyed.

Adams and Jefferson, we remember them now in this great autumnal correspondence — they're the great rivals who came back together and exchanged almost two hundred letters in their retirement. But Adams never really got over how, as he put it, the Declaration of Independence was a theatrical show and Jefferson ran away with all the glory of it, and so that was part of the rivalry that really never went away.

Jefferson's rough draft of the Declaration of Independence from June 1776 includes edits made by John Adams and Ben Franklin, among others.

The Declaration of Independence has three parts to it. First is the preamble, which I gave a little bit of before: "We hold these truths to be self-evident." Nobody paid attention to that. That was not important then because it was just a preamble.

The part that was most important was the section that listed the faults of King George III. That was what most of the document dealt with. The mutilation that occurred was the Congress's taking out Jefferson's view that King George should be blamed for the slave trade. He blamed King George for forcing slaves into the United States. It was taken out because many of the people in the Congress were slave owners, and they didn't really like to criticize King George for it.

Then the third part of the Declaration stated that we're going to become independent. Those were the three parts.

Thomas Jefferson, not being unlike many of us, perhaps — at least, not unlike me — he would send his friends a copy of his draft and say, "Don't you think my draft is better than what these guys did?" So he wasn't above all that.

Let me describe what you're actually seeing when you see a copy of the Declaration of Independence. The language of the Declaration was agreed to on the Fourth of July. In those days, they didn't have typewriters and things like that, so once they mutilated the language — I should say that Jefferson was so upset that for nine years he didn't admit that he wrote the Declaration of Independence. He wouldn't tell anybody, he was so upset about it. Later he said it was the most important thing he did, and he put it on his tombstone.

But, okay — the language has been agreed to. They went next door to a man named Mr. Dunlap and said, "Print up a hundred copies of this" as a broadside — a Dunlap Broadside, as they are now known — and they took these hundred copies and distributed them around — one to King George, one to George Washington to read to the troops at Valley Forge, and then they were sent around to the states.

There were two hundred of them. There are twenty-seven known copies. They probably are worth about $25 million apiece now.

The broadside version doesn't have any signatures. It just was the text. They had to inscribe it, so what happened?

Well, they told all the members who agreed to the final document on July 4, "Go home, because one of the states hasn't agreed to it." New York State had been invaded by the British, so the legislators were hiding, and they hadn't agreed to the independence. So the Congress ultimately said, "Let's get all thirteen states together. We'll come back at another time when New York can be in favor of it and everybody can sign it."

They came back, more or less around August 4. There are debates on whether it was signed then or not, but let's just assume for a moment it *was* signed on August 4.

That document was kept as part of the

United States government. It was moved to New York and back to Philadelphia; it was wrapped up for a time, hidden in a box. When the British invaded in 1814, it was wrapped up and taken in a cloth bag down to Leesburg and hidden there. At one point it was displayed for thirty years in a building in Washington — the Claims Building.

The original is now in the Archives. If you go to the Archives, what you see is a very faded document. One of the reasons it's so faded is because it was exposed to sunlight — nobody preserved it — but another thing also happened.

In 1820 John Quincy Adams, the secretary of state, said, "We're not going to have a copy that everybody can see, because it's getting faded." He hired a man named William Stone and said, "Figure out how to make a perfect copy of the Declaration of Independence."

So Mr. Stone, in a three-year process, came up with a process that essentially involved taking a wet cloth and putting it on the original. That took half the ink off, and that was then made into a copper plate. That copper plate was then used to make two hundred perfect copies — two hundred — two were given to each living signer of the Declaration, and two or more to each state or governor.

There are fifty or so of them left. When you see the *New York Times,* on the Fourth of

July, printing a copy of the Declaration of Independence, what you're seeing is a Stone copy. It's a perfect replica, but it's a Stone copy because the original one is so faded. So today, when people talk about the Declaration, there's the original in the Archives, there is the Stone copy, and then there are the Dunlap copies that were printed the day after, which don't have signatures.

And the signatures had no binding effect. The Declaration was a propaganda document, but everybody wanted to make sure that, in effect, the signers were really standing behind it. They all knew when they signed it they might be signing their death warrant, because it was treason. So that's more than you might want to know about the Declaration.

Now, how many Stone copies do you have?

DR: I own four of them [now seven], and I've given one on permanent loan to the State Department.

JM: That's one more than me.

DR: One is in the permanent display at the State Department. If you go to the Diplomatic Reception Rooms, it's there. One is at the Archives, one is at Mount Vernon, and one is now at the new Constitution Center in Philadelphia. I put them on display so people will see them.

JM: Can I give you one treason story?

DR: Go ahead.

JM: When the signing of the Declaration was going on — I have this vision in my mind that it was on a table in the corner and you would come in for a roll call and they would say, "Have you signed this?" — it was like a birthday card — "Have you signed it yet?" and they would go over and do it.

There was a great fat Virginian named Benjamin Harrison and a little, little guy from Massachusetts named Elbridge Gerry, of gerrymandering fame, a wispy fellow. And as they were taking their turns, Harrison turned to Gerry and said, "You know, when the British catch us and hang us, it'll all be over with me. You're going to dangle for days." So there was the sense that if they didn't hang together, they would hang separately.

DR: Thomas Jefferson, when his document was being mutilated, never said a word because he didn't like to talk. As president of the United States, he gave one speech in public. He hated to talk in public. Why was that?

JM: He wasn't very good at it. Honestly, he

did not have a voice that carried.

As keen an observer of Jefferson as John Adams — and as we all know, our frenemies are often our best critics and the most precise ones — believed that Jefferson's political power was enhanced by his failure to be a great speechmaker. Remember, in those days, the largest group he would have addressed — outside of the presidential inauguration, which would have been a big crowd — would have been the House, the Continental Congress, or the Confederation Congress. It would have been a group of people fewer in number than are in this room.

Adams — and Franklin also agreed with this — said that because Jefferson was such a good committeeman, he was a good draftsman, he would exercise a certain amount of power in being the fellow who wrote the report. It enhanced his power, because no legislator had ever changed his mind.

Adams spent most of his time getting up and giving speeches saying the other guy was wrong, and it never changed anyone's mind. And so both Franklin and Adams, on reflection, believed that Jefferson had been wise not to pursue the art of rhetoric.

DR: In those days, you ran against each other for president, and whoever came in second became vice president. In this case, when Adams ran against Jefferson in the election of

1800, Adams got the highest number of votes, and he became president. How was it to be serving as vice president for somebody you ran against?

JM: It didn't work out very well, surprisingly. This was the first great contested election in U.S. history, because Washington had not faced any opposition and yet was so sensitive to criticism that he almost left after one term because he didn't like being criticized at all. I certainly never have that reaction to criticism.

Adams came to call on Jefferson when he arrived after the 1800 election and said, "I very much want you to be part of the councils of the administration." They talked about several issues, and then Adams went off to have dinner with a bunch of Federalists and, as Jefferson put it, "We never again had a substantive discussion about any measure of the administration."

The Federalists are holdovers. John Adams kept Washington's cabinet, and later said it was one of his greatest mistakes because they were more loyal to older policies than to Adams's.

DR: So when Adams ran for a second term, he was defeated by —

JM: Thomas Jefferson.

DR: And Jefferson's vice president was?

JM: Aaron Burr.

DR: And Aaron Burr shot Hamilton while he was vice president?

JM: In 1805.

DR: When Aaron Burr was vice president, was he preparing an insurrection against the president because of the Louisiana Purchase?

JM: There were several insurrections. In 1801, beginning in February, there were thirty-two ballots cast in the House of Representatives for the presidency of the United States. There had been a mistake. It took the Twelfth Amendment to correct it, but in 1800 the number of electoral votes for Jefferson and Burr turned out to be the same.

In the past, they would figure out a way to throw away a vote, vote for someone else, just symbolically. It hadn't happened this time.

There's a great debate about this, but Burr was not as eager to stand down as a possible president as Jefferson had hoped, and so you had this entire intrigue in February. There was a snowstorm in Washington. Jefferson was in a quiet agony over at Conrad and Mc-Munn's boardinghouse at C Street and New

139

Jersey Avenue, a fancy new boardinghouse, just trying to figure out how to survive this great political intrigue. Burr let it be known that perhaps he would accept the presidency.

In one of the moments that helped feed an existing rivalry between John Marshall, a cousin of Jefferson's, and Jefferson, there was talk that Marshall might become president for a year while they settled this. You can imagine how that made Jefferson feel about Marshall.

As someone once said, for some reason God loves drunks, little children, and the United States of America. This was the fourth election we'd ever had. Thomas McKean of Pennsylvania and James Monroe of Virginia were governors who prepared to send militia to Washington if, in fact, Thomas Jefferson was not made president. It was a remarkably conditional moment.

DR: Jefferson lived in the White House for eight years — two terms — and his hostess was Dolley Madison because he didn't have a wife, is that right?

JM: That's right.

DR: He didn't give speeches, so members of Congress would come to the White House for salons, and he would greet them in his slippers. What was that all about?

JM: He very much wanted to establish a republican — lowercase — ethos. A lot of debates in the first four, five, six years, even the first decade of the Republic, were about these questions of style and etiquette.

Washington was much more monarchical than a lot of Republicans believed he should be, understandably. General Washington wore a sword when he took the oath of office both times; John Adams also wore a sword. I always have visions of the Gilbert and Sullivan operetta *The Pirates of Penzance* in my mind with that.

Jefferson refused to do that. Jefferson walked from Conrad and McMunn's to the Capitol to take the oath of office and then returned after his inaugural address and sat down at the common boardinghouse table to have lunch, a very conscious way of signaling that this was a republic, not a proto-monarchy.

The way in which he entertained at the White House was very much like this, and also classically contradictory in a Jeffersonian way. There had never been better food, there had never been better wine — he went broke buying wine for the White House to keep members of Congress happy — but he would show up in these sort of Virginia plantation-house clothes, showing that any farmer could become president.

DR: Jefferson almost went broke all the time. He would die bankrupt, more or less. Why was he always borrowing money, and how come he was so bankrupt if he was so smart about so many other things?

JM: You're a private-equity guy. You know farmers.

He was a plantation owner, and he was not very good at it. He spent a lot of time creating new things. He created new species of apples, he loved grapes, he was always trying to bring Italian musicians to Albemarle County, Virginia. It was all very charming, but he didn't actually get a crop to market very often.

DR: You spent five years studying him. If Thomas Jefferson were sitting right here now and you had a chance to ask him one question, what would that question be?

JM: "Why, given your clear moral sense that slavery was the fire bell in the night that was going to lead to a civil war someday, did you not use any political capital in the twenty years of your political dominance to try to ameliorate the situation?"

He just gave up. Again, no one was more eloquent, even in retirement. If you go to the Jefferson Memorial, all those quotations, almost all of them, are about slavery: "I tremble for my country when I reflect that God is just." "Nothing is more certainly written in the book of fate than that these people shall be free."

These are all about slavery, but these were always in letters in which he then said, "But I can't do anything about it. It'll be the work of another generation."

Thomas Jefferson was the dominant political figure of the first half of the American Republic. I absolutely believe he was the most important president — Washington, Jefferson, Jackson, Lincoln.

From 1801 through 1840, for those forty years, either Thomas Jefferson himself or a self-described Jeffersonian was president of the United States, except for four years during the administration of John Quincy Adams. For thirty-six years there was a de facto Jeffersonian dynasty. No other president has done that. Lincoln didn't do it, Roosevelt didn't do it, Reagan didn't do it. It's an unmatched achievement.

If I'm right about that, then you have to take unpopular positions at times to move the country forward in places they don't want to go, and Jefferson just never tried. So "Why, Mr. President, did you never try?"

DR: I wish I knew the answer. One last question. Jefferson lived to be eighty-three years old — a very old age in those times, when

143

James Hemings, a relative of Sally Hemings, was trained as a French chef. He prepared this inventory of kitchen utensils in 1796, two weeks after he was emancipated by Jefferson.

the average life span was forty-five or forty-seven. He would attribute that to riding horses and walking, but he also did something with water every day with his feet. If you want to live to eighty-three or longer, what is the secret that he used?

JM: I'm glad you asked that, because I'm investing in a small company to create foot bowls.

I was allowed, through the good graces of

Monticello, to spend the night in Jefferson's bedroom in the course of doing this book. Nothing inappropriate happened with anyone, I quickly, quickly add.

But one of the things I learned, because I slept on the floor next to the bed, is there was this groove next to the bed. I asked the curator — marvelous staff there, marvelous people — I said, "What is that?" And she said, "Oh, that's from the foot bowl," as if I were a lunatic for not knowing this.

Every morning a bucket of cold water was brought to Jefferson's bedside and he plunged his feet in. And they were little feet. We looked at his boots recently, actually. They were tiny, but he was tall, above six feet. He plunged his feet into cold water and left them in for a few minutes. Benjamin Franklin did the same thing, and he lived a long time too.

He also didn't eat a lot of meat, and he avoided hard liquor, although four glasses of wine was just the beginning of a good time in Jefferson's house. Soak those feet in cold water, and you too can live to be eighty-three years old.

4
RON CHERNOW
ON ALEXANDER HAMILTON

"Alexander Hamilton was someone who radiated genius."

BOOK DISCUSSED:
Alexander Hamilton (The Penguin Press, 2004)

Some biographers write books that are well regarded by serious scholars but that may be too detailed and too long to attract enormous popular interest. Other biographers write books that are quite popular with the book-buying public but that serious scholars feel lack original or serious scholarship.

Then there is Ron Chernow. He is the rarest of biographers: able to write books that are best sellers but that are also praised by scholars. This has been true of all of his biographies, which include books on the House of Morgan, John D. Rockefeller, the famous Warburg banking family, George Washington (a book that won a Pulitzer Prize), and Ulysses S. Grant.

And there is that other biography on a heretofore important but not all that well known Founding Father, Alexander Hamilton.

When it was first published, it not only sold well, but it also was an important contribution to the scholarship on Hamilton. Of greater significance, it was read on a Mexican vacation by Lin-Manuel Miranda, who then used it as the basis for the biggest theatrical phenomenon of recent decades: the musical *Hamilton*.

When I interviewed Chernow, *Hamilton* had just debuted on Broadway, but its now well-known spectacular success as a rare cultural force had not yet occurred, and everyone in the country was not yet familiar with the incredible story of Alexander Hamilton. Chernow does an excellent job of conveying the key elements of that story in this interview.

A footnote: A few years ago, I received the Alexander Hamilton Award from the Museum of American Finance. The director of the museum asked if I would mind if the creator of a then off-Broadway show could sing a few hip-hop songs about Hamilton before I was given the award. I said fine, and a then unknown (to me) Lin-Manuel sang two songs from the musical, which I was told he was still fine-tuning.

I listened, and told the museum director that I knew one thing about Broadway — a hip-hop show based on our first treasury secretary was doomed to fail, and I was glad I had not invested in it. I guess this is why I have not been an investor in Broadway shows. I have absolutely no talent in assessing potential winners.

Chernow's recounting of Hamilton's life makes one realize what Lin-Manuel Miranda found so interesting, if not unbelievable: an illegitimate and orphaned young man from the Caribbean came to New York and, not too long thereafter, became General Washington's top aide during the Revolutionary War, the principal author of *The Federalist Papers,* the first treasury secretary, and the architect of the country's financial system.

How did he pull this off? Chernow makes it clear that Hamilton was not only intellectually gifted but also a truly driven man (a workaholic in today's terminology).

But how could such a smart man, who was driven to accomplish so much more than he had already done, allow himself to die at the age of forty-nine in a duel with Aaron Burr, vice president of the United States? There is no good answer. But Chernow suggests that Hamilton did not intend to shoot Burr — that he was prepared to "waste his shot," perhaps in the expectation (or hope) that Burr, a well-educated "gentleman," would do the same.

One wonders just how history might have been changed, or how many other brilliant feats Hamilton might have accomplished, if he had lived to a ripe old age, as so many of the other Founding Fathers did. We will never know.

We will also never know what George Washington would think of Hamilton becoming so famous because of the success of *Hamilton*. Is he in heaven thinking that *he* was the Revolutionary War general, the president of the Constitutional Convention, the unanimously elected two-term president of the United States, while Hamilton was always subordinate to him? Why did Lin-Manuel not write a show about him? After all, Chernow's book on Washington actually won the Pulitzer Prize.

One suspects, though, that any concern

Washington might feel about Hamilton becoming so popular is a fraction of the concern that Thomas Jefferson must be experiencing.

MR. DAVID M. RUBENSTEIN (DR): We're going to delve into a conversation on our first treasury secretary, Alexander Hamilton, with the man who's written what I think is the definitive biography of him. How many people here have read the biography? How many people have seen the play? How many people are looking for tickets to the play?

When you were writing this book, did you ever think it would be made into a show?

MR. RON CHERNOW (RC): I think it's safe to say, David, I never thought it would be made into a musical, much less a hip-hop musical.

DR: But *Hamilton* was based on your book.

RC: Yes, it's very faithfully based on the book.

DR: The producer read your book, or the lyricist read it?

RC: Lin-Manuel Miranda, who stars in it — he wrote the lyrics, the music, and the book for the show — read the book back in 2008. When I met Lin-Manuel, he told me that he had been reading my Hamilton biography on vacation in Mexico, and he said that as he was reading it, hip-hop songs started rising off the page. Needless to say, this was not a typical reaction to one of my books. But he has produced the most extraordinary show

I've ever seen.

DR: How long did it take you to research the book, and how long to write it?

RC: The book took me five years to write, which seems like a long time, but you have to understand that Alexander Hamilton was the most prolific author of all time. He died at age forty-nine, and yet he left behind thirty-two thick volumes of personal, political and business papers. *The Papers of Alexander Hamilton* was published by Columbia University Press, and the chief editor, Dr. Harold Syrett, made the facetious statement that he wanted to dedicate the volumes to Aaron Burr, without whose cooperation the project could never have been completed.

DR: When we talk about the Founding Fathers, we often say Washington, Jefferson, Adams, Franklin. But Hamilton hasn't historically gotten the deification the others have. Why do you think he wasn't as well recognized for his accomplishments, given all the things he did?

RC: When I tell you, David, that Alexander Hamilton's political enemies were John Adams, Thomas Jefferson, James Madison, James Monroe — and I'll even throw in John Quincy Adams and Andrew Jackson — what do you notice about that list? It sometimes seemed like the fastest road to the White House was to be a political opponent of Alexander Hamilton.

What happened is that Hamilton died in 1804. He never reached the age of fifty. If history is written by the victors, the victors were certainly the Jeffersonians who dominated American politics in the years leading up to the Civil War. No less important, I think, is that Hamilton's party, the Federalist Party, disappeared in the first quarter of the nineteenth century, so there wasn't an institutional structure perpetuating his memory.

DR: Of all the Founding Fathers I mentioned, the only one who was not born in the United States was Alexander Hamilton. Can you go through the story of his birth and how he was considered by some to be illegitimate, and how that affected him?

RC: This was a really ghastly Dickensian childhood. Hamilton was born on the Caribbean island of Nevis and spent his adolescence on the island of St. Croix. Hamilton's father, James Hamilton, abandoned the family when Alexander was eleven. His mother, Rachel, died when Alexander was thirteen. He was lying there inches away from her, deathly sick himself.

But he survived. He was farmed out to a

Hamilton's birthplace on the Caribbean island of Nevis.

first cousin, who committed suicide a year later. He was then sent to live with a planter named Thomas Stevens, whose son, Ned Stevens, became his best lifelong friend. Everyone who saw Ned in later years was shocked by the uncanny resemblance between him and Alexander Hamilton, so in all likelihood, Hamilton's biological father was actually Thomas Stevens.

He was clearly illegitimate. His mother, Rachel Faucette, came from a French Huguenot background. She had already been married when she met James Hamilton and, under the terms of her divorce, she could not legally remarry, so any children she had were illegitimate, and there was a tremendous stigma to that at the time.

DR: How does somebody whose mother was gone and whose father abandoned him make it from the Virgin Islands to the United States? How did that happen?

RC: What happened was that Hamilton was a poor clerk working at a trading house on St. Croix when a killer hurricane hit the island in 1772. It was a monstrous hurricane. It's thought that a tsunami rolled across the island. Hamilton sat down and he published a description of the hurricane in the local newspaper, and it was almost Shakespearean in its vividness.

The local merchants read this, recognized the extraordinary literary flair of this young man, banded together, and took up a collection to educate him in North America. He came to America around 1773 — in other words, right on the eve of the American Revolution. He didn't know a soul, just came armed with a few letters of introduction. He was briefly educated in New Jersey and ended up in King's College, now Columbia University, which was then on the southern tip of Manhattan.

DR: He was in New York and going to college, paid for by friends and admirers. When did other people realize that he was a gifted writer and talker?

RC: Almost immediately. Alexander Hamilton was someone who radiated genius.

I remember a wonderful statement that Dr. Samuel Johnson made about Edmund Burke. He said that if there was a rainstorm one day and you sheltered under an awning with Edmund Burke, whom you had never met before, if you sheltered under an awning with him for five minutes, you would know that you had been in the presence of a genius. That describes the reaction people had to Hamilton.

He was an undergraduate at King's College, but he was already publishing fiery essays against the British and making rabble-rousing speeches in what today is City Hall Park. And then, as the Revolution started, he became the head of an artillery company, drilling in St. Paul's churchyard.

DR: Did he just start the artillery company himself and say, "Join me"?

RC: Originally it was a group of students.

DR: He was in the artillery company, fighting in the Revolutionary War. How did he wind up as the chief of staff to George Washington?

Alexander Hamilton at the age of fifteen.

RC: As a soldier and as the head of this artillery company, Hamilton was a daredevil. He was physically fearless at the Battle of White Plains in 1776, and as the Continental Army was retreating across New Jersey to the Delaware after the battle, Hamilton was covering the retreating soldiers. He was spraying the British and Hessian soldiers with fire.

So he came to Washington's attention first, I think, for his derring-do, but also because of his brilliance. There were four generals who tried to recruit Hamilton onto their staff, because he was so literate and capable. From

157

Washington's standpoint, Hamilton had an ideal combination of talents. He was already a very skilled soldier, but Washington's most pressing need was for someone to write letters for him.

DR: Because the generals in those days were writing dispatches all the time, and Washington had something like four people doing this for him?

RC: He had a number of people doing it. To give some sense of how important these letters were, during the eight and a half years of the Revolutionary War, Washington was serving fourteen different political masters. He was keeping up extensive correspondence not only with the Continental Congress but with the governors of the thirteen states.

Hamilton was handling this correspondence, which was even more important once we forged the alliance with France. Hamilton's mother was a French Huguenot and he was therefore bilingual. When he was exchanging letters with the marquis de Lafayette, he would write to Lafayette in faultless French. Lafayette would send back letters that even I could see were full of spelling and grammatical mistakes in French.

DR: So Washington brought Hamilton onto his staff, and he quickly rose up to be not just a letter writer but, in effect, the chief of staff?

RC: It was quite remarkable. When you look at the lists of generals at the different war councils before the major battles, you have something like eleven generals, and then it will say "Colonel Hamilton" on the bottom. This was very important in terms of Hamilton's career, because he was getting a really expansive view of the Revolutionary War, both from a military and also a political standpoint. This was his school.

DR: So he was running the war, practically, for Washington. He was Washington's mouthpiece.

RC: Well, not exactly running the war, but weighing in on all sorts of issues.

DR: Why was he not happy with that? At one point he said, "I want to do something else." What was it he wanted to do?

RC: Alexander Hamilton realized from the very beginning of the war that postwar political glory would not go to the person who had written the most beautiful letters for Washington during the war but would go to battlefield heroes. Throughout the war, he was lobbying Washington to give him a battlefield command. It produced real friction between them, and Hamilton ended up leaving Washington's staff.

Hamilton finally got Washington to give him a field command at Yorktown, and at last he had the moment he'd always fantasized about. He was assigned to take a defensive fortification.

It was at night. He rose up out of the trenches, with shells exploding in the air, and led his men across this rutted battlefield. When they got to Redoubt No. 10 [a key part of the British defenses], Hamilton had one of the men in his company stoop down. He stood on the guy's shoulders, sprang up on the parapet, and yelled to the other men to follow him. It was almost like a scene from a Hollywood action flick. That was the life of Hamilton.

DR: And he became a bit of a hero for this.

RC: Absolutely.

DR: The Treaty of Paris took another two years or so to negotiate, but after Yorktown the war was over, more or less. What did Hamilton do?

RC: What happened was Hamilton went back to New York. He was a great one for taking advantage of opportunities. Robert Morris, who was the superintendent of finance for the United States, appointed him tax receiver of New York.

This would have been a very lowly job for anyone else, but Alexander Hamilton lobbied the New York legislature to create a special committee on how to make tax collection more efficient. Hamilton so impressed the New York State Legislature with his presentation that he was appointed one of the five New Yorkers at the Confederation Congress [the U.S. governing assembly from 1781 to 1789].

DR: He was also practicing law. He got to become a lawyer without going to law school, right?

RC: It was amazing, because at the time you became a lawyer by serving a two-year apprenticeship with an older lawyer. Hamilton passed the bar in New York after six months of self-study. He cobbled together a digest of New York legal precedents and procedures that was so expertly done it became a crib sheet for law students for another two or three generations in New York.

DR: In those days, if you came from a foreign country and you were, let's say, illegitimate, you were not likely to rise up in New York. How did he manage to get to the top of New

York society?

RC: He married Elizabeth Schuyler, whose father, Major General Philip Schuyler, was not only one of the leading generals in the Revolution, he was a close friend of George Washington, and one of the leading landholders in New York State.

I think what happened, David, was that because Hamilton was Washington's chief of staff, even though he was this illegitimate orphaned kid from the Caribbean, it was like being chief of staff of the White House. It gave him tremendous standing.

When Hamilton married Elizabeth Schuyler at the Schuyler mansion in Albany, the place was teeming with all her rich relatives — the Van Cortlandts, the Van Rensselaers, the Beekmans. They were the Anglo-Dutch royalty of New York State.

Hamilton didn't have a single family member there. He had only one friend, a James McHenry from Washington's staff. So you can imagine the discrepancy in status. He was marrying into the most social and prosperous family in New York, and he had only one friend present.

DR: He had a bit of an amorous reputation. In fact, what did Martha Washington call her tomcat?

His marriage to Elizabeth Schuyler, a member of one of New York's wealthiest families, raised Hamilton's social status considerably.

RC: Hamilton. Yeah, it was a big joke. She had this feral tomcat that she called Hamilton, although historians have disputed the accuracy of this.

Everyone noticed early on that the ladies were fatally attracted to him. In fact, Abigail Adams, after she met Hamilton, said, "The devil is in his eyes. His eyes are lasciviousness itself" — what we would call "bedroom eyes." Hamilton clearly had a roving eye.

DR: So the war was over. We signed the Treaty of Paris. The Articles of Confederation were governing the country, and Hamilton was a member of the Congress. What could be better than that? He was making a lot of money as a lawyer. He'd married into a prosperous family. Why did he decide to try to overturn the Articles of Confederation?

RC: For one thing, throughout the war, Hamilton and Washington were constantly writing letters to the Congress and the state governors, pleading for men and money. The Continental Congress did not have the power to demand money from any of the thirteen states. They did not have the power to demand men from the states. They could only request. And of course all of those thirteen state governors decided that they would rather keep the money and men in their own states. So Hamilton already saw the weakness of the Articles of Confederation.

When he was in the Confederation Congress, it had no independent revenue source. They tried to enact a 5 percent impost — a 5 percent customs duty. They could not get that passed. Hamilton, I think, despaired of the Articles of Confederation as ever being the framework for a real government.

DR: So he and Madison caballed to put together an effective request for a constitutional convention.

RC: They met in Annapolis, Maryland, in late 1786. There was a small conference called to try to iron out trade disputes. There was no common trade policy, so Connecticut had its own import duties, as did New York, as did New Jersey, etc.

What happened at this little conference in Annapolis was that they realized the disputes over trade policies were just symptomatic of the basic problems with the Articles of Confederation. Hamilton personally wrote and issued the plea for a constitutional convention to meet in Philadelphia in May of 1787.

DR: Congress agreed to have a constitutional convention that might modify but not completely change the Articles of Confederation. The trick was getting George Washington to show up. Why was that so important?

RC: They realized that Washington would give the convention a cachet it couldn't possibly have otherwise. Hamilton and Madison at that point were comrades in arms, but that changed. This was the one relationship where someone went from being Hamilton's political friend to political enemy.

But at that point they were working very, very closely together, and they realized that technically the Constitutional Convention was supposed to revise the Articles of Confederation. Hamilton and Madison saw that was ridiculous — that they needed to scrap the Articles of Confederation and create a brand-new constitution. That was obviously going to be something that would be hard for the general public to swallow, so they felt that it required someone of George Washington's stature to reassure the country that this was not some sinister plot being hatched in Philadelphia.

DR: Hamilton convinced Washington to go, and he showed up at the Constitutional Convention. They met for three months. What was Hamilton's role in the convention? He wasn't really that powerful, was he?

RC: In the opening weeks of the convention, Hamilton didn't make a single speech. When he finally opened his mouth, being Alexander Hamilton, he spoke for six straight hours. He presented his own plan for a new form of government, and it was frankly pretty wacky. It was not his greatest moment.

For the presidency, he wanted to have an elective monarch, essentially. He wanted the president to be elected but then to serve for life, subject to impeachment or recall. It was a terrible idea, but luckily it was not taken seriously. Then Hamilton got down to the serious business of passing a more realistic proposal.

DR: At the Constitutional Convention, each state had one vote, and there were two people in the New York delegation who were against his views. Hamilton was always outvoted, so he didn't show up that much, did he?

RC: Right. The New York State governor was a man named George Clinton, who was a real local boss. George Clinton loved the Articles of Confederation. The weaker the central government, the more he liked it, so he was afraid of the Constitutional Convention.

There were three delegates from New York: John Lansing Jr., Robert Yates, and Hamilton. Lansing and Yates were sent by Governor Clinton essentially to sabotage the Constitutional Convention. It wasn't until a certain point, in the middle of that summer, when Lansing and Yates left the Constitutional Convention for good, that Hamilton suddenly came back, realizing his moment had come.

DR: When the convention agreed on the Constitution, Hamilton agreed to it even though he thought it wasn't perfect. Why?

RC: People often say, "Well, the final document was so different from his speech," but the final version of the Constitution differed in significant ways from the views of every single person there. Hamilton's elective monarch was wacky, but Madison wanted the federal government to have a veto over every state law — not exactly a great idea either. Benjamin Franklin wanted a plural executive — that is, instead of one president, we would have a council of three, which I think we will all agree was not a great idea. The beauty of this situation was that all of these men were able to then rally around this compromise document.

DR: As drafted, the Constitution said that it would go into effect if nine of the thirteen states ratified it. What was Hamilton's role in the ratification process?

RC: Major. First of all, it was Hamilton who originated the idea for *The Federalist Papers,* basically because New York was one of the states with significant opposition to the Constitution.

The Federalist Papers were eighty-five essays published over a six-month period. [Written by Hamilton, Madison, and John Jay and published under the pseudonym Publius, the essays argued the case for ratifying the Constitution.] Alexander Hamilton wrote fifty-one of them, and he was doing this as a sideline. He had a full-time legal practice. We have anecdotal evidence of the printer sitting

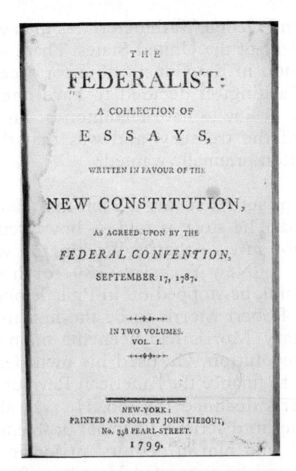

Alexander Hamilton, James Madison, and John Jay made the case for the Constitution in a series of eighty-five public essays, The FedAveralist Papers. *Hamilton wrote fifty-one of them.*

in the outer office as Hamilton was finishing the final lines, and then the printer would run off to publish them.

DR: *The Federalist Papers* were written, the Constitution was ratified and went into effect, and George Washington was then elected president of the United States. There was no provision in the Constitution for a cabinet, but Washington decided to have one. Why did he decide to have Hamilton be his secretary of the treasury, and was that the job Hamilton originally wanted?

RC: I'm sure that was the job that Hamilton wanted. The story is told — how accurately I'm not sure — that as Washington was en route to New York in 1789 for his first inaugural, he stopped off in Philadelphia and asked Robert Morris to be the first treasury secretary. Morris had been the financier of the Revolution. He used his own personal credit to finance the American Revolution.

Morris declined the job. He was already running into serious financial problems that would land him in debtors' prison in a few years, and he suggested Hamilton. Washington supposedly said to Morris, "I didn't realize that Alexander Hamilton knew so much about finance," and Robert Morris said, "To a mind like his, nothing is amiss."

I think Washington knew all about Hamilton's knowledge of finance. So Hamilton, at age thirty-four, became the first treasury secretary, which was far and away the most important job in the cabinet.

DR: The cabinet then had three people.

RC: Effectively, yes. Even the attorney general was a part-time legal advisor. There were three cabinet secretaries. Thomas Jefferson, the secretary of state, started out with six people in his department. Henry Knox, the secretary of war, started out with twelve. Alexander Hamilton, because he had customs inspectors and revenue collectors, suddenly had hundreds of people, so his department was more than 90 percent of the entire government.

DR: He created the U.S. Mint and the U.S. Coast Guard at the same time. How did he do that?

RC: The main source of government revenue at the time was from customs duties, so Hamilton created a customs service. There was a lot of smuggling, so he created a fleet of revenue cutters to intercept smugglers. That fleet of revenue cutters became the Coast Guard. Hamilton was really more like the prime minister than just treasury secretary.

DR: One of the big issues was who was going to pay off seventy-some million dollars of Revolutionary War debt. Hamilton had a plan, and ultimately there was a compromise at a famous dinner. Can you describe what happened?

RC: Again, just let me say that the United States was literally bankrupt when Washington was sworn in as the first president. American debt was selling at ten or fifteen cents on the dollar.

Any other regime after a revolution would have just repudiated the debt. Hamilton felt that, as a matter of both American honor and American pride and American credit, that debt had to be paid off in full at par value. The centerpiece of his plan was to assume state debt. There was $50 million in federal debt, $25 million in state debt.

It seems counterintuitive. Why would any treasury secretary voluntarily take on additional debt? Hamilton realized that, if he assumed state debt, the federal government forever after would have a lock on the main revenues of the country. To this day, I think that that assumption of state debt is the reason we pay more in federal taxes than in state and local taxes.

Now, Hamilton had a lot of trouble getting that through Congress, but he struck a deal over dinner with Jefferson and Madison. He agreed to have the new U.S. capital on the Potomac River if they would get him a few extra votes from the South on the assumption of state debt by the federal government.

Thomas Jefferson later said it was the single biggest mistake of his political career. It sounded like a technocratic thing, the assumption of state debt. He didn't realize that Hamilton had a whole political agenda buried in that to strengthen the central government.

DR: At the time, the capital was New York. The agreement was it would then go to Philadelphia for ten years. And after those ten years, Washington, D.C., would be built. We're here because of that dinner. After George Washington got reelected, Hamilton decided to stay for how much longer?

RC: Hamilton stayed one year into the second term and went back to being a lawyer in New York.

DR: Why did he leave?

RC: This will not come as a surprise to anyone in this room. He'd made tremendous financial sacrifices for public service.

DR: The salary of the secretary of the treasury in those days was —

RC: It was very low.

DR: Two or three thousand dollars?

RC: Yes. He could make much, much more money as a lawyer in New York. Alexander and Eliza Hamilton ended up having eight children, so he had a lot of bills.

Also, to give you some idea of the success of his program, when he became treasury secretary, we were the deadbeat of world finance. We were in arrears on both the principal and interest on our debt. By the time that Alexander Hamilton left the Treasury five years later, we commanded interest rates as low as any country in the world. Our credit was as high as any of the Western European powers.

DR: When they were in the cabinet, Jefferson was secretary of state and Hamilton was secretary of the treasury. How bad was the relationship? Did they ever get along?

RC: No. Hamilton later said that from the day Jefferson arrived in New York, Jefferson was gunning for him. It was partly there was certainly a personality difference between them. Jefferson was a rather shy, courtly person. Hamilton had a real zest for political combat and polemics.

But they also had two fundamentally differing visions. In terms of the economy, Jefferson wanted a nation based on small towns and traditional agriculture. Hamilton wanted that plus large cities, stock exchanges, banks, factories, corporations — in other words, the world that we know today.

Then there was also the political difference.

Jefferson wanted a weak central government, legislative power, strict construction of the Constitution. Hamilton wanted a strong central government, executive power, and a very expansive interpretation of the Constitution. They really started the debate we still have.

DR: In those days, even if you were in the same president's cabinet, you apparently hired surrogates to write negative articles about other people in the cabinet.

RC: While he was treasury secretary, Hamilton liked writing articles under Roman pseudonyms, which was fairly common at the time. In the middle of one controversy, he started secretly writing essays praising the treasury secretary under the pen name of Camillus.

Then he launched another series under the pen name of Philo Camillus. And Philo Camillus kept praising Camillus, and they both kept saying that the treasury secretary was the most brilliant man in America.

DR: What did they say about Jefferson?

RC: Much less complimentary things.

DR: Madison and Hamilton cooperated on writing *The Federalist Papers*. How did that relationship go later on?

RC: It sank over an issue that was known as discrimination. I mentioned that the debt was selling for ten or fifteen cents on the dollar. Hamilton announced his plan to redeem all the debt at face value, and the value of that debt soared.

A lot of it was originally in the form of IOUs that had been given to soldiers during the Revolutionary War. Many of them, desperate for money after the Revolution, sold those pieces of paper at depressed prices. Speculators gathered them up and made a killing on Hamilton's plan.

Madison said, "Let's track down those original soldiers who sold their IOUs. They should be the ones who profit from the appreciation in value." Hamilton opposed the idea, even though he was the one who had been a soldier during the war, not Madison.

Hamilton said two things. He said, number one, tracing back all the owners of a security administratively would be a nightmare. The second point was much more important. He said, "I understand that this is hard to swallow, but we have to establish forever the principle that anyone who owns a stock or a bond or any kind of security has, in purchasing that security, assumed all of the risk and all of the reward for it." So it's really the basis of our modern financial markets.

DR: George Washington decided not to run for a third term, and he gave a farewell address. Did Hamilton write that farewell address?

RC: Yes, Hamilton did write the farewell address.

Washington gave him two options. He had thought of stepping down at the end of his first term, and he'd had Madison write a farewell. He gave Hamilton Madison's farewell address and said, "You can either revise Madison's farewell address or trash it and start anew."

Anyone who knew Alexander Hamilton knew what decision he would make in that situation. He wrote a completely new farewell address.

He used to tell the story that he and Eliza were walking down the street in New York one day after it had been published in pamphlet form, and a vendor on the street tried to sell him a copy of Washington's farewell address. He turned to his wife afterward and laughed. He said, "That man tried to sell me a copy of my own writing."

DR: Hamilton wanted to retain political influence. When Washington stepped down, the next election was between John Adams and Thomas Jefferson. What role did Hamilton play in that election?

RC: Hamilton and John Adams were the two leading figures in what was known as the Federalist Party. Hamilton had started out with a lot of respect for Adams as one of the original venerable figures of the Revolution, but their relationship became really pathological.

Adams saw Hamilton as this conceited upstart who had overshadowed him. Hamilton saw Adams as crotchety and temperamental and difficult. So their personal relationship was very bad.

Two things that Adams said about Hamilton — one was that "Hamilton has a superabundance of secretions which he cannot find whores enough to draw off." And we think the style of political play is rough nowadays.

He also — and this, I think, was far more painful to Hamilton — called him "the Creole bastard," which was simultaneously sticking it to him in terms of saying he was biracial, which some people imagined he might have been, and also that he was illegitimate. And nothing pained Hamilton more than that.

Hamilton, of course, gave as good as he got. He said of Adams, "I think the man is mad and I shall soon be led to say as wicked as he is mad."

DR: They were both members of the Federalist Party. Did Hamilton get Adams elected president?

RC: No. Adams ran in 1796. Under the rules of the day, Jefferson was the runner-up and therefore became vice president.

Adams and Hamilton continued to have a very stormy relationship up to the point in 1800 when Adams ran for reelection. Hamilton — again, not one of his finest moments — published an open letter to John Adams. It was really a pretty cruel diatribe about him that, I think, injured Hamilton much more than it injured Adams. But, of course, Jefferson won the election.

DR: Adams was elected to the White House just once. During that period of time, there was in effect a quasi war. We thought the French were going to invade the United States, and Adams asked George Washington to lead an army to repel them. What did Washington say about what he needs to do to pull it off?

RC: Washington was, after forty years of public service, happily retired in Mount Vernon at that point. Adams sent Washington's name to the Senate before Washington even knew what was happening.

Washington then did something that flabbergasted Adams. He said, "I will only take the job" — which was to lead a provisional army of ten thousand people in case France invaded — "I'll only take the job if I can have Alexander Hamilton as my inspector general," which was the number-two job.

By this point Adams loathed Hamilton, and suddenly George Washington, the great political untouchable, is saying, "I'm not going to take this job unless Alexander Hamilton can be my major general," which is what happened. And that really stuck in Adams's craw.

DR: Adams ran for reelection in 1800, and he was running, in effect, against Thomas Jefferson, his vice president. What role did Hamilton play in helping Jefferson get elected?

RC: Enormous. However strange it sounds now, under the rules of the time there were not separate elections for president and vice president. Thomas Jefferson and Aaron Burr were ostensibly on the same ticket — that is, everyone understood that Jefferson was the presidential candidate and Burr was the candidate for vice president. But there was only one election, and they tied.

At that point, Aaron Burr thought, "Well, it might be very nice to be president of the United States instead of vice president." The vote went to the House, which was still controlled by the Federalists.

And Hamilton did something that Aaron

Burr would never forgive and that may have cost Hamilton his life. He advised the Federalists in the House to vote for Jefferson, even though Jefferson had been his bitter enemy. He said, "It's better to have Jefferson, who has the wrong principles, than Aaron Burr, who has no principles," which Burr never forgave.

DR: So Jefferson became president and the vice president was Aaron Burr.

RC: Yes. But Jefferson felt that during that period when the election went to the House for a vote, Burr had angled to become president. Even though he was forced to have Burr as vice president for four years, when Jefferson ran for reelection in 1804, he dropped him from the ticket.

Burr then went back to New York — both Hamilton and Burr were from New York — and ran for governor, and Hamilton again blocked Burr in his attempt to win office.

If you were Aaron Burr, Alexander Hamilton stopped you from becoming president, then stopped you from becoming governor of New York. I think that was really the political context of the duel.

DR: Hamilton was having a conversation with somebody. He said something negative about Aaron Burr, as if he needed to say more than he'd already said. This got put in a letter, and the letter was read by Burr. What happened?

RC: There was an Albany dinner party, and someone reported, in a letter that was published in a newspaper, that Alexander Hamilton had uttered a despicable opinion about Aaron Burr. Historians for two hundred years have been trying to figure out what the despicable opinion was. I came up dry, unfortunately, like all my predecessors.

As strange as it sounds, very often politicians in those days had duels as a way of trying to rehabilitate their careers. So Aaron Burr challenged Hamilton to a duel.

Hamilton's son had died in a duel, also in New Jersey, about three years earlier. Because of that episode, Hamilton on the one hand had a principled objection to dueling, but on the other hand he felt that, as a political figure and a military man, if he was challenged to a duel and spurned it, he would look like a coward. This would destroy his political and military usefulness.

I think this was more in his head than in other people's: How could he resolve this conflict? He decided he was going to go to the dueling ground in Weehawken, New Jersey. He would show his bravery by showing up for the duel, but then, when they squared off, he was going to waste his shot.

DR: At the time they often had seconds who would be negotiating to avoid the duel, but the seconds were unable to negotiate a resolution this time. They were in New York. Why did they go across the river to New Jersey?

RC: Dueling, on paper, was illegal in both New York and New Jersey, but it really wasn't prosecuted vigorously in New Jersey, so duelists would row there across the Hudson — although after Burr killed Hamilton, he was wanted for murder in two states.

In fact, it's a bizarre story. He was wanted for murder in New York and New Jersey, so where did he flee? He fled to Washington and, because he was still vice president, he presided over the impeachment trial of a Supreme Court justice in the U.S. Senate, even though he was wanted for murder in two states. Strange.

DR: What happened in the duel was that Hamilton put up his gun and shot first but didn't try to hit Burr?

RC: One of two things could have happened. Hamilton's second said that Burr fired first. If Burr fired first, what must have happened was that Hamilton, who had the pistol in his hand, as the bullet hit reflexively squeezed the trigger. Because Hamilton's bullet went about twelve feet high, it hit tree branches above Burr.

If Hamilton fired first, he must have aimed in the air because, again, it went many feet above Burr, and Hamilton had been a soldier, so he was a decent shot. Either way, there is evidence that Hamilton did not aim his pistol at Burr, who may have aimed to kill.

DR: Hamilton didn't die instantly. They rowed him back to Manhattan. What happened? Everybody came to say good-bye?

RC: It was an extraordinarily dramatic scene. He was rowed back to the Bayard Farm, in what's now the West Village of Manhattan.

Hamilton was lying in the bed, and he asked his wife, Eliza, to have all of the children line up in a row at the foot of the bed. And he took one last look at them, and then he shut his eyes. It was heartbreaking. We have a lot of descriptions. There were people on their knees weeping and gnashing their teeth. It was an incredible moment.

DR: Is the home that Hamilton built and lived in in his later years in New York still there?

RC: Yes, it's called the Grange. It's now in Harlem, or what's called Hamilton Heights.

DR: After his death, his wife tried, with his family, to perpetuate his image. How much longer did Eliza live?

RC: She lived another fifty years, to the age of ninety-seven. One of the most touching things, for me, about the later years of Elizabeth Schuyler Hamilton is that she not only did everything in her power to try to honor her husband but Washington as well.

In 1848, she attended the laying of the cornerstone for the Washington Monument. She'd become very close friends with Dolley Madison, even though their husbands had been political opponents. And in the crowd that day with Eliza Hamilton and Dolley Madison was a one-term congressman from Illinois named Abraham Lincoln.

It was an amazing moment. It's the only moment of that sort I'm aware of where the founding generation touches the Civil War generation.

DR: Can you explain why the ten-dollar bill will not have Hamilton on it?

RC: I can't. I pray to God that he'll stay on the ten. I feel it has been his claim to fame. I'd love to see a woman on the currency, but on the twenty. I think maybe it's a good time for Andrew Jackson to retire. [The Treasury Department ultimately decided to keep Hamilton on the ten-dollar bill; as of spring 2019, Jackson remained on the twenty after the U.S. Treasury Department announced that replacing him with Harriet Tubman would be delayed until at least 2026.]

Hamilton doesn't have an obelisk near the White House. He doesn't have a temple on the Tidal Basin. There's a tiny little statue of him behind the Treasury Department that I think maybe one visitor in a thousand sees.

DR: After *Alexander Hamilton,* you subsequently wrote a book on George Washington, which won the Pulitzer Prize. In it you say, in effect, that Washington is the indispensable man to the beginning of the country. Where do you think Hamilton stands in that pecking order?

RC: I would also call him an indispensable man. Remember, this is somebody who created the first fiscal system, the first monetary system, the first accounting system, the first tax system, the first central bank, the first mint, on and on and on and on.

He was uniquely qualified to do it, because the first treasury secretary had to be someone with extraordinary financial sophistication. Hamilton had that. It had to be someone who was a great legal scholar and could argue that the Constitution permitted these activities. He also had to be a great enough technocrat

In spite of his many contributions to the nation, including the creation of its first fiscal system, Hamilton does not have a monument in Washington, D.C. His final resting place is in the Trinity Church Cemetery in New York City.

to craft these policies, and then he had to be a great enough political theorist to see them as consistent with the American Revolution and the Constitution.

DR: Who is your next book on? What great American are you working on?

RC: Ulysses S. Grant.

DR: And how many more years will that take you?

RC: I'm hoping it will be out in a couple of years. But I've been a little distracted by a certain show. [Chernow's *Grant* was published by The Penguin Press in 2017.]

5

WALTER ISAACSON

ON BENJAMIN FRANKLIN

"The Founders are the greatest team ever fielded. You have somebody of great, high rectitude: George Washington. You have a couple of really brilliant people: Madison, Jefferson. You have very passionate visionaries: Sam Adams, his cousin John. And then you have somebody who can bring them all together: Ben Franklin."

BOOKS DISCUSSED:
Benjamin Franklin: An American Life
(Simon & Schuster, 2003)
Kissinger: A Biography (Simon & Schuster,
1992)
Einstein: His Life and Universe (Simon &
Schuster, 2007)
Steve Jobs (Simon & Schuster, 2011)
*The Innovators: How a Group of Hackers,
Geniuses, and Geeks Created the Digital
Revolution* (Simon & Schuster, 2014)
Leonardo da Vinci (Simon & Schuster,
2017)

The phrase "Renaissance man" is not used to describe many individuals today, for there are so few who, in the era of specialization, can do many different intellectually challenging acts in an enviable way. In the modern era, one such man is Walter Isaacson: Rhodes Scholar, member of the Harvard Board of Overseers, former editor of *Time* magazine, past president of CNN, past president of the Aspen Institute, a member of the Tulane Board of Trustees, the founding chairman of Teach for America, and the author of best-selling books on Henry Kissinger, Albert Einstein, Steve Jobs, and Leonardo da Vinci, among others.

One of Isaacson's books is about America's first, and perhaps most gifted, Renaissance man — Benjamin Franklin. During his era,

Franklin was America's best-known and most admired person, in the colonies as well as in Europe: publisher, printer, political theorist, humorist, author, scientist, inventor, postmaster, signer of the Declaration of Independence and the Constitution and the Treaty of Paris (the only person to sign all three), university founder, library creator, friend of kings and government leaders, the colonies' overseas representative and negotiator, prominent figure of the day in science and literature and the arts, and, of course, skilled raconteur and well-known lover of life.

Perhaps it takes a Renaissance man to fully understand and write about another Renaissance man. That may account for the insightful, hard-to-put-down biography that Walter Isaacson wrote about Benjamin Franklin.

I have worked with Isaacson on a variety of Aspen Institute matters over the years and have interviewed him in various settings about most of his books. His admiration for Franklin, as well as his appreciation of Franklin's flaws, comes through in this interview. A reader of it would be hard-pressed to not also read the entire biography. I hope some skilled author will, not long from now, write the biography of Walter Isaacson.

In our conversation, Isaacson first addresses the fascination he has with Renaissance men or "geniuses." He enjoys trying to understand how the creative mind really works, and what enabled some individuals to think outside of the box so creatively that they could develop theories of relativity, create the iPhone, or discover electricity.

But he notes that even the greatest of geniuses have usually been building on the earlier work of others, and many have had partners to enable them to make their "genius" breakthroughs.

Franklin is in that category. An inventor and a creator of enormous breadth and scope, often he was working with others or building on the work of others. Still, as Isaacson points out in the interview, however Franklin did what he did, the scope of his creations in the sciences, and in so many other areas, made him the country's best-known individual before the Revolutionary War. He was also the most admired American in Europe, where he lived for nearly two decades, in London and in Paris, representing various colonies and ultimately the new country as it sought to negotiate the end of the war.

Isaacson did note one of Franklin's secrets: he could spend much of his long life (he lived to the age of eighty-four) without having to work for a living.

Although born poor and educated only for two years, Franklin was able to retire from his successful printing operation in his early forties, having his employees and his common-law wife continue to run the business throughout much of the rest of his life. That provided him with income as well as the freedom to create, think, negotiate, and charm.

Part of the charm was the homespun wisdom often seen in *Poor Richard's Almanack,* an example of an exceedingly popular and profitable Franklin venture. And part of the charm was due to Franklin's ability to appear as a common man, for instance, not wearing the kind of wig favored by aristocrats to cover their baldness.

His flowing long hair became his trademark. Little could he have imagined how, centuries later, that look would adorn the most commonly printed U.S. paper currency — the hundred-dollar bill.

MR. DAVID M. RUBENSTEIN (DR): Walter, thank you very much for doing this. Is this one of those rare times that you're not writing a book?

MR. WALTER ISAACSON (WI): Correct. It's great to be here at the Library, because you can see the back of Ben Franklin's head when the sun is coming through the window in the Great Hall, and there's the bust of him. And let me also say that David Rubenstein has invented patriotic philanthropy, and this is all part of it. So thank you, David.

DR: Thank you very much. Walter, you have tended to write books about people that others would say are more or less brilliant people — Henry Kissinger, Benjamin Franklin, Steve Jobs. Oh, and Albert Einstein. Why did you pick geniuses as kind of a theme? Of those geniuses, who do you think was actually the smartest?

WI: Einstein was the smartest. That one is easy. He was the smartest because he had that quality of genius that allowed him to think out of the box, to be totally imaginative. But he was also somebody who knew what was in the box better than anybody. He was a great physicist.

I like the life of the mind and how the creative mind works. Some people write about great military heroes or sports heroes or literary people. To me, somebody who can think creatively, be imaginative, that's an interesting thing to wrestle with — somebody like Franklin.

DR: Is it easier to write about a dead genius or a living one?

WI: When I did Henry Kissinger, who of course is a genius, as he will tell you and probably has told you —

DR: A few times.

WI: Right. And he actually was.

He comes up with this whole balance-of-power theory for how to extricate the U.S. from Vietnam and play Russia and China off against each other. But having dealt with him, when the book was over, I got nine letters in one day, hand-delivered by his assistant Paul Bremer, who went on to be viceroy in Iraq. [In 2003–04, Bremer led the Coalition Provisional Authority, which ran the country after the U.S. invasion.]

This was so difficult, in some ways, to deal with that I said, "I'm going to do somebody who's been dead for two hundred years." And that's why I did Franklin.

But there are challenges when you do someone who is in the far past such as Ben

Franklin. Let's take the most ingenious thing he did, which was the kite-flying experiment that led to figuring out the single-fluid theory of electricity. [One popular theory at the time held that electricity was composed of two fluids that worked together to produce a charge.]

We have one newspaper article, one letter to Peter Collinson [a Fellow of the Royal Society in London who corresponded with Franklin about electricity], and one textbook written about ten years later that tells you about it. [Franklin's *Experiments and Observations on Electricity, Made at Philadelphia in America,* was published in 1751.]

With Steve Jobs, if we were doing the iPad, he would tell me for an hour how he made the curve in the chamfer [the curved edge where the two sides of the computer meet]. So you know a thousand times more from somebody living.

DR: After the Kissinger experience, you wrote about some dead geniuses, Franklin and Einstein. Why did you then pick a person who at the time was living, Steve Jobs? How did that come about, and how difficult was it to write that book?

WI: Partly it came about because I had done the Ben Franklin book, just finished Einstein, and Steve gave me a call. And he said, "Do

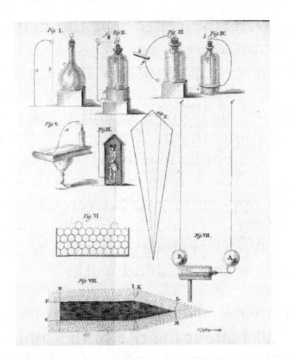

Franklin described his famous electrical experiments in a series of letters that became a highly influential scientific textbook.

me next." My reaction was: "Sure, you arrogant —" Never mind.

I had known him since 1984. We are about the same age, and when he was doing the original Mac computer, he used to come to *Time* magazine where I worked and show it off. I said, "I'll do you in twenty or thirty years when you retire."

But then somebody close to him said, "If you're going to do Steve, you have to do him now." I said, "I didn't realize he had cancer." And this person said, "He had been keeping it secret. But he called you the day after he was diagnosed."

So I thought about it. We don't often write about great business leaders, people who take technology and business and design and art and combine them. We very rarely get up close to somebody like that. We do politicians, presidents. You see them every day. I realized I had an opportunity to get very close to Jobs for two years, at times almost living with him, and to say, "How does a business/technology/engineering/artistic mind work?"

DR: You've written a book, *The Innovators,* which talks about the rise of the Internet and personal computers and so forth. In it, you talk about a lot of geniuses. One you have a fair bit on is Bill Gates. How do you compare Gates to Steve Jobs? Who was smarter?

WI: In the Steve Jobs book I have a chapter on that. They're both born in 1955. They intertwine often. In the 1970s, when the Apple II comes out, the software writer who does the most for the Apple II is Bill Gates. So they intersected quite a bit. They were the type of friend-rival combination that you see in business.

And they had totally different minds. Bill Gates was smarter than Steve Jobs in a conventional sense. He had more mental-processing power. He could look at two different computer screens with four different flows of information and process things in an analytical-processing-power way that was awesome.

But Steve was more of a genius. Steve had an intuitive imaginative ability to just see around corners, to know what we wanted before we did, and to have a feel for beauty. In the end, Bill Gates creates the Zune. Steve creates the iPod. He's the creative genius.

DR: In *The Innovators,* you talk about the history, over several hundred years, of the development of the computer. Is it your view that computers, the Internet, and smartphones came about because of geniuses sitting in their own rooms, or was it because of some other process?

WI: We biographers know deep inside that we distort history a little bit. We make it sound like there's a guy or a gal who's a genius sitting in a garage or a garret and they have a lightbulb moment and, boom, innovation happens, an invention is born.

In fact, in the digital age in particular, most people wouldn't even know — with all due respect to Al Gore — who invented the Internet, who invented the computer or the microchip. The reason is because innovation was done collaboratively.

Bell Labs was a great example. To develop

the transistor, they've got a quantum theorist like John Bardeen. They have really great physicists like William Shockley. They have deft experimentalists such as Walter Brattain, who knows how to take a piece of silicon and dope the surface of it with boron, so it becomes a semiconductor, and put a paper clip through it and make a transistor based on the theories. You have Claude Shannon — who juggled balls on a unicycle in the Bell Labs corridors — because he's this great information theorist.

But you also had people with grease under their fingernails who would climb telephone poles and knew how to amplify a signal. It takes a team to put something together. That's what I wanted to show in *The Innovators.*

DR: One last question before we get to Benjamin Franklin. How do you actually have time to write these books? You are the president of the Aspen Institute, which is a very active organization. That's a big day job. When do you write these books?

WI: When I was writing *Benjamin Franklin,* I was running CNN — which is harder than running the Aspen Institute. But I like to write at night. To me, writing is fun. It's an escape, because you get to meet people in your mind and do things.

I work from 9 p.m. until 1 or 2 in the morning. Cathy, my wife, is always indulgent. The smart move is that if you're a night person, you should marry a morning person. Cathy gets up at 6. I like to get up at about 8:30 or 9.

The good thing about the Aspen Institute too is that it's a think tank. I discovered that nobody ever had a good idea before 9 a.m., so we don't start that early.

DR: Who will be the next genius you're going to write about? There are some rumors that you're thinking about Leonardo.

WI: Leonardo da Vinci is the ultimate genius. You look at his notebooks and realize that everything that I've tried to write about, when it comes to creativity, comes from the ability to connect the humanities to the sciences. I know that seems odd — "I'm a humanist. I don't need the sciences," and vice versa.

But Ben Franklin flying the kite in the rain, that wasn't some doddering old dude. He's a humanist. He knows how to put together humans and science.

The Vitruvian Man, the great drawing by Leonardo da Vinci, is the ultimate symbol of the connection of the sciences to the humanities. So I would love to take on Leonardo, not just as an artist. [Isaacson's biography of Leonardo da Vinci appeared in 2017.]

When he applies for a job with Ludovico il Moro who in 1494 becomes the Duke of Milan, Leonardo writes a twelve-paragraph letter — eleven paragraphs on "here's my engineering skills, here's how I helped build a dome on a church, here's my military skills, everything else." And the last paragraph is: "I can paint and sculpt if you need me to as well." So he does the *Mona Lisa* while he's there in Milan, but he considers it all one thing, not like "I'm an artist on one day and an engineer the next."

DR: Let's talk about Franklin.

WI: I wrote about Benjamin Franklin at first because I'd done Henry Kissinger, and I realized that the great balance-of-power diplomat we had in our history was Ben Franklin. Most people write about him as a writer, as a newspaper editor who writes wonderful essays. I realized he was a great diplomat.

But then I realized he was also a great scientist. That, to me, was sort of the revelation — that if you're going to be an Enlightenment thinker, if you're going to work for the balance of power as a diplomat or the balances that we see in the Constitution, it helps to know Newtonian mechanics, which he loved. That's what got me very excited about a person who could do science and engineering as well as the humanities and art.

DR: Franklin wasn't educated to be a scientist. In fact, he only went to school for two years. He was born in Boston, then came to Philadelphia. How did that come about?

WI: Well, he was the tenth son of a Puritan immigrant. As the tenth son, he was going to be his father's tithe to the Lord. They were going to send him to Harvard to study for the ministry. It was a long time ago, when Harvard knew how to train ministers.

Ben Franklin wasn't exactly cut out for the cloth. At one point, they're salting the provisions at his house in Boston, and he was tired of the fact that they had to say grace every night. So he asked his father if he could say grace when they put the provisions away and they could get it done with once and for all for the entire year. His father realizes, "Man, this guy is never going to be a minister," and doesn't send him to Harvard.

He gets the next-best education, which is as a newspaper reporter. He's apprenticed to his brother James. He writes the wonderful Silence Dogood essays — fourteen humorous essays he did for his brother's paper — about what a waste of money it is to go to Harvard. He says, "Harvard knows only how to turn out dunces and blockheads who can enter a room genteelly, something they could have learned less expensively at dancing school."

If you were a printer and a newspaper publisher, you were also a bookseller. And so Franklin would take, late at night, all the books from the shelf without his brother knowing it, and he would read Addison and Steele. [Joseph Addison and Richard Steele's witty newspaper the *Spectator* appeared in 1710–11 and was highly influential in the early eighteenth century.]

Daniel Defoe was one of his favorites, Bunyan's [*The*] *Pilgrim's Progress,* Cotton Mather's *Essays to Do Good,* other things you and I were reading when we were fifteen. He sort of becomes a scientist because Cotton Mather and others were too.

DR: So he's working for his brother, who is a printer in Boston. And then around age seventeen he decides to run away. He goes to Philadelphia. How does he manage to make himself a living in Philadelphia?

WI: He runs away, arrives in Philadelphia — in the most famous scene in autobiographical literature — with three coins in his pocket. Tips the boatman very generously because he says — here's something you wouldn't understand — "When you're really poor, you're more generous than when you're really rich because you don't want people to think you're poor."

DR: I've been poor.

WI: Okay, okay. And then he buys the three puffy rolls [another famous scene in Franklin's *Autobiography*] and he decides to become a printer. Now, this is really cool. There are about seven newspapers in Philadelphia, a town of three thousand. He says, "I'll start another newspaper." These were the good old days for newspapers. He starts a very funny, spunky newspaper, and he's really good as a media mogul.

Instead of printing the Bible at his printshop and making that one of the books he sells, he says, "People only buy a Bible once a year." So he invents *Poor Richard's Almanack,* so you have to buy it every year.

Then he helps start the colonial postal system because he wanted to make sure that he could sort of franchise his printshops up and down the East Coast, and he would get preferred carriage in the colonial postal system.

DR: So as he's building this printing business —

WI: And becomes incredibly wealthy.

DR: On the side, he experiments with various

scientific things. Let's go through some of the things he supposedly invented. Bifocals?

WI: Absolutely. He was not only a good theorist, he was a good engineer. When he would ride in the carriages on the postal inspection tours he took, he loved to read. Then he would look up and see the scenery, and it was hard for him. He had to switch glasses.

DR: So he did bifocals. What about the famous Franklin stove?

WI: It was actually not as successful as it should have been. One of the problems in that period was smoky stoves and waste of heat. So he invents an enclosed stove that recirculates the air, and he starts making money off of it, but it doesn't succeed too well, because it was so efficient that the smoke didn't go up the chimney much and it smoked up houses.

DR: What about electricity? Did he actually discover it?

WI: He comes close. Up until then, electricity was some parlor trick where people would take little balls of amber and put cloth on them and sparks would come out. [Rubbing the amber with the cloth produced static

Among Franklin's many inventions: bifo-cals, sketched here in a letter to George Whatley, May 23, 1785.

electricity.] People couldn't figure out what electricity was. So Franklin does the great electricity experiments in the 1740s.

DR: Did he actually go out with a kite, or is that apocryphal?

WI: He did. Totally true.

DR: Isn't that kind of dangerous?

WI: It was very dangerous. He said one of the great things about the electricity experiments and the kite experiments was that you kept getting shocked and knocked down. He said it was useful because it made a vain man humble. He was always trying to pretend to be more humble.

DR: He discovered that lightning was electricity?

WI: There are three things he discovers that are incredibly important. The first is called the conservation of charge, which even Newton hadn't discovered. If you read I. Bernard Cohen's *Revolution in Science* textbook, this is the most important discovery of that period.

They used to think that electricity was two fluids. Franklin discovered that it's not two fluids. You're just taking one charge and another charge and then when you put them back together it's called the conservation of charge. He even invents terms — *positive* and *negative* — and a word, *battery,* to describe putting Leyden jars together so he can store a charge. [Leyden jars were an early kind of capacitor for storing electrical charges.]

Secondly, he looks at sparks. He's making sparks. He looks at lightning, and he has a wonderful notebook entry that says: "Here's the characteristics of a spark [snaps fingers], a quick thing like that, sulfurous smell, whatever. Here are the characteristics of lightning. They're all the same."

And at the very bottom he puts: "Let the experiment be made." So he goes out and flies a kite.

DR: The value of this experiment, among other things, was it led to the lightning rod. Can you explain what that was?

WI: The lightning rod was the most important invention of the eighteenth century. I was stunned, when I researched this book, at the number of lightning strikes that just totally destroyed things.

DR: All over the place. Houses, churches.

WI: All over Europe. One of the great dangers of that period was lightning. They used to consecrate church bells. They used to pray over the church bells and put them in the steeples so that lightning wouldn't strike there. And they even sometimes stored gunpowder under the steeples. And yet the lightning kept striking the steeples and everything would blow up.

Franklin, in his wry way, in the same notebook with "Let the experiment be made," writes: "You would think we would try something different after a while."

He realizes through the kite experiment that lightning is actually an excess of negative charge in the cloud that suddenly discharges to the ground. The kite with its wet string actually brings the charge down, and he captures it with a key and transfers it into a Leyden jar.

By doing that, he realizes that a pointed, grounded, metal rod will capture the excess electrons, or the negative charge of the cloud, and keep it. When he publishes that in the *Pennsylvania Gazette,* that summer in Philadelphia, forty-two lightning rods go up, and those buildings no longer get hit by lightning.

They actually do the full experiments [that Franklin proposed on electricity] first in France. He does the kite experiment himself, but he hasn't heard the fact that they've done it in France. But he becomes an unbelievably important international celebrity.

DR: He became the most prominent American in the world. He was better known than George Washington and Thomas Jefferson.

WI: By far. The French sculptor Jean-Antoine Houdon has a wonderful epitaph for him — I think it may be on the Houdon bust on

Franklin as scientific investigator: Lightning strikes outside the window as the scientist takes notes during an experiment in this 1763 portrait.

display at the Library — which is: "He snatched the scepter from tyrants and lightning from the gods."

DR: Think about some of the other things he did. He created the first hospital in the United States.

WI: When he was a young newspaper tradesman printer, he started something called the Leather Apron Club, or the Junto. It's for civic improvement, because he was the ultimate in what you want as a civic leader. He wasn't looking for big expenditures. He would just get people together and start things.

Every Friday when they met, they said, "What does the town need?" They start, I think, with the Hospital Company of Philadelphia. Then they have a militia, a street-sweeping corps, the Library Company of Philadelphia. On his deathbed, he still has his leather fire bucket from the Union Fire Company [the volunteer fire brigade he helped start], because you're supposed to sleep with that for safety. Sixty years later, when he's dying, he still has that.

DR: On the side, he created the university that's now the University of Pennsylvania.

WI: And you should read the document for it. It's called *Proposals Relating to the Education of Youth in Pennsylvania,* and it starts the academy.

It's a particularly interesting thing because Franklin and Jefferson were really close, but they had separate theories of education. Jefferson believed — and if you read the founding documents of the University of Virginia, you see it — it was to take the best of the best and skim the cream and create what Jefferson calls "a natural aristocracy."

But *Proposals Relating to the Education of Youth in Pennsylvania,* which becomes the founding document of what is now the University of Pennsylvania, says this is not just to skim the elite, this is so that every person, whatever their abilities or whatever their station in life, can reach fulfillment by having a better education. I'll let Jon Meacham come back and defend Jefferson later.

DR: The printing business is a very big business, and so, at the age of forty-two, Franklin says, "I'm done. I'm retired."

WI: Sort of. He has franchises with all of his apprentices up and down the coast. Something else you would understand — he is getting an equity stake in each one of these but he's not going to work every day.

DR: He has a deal with his partner where I think he gets half the profits for eighteen years or something like that.

WI: Not bad.

DR: So now he has time for public affairs. How does he get involved in governmental matters? Why did he actually decide to leave Philadelphia and go to London?

WI: He gets appointed. First of all, he hates the proprietors of Philadelphia and Pennsylvania. There's a complex situation there. It was not a Loyalist colony.

DR: The Penn family owned the state, essentially.

WI: Essentially, although Franklin would not have agreed with that. But the Penn family thought they owned it outright.

Franklin's newspaper was an independent newspaper, but he becomes involved with the Pennsylvania Assembly, which thinks that you should not be able to tax people, as the Penns were trying to do, without the assembly agreeing to it. Franklin becomes the envoy of the Pennsylvania Assembly to London, to be a lobbyist, basically, to get the ministers to agree to allow the colonies to have their own governance. He also then becomes the envoy for Massachusetts and two others.

DR: So he eventually moves to London. Does he come right back?

WI: No. It's kind of odd. He loves it, and he brings his illegitimate son, William, who loves it even more and becomes very aristocratic.

But Ben Franklin is not an aristocrat. He loves "we, the middling people," so he becomes friends with all the printers and Dr. Johnson and David Hume, the great thinkers of the British Enlightenment. He is already a bit of a celebrity. And, weirdly, he replicates

"Join, or Die": *Franklin published this famous early example of editorial cartooning in his* Pennsylvania Gazette *newspaper to encourage the colonies to band together to defend themselves.*

his home life in England, because he has Deborah Franklin as his common-law wife in America. And in London he has Mrs. Margaret Stevenson, who sets up house with him, and he lives with her there.

DR: With his common-law wife, he had two children, a son who dies young —

WI: Frankie.

DR: — and then a daughter, and then he had the illegitimate son with somebody whom we don't know. And over in London —

WI: He has no children there, but he has a family and basically adopts Polly Stevenson, who is Margaret Stevenson's daughter.

DR: While he's over there, he's trying to make the case that we shouldn't tax the colonies so much. Then he gets into a problem because the Stamp Act is proposed by Parliament, and Benjamin Franklin is supposed to be against it. [The Stamp Act, passed in 1765, taxed the paper used by the colonists for printed documents and newspapers.] What happens?

WI: This is something everybody in this room can relate to. His great strength, but sometimes his problem, was that he always believed you could find a middle ground and compromise on things.

DR: You can't do that?

WI: You cannot on the Stamp Act, apparently. He sort of goes along with it and then there's a blowup in Pennsylvania: "Hey, you were supposed to fight taxation, and look what you're doing. You're kowtowing to Parliament." By having left the colonies and gone to England, he has lost touch with his constituents.

DR: He's over there for more than a dozen years.

WI: Yeah. And he's lost touch with the fact that they're becoming more and more radical. Then he has to get the Stamp Act repealed, which he does.

DR: He gets it repealed, and then people in England say, "You're going to stay here. You're one of us now. You're more of an Englishman than an American." But then what happens? Why does he become unpopular in England and have to leave?

WI: He becomes more radicalized by the late 1770s, because various ministers for the colonies like Wills Hill, Earl of Hillsborough [later Marquess of Downshire] and others keep imposing taxes from London. [Hill served as secretary of state for the colonies from 1768 to 1772.]

And then he gets involved in a complicated affair I won't get into, which involves some letters from the royal governor of Massachusetts called the Hutchinson Letters, which he leaks. [Franklin leaked the letters to Samuel Adams, and they were published in the *Boston Gazette,* creating a political uproar.]

He gets called in front of what's called the Cockpit in Parliament. Imagine the Senate

Foreign Relations Hearing Room but writ large as a battlefield.

He's called for a hearing and is humiliated. He's refusing to dress up for the proceedings. He's wearing this blue frock coat. And he gets so upset that in April of 1775 he sails back to America.

And when he gets home, nobody knows quite if he will declare for independence. Because in 1775, two-thirds of the people in the colonies were in favor of sticking with Britain.

DR: Because he had lived in England so long, did some people in the colonies think he was a spy?

WI: They think he is a spy. They're not sure which way he's going to go. Sam and John Adams are like, "Whoa, is he going to be with us or against us?"

The reason it's complicated is that illegitimate son we talked about, who I said was becoming very aristocratic, does indeed become the Loyalist governor of New Jersey. Franklin is waiting to have a meeting with his son William, and he tells William, "I'm now abandoning the cause of unity and I'm going to become a rebel," and then makes a big declaration in 1775 that he's on the side of independence.

DR: He gets elected to the Second Continental Congress, and he's appointed to a committee to draft the Declaration of Independence.

WI: That's been one of the times that Congress really created a good committee. It has Jefferson, John Adams, and Franklin on it, along with two others.

DR: Jefferson writes the Declaration, but Franklin is a printer and a writer, so he edits it.

WI: In this building is the coolest document I've ever dealt with. It's the first draft of the Declaration of Independence — Jefferson's first draft that he submits to Franklin and Adams.

He writes a wonderful letter to Franklin — even though they're living next door in Philadelphia — saying, "Would the good Dr. Franklin, in all of his wisdom, please look over this draft?" People were nicer to editors back then than when I was an editor. Franklin looks at it, and as you know, there's that second paragraph, which is awesome.

DR: Jefferson writes, "We hold these truths to be sacred and undeniable," and Franklin as an editor says, " 'Sacred and undeniable' is three words. Let's make it 'self-evident.' "

WI: If you look at the draft, there's Franklin's printer's pen — you know, heavy black printer's pen that you use to do backslashes. If you're an old editor like me, you know how to backslash something, which means you're really taking it out. And he writes "self-evident," not simply to save words, but because he wanted to show that we were creating a new type of nation based on rationality and reason, not on the dictates of a religion.

He had been friends with David Hume, as I said, when he was in London, and Hume had come up with the notion of "self-evident truths." But then the sentence goes on, and it says that all men are created equal, and you see what I am pretty sure is and most historians think is John Adams's insert: "They are endowed by their Creator with certain inalienable rights." So in the editing of this document you can see them balancing the role of divine providence and the role of rationality and reason, just in that half sentence.

DR: Jefferson is much younger than Franklin — about thirty-seven years younger. He looks up to him. He takes his edits. When the Declaration of Independence is approved, and we declare independence, what happens to Franklin? Does he remain in Philadelphia?

WI: Well, no. First of all, he gets to help print it, because he's a printer. They use what we now call Franklin Gothic as the font. It's a great thing.

But in order to make that document any good, we had to get France in on our side in the war — even back then, France was a bit of a handful — and there's only one person who can do it. He's in his seventies. But he is larger than life.

Other than Jerry Lewis, we have never produced somebody that the French were so gaga for. *Poor Richard's Almanack* is selling more in France as *Les Maximes du Bonhomme Richard. Bonhomme Richard* is the name of U.S. naval commander John Paul Jones's ship because Franklin, when he gets there, gets it funded.

They send Franklin over in a wartime journey across an ocean that is controlled by the enemy, meaning British warships. He goes to try to convince France to come in on our side.

He does it in two ways. First of all, he realizes that the American Revolution, with all due respect to us, was not the central act in this play. This was part of a long war between Britain and France that had played out in the French and Indian War and had played out all over Europe, and that, naturally, we should get France in on our side. Like Henry Kissinger, he's a brilliant balance-of-power diplomat.

Charles Gravier, comte de Vergennes, is the French foreign minister. Franklin writes these letters that say, "Here's the balance of power. If you and the Bourbon pact" — meaning France, the Netherlands, and Spain — "come in with us against England, you'll have navigation rights on the Mississippi." It is a perfect triangular balance.

But then he does something really cool. He builds a printing press at Passy, his place in Paris, because he realizes you have to win the hearts and minds of the people. It was a battle for public diplomacy. He prints the Declaration and the Virginia Declaration of Rights, all the documents coming out of America, because the notion of liberty, equality, fraternity is welling up in France.

He wins the battle for French opinion. He brings one of these things to the steps of the Académie Française and hands it to Voltaire, who hugs him. There are about twenty thousand people there to watch this great meeting, at which point the French say, "Okay, okay, we're in on your side."

DR: So France supports the United States, and we win the war. Does Franklin come back?

WI: He doesn't come back right away. [Franklin returned from Paris in 1785.]

He has done this remarkable thing of weaving what you would call realism, meaning balance of power and diplomacy, and idealism, which is appealing to the ideals of people around the world. That's what we still try to do today, but he does it better. So after the war, he negotiates a treaty with England.

DR: By himself or with other people?

WI: He does it with John Adams and John Jay.

A spy who was working for the British, Edward Bancroft, is his valet. Franklin uses that by allowing the British to know that we might still stick with the French if they don't sign fast.

DR: They sign the Treaty of Paris in 1783, and he stays.

WI: He loves science, and they're doing balloon experiments and he can't leave. So he and his grandson are there during the balloon experiments. They're also all into this new romantic science, like mesmerism [a system of hypnotic induction], created by Franz Mesmer, and the king asks him to test out these things. So he becomes a scientist there for two years before he returns home.

DR: His illegitimate son had an illegitimate son. That's the grandson you mentioned?

WI: Right. And he and his son are fighting over the affection of Temple, the grandson. When he finally does go home, William, the royal governor of New Jersey and estranged son of Ben Franklin, is now living in England in Portsmouth as a refugee Loyalist who had been traded to England. On the way home, taking Temple with him, the grandson, Franklin stops in Portsmouth, they divvy up the family proceeds, and he and the grandson head off to America.

DR: He comes home, and what he finds in America is that the Articles of Confederation aren't working so well.

WI: They're terrible. It's a mess.

DR: So they have a constitutional convention, and he managed to get invited to that.

WI: He is eighty-one years old in 1787, and so he's exactly twice as old as the other people — as the average age there — and he becomes the great sage at the Constitutional Convention, the person who pushes this notion of "we can find the common ground here."

He has a huge impact. The famous speech

was the call for prayers, which he does partly because he just thinks it will calm everybody down. But the main thing he does is that the convention, as you know from your high school history, had broken down in that long, hot summer on the big state / little state issue and proportional representation, an equal vote for each state. And it's unclear whether they're going to get a constitution.

Franklin gives one of the best speeches, which everybody here should read because you have to deal with this every day. He finally gets up. He's been pretty quiet.

He's actually been in favor of a single house — just an elected House of Representatives, not the Senate — but he proposes a full compromise: a House of Representatives to provide proportional representation, direct election, and a Senate that has equal votes for all the states.

He says, "When we were young tradesmen in Philadelphia, we had a joint of wood that didn't quite fit together. You'd take a little from one side and then shave a little from others until you had a joint that would hold together for centuries. And so too, we here at this convention must each part with some of our demands if we're going to have a constitution that will hold together."

And he makes the argument that compromisers may not make great heroes, but they do make great democracies. That's the essence of how you put things together. Then he asks them to line up by state to sign on to it.

And they do, every state. It was clever, because there were a lot of people against it, but the people who were against it were the ones who wanted voting by state. So, by voting by state, he gets basic unanimity.

DR: So Franklin becomes the only person to sign the Declaration of Independence, the Constitution, the Treaty of Paris, and the 1778 Treaty of Alliance with the French. Is that right?

WI: The four great documents — and the fifth, which he wrote, is the Albany Plan of Union in 1754. It was the first time somebody had proposed that the colonies should unite and form their own government.

DR: When it's over, he walks out of Independence Hall, and a woman comes up to him and says, "Mr. Franklin, what have you done?"

WI: "What have you wrought in there?" Mrs. Powell says. "What have you given us?" And he says, "A republic, madam, if you can keep it."

DR: He only lives a few more years after that.

He dies at eighty-four. Was he a religious person? Was he a deist? Was he a Christian?

WI: He wrestles with it like we all do. In the book, I talk about each phase of his religious thinking.

For a long while, as a young person, he's a deist, which is sort of the Enlightenment science view of religion that there's a Creator who made everything beautiful with all the laws of the universe, but our Creator is not a personal god that you can pray to really hard and the Seahawks will win the Super Bowl or something. God doesn't intervene. He's just the great Creator.

Then Franklin says something interesting. He decides that deism is not for him. He said, "Even if it happens to be true, it's not useful" — meaning it's more useful to have a more fervent religious received wisdom from God.

That was the interesting thing about Franklin. Almost everything he did, his first question was, "Is it useful?" He said, "I can't wrestle with all the metaphysical questions of whether God exists or not, but I know what the most useful way is to have a religion." And so he becomes nondenominational. During his life, he donates to the building fund of each and every church built in Philadelphia.

DR: What was his view on slavery? Was he not a slave owner at one point?

WI: Yeah. And that's interesting too, of course. He made a lot of errors in his life. He called them "errata," and he kept a chart of them.

The first error he makes is running away from his brother James when he was apprenticed to him and going to Philadelphia without permission. Then he has a second column in which he says, "How did I make up for it?" The way he makes up for it is that when James is dying, Franklin promises to educate his son. And he does, and puts him in business.

All through his life he does this. But he made one great mistake that he said was larger than them all, which is he compromises on the issue of slavery.

In his newspaper, the *Pennsylvania Gazette,* he had allowed advertising related to slavery [including slaves for sale and runaway alerts]. In fact, one of the ads says, "Inquire at the house of Deborah Read," meaning his father-in-law's house. He'd owned two household slaves. He frees them — one of them just leaves — and he frees them in his will. But he realizes he had compromised at the Constitutional Convention.

He said, "Look, we're going to not be able to solve this in the Constitution until you have the compromise." That's the one thing left. And so, at age eighty-one, he becomes president of the Pennsylvania Society for Promoting the Abolition of Slavery, because he wants to try to rectify the moral error he had made.

DR: His image is very well known because he had this long hair and kind of a balding head. Was that an affectation?

WI: It was an affectation because he did not want to be pretentious, did not want to put on airs. He said, "We're trying to create a new type of people who don't have aristocratic habits."

DR: No wigs.

WI: No powdered wigs. And we don't have titles. It's all going to be common people wearing [working clothes like the printer's traditional] leather apron, including the blue coat he wears when he's at the Cockpit, which he puts back on when he signs the Treaty of Paris — as a symbol, this old coat.

But when he goes to Paris for the first time, he's lived in Philadelphia, London, and Boston. He's not a wilderness dude. He likes Market Street, not the backwoods.

But he realizes that the French have read Rousseau once too often, and they sort of think of Americans as the natural philosophers prancing around in the wilderness — "the natural man" of Rousseau. [The philosopher Jean-Jacques Rousseau (1712–1778) associated virtue with the natural state.]

So when he goes to France, he wears no wig, but he wears a coonskin cap and a backwoods coat that somebody had given him. And in Paris, all the women start doing the coiffeur à la Franklin, which is making your hair look like a coonskin cap. I mean, he was pretty good.

DR: If you look back on the Founding Fathers — let's say Washington, Adams, Jefferson, Madison, Franklin — who do you think actually had the biggest impact on the country at the time, and how would you assess Franklin?

WI: Washington, probably. But let me answer in a slightly different way, which gets back to the innovators.

When I was doing Franklin, I realized it wasn't about one person. What you do, especially in business, but also in politics, is you build a team.

The Founders are the greatest team ever fielded. You have somebody of great, high rectitude: George Washington. You have a couple of really brilliant people: Madison, Jefferson. You have very passionate visionaries: Sam Adams, his cousin John. And then you have somebody who can bring them all together: Ben Franklin.

If you look at Intel, it's like having Andy Grove, Bob Noyce, and Gordon Moore, Intel's cofounders. You have to have a team that holds together. So I would be loath to say who's the most important, but I think Franklin is indispensable, because there was nobody else in that role.

One of the halls in the U.S. Capitol has beautiful pictures of our history. And one of them is Benjamin Franklin in Philadelphia, at the Constitutional Convention, under the mulberry tree. He's got Adams and Hamilton and one other person I can't remember, and a couple of people are standing around.

He said that under the shade of the tree in his backyard, which is two blocks from Independence Hall, "I can bring people together and the tempers cool down and I can make sure we can get things done." Sound familiar?

DR: Why do you think that in Washington we have memorials for a lot of great people, but we don't have any real big memorial for Benjamin Franklin?

WI: Every now and then, you get David McCullough saying, "Sign up to get a John Adams memorial, sign up to get a Franklin memorial." I think we see Franklin all around us. Wherever I am, I see the fingerprints of Dr. Franklin. It's like the epitaph on the stone slab in St. Paul's Cathedral where its architect, Christopher Wren, is buried: "If you seek his monument look around you."

6
Cokie Roberts
ON FOUNDING MOTHERS

"The letters that the women write, where they have absolutely no expectation that we're going to be reading them two hundred years later, are just completely unvarnished, frank, and real. You get a much more complete view of the society as a whole."

BOOKS DISCUSSED:
Founding Mothers: The Women Who

Raised Our Nation (HarperCollins, 2004)
*Ladies of Liberty: The Women Who
Shaped Our Nation* (HarperCollins, 2008)
*Capital Dames: The Civil War and the
Women of Washington, 1848–1868*
(HarperCollins, 2015)

Much of the traditional writing about the great events of history has focused on the accomplishments of men. Perhaps that is why it is called "his" story and not "her" story.

This is certainly evident in so much of the written history of the United States in the eighteenth and nineteenth centuries. Written history has generally focused on Founding Fathers, generals, presidents, senators, and secretaries of state. By and large, that history has overlooked the women of these eras. They held none of those visible positions; they were not, if married, allowed to own property in their own names; and, of course, they were not allowed to even vote. They were very much behind the scenes.

In fact, the women associated, through family or social relationships, with the well-known men of the eighteenth and nineteenth centuries were quite influential. They were just not as publicly visible, and they exercised influence in areas the men did not understand as well.

All of this is made clear by Cokie Roberts in three books devoted to the influential women of three historical periods: the pre-Revolution era, the early years under the Constitution, and the Civil War. In writing about these women — including Martha Washington, Eliza Hamilton, Abigail Adams, Dolley Madison, Mary Todd Lincoln, Julia Grant, and Clara Barton — Roberts used a treasure trove of letters, some not previously well known, written by and to these women. The result is a look at a side of American history that even diligent students of the subject may know little about.

Cokie Roberts's role as a book author also may not be as well known to the public as many of the other roles she has held or pursued: daughter of two congressional leaders (House Majority Leader Hale Boggs and his successor Lindy Boggs), NPR and ABC commentator, PBS journalist, and coauthor, with her journalist husband, Steven Roberts, of a weekly news column.

I have known Roberts and her family for many years and have interviewed her many times. On the occasion of this interview, she was really at a homecoming, since both of her parents were so highly respected by the members of Congress.

As the interview shows, Roberts is as adept at being an interviewee as she is at being an interviewer. She clearly conveys that the wives of the Founding Fathers, and of other American political leaders through the Reconstruction period, were not merely social adornments to their prominent husbands, as some readers of traditional accounts of these periods might have thought.

In fact, they had clear impact on their husbands' work, and thus on the outcome of so much of American history. And they did so despite having virtually no legal or political rights; typically getting married at very young ages; being often pregnant because of the lack of reliable birth control; and having to run businesses and raise children while their husbands were overseas, running the government, or fighting a war.

Roberts provides a number of vivid illustrations of her general view that the women had real impact even though they received little credit for it. For instance, Martha Washington, at great physical risk, visited her husband's troops every year during the eight-year Revolutionary War, to the great delight of the troops — she helped with replenishment of food and clothing — while also continuing to run Mount Vernon and raise their grandchildren.

Abigail Adams, who was actually a stronger advocate of the break with England than her husband, managed to exchange more than a thousand letters with her husband. The most famous of the letters urged that he "remember the women" when creating laws for the new government. (He did not.) Many of her letters were written while her husband was overseas for years at a time and she was raising their children, running their farm, and fending off potential British attacks.

Dolley Madison became one of Washington's most influential figures, serving as the widowed President Jefferson's White House hostess, subsequently as her husband James Madison's hostess, and, in her later years, as the capital's most beloved and quite influential figure.

Harriet Lane, the unmarried President James Buchanan's niece, acted as his hostess and was so involved that she became the first woman to be deemed "First Lady."

Mary Todd Lincoln was not beloved by anyone, it seemed. But she had enough of an iron will to be able to influence her husband's views and practices in a number of areas, though not always to Abraham Lincoln's or the country's benefit.

Because Julia Grant did not want to be around the volatile Mrs. Lincoln, General Ulysses S. Grant declined to go with the Lincolns to Ford's Theatre on the night the president was assassinated. Had he done so, Grant might have been in a better position than the young military aide who ultimately accompanied the Lincolns to thwart John Wilkes Booth.

MR. DAVID M. RUBENSTEIN (DR): Let me ask you this, Cokie. In your book on the Revolutionary War era, you point out that you are descended from somebody who was the first governor of the Louisiana Territory, appointed by Thomas Jefferson. Your mother was a member of Congress. Your father was a member of Congress. Your sister was mayor of Princeton, New Jersey. Your brother ran for Congress. Why did you decide not to pursue politics as a career yourself?

MS. COKIE ROBERTS (CR): I have an answer to that that should please you, which is that I feel very guilty not having done that. I have to tell you, there's been many a time when I've been covering Congress when I would like to get down on the floor and just slap you all. It's the mother thing: "I don't care who started it, I'm stopping it."

But I met my husband when I was eighteen years old, and he was always going to be a journalist. He knew that from the time he was nine or ten, and it would have been very hard on him for me to go into politics. So I didn't.

I would like to say — and I could not mean this more strongly — I am such an admirer of people in public service of all kinds, but particularly people in elected office. It is hard work. You are constantly called upon to respond to the needs and desires, crazy as they can be sometimes, of your bosses, the voters. And I believe that all of you are serving the country by your lights as well as you can, and I admire you.

I do have to tell a story, though, because it does give some perspective on all of this. The ancestor you're talking about, the guy named William Claiborne, he was interested in politics as a young man. He worked as an enrolling clerk in the first Congress. [Enrolling clerks keep track of passed legislation and handle related correspondence with the Senate.]

And he said he wanted to run for office. He was from Virginia, and the Clerk [the top person in charge of record-keeping for the U.S. House of Representatives], who was a very powerful person named John Beckley, said to him, "Well, hello, Virginia has Madison and Monroe. You're not going to win."

Tennessee became a state very fast. The Clerk said, "Go to Tennessee, there's nobody there." So William Claiborne went to Tennessee. Andrew Jackson had been in the House, then took a Senate seat that came open. So there's an open House seat. There's nobody in Tennessee.

This kid was twenty-three years old. As you might know, the constitutional age for running for Congress is twenty-five. He ran for the House and was elected, because there wasn't anybody else. He comes to Congress

239

and they seat him — it's still in the National Archives — they seat him in contravention of the Constitution, because he was only twenty-three. That was 1797.

Then the election of 1800 happens. He's the sole representative from Tennessee. His one vote is the equal of everybody from Massachusetts, everybody from Virginia, all of that. He's got incredible power. And the view among Alexander Hamilton's people was that his head could be turned because he was young and vain. [Hamilton eventually supported Jefferson for president after trying to negotiate on some issues in exchange for Federalist support. Jefferson in the end did all of the things Hamilton asked for.] He stayed with Jefferson through thirty-six ballots. One month later, he was made governor of the Mississippi Territory.

So there you go. Political payoffs have always been with us.

DR: We have a lot of histories of the Revolutionary War period and the post–Revolutionary War period, and the world doesn't lack for Civil War books. What made you think you needed to write a book about each of these periods, and what made you focus on women?

CR: Well, I am a woman. You might have noticed that. But the truth is — this crowd will understand the answer to this question better than most — my mother is the real answer.

My mother was not only a remarkable woman, but I grew up with Betty Ford and Lady Bird Johnson and Pauline Gore. I grew up with all these remarkable women who were incredibly powerful. They had no titles, but they were very, very influential. I saw them running the political conventions, voter registration drives, their husbands' campaigns, and raising all of us kids.

They also worked with African American women in Washington and ran all of the social-service agencies in the city, because it was before Home Rule. [The Home Rule act of 1973 gave the residents of Washington, D.C., the ability to elect their own mayor and city council.] And I knew how important and influential they were.

I spend a huge amount of time with the Founding Fathers, whether I like it or not, because if you cover Congress and politics as long as I have, you have to get to know them.

I shouldn't say this in this audience — I hear the Founders quoted on the floor of Congress all the time, and almost 100 percent wrong. I have to go back and read what they actually did say. So I got to know them, and then I realized how incredibly crucial this period is in our history, and I wanted to know what the women were doing.

241

DR: How long did it take you to research and write *Founding Mothers*?

CR: It's really hard for me to know the answer to that, because I have a day job. I was working very, very hard daily. The book came out in 2004, and I had already had a book come out in 1998 and a book come out in 2000.

DR: One of the things I was struck by in *Founding Mothers* is how every woman you write about wrote long letters to her spouse or boyfriend or relatives. For those of you who are not familiar with letters, a letter is something that you actually have a pen and you put it on paper and you write and you mail it. Were you struck by how long and detailed and perceptive these letters were?

CR: They were extraordinary. By the way, I have had wonderful help from the Manuscript Division here at the Library of Congress. But, you know, even when I was growing up, David, we wrote long letters. This is not something that is foreign to me as a human.

The wonderful thing about the letters we have — and that's a whole nother question, because there are many, many letters we don't have — but here's the thing to know about women's letters: women's letters are really so much better than men's letters.

The Founders knew that what they were

242

doing was extraordinary. They were self-aware men, and they knew that if they failed, they'd be hanged, but if they succeeded, they would be held in acclaim, that their writings would be published, and they wrote with that in mind.

I always joke that we see our Founders as bronze and marble statues, and their letters read like they were written by the bronze and marble statues. They are edited, and they are considered, and they are in some cases pompous.

Whereas the letters they write to the women, which they don't expect to be saved, are much more human. We get to know them as flesh-and-blood people with all the flaws and feelings that a husband, a lover, a son, a brother have.

And the letters that the women write, where they have absolutely no expectation that we're going to be reading them two hundred years later, are just completely unvarnished, frank, and real. You get a much more complete view of the society as a whole. So in the same sentence you might hear about how we really have to declare war against France, and so-and-so's pregnant again and it's so scary because her last baby just died, and by the way I need that bonnet I left at home.

So you get a much fuller picture of society, and also you get a much truer sense of the men. I actually think that we can admire the

Founders more as flesh-and-blood people. Because it's easy for a deity to do something extraordinary, but for just a guy to do something extraordinary is hard. And that's what they were. They were guys.

DR: Let me ask you about one of the most extraordinary series of letters I've ever read — the John Adams / Abigail Adams letters, about a thousand letters. They didn't see each other for eight years or so, but she writes to him saying things like, "Maybe you could say you love me."

CR: "You're a cold Laplander."

DR: He seems to write letters just ignoring everything she asks for.

CR: Well, he had had his letters intercepted. And he had written some unpolitic things, you know — the era of e-mail's not the first time when people have written unpolitic things — about his fellow members of Congress. He did talk endlessly about how they're all great men here and they talk on and on. This is the Continental Congress he's talking about.

His letters had been intercepted, and he had been embarrassed. He was very concerned that his letters would be intercepted again, and that not only would he be embarrassed by talking about his colleagues but that what she wanted was what he called "sentiments of effusion," and if he revealed such sentiments, he'd be humiliated.

But he did do really stupid things. Think about this. So he's in France, right? She's in Braintree, Massachusetts, trying desperately to keep body and soul together. She's suffering tremendously. There's want, and she's got these four little kids. She's taking care of the parents, and there are periods when there really isn't enough to eat and all that.

And he writes to her about how wonderful the women in France are. I mean, this is death time. But she never misses a beat. She writes right back — of course, the letter takes a while to get there — and says, "Well, if the women of America were able to have the same kind of education as the women of France, we'd be so fabulous too."

DR: How long did it actually take to get a letter?

CR: It could take six weeks. It could take a long time. But everybody got used to that.

DR: What I'm also struck by in that period is that the women got married very, very young — the men were often older — and then they seemed to have children every year. And the children, as you point out, died a lot. Can

245

you talk about that experience?

CR: It's really striking how much death you were dealing with all of this time. The book I've just finished, the Civil War book, of course it's death everywhere. Think of it — six hundred thousand–plus Americans killed in that war.

Just a normal week could take your six-year-old and your ten-year-old, because typhoid fever would come through. Living in the eighteenth and early nineteenth centuries was tough. Just getting through the day was tough. Even if you were elite, it was a very difficult life.

That's one of the reasons I admire these women so much. You're right — the men would come home just long enough for the women to get pregnant. They were having babies, losing babies, raising babies, taking care of the old people, all of that.

But still they were such devoted patriots. It's just incredible. Abigail Adams would sit at night in this teeny house — if you've ever been to the Adams homestead in Quincy, Massachusetts, the original house that they lived in is half the size of this room — no, a quarter the size of this room, this gorgeous room — and there she was with four little children and dogs, and American soldiers would come stay because the British were occupying Boston, and still she would sit up at night by candlelight and write these letters that were so filled with patriotism and enthusiasm about the cause. You'd think she'd just want to go to bed.

DR: The most famous letter of the thousand that she wrote is the one she writes to her husband when he's at the Second Continental Congress. Why is the letter so famous, and what was his response to it?

CR: The letter is so famous because it says, "Remember the ladies." She had been militating, Abigail had, for independence for a full year.

Now, keep in mind that the British were in Boston. The Battles of Lexington and Concord were in April 1775. It takes until July 1776 for the men to have the courage to declare independence. And the women are writing these letters — she and Mercy Otis Warren and then later Esther de Berdt Reed — writing these letters saying, "For God's sake, what's wrong with you guys? Do this. You know, the British are here."

And John Adams writes to Abigail and says, "If it gets really dangerous, take our children and fly to the woods." Thank you, John. Hope you're having a nice dinner in Philadelphia.

John Quincy Adams did write later, "My mother for the space of twelve months, with her infant children, was in danger of being killed or taken hostage into Boston by the British." Because patriot women were taken hostage, and some were killed.

She is realizing that, finally, they're going to declare independence. And so she writes to John and says, "If we're going to become a country, we're going to have to have a code of laws. And in your new code of laws I want you to remember the ladies because all men would be tyrants if they could."

And he laughed at her. He just laughed at her.

DR: He didn't take seriously the idea of women being educated or having any political rights?

CR: No. In terms of education, it was very interesting that she did make sure that their only daughter learned Greek and Latin. And he said, "It's fine as long as you don't tell anybody."

DR: Let's talk about another woman who was very famous at the time, Martha Washington. The image people have of her is that she was hanging out at Mount Vernon. George Washington spends eight years running the war. But it turns out in your book that she was actually with him much of the time.

CR: All the time. I think Martha Washington

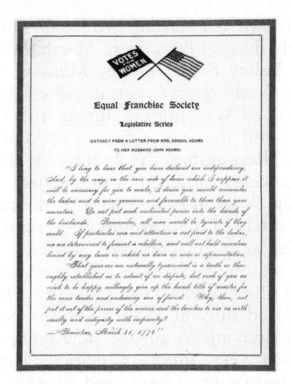

During the fight for women's suffrage in the early twentieth century, the Equal Franchise Society saluted Abigail Adams's famous "Remember the ladies" letter to John Adams.

has done herself a disservice by wearing that cap in the famous Rembrandt Peale portrait of her. We see her as elderly. Of course, "elderly" then was a lot younger than I am. That's one of the reasons when you talk about getting married young, you died young, and some of these men did have several wives.

But Martha was called upon by her husband, the general, to come to camp every winter of the war. When I was growing up —

actually, when I started writing this book — the only things I knew were Martha Washington at Valley Forge, Dolley Madison saving George Washington's portrait [when the British burned Washington during the War of 1812], and then, as a grown-up, I learned about "Remember the ladies" during the resurgence of feminism in the 1970s.

Valley Forge was one winter of the eight long winters of the Revolution — eight years. And she went to camp every winter.

The reason she went — she hated going — first of all, she was leaving behind what she considered duty at Mount Vernon. Second, she was having to go over terrifying roads. She was very much a prime target for hostage-taking. There had already been threats that she would be kidnapped and taken. And camp wasn't so pleasant once you got there. But the general would call and she would answer.

Over the summer, the enslaved people at Mount Vernon would work with her, making cloth and preserving foodstuffs and all that. She would then come to camp, and she was cheered. The troops adored her. She was cheered into camp — "Lady Washington is here!" — and bring all of these things from Mount Vernon, one of the many contributions of African Americans to the Revolutionary cause.

She would then organize the other officers'

"Lady Washington is here!" Martha Washington boosted the morale of her husband's troops, bringing them clothes and food in camp and organizing other officers' wives to help cook for and nurse soldiers.

wives to cook for the soldiers, sew for the soldiers, nurse the soldiers, pray with the soldiers. That was key, because they were threatening to desert by regiment at various times since they were unpaid, unhoused, all that.

Then they'd put on great entertainments, all to keep up troop morale. Washington thought she was absolutely essential. It's also good that she was there because he could be a little indiscreet, and there was the one time that he danced for three hours straight with the very pretty and flirty Catharine Littlefield Greene, the wife of Nathanael Greene. So it was good that Martha was on hand to keep an eye on the situation.

DR: She was watching him as well as helping him.

CR: Watching him. She also had a sense of humor. She named her tomcat Hamilton —

DR: Because Alexander Hamilton was such a —

CR: Tomcat.

DR: We have a thousand letters from John Adams and Abigail Adams. We have no letters between George Washington and Martha Washington. Why is that?

CR: Well, we have two that George wrote to Martha, which were found stuffed in a desk drawer of a house of a descendant. We believe that she burned all their correspondence. And that did happen then.

In her case, I think it's for two reasons. One, she was embarrassed that her punctuation and grammar were not perfect. But also the letters were personal, and she didn't much want them published.

The other two Founding Mothers whose letters we don't have are Martha Jefferson and Elizabeth Monroe. In each of those cases, their husbands burned their letters.

In the case of Martha Jefferson, Thomas Jefferson said that he was burning her letters because he was heartbroken. Now, that's his story and he's sticking to it, but I don't think that's what you do when you're heartbroken.

DR: So let's talk about Martha Washington as the first lady. We have no tradition of first ladies, so are you supposed to be a queen? Are you supposed to be something else? How did she figure out how a first lady was supposed to act?

CR: She had to do it on the job. She was in a good position to do it. Abigail Adams would have been a terrible first first lady. She would have been telling everybody what she thought all the time. Martha Washington was a well-bred southern lady and understood indirection. But she was very political. She understood politics quite well.

When George Washington goes to New York to become president, he arrives on a barge — this big, elaborate barge from New Jersey. So then she goes up. They've got two little children — their grandchildren, who lived with them, had just turned eight and just turned ten when she occupies the equivalent of the executive mansion in New York. And she's got these little kids.

She has sort of a grand procession up from Mount Vernon to New York and is called upon to stop in places and make speeches and all that. When she gets on the barge to come across from New Jersey, she wears homespun [meaning cloth made from homespun yarn]. Now, this is a woman who loved her silks. But she had a PR sense that's the equivalent of Pat Nixon's good cloth coat. [During his famous Checkers speech in 1952, made while he was running for vice president, Richard M. Nixon celebrated his wife, Pat's, "respectable" cloth coat.]

Martha wore homespun to come across the river. But the minute they get across the river, the little boy, George Washington Parke Custis, gets lost in the crowd and she's got to find him, get them in school, and, within something like two days, do the first levee, as the formal reception ceremonies were called, where she has to be courtly enough and formal enough to satisfy the courts of Europe.

Think of it. This is this little tiny upstart country along the Atlantic coast of America, and you're talking about France and England and Prussia and all of that. You have to create some sort of sense that we're regal enough that they will pay attention. But we've also just fought a war knocking off a monarch. So you have to be republican enough to satisfy the voters. It was a very tough balancing act.

She did write at one point that people called her the "First Lady of the Land," which was surprising to see because the term *first lady* was not officially applied until the Buchanan administration. But she said, "I really think of myself as the chief state prisoner." I think a lot of first ladies have felt that way since.

DR: So she came up with a tradition of entertaining. They entertained a lot, but they would not go visit anybody else, because they didn't want to pick and choose.

CR: Also — you all can relate to this — if you went to somebody's house to dinner, were you beholden to them? So George and Martha Washington had everybody in. The dinners sound just grim.

DR: The capital was initially in New York, then they moved it to Philadelphia, so she had to move from New York to Philadelphia. Then they moved back to Mount Vernon after eight years. How long does it actually take to go from Philadelphia to Mount Vernon by carriage or whatever they used?

CR: A lot of the travel was by boat. We used the ocean and the rivers to get everywhere.

But it would take about a week.

DR: A week. You mention in one of your books how long it took to go from George-town to Capitol Hill in those days.

CR: It was a mess. It was all muddy and hor-rible. And when they started building Wash-ington, they just willy-nilly chopped down trees, so there were tree stumps everywhere. That made it very hard to get around.

DR: Like a pothole.

CR: But a pothole you could trip over. So the trip took a couple of hours.

Let's talk about Mount Vernon for a second. Between the Revolutionary War and the Constitutional Convention, they're at Mount Vernon. This is between 1783 and 1787. Everybody comes to Mount Vernon. The whole world comes to Mount Vernon.

On Monday I gave the first Martha Wash-ington Lecture at Mount Vernon. I have been bugging them for years, because everything there says "George Washington's Mount Vernon." And I keep saying, "Really? He did this all by himself?"

First of all, it was all her money. But secondly, she had to do all of this.

The one person he didn't want to come to Mount Vernon was his mother. He was terrified that his mother was going to move in.

He had worked it out that she was going to move in with a brother, and then the brother had the bad grace to die, and so he writes his mother this letter that's just a riot where he says, "You know, this is like a well-resorted tavern — everyone going from north to south or from south to north stops here. And if you came, you would have three choices. You would either have to get up every day and get dressed for all the visitors, which you wouldn't like, or you would be around in dishabille, which I wouldn't like, or you would be confined to your room, which neither one of us would like."

Isn't this a nice letter? And so she didn't come. But Martha is having to do this entertaining.

Then he leaves the presidency after two terms — which is an interesting story all in itself — in 1797. They get back to Mount Vernon. He dies at the end of 1799, and she still has all these people coming through.

Any politician who wanted to prove his bona fides, you know, to show what a great patriot he was — things have not changed — goes to visit Mount Vernon to represent himself to Mrs. Washington. She would take them all in, even though she thought Thomas Jefferson was "the most despicable of all mankind." That was a quotation.

DR: In your book you point out how many guests they had one year — four or five hundred guests who came for dinner or wanted to stay over.

CR: And you don't think George was doing that, do you?

DR: George Washington never lived in the White House. It's finally built at the time that John Adams is the president, and he and Abigail move down here from Philadelphia. They're here for about a year or so.

CR: It's really kind of November till March.

DR: Did Abigail Adams come down and serve as first lady?

CR: Yes. The White House famously was unfinished, and Mrs. Adams was hanging the laundry and all that. But she did write a letter to her daughter saying that Georgetown is a filthy hole. But still the ladies all expected her to entertain and came by. She said to her daughter, "Tell people that I say it has a very nice view, because that's true."

DR: They leave, and the next president is Thomas Jefferson, but he's not married. His wife had died. What did he do for entertaining? Did he have a hostess?

CR: He had various ways of entertaining. You all will respond to this. He had the Democratic-Republicans over one night and the Federalists another night. He did not have them together to dinner. It was really dangerous for him to do that because the country was not in a position where it could survive the kind of partisanship and regionalism that was fierce at the time. It was way too young and fragile a country.

But fortunately, Dolley Madison was on the scene. And she did do some hostessing at the White House, but what she mainly did was set up a completely separate power center at the secretary of state's house on F Street. She had Federalists and Republicans come together and break bread together, have some wine together and behave.

Every so often — and this continued when she went to the White House — the Federalists would say, "We're going to boycott it." Then they'd discover they couldn't because those evenings were where all the trading, all the deals got made, all the information got exchanged.

DR: What about the famous story that while the War of 1812 is happening, and we're being invaded by the British, Dolley Madison is getting ready to cook a dinner, and all of a sudden, she decides she should leave. She writes a letter while she's getting ready to

A power player in Washington even before she became first lady, Dolley Madison hosted must-attend parties for politicians in search of the latest inside information.

leave and then takes the painting of George Washington down. Is that all true?

CR: It's sort of true. It's true enough. She is in the White House by herself — well, not by herself. She's got servants and her wonderful enslaved man Paul Jennings. Madison has gone out to Bladensburg, where the war is being fought, and she expects him to come back to the White House with the generals and the cabinet and have dinner.

She's not cooking, but she's planning it.

And she goes up to the roof and she starts to see the British are coming. People start saying to her, "You've got to go. It's getting dangerous."

She's hoping that Madison will get home before she goes, but finally she is convinced that she has to go. She packed up not just the portrait but government papers and whatever she could get out that she wanted to get out.

But she did insist that the portrait be secured. She didn't roll it up and take it out, but she insisted that it be secured. It was cut out of the frame, and a gentleman traveling to New York took it with him on his carriage.

DR: And that's the Gilbert Stuart painting of George Washington that's now back in the White House.

CR: That's right. What was significant about that when you think, well, it was a painting? Think of all the images we've seen of Saddam Hussein's statue coming down or Lenin's statue coming down.

If Washington's portrait had been in the hands of the British, they could have desecrated it, which would have been very demoralizing. What Dolley did was make sure that that did not happen. What they did instead was desecrate *her* portrait, and then they sat down and ate her meal. It's like Goldilocks. One of the soldiers actually wrote about it — about eating her meal and feeling a little bit guilty but liking it.

DR: In those days, how big was Washington? How many people lived in Washington in the Revolutionary War period?

CR: Oh, in the Revolutionary War period, nobody was here. The government was "removed" to Washington in 1800. Georgetown was a town. Alexandria was a town. But there was no Washington. There were some farms. And when they bought the property here where we are and started building a capital, a few little boardinghouses and liquor stores opened up around here.

DR: And the members of Congress tended to live in —

CR: Boardinghouses. They tended to live in boardinghouses with people either from their delegations or like-minded people.

In fact, Albert Gallatin wrote to his wife — he was later secretary of the treasury, that was his most famous role — but he was a congressman from New York at the time. He wrote to his wife and said, "You know, we all think alike. We don't talk about anything but politics." It's not exactly likely to bring about moderation.

DR: Did they bring their wives down here?

CR: No. Very few wives were here. There was no place for them to stay. But some of the cabinet brought their wives, and the wives played a very key role, because they were the people that brought everybody together.

Dolley Madison, by the way, was not here just in that period. Dolley Madison reigned over this city basically from 1801 to 1848–49. She had a brief period where she went back to Montpelier with James during which she would write these letters saying, "What's going on?"

But she then came back as a widow. Every head of state from all over the world would come to call on her, every president relied on her. She was absolutely the unifying force. Daniel Webster once said, "There's no permanent power in Washington but Dolley Madison."

DR: She was succeeded as first lady by Liza Monroe and then later Louisa Adams. Did they change very much what the first lady did?

CR: Liza Monroe was nowhere near as warm and loving as Dolley. Dolley Madison was just this unbelievably effusive person. Everybody loved her. Henry Clay said to her once, "Everybody loves Mrs. Madison," and she said, "That's because Mrs. Madison loves everybody."

Now, I have read her mail. It's not true, but that was how she portrayed herself. In his inaugural address Jefferson had said, "We're all Federalists, we're all Republicans," which he didn't mean for a minute. When Dolley left, the newspapers wrote that she gave meaning to that statement because no one could tell how she felt about things, she was so welcoming and so generous. But she was all the time working for her husband and for his reelection.

And if you think things are bad now in terms of press, when Jefferson was running for reelection, the newspapers wrote that he had pimped Dolley Madison and her sisters in exchange for votes in Congress. It was nasty stuff. And they wrote that she had unsexed Madison because she was so sexy. John Randolph, who was crazy as a coot, kept threatening to "reveal the men in her life" on the floor of the Senate, things like that.

DR: Moving forward to the Civil War period, what did James Buchanan, the only never-married president, do for a hostess? Did he have one?

CR: He actually had a very good hostess.

We had this period before Buchanan where we had a new president every few years. We had Zachary Taylor die after a year in office, and Millard Fillmore come in. Then Franklin Pierce comes into office, and his wife, Jane Pierce, was devastated because they had three children, two of whom had already died. Then, as they were coming to Washington for her to become first lady, their only surviving child was killed by a train, which she witnessed. And she understandably never got over it.

One of her husband's best friends, Nathaniel Hawthorne, wrote about "that death's head in the White House," so she didn't get much sympathy. And so she didn't preside over White House social events.

So Buchanan really was the first in a while to have a White House that had entertainment and brought the city in. His niece Harriet Lane was his hostess. She was the first person to be called, in the press, "First Lady."

And she managed the first Prince of Wales visit. He went to Mount Vernon with her. Think of it — it was just his great-grandfather who had been defeated by George Washington, so it was very close in time to the Revolution.

The newspapers at the time are such fun to read. The Library of Congress has them online. Go to the Chronicling America website [URL: https://chroniclingamerica.loc .gov/] and you can read all these newspapers

Mary Todd Lincoln did not hide her political views or her likes and dislikes, a trait that likely contributed to her reputation as a "complicated" personality.

from the time. It's just wonderful.

The Prince of Wales goes to Mount Vernon, and the story says — it was ridiculously formal — "and they showed him the key to the Bastille, but he seemed much more interested in Miss Lane."

DR: For those who have ever been to Johns Hopkins, you will know that the Children's

Center there is named the Harriet Lane Clinic in part because of the work she did at Johns Hopkins. Going forward to the next first lady, that was a woman named Mary Todd Lincoln. She was an easygoing person. Is that right?

CR: *[Laughs.]*

DR: Very easy to get along with?

CR: Complicated lady.

DR: How did she change the first lady's role?

CR: I don't think she necessarily changed the role. She was more out-front than her predecessors about her political views and who she liked and didn't like. I think a lot of the others had had the same kind of role, but she just made it known to everybody, and therefore made people unhappy.

DR: Including her husband at times.

CR: It was a true love match, but they were both difficult people.

You know, in doing these books, frankly, I really get to the point where I lose all patience with the men. Benjamin Franklin and his wife, Alexander Hamilton and his wife, and all that.

Abraham Lincoln I really like. I didn't really know him until — well, of course I knew him, but I didn't *know* know him until I wrote this last book, and I've come out of it liking him.

Part of the reason I like him is that he put up with her even as 100 percent crazy as she was. When she died, the obituaries of her said she was a wacko. Not good.

DR: Franklin went to London and Europe and in ten years didn't come back and visit his wife. He was told his wife was going to die and he still didn't come back.

CR: Think about it. What do we learn about Benjamin Franklin as children, other than the kite? We learn that he was postmaster general of the United States.

But he was not in the United States. He was in England. His wife, Deborah Franklin, ran the postal system and their businesses, which were basically franchise printing offices that went out to the frontier, which was Pittsburgh — which was far at the time. And he's off in England having a wonderful time.

He's the lobbyist for the Pennsylvania Colony in London, and his friends and neighbors feel that he does not sufficiently oppose the Stamp Act. They're furious, and they come to burn down his house.

Everybody tells Deborah, "Get out! Get

out! They're about to burn down your house!" And she says, "I have not given anybody any offense." She gets a gun and she gets some relatives, and they stave off the neighbors.

Ben writes to her and says, "Well done, Deborah. Thanks for saving the house." But he still wouldn't come home, although she's begging him to.

Their only daughter gets married. He says, "Keep the wedding cheap." He still doesn't come home.

Finally, she dies, and he writes to friends and says, "My wife, in whose hands I have left the care of my affairs, has died, and so I have to go home." Poor Ben.

Now, when he got home, I have to admit, he signed the Declaration of Independence and then he went back to France and forged the alliance that saved the war, so I can't be totally mad at him. But he did not treat his family well.

DR: Of all the women you wrote about in your three books, which one would you say is the most impressive to you? Which one would you like to have met, and what would you ask that person if you could meet her?

CR: I'm not good at "most impressive" in the same way in modern times people always ask me, "Who's your best interview?" I'm never

Deborah Franklin kept the family printing empire going while her husband pursued diplomatic (and romantic) affairs in Europe.

able to answer that because people are so different from each other, and you learn different things from different people.

Some of these women are impressive in their ability to bring people together. Some of these women are impressive like Mercy Otis Warren with her propaganda and her ability to sway opinion. Some are impressive like Abigail Adams with their clear thinking. Different people do different things.

The one woman of the founding period that I'd like to just sit down to dinner with would be Sarah Livingston Jay, John Jay's wife, who was just delightful. Her letters are funny and fun, and we have her menus, and they were good.

7
DORIS KEARNS GOODWIN
ON ABRAHAM LINCOLN

"If I could talk to Lincoln, I'd tell him, 'See what you did? You were a model for all of us. You bring us here together tonight, both sides of the aisle.'"

BOOKS DISCUSSED OR MENTIONED:
Team of Rivals: The Political Genius of Abraham Lincoln (Simon & Schuster, 2005)
Leadership in Turbulent Times (Simon &

Schuster, 2018)
The Bully Pulpit: Theodore Roosevelt,
William Howard Taft, and the Golden Age
of Journalism (Simon & Schuster, 2013)
No Ordinary Time: Franklin and Eleanor
Roosevelt: The Home Front in World War II
(Simon & Schuster, reissued 2013)
The Fitzgeralds and the Kennedys: An
American Saga (Simon & Schuster, 1987)

Doris Kearns Goodwin first came to public attention as the author of a *New Republic* article about how a third-party candidate might help beat Lyndon Johnson in his presumed 1968 run for reelection. The article was published just days after the author had been selected as a White House Fellow during the Johnson administration. Upon the fellows' selection to this prestigious program, there was a celebration, and President Johnson danced with Doris — there were only three women and thirteen men chosen as fellows that year. Johnson whispered that she would be assigned to work directly for him.

But after the *New Republic* article appeared, she was reassigned to the Department of Labor. Later, Johnson brought her down to work in his office. "If I can't win her over, no one can," he said. She became a valued advisor to the president, and later spent a good deal of time working with him on his presidential memoirs.

How did the *New Republic* article author become such a close advisor to Johnson? With her extraordinary knowledge and brilliance, her commitment to hard work and long hours, and her infectious enthusiasm for whatever project she was pursuing.

Those qualities led Doris, post-Johnson, to a successful teaching career at Harvard, as well as to a multi-award-winning career as a biographer of Lyndon Johnson, the Kennedy-Fitzgerald family, Eleanor and Franklin Roosevelt (a book that won the Pulitzer Prize), Abraham Lincoln, and Teddy Roosevelt and William Howard Taft.

Doris's work on Lincoln, *Team of Rivals: The Political Genius of Abraham Lincoln,* is without doubt her best-known (and best-selling) book. It is the product of ten years of research and writing and was the basis for Steven Spielberg's award-winning film *Lincoln.* (The movie focused on the House passage of the Thirteenth Amendment, which ended slavery.)

It is said that more books have been written on Abraham Lincoln than on any other American. So it might seem an unenviable task to embark on a new book on him and try to find an angle or perspective that no one else has captured.

But Doris managed to do this. Early in her research, she recognized that Lincoln had, to the dismay of his closest friends and advisors, given his key cabinet positions to those who had sought the 1860 Republican nomination against him — and who initially had a relatively low regard for him.

I have known and greatly respected Doris for a good many years and have interviewed her on a number of occasions. In this interview, as in all of the others, Doris's knowledge of the subject matter and ability to enthusiastically recount its essence is evident from the start. There are few if any authors who are more enjoyable to interview.

MR. DAVID M. RUBENSTEIN (DR): We're going to talk briefly about a new book that Doris has written — *Leadership in Turbulent Times.* But principally we're going to talk about her book on Abraham Lincoln, *Team of Rivals,* and then a little bit at the end about a subject that everybody cares about and that Doris knows a lot about as well — baseball.

In the new book, you have taken four presidents you've written about and put together their leadership styles — Lincoln, Teddy Roosevelt, Franklin Roosevelt, and Lyndon Johnson. Of those four, which one was the smartest?

MS. DORIS KEARNS GOODWIN (DKG): Smartest in terms of intellectual breadth would probably be Teddy Roosevelt.

But there's a different definition of "smart." People thought that FDR was kind of a lightweight intellectual. Oliver Wendell Holmes said, "He had a first-rate temperament but a second-rate intellect." But he was a problem-solver. He could see how things fit together, which is another definition of intelligence.

DR: Let's suppose you had a chance to have dinner with any of them. Who would you want to have dinner with?

DKG: I think it would be whomever I had been living with at the time. It takes me so long to write these books that I feel like I'm waking up with the guy in the morning, sleeping with him at night. Ten years with Lincoln, seven years with Teddy and Taft, six years longer than the war itself lasted with Franklin Roosevelt in World War II.

My only fear is that in the afterlife there's going to be a panel of all the presidents that I've ever studied and every one is going to tell me everything I missed about them. The first person to scream will be Lyndon Johnson: "How come that damned book on the Kennedys was twice as long as the book you wrote about me?"

DR: If you could ask Abraham Lincoln any question, what would you ask him?

DKG: Instead of asking what I know I should as an historian — "What would you have done differently about Reconstruction?" — I would want him to come alive. If I could ask him to tell me a story, his whole demeanor would change, because when he told a funny story, he would just lighten up.

He loved to tell a story about the Revolutionary War hero Ethan Allen, who went to England after the war. They decided to embarrass him by putting a huge picture of General George Washington in the only outhouse that was connected to the dinner party. He goes into the outhouse and he comes out and he's not upset at all.

And they said, "Well, didn't you see George Washington there?"

"Oh, yes," he said. "It was the perfectly appropriate place for him."

"What do you mean?"

"Well," he said, "there's nothing to make an Englishman shit faster than the sight of General George Washington."

If I had the chance to talk to Lincoln, what I would like to do instead of asking him something is to tell him something. He dreamed, at the age of twenty-three, that he would do something that would allow other people to remember him — something good for the world. And then he died. He knows that the war is won, but he could never have imagined how much he was remembered.

If I could talk to Lincoln, I'd tell him, "See what you did? You were a model for all of us. You bring us here together tonight, both sides of the aisle."

DR: What would you like to ask FDR?

DKG: The hardest question would be, "Was there more you could have done to bring more refugees into the country before Hitler closed the door forever?" It's the scar on his legacy. Or "Could you have gotten by without

278

incarcerating Japanese Americans?"

Everything else he did makes him one of the most extraordinary leaders we've ever had. I'd be much happier talking to him about the New Deal.

DR: Then you would ask him, "What was it like having all those people living in the White House?"

DKG: I'd like to ask him if I could have lived up there with him.

What happens is he wants a cocktail hour every night in the White House during World War II so that he can enjoy himself and relax. The rule was you couldn't talk about the war. You could have gossip. You could talk about movies you'd seen, books you'd read, as long as you didn't mention the war.

After a while, this cocktail hour was so important to him, he wanted guests to be ready for it. So he invited his best friends and associates to live on the second floor of the White House.

His foreign policy advisor Harry Hopkins comes for dinner one night, sleeps over, and never leaves until the war comes to an end. His secretary, Missy LeHand, is living with the family in the White House. Lorena Hickok, who has a friendship with Eleanor, is living on the second floor. And Winston Churchill comes and spends weeks at a time in a room diagonally across from Roosevelt.

When I was writing the book, I kept imagining how it must have been at night, when they're all in their bathrobes and they meet in the corridor, and what incredible stories they must have told.

I happened to mention this on a radio program in Washington, and it happened that Hillary Clinton was listening. She promptly called me up at the radio station and invited me to sleep overnight in the White House, so I could wander the corridor with her with my map in hand and figure out where everyone had slept.

So my husband and I sleep over there in the White House, and it turned out the room we were given that night was Winston Churchill's bedroom. There was no way I could sleep. I was certain he was sitting in the corner drinking his brandy and smoking his ever-present cigar.

In fact, my favorite story about Churchill was that he came to Washington right after Pearl Harbor, and he and Roosevelt were set to sign a document that put what they were calling the Associated Nations against the Axis powers. That morning Roosevelt awakened with a whole new idea of calling them the United Nations against the Axis powers.

He was so excited, he had himself wheeled into Churchill's bedroom to tell him the news. But it so happened that Churchill was just coming out of the bathtub and had nothing on.

Roosevelt said, "I'm so sorry. I'll come back in a few moments." But Churchill, dripping from the tub, has the presence of mind, with nothing on, to say, "Oh, no. Please stay. The prime minister of Great Britain has nothing to hide from the president of the United States."

The next morning, I couldn't wait to go in the bathtub, and I thought, "I'm in the presence of the greatness of the past."

DR: You knew Lyndon Johnson, and you helped on his memoirs. You worked at the Johnson White House as a White House Fellow. In hindsight, what would you like to ask him?

DKG: First, it was the most extraordinary experience for me as a twenty-four-year-old White House Fellow to work for Lyndon Johnson. I had been a graduate student at Harvard. I got this White House Fellowship.

The night we were selected, we had a big dance at the White House. Johnson did dance with me. That was not that peculiar, because there were only three women then out of the sixteen White House Fellows.

In the months leading up to my selection, like many young people, I'd been active in the anti–Vietnam War movement, and had written an article with a friend of mine that we'd sent to the *New Republic* that they suddenly published. The title was "How to Remove Lyndon Johnson from Power."

I was certain he would kick me out of the program. Instead, surprisingly, he said, "Oh, bring her down here for a year, and if I can't win her over, no one can." I did eventually end up working for him in the White House, and then accompanied him to his ranch to help him with his memoirs the last years of his life.

I must say I saw him at a time when all of that energy and the extraordinary skill and legislative wizardry that he had in the mid-1960s was over. There was a sadness in him at the ranch, which is probably why he ended up talking to me so much. If I'd known him at the height of his power, I never would have had that experience. But he knew that the war in Vietnam had cut his legacy in two.

Again, rather than asking him a question now, I'd like to tell him that fifty years later, people are beginning to remember the extraordinary things that he did — Medicare, Medicaid, voting rights, the Civil Rights Act, aid to education, fair housing, immigration reform. Any one of those legislative achievements would make a president today. He went to his death, sadly, not knowing that that was going to be.

DR: I've listened to all of the Johnson tapes over the years. I always heard about the "Johnson treatment" — that he could be difficult and vile in person — but I never heard any curse words on the tapes. Where are the curse words?

DKG: The curse words are more in the stories people tell about him. He did use them. I must say I heard that.

But the Johnson tapes show an extraordinarily brilliant one-on-one figure. He could persuade anybody to do anything.

When you hear the tapes that focus on his relationship with Republican minority leader Senator Everett M. Dirksen, you hear how he needs to get the Republicans to join with the Democrats from the North to break the filibuster on the Civil Rights Act of '64. You hear him saying to Dirksen, "What do you want for Illinois? Public works projects, dams, pardons, whatever you want."

But then, most importantly, he says, "Everett, you come with me on this bill, and two hundred years from now, schoolchildren will know only two names: Abraham Lincoln and Everett Dirksen."

Years later, I met the CEO of Pepsi Cola, Don Kendall. When Nixon first went into office, he asked Kendall, who was a good friend of his, to go down and talk to Johnson at the ranch about some sensitive matter.

Kendall gets to the ranch. Johnson's working on his memoirs, and he's saying, "How am I going to remember what happened forty years ago, thirty years ago? The only chapters that are any good at all are from this little taping machine in the Oval Office. I could turn it on when I was having an important conversation. So you go back and tell your good friend Nixon, as he starts his presidency, there's nothing more important than a taping system."

DR: Let's talk about *Team of Rivals.* It's said that more books have been written about Abraham Lincoln than any other American. Why did you think that the world needed another book on Lincoln?

DKG: I don't think I thought that the world needed another book. I just knew that I wanted to live with him. Because it takes me so long, as I was saying, to write these books, and because I get so involved with whoever it is — I haven't written twenty books like a lot of my historian friends. I knew that I wanted to live with Lincoln.

I wanted to learn about him. I wanted to know about him. I'd written about Franklin and Eleanor in World War II, and I thought, "What more exciting era to live in than to try to understand the Civil War?"

When I started, I was really scared. I wasn't

sure I could produce anything different. I went with my confidence at the beginning that I would write about Abe and Mary like I had Franklin and Eleanor. But after two years, I realized that Mary couldn't carry the public side of the story the same way Eleanor could.

Just luckily, I went up to Auburn, New York, and I happened to visit William H. Seward's house there, and then I found out that he'd written thousands of letters to his wife. I knew what an important part of the cabinet he was. [Seward served as Lincoln's secretary of state.]

I started reading those letters, and they talked about Salmon P. Chase [Lincoln's secretary of the treasury], and they talked about Edward Bates [Lincoln's attorney general], and I realized that if I could learn about Seward's relationship with Lincoln, and Chase's and Bates's relationships with him, maybe I could get at Lincoln that way. Eventually that became *Team of Rivals.*

DR: You start the book with the 1860 Republican National Convention in Chicago. At the time, Abraham Lincoln was not thought likely to get the nomination. Why were the other three candidates you just mentioned considered likely to get it, and how did they not get it?

DKG: The nomination struggle is such an extraordinary moment. There is a picture of the contenders, probably taken in 1859. Lincoln's not even mentioned, which is an extraordinary thing.

Seward had been the governor and then U.S. senator from New York. He was the most important orator in the Whig Party and then the new Republican Party. He was considered at that time a liberal, almost a radical.

Everybody thought Seward would be the nominee. So Lincoln, brilliantly, knowing that he is never going to be the first choice of any of the delegates, says to his managers, "Just tell everybody if they can't get their first love, I'm there. I'll be the second love."

He never attacked any of the other three, while they attacked one another. Also, he made sure that the convention was in Chicago, which seemed like neutral ground. Of course, it helped Lincoln [who was from Illinois] that the convention was in Chicago.

When Seward misses getting the majority on the first ballot, and people are trying to figure out where to go, they peeled off to Lincoln, because he was the one who hadn't attacked their man. It was an incredibly brilliant strategy.

DR: He gets the nomination on the third ballot. Does he reach out to these other men or just ignore them?

DKG: That's the incredible thing he does. Right away, he knows that the way the Republican Party's going to win — and the way they absolutely can win, because the Democratic Party is split in two — is to stay united.

So he reached out to each one of his rivals. He wrote letters that said, "I'm the humblest of all of you. I need your support."

Seward finally came along and did a grand tour for Lincoln on a train trip. Chase supported him. Bates wrote a public letter about him.

And so Lincoln united the Republican Party behind him, in part because of who he was and because he had the confidence and the humility to reach out to his rivals. They were all better known, better educated, more celebrated. They each thought they should have been president instead of him. But he was able to bring them aboard.

DR: How do you campaign for president in 1860?

DKG: Well, you don't leave the place where you're from — which is an amazing thought, right? Lincoln just stays in Springfield.

Surrogates are on the campaign trail for him. It was considered unseemly in that time for a candidate to campaign on his own behalf. Delegations would come to Springfield.

What he campaigns on is he understands the importance of the Republican Party not being too far to the right or the left. He keeps them moderate, because he knows that's the way they're going to win. He's writing letters to them. He's making public statements. But he's still staying in Springfield while these other guys run around the country.

DR: A principal issue facing the country then was whether slavery should be extended past the original southern states. What position did Lincoln take on that?

DKG: The main issue that the Republicans ran on, and that Lincoln ran on, was not ending slavery. There was very little thought — except among the abolitionists, who didn't have anywhere near a majority, even in the states in which they were popular — about ending slavery itself, because the Constitution protected property. [Enslaved people were considered property.]

The main issue was whether you extended slavery to the western territories. An act that had been passed by the Congress in 1854, the Kansas-Nebraska Act, allowed it to extend there.

That's what mobilized the Republican Party. They always thought that if we could keep slavery in the South, someday it might die out, but if you brought slavery into the western territories, slaves would continue to be used in the West, and then those states that were new would become slave states. That was the theme of the Republican Party — not to end slavery, but to end its movement out west.

DR: Lincoln was running against the candidate that he'd lost to before, Stephen Douglas, who was the Democratic candidate. But the famous Lincoln-Douglas debates did not occur during that campaign. When did they take place?

DKG: What happens is that Lincoln runs for the Senate in 1855 and loses. Then he runs again in 1858 and his main opponent is Stephen Douglas, whom he's known ever since they were young.

In fact, at one point Lincoln said, "Stephen Douglas's life has been this extraordinary success and mine has been a flat failure compared to him." He'd watched the rise of Douglas, who was an extraordinary debater and a really strong, pugilistic kind of character.

Douglas agreed somehow to have these seven debates with Lincoln, and this is what made Lincoln a national figure. Debates in those days — when you think about it today, how incredible it must have been — were the biggest sporting event of the times. Before we had a lot of professional sports, people would go to debates by the thousands.

The first guy would speak for an hour and a half, the second guy would speak for an hour and a half, then there'd be a rebuttal for an hour, and another rebuttal for an hour. They're sitting there for six hours. There are marching bands. There's music. And the audience is yelling, "Hit 'im again! Hit 'im again! Harder!" It's an extraordinary thing, these debates.

Lincoln did great in the debates. They published them afterwards. People saw what an extraordinary debater and character he was in terms of understanding the issue of slavery and the Kansas-Nebraska Act.

But in those days, there weren't really national newspapers yet, so the way you got your news, much like today, was by reading your own partisan paper. You would subscribe to the Republican paper or the Whig paper or the Democratic paper.

So when the papers would describe the debates, if it's the Democratic paper, they would say, "Douglas was so amazing that he was carried out on the arms of the people in great, great triumph! And Lincoln, sadly, was so terrible that he fell on the floor and his people had to carry him out just to get him away from the humiliation." So we had a certain partisan press in those days.

DR: So the general presidential election campaign is won by Lincoln. Did he win any southern states?

DKG: No southern states.

DR: He won the election, but he didn't say he was going to abolish slavery. In fact, he supported what was then called the Thirteenth Amendment, which reaffirmed that slavery was part of the Constitution. So why did the southern states begin to secede?

DKG: Because the secession was in the works. It was afoot for years before that. The South and the North were pulling too far apart. The cultures were different. The economics were different. And the whole idea of what future slavery was going to have had torn the country apart already.

You could see that in the moment when Preston Brooks, a congressman from South Carolina, hits Massachusetts senator Charles Sumner over the head with a cane. [The incident took place on the floor of the U.S. Senate in 1856, after Sumner made an anti-slavery speech.] Sumner was really hurt, out of action for several years.

The incredible thing is it mobilized the people in the North. They had mass meetings against it. But Preston Brooks was made a hero in the South. They carried golden canes in his honor. That kind of division in a country was not going to be healed.

The South understood that demographics were not on their side. If the North could keep slavery from moving to the western territories, the antislavery population in the West would add to that in the North, overwhelming the southern proslavery population. So they saw the writing on the wall.

DR: A number of states secede. Why doesn't Lincoln say, "Go away if you want to go away. We'll just have our country be the North"? Why did he feel so determined that the country had to stay together?

DKG: Lincoln believed that what America stood for, what made us a beacon of hope to other countries in the world ruled by kings or queens or dictators, was that we believed ordinary people could govern us, and that we could have an election and people would abide by the rules of that election.

If the South was able to secede, that meant the idea that ordinary people could govern themselves would not be true, and maybe someday the West would secede from the East. The whole idea that you could have a mass democracy in an area like the United States would be undone, and we no longer would be a beacon to the world.

DR: As he puts his administration together, the top jobs go to his former rivals. So the secretary of state is Seward. The attorney general is Bates. And then Salmon Chase becomes the secretary of the treasury. And the secretary of defense or war — who was that initially?

DKG: Originally it was somebody — a businessman named Simon Cameron — who had to be let go from his job because he let contractors give the Union troops horses that were blind — he didn't know it was all happening — and knapsacks that fell apart in the rain. So he was pushed out of the job, and then Stanton comes in.

That's the most amazing story. Edwin Stanton had been a famous lawyer in the 1850s, and he had a patent case that was going to be tried in Chicago. He came from Ohio. They thought they needed someone who would know the judges in Chicago. This is in 1855. They came and interviewed Lincoln. They thought he'd be good for the case.

Lincoln was so excited at the thought of working with this nationally famous lawyer, Stanton. But the judge changed the case from Chicago back to Cincinnati, Ohio, so they didn't need Lincoln anymore — but they forgot to tell him.

He kept working on his brief. He went to Cincinnati all on his own. He goes right up to Stanton and Stanton's partner on the street corner, and he says, "Let's go up to the courthouse together in a gang."

Stanton took one look at Lincoln — this was recorded at the time — and he said to his partner, "We have to lose this long-armed ape." Lincoln had a stain on his shirt. His hair was disheveled. His sleeves were too short for his long arms.

And they turned away from him. They never opened the brief he had painstakingly prepared. He was humiliated. In fact, he said he never wanted to go back to Cincinnati again.

But he stayed that entire week to listen to Stanton deliver the case, and he was so impressed by Stanton's way of doing it that he went back to Illinois and he said, "I have to educate myself even more. I thought I was a good lawyer."

He would go on the circuit with his fellow lawyers, stay up at night studying Euclid, reading books. He said, "I'm going to become even more than I was," which is an extraordinary thing.

Anyway, when Cameron, the first secretary of war, has to leave, everybody says to Lincoln, "The only man for this job is Edwin Stanton." Somehow Lincoln is able to forgive that resentment that he must have felt against Stanton and make him his secretary of war. Stanton ends up loving him more than anyone, outside of his family.

Lincoln had that ability to forget past resentments and to appoint somebody not because they hurt you in the past but because they are the best man for the present — and the two of them were perfect together because they were so opposite.

Stanton was blunt and intense. He could be mean-spirited. Lincoln was always compassionate and giving people too many chances. But they worked together brilliantly, and Stanton became, along with Seward, one of his closest friends.

DR: Seward, Stanton, Bates, and Chase become the leading members of the cabinet. They're all well educated — college, law school. Lincoln basically didn't go to school. How did he get to be so well read and such a good writer?

DKG: Some of it is probably a gift. Teddy Roosevelt one time wrote an essay arguing that there are two kinds of success in the world. One comes from people who have a talent that is just given to them as a gift: Keats's poetry, Lincoln's gift for writing.

But the other kind of success comes from people — of whom he thought he was one, and most people are — who have ordinary talents but an extraordinary ability for hard, sustained work, to bring everything possible out of those ordinary talents.

Lincoln had both. He had a gift for language that must have been inborn. There's a poet in that man.

But as a child, he only went to school for less than twelve full months, he later figured out, because his father needed him to work on the hardscrabble family farm. But he scoured the countryside for books, and he read everything he could lay his hands on. It was said when he got a copy of the King James Bible or *Aesop's Fables* or one of Shakespeare's plays, he was so excited he could not eat, he could not sleep.

He learned to read early on. He would read aloud. He learned to love poetry. He would stay up as late as he could at night reading. When he's plowing in the field, he's got a book with him by the tree.

And he learns to tell stories when he's a young boy. That becomes part of his stock-in-trade later. He would listen to his father and their friends tell stories at night, and he would not be able to sleep until he could recount the story to his little friends in the field. He'd listen to ministers giving sermons. Eventually, on the circuit in Illinois, he became the storyteller that everybody wanted to come and hear.

DR: Lincoln becomes president. How does he get into Washington, D.C.? There's a rumor that he snuck in dressed as a woman. Is that true?

DKG: What is true is that he was taking the train from Springfield to Washington. He came early because he thought he had to be closer to Washington as everything was happening.

But the Secret Service, or whatever they were called at the time, heard a rumor that there were thugs in Maryland who were going to stop the train as it was passing through.

I don't think he was wearing a skirt, but the Secret Service did bring him in secretly. He was always later sad that he had done that, because it was made into a big story that he came in without being openly who he was, but he was just listening to them in terms of security.

DR: He's president of the United States. The South secedes. There's going to be a fight. Is it true that he asked Robert E. Lee to be the general for the North?

DKG: Absolutely. He respected Robert E. Lee. They met in the Blair House, near the White House, and Lee said he needed a little time to think about it.

In the end, he had to go where Virginia went. That was his home state. But things might have been so different. If the North had had the generals from the South and the political leadership of Lincoln, it would have been a much shorter war. As it was, the South had the generals but not the political leadership.

DR: When the war starts, the North is considered so likely to win that at the First Battle of Bull Run, people come out with picnic tables and carts. They're going to watch the North annihilate the South. What happened?

DKG: Many of the soldiers ran away from the battle, and it was a humiliation for the North. That night, Lincoln couldn't sleep, and he saw the soldiers and people coming through Washington and knew what had happened. So he stayed up all night.

This is what Lincoln was like. He just had to figure out what went wrong. He would always write down what he could when something went wrong so that he could learn from mistakes.

He realized the three-month term of army service was too short. Many of these people were about to be out of the service, so they ran away from the battle. He realized the general wasn't right. The discipline was wrong. As long as he could figure that out and start to change what had happened, then he was able to finally go to sleep.

Always that was his mantra. He said, "As

"The President and General McClellan on the Battle-field of Antietam."

long as I can figure out what I've done wrong, I'd like to believe I'm smarter today than I was yesterday because of what I've understood about what happened."

DR: His general at the beginning was George McClellan. Why was McClellan not so effective? Why did he not attack the South?

DKG: Oh, McClellan. When I say I want to live with the people that I love — I did not love George McClellan.

He was very popular among the troops.

They loved him. But unlike Grant later, he was always assuming he didn't have enough troops and that he didn't have enough supplies. There was a lack of forward movement on his part.

Worse than that, when you read his diary, or you read the letters that he wrote to his wife — which she should never have allowed to be published; his reputation might have been different — he says terrible things about everybody. He says, "The whole cabinet are geese, Lincoln's stupid. I could be a dictator if I wanted to, they love me so much."

There's a famous story where Lincoln went to McClellan's house one night. This is in 1861. McClellan is coming home from someplace, and he's supposed to be home soon, and Lincoln's waiting in the parlor.

McClellan knows that Lincoln is there, but he goes straight up to bed. John Hay, Lincoln's secretary, was there, and he said, "This is the insolence of the epaulet." And Lincoln says, "I will hold his horse if he wins a battle. That's all that matters."

He gives McClellan too many chances — always wanting somebody to have a second chance was one of the weaknesses that he had — keeps him on too long, until finally he decides that McClellan has to go and fires him.

DR: Toward the end of the war, Lincoln gets

a general he likes — Ulysses S. Grant. But initially he resisted efforts to free the slaves. Why was that, and why did he issue the Emancipation Proclamation?

DKG: He initially resisted it because he didn't think that the federal government had the power to do anything about slavery, because of the Constitution.

But after the defeat of the Peninsula Campaign of 1862, when McClellan was so outgeneraled by Lee, Lincoln said that we were at the end of our rope and that something had to happen. So he went to his summer cottage at the Soldiers' Home, which is where he would often go to think just to get away from Washington.

In those days, people who wanted to see Lincoln could come in the mornings. They would be lining up outside his office to ask him for a job. These are the days before the Civil Service.

He would spend two hours with these ordinary people. When his secretary said, "You don't have time for these ordinary people," he said, "I must never forget the popular assemblage from which I have come."

But he knew he needed time to think about what to do, so he went to the Soldiers' Home, and it was there that he began drafting, in the summer of 1862, the Emancipation Proclamation.

He had visited the troops at least a dozen times and realized, as he talked to the soldiers, that slaves were an enormously positive force for the Confederacy. They were working in the camps, they were tending to the kitchens, and they were helping the Confederates in the balance of power.

He began to realize that "I'm commander in chief of the army, and if I can emancipate the slaves to help the war struggle, then I can issue an emancipation proclamation."

He comes back to his cabinet and he tells them. They've been debating for months what to do about slavery. Several people in the cabinet thought he should have done it right away. There were others who thought, "If you do it, the South will never, ever stop fighting. This war will never end."

Lincoln tells them, "I'm issuing an emancipation proclamation, and I will listen to your advice about its timing and its implementation, but I want you to know I've made up my mind about it."

Seward comes back and says, "I'm with you on this, but you can't issue it now. It'll look like it's part of the defeat of the Peninsula Campaign. Wait until the eagle of victory takes flight." That's the way they talked in those days — "Wait until the eagle of victory takes flight."

So Lincoln waits until the Union victory at Antietam in September. He doesn't issue it in July. When Lee's forces are pulled back, he issues the Emancipation Proclamation.

The amazing thing is he meets with the cabinet again, and at that point — even though several of them are still not happy with what he's doing, and he tells Montgomery Blair, his postmaster general, "I'll let you file your written objections to anybody" — none of them go against it publicly. So much do they by that time respect Lincoln, they present a united front to the country, which was essential — that the cabinet be together in that important moment.

DR: The Gettysburg Address is very eloquent, and so is Lincoln's second inaugural address. Why is the Emancipation Proclamation just boilerplate?

DKG: He meant the Emancipation Proclamation to be a legal document, not a speech. Also, he knew that it was so important that this be accepted by as many people as possible in the North. He knew, and was told, that a lot of soldiers would leave the army if he freed the slaves. They were just fighting for the Union, not against slavery.

There were states in the North that passed resolutions saying they might secede from the Union because New England was pushing us into this emancipation. So he wanted the proclamation to be the least incendiary

"The First Reading of the Emancipation Proclamation Before the Cabinet."

document it could be, so as not to spark the tinder that was already there.

DR: While there are slaves who are freed, and some of them do fight for the North, it still takes a long time for the war to come to an end. The final, critical battles take place in Gettysburg. What happened there?

DKG: They begin to make Lee's army retreat. But the hard thing for Lincoln about Gettysburg was that they were sending telegrams to General Meade and saying to him, "Just don't let Lee's army escape, no matter what you do." Unfortunately, Meade did let Lee's army escape.

The soldiers from the North were decimated as well. They were exhausted. Lincoln later understood why that might have been so, but it was one of the biggest moments of depression for him when they heard that Lee's army had escaped.

He wrote a long letter to General Meade saying, "I'm immeasurably distressed you didn't do what we asked you to do. Had you been able to get Lee's army, the war might have ended in a few months. Now it could go on year after year."

But he knew that that would paralyze the general, who was in the field, so he did what he often did in these moments: he wrote what he called a "hot letter" to General Meade. He would then put these hot letters aside, hoping he would cool down psychologically and never need to send them.

When his papers were opened in the twentieth century, underneath this one to Meade was written "Never sent and never signed." He did that dozens of times.

It seems to me that would be a good thing for people in today's world of Twitter to learn. Just write a hot Twitter account, don't post it.

DR: After Gettysburg, although Meade did not pursue Lee the way Lincoln would have preferred, ultimately the North does prevail. Grant becomes a great general. He defeats Lee. Was Lincoln's view that Lee and the

South should be humiliated at the surrender at Appomattox?

DKG: Without question, no. Lincoln understood early on — and he made it known to Grant — that he wanted to treat the South with as much leniency as possible, even in terms of what he hoped would happen to the Confederate leaders. He knew that if they stayed in the United States, there would be a wish to put them on trial. He didn't want that.

He hoped they would kind of escape — go somewhere else, so that they didn't have to be caught. He hoped that the government could give the soldiers in the South guns so that they could go back to their farms, give them back their horses, not take away their personal property.

And indeed, on the last day of Lincoln's life, when Grant came to the cabinet to talk about the terms that he had given to Lee's army and to the soldiers, that was what Lincoln wanted, and he was so happy.

That's what's so sad. That day was probably the happiest day he'd had in his life. His son Robert was back from the war. He and Mary went together that afternoon on a carriage ride and talked about how difficult the years had been for her. They'd lost their son Willie, the favorite kid in the family, at ten years old.

And the Lincolns said maybe they could dream about what would happen after the presidency. He wanted to go to California more than anywhere, over the Rockies. She wanted to go to Europe. They had the sense of a future before them.

He's at the White House talking to a bunch of his friends that night. He used to go to the theater for recreation. He went a hundred times, during the Civil War, to the theater — more than a hundred times. He said, like Roosevelt with his famous cocktail hours, that for a few precious hours he could go back to another time and forget the war that was raging.

But that night he didn't want to go, he was so happy talking to his friends in the White House. But he had given his word, and it was in the newspapers that morning that he was going to go. So he said to them, "I'd rather stay, but I've given my word, so I have to go to the theater."

DR: The night before he goes, he gives his last speech at the White House, and he talks about incendiary things. John Wilkes Booth was standing there, listening. What made Booth so upset?

DKG: What Lincoln talked about that night was the possibility of giving the vote to black soldiers. John Wilkes Booth turned to the person next to him, one of the conspirators, and said — in worse words — "That means Negro citizenship. We have to get him."

DR: He plotted not just to kill Lincoln but to kill three people. Who were the three?

DKG: He was going to kill Seward and Andrew Johnson, the vice president, and Lincoln. The conspirators did actually go to Seward's house. It's an extraordinary scene. Seward lived with his wife and his daughter and son in a mansion that's right where the Hay-Adams hotel is right now.

The guy comes in with a knife and pretends that he's bringing a prescription medicine for Seward, because Seward had been in a carriage accident several weeks earlier and had broken his jaw. The attacker goes into Seward's room and he slashes Seward's jaw. The only reason Seward lived was that his jaw had been wired, so the assailant didn't hit the artery that he would otherwise have.

The guy who was supposed to kill Andrew Johnson was staying at a hotel. At the last minute he goes and has a drink at the bar, and he decides not to do it.

But, of course, John Wilkes Booth comes to the back of the Lincolns' box at the Ford's Theatre because he was known in the theater as an actor. His brother Edwin Booth was the most famous Shakespearean actor at the

The famous editorial cartoonist Thomas Nast offered a rosy view of post–Civil War life for emancipated African Americans, contrasting scenes of freedom with scenes of the horrors of slavery.

time, whom Lincoln had met and admired.

They let him into the back of the box. He shoots Lincoln, as we know, in the back of the head.

The doctor said Lincoln should have died instantly, but he didn't die, he was so vital. They said he stayed alive until that next morning, and then Stanton gives the words that have come down to us. "Now," Stanton said, "he belongs to the ages." The very thing he had dreamed of — that he'd be remembered over time.

DR: It took you ten years to write this book.

At the beginning, you mentioned to Steven Spielberg that you were doing this, and he said he was going to make a movie out of it, and he did. What part did he choose, and were you upset that he only used four pages out of your seven hundred?

DKG: No, no! The whole point is, did he get the man, Lincoln, that I thought I knew? He got this man who was an incredibly great political genius, who was able to trade for what he wanted yet was a transformative leader.

I'd met Spielberg because he was doing a documentary on the century that had just passed. He'd always wanted to make a movie about Lincoln. He said it would be the culmination of his life. He had read *Franklin and Eleanor,* so he asked me if he could have first dibs when I finished the Lincoln book — like there's going to be twelve Steven Spielbergs wanting to do this book. Of course I said yes.

Then, whenever he was on a movie set, he would call me — he hadn't bought the rights yet, he had just optioned them at this point — and he would say, "What did Lincoln do today?" And I'd tell him, "Lincoln was at the courthouse today," "He's on the legal circuit," or "He was telling a funny story." That's the way Spielberg would relax between his other movies.

He finally put two scriptwriters on it even before I finished the book, and they both wrote really good scripts. But to neither of those scripts did Daniel Day-Lewis [who had been cast as Lincoln] say yes.

Finally Tony Kushner started working on the script, and I worked with him. At first he had something like a seven-hundred-page script. Chase was a big figure in it. The cabinet was a big figure in it.

But the filmmakers knew they had to focus on a smaller subject instead of telling a bigger story where you wouldn't get into his character. The plot was less important than what it showed about Lincoln.

Finally Daniel says yes to the screenplay, and Spielberg called me the next day and he said, "Daniel wants a year to become Lincoln, so we're not going to announce that he's Lincoln yet, but I want you to take him to Springfield. He going to come under an assumed name, and you'll take him around and show him all the sights."

We get to the hotel, and I say, "We're just supposed to eat in the hotel, right, with you under this assumed name?" He said, "Oh, no, let's go to a bar."

So we went to a bar, and immediately somebody bought us drinks, and I thought, "Oh my God. It's already over." But they didn't recognize him; they recognized me. It became a huge joke between us.

For an entire year, as he's preparing for the role, I'm sending him books, and we're talking, we're texting each other, and he's becoming Lincoln. He's reading about Henry Clay and John C. Calhoun and Daniel Webster.

I went to the filming in Richmond, Virginia — it was great the way that Richmond opened its doors to this film. It felt like a reconciliation between North and South.

Daniel was by now Lincoln. He never was out of character. Even the other actors had to call him Mr. President or Mr. Lincoln. It was an extraordinary experience to watch Lincoln come to life.

DR: Let's go to baseball for a moment. Why do you care about baseball?

DKG: I grew up as a Brooklyn Dodgers fan in Long Island when the Dodgers, the Yankees, and the Giants were all there at the same time. My father came from Brooklyn and loved the Brooklyn Dodgers. He taught me how to keep score when I was six years old. He would come home, and I would recount every single play that had taken place that afternoon.

It made me think, "There's something special about history, even if it's only five hours old, keeping my father's attention." I'm convinced I learned the narrative art from those nightly sessions with my father, because at first, I'd be so excited I would blurt out, "The Dodgers won!" or "The Dodgers lost!" which took the drama of this two-hour telling away. I finally learned you had to tell a story from beginning to middle to end.

My father died before I got married and had my three sons. But I have given them that love of my father through the stories I've told and through baseball. I then went to Harvard and became an equally irrational Red Sox fan. My kids are now Red Sox fans. I can sit there at a game with the kids and just imagine myself a young girl once more in the presence of my father watching my players — Jackie Robinson, Pee Wee Reese, Duke Snider, Gil Hodges — and it's a magical thing, because then I can feel as if my father is still there.

Even though they never met their grandfather, they've heard about him through the stories I've told, which is why I love history. We make these people who were part of our families and part of our country's history come back to life.

8
A. Scott Berg
ON CHARLES LINDBERGH

"He was human quarry all his life."

BOOK DISCUSSED:
Lindbergh (G. P. Putnam's Sons, 1998)

Most of the biographies in this series involve government officials or those who influenced government policy. Charles Lindbergh (1902–1974) is in a different category, but his impact on history, and on the United

314

States and Europe, was truly unique.

In May 1927, a little-known twenty-five-year-old airmail pilot named Charles Lindbergh made history when, responding to a $25,000 prize challenge, he became the first person to fly solo across the Atlantic, piloting his plane, the *Spirit of St. Louis,* from New York to Paris in a thirty-three-and-a-half-hour flight. The feat made him an instant celebrity around the world — perhaps the most famous human in world history up to that point — and, as award-winning biographer A. Scott Berg explains, it ushered in the modern era of media superstardom.

Lindbergh spent the rest of his life uncomfortably in the glare of public attention, by turns a figure of admiration, sympathy, and controversy. He and his wife, the writer Anne Morrow Lindbergh, found themselves at the center of a media frenzy in 1932, when their baby son was kidnapped from the family home in New Jersey and killed. Bruno Richard Hauptmann, a German immigrant, was convicted of the crime during "the trial of the century" in 1935 and later executed.

To escape the publicity, the Lindberghs moved to Europe. Lindbergh spent time in Germany and became an ardent noninterventionist, accused of being an anti-Semite and a Nazi sympathizer. A key figure in the growth of commercial aviation, he became a dedicated conservationist late in life.

Written with unprecedented access to the Lindbergh family papers, Berg's *Lindbergh* won the 1999 Pulitzer Prize for Biography. Berg's other books have chronicled the lives of some of America's most notable figures, including legendary editor Max Perkins, Hollywood mogul Samuel Goldwyn, actress Katharine Hepburn, and President Woodrow Wilson. He is currently working on a biography of Justice Thurgood Marshall.

In this conversation, Berg explains how a shy kid from an unhappy family became the world's most famous aviator; how obsessive attention to detail and a paper cup helped Lindbergh make his successful transatlantic flight; and how his fame helped create the lifelong focus by the media on everything Lindbergh — a focus that Lindbergh largely abhorred.

Berg also delves into Lindbergh's controversial political stances, including his links to the America First movement, the perception of his anti-Semitism, how he served the country in World War II (despite President Franklin Roosevelt's ban on his serving in the military), his role in the growth of commercial aviation and space exploration, and the complicated private life of a man who lived most of his life in the public eye.

For those who did not live in the era of Lindbergh's transatlantic flight, it may be hard to understand how a solo flight of thirty-three and a half hours between New York and Paris could create the world's greatest celebrity ever (and, for a long time, its most admired person). The first men to climb Mount Everest or to circle the globe from space or to land on the moon, while celebrated, never came close to Lindbergh's global and enduring fame.

In the interview, Berg explains the phenomenon this way: there had been a well-known cash prize available to individuals who could make the flight between the two cities; several had died trying; Lindbergh seemed like the perfect hero: young, handsome, unmarried, shy, and polite; he decided to do the flight solo; the world was at peace and seemed unconcerned about national bragging rights (and so the French were just as excited as if the prizewinner had been from France); and, perhaps most important, this time period was essentially the first time that the world was linked instantly through electronic communication. Everyone essentially knew everything at almost the same time, producing a snowball effect of fame.

Berg also discusses something that surprised him even after he had spent ten years researching and writing the book. Lindbergh managed to keep secret from the world, his family, and his biographer that he had fathered seven children with three German women. Berg discovered this only when one of those children, having read his book, wanted him — and presumably others — to know that there were seven other heirs to the Lindbergh name.

A final note on the interview: Scott Berg is essentially a writer, and clearly a gifted one. But his ability to tell a story orally, with enthusiasm and detail and suspense, is rivaled by few biographers I have ever interviewed. I think that is apparent here.

MR. DAVID M. RUBENSTEIN (DR): Why did a thirty-three-and-a-half-hour flight from New York to Paris make Lindbergh the most famous person in the history of the world? He got more adulation than anybody had ever gotten. Why was such a big deal made of something that wasn't like going to the moon?

MR. A. SCOTT BERG (ASB): It was so much bigger than going to the moon. It represented the convergence of so many things in the world in that moment, not the least of which were advancements in communication. This was the first moment in which sound footage was attached to newsreels, in which radio reached the entire civilized world, in which photographs could be sent by wire across the ocean.

And so, in May of 1927, when Charles Lindbergh flew from New York to Paris, it was the first moment in history that could be shared instantaneously and simultaneously around the globe.

The second factor is that he was impossibly handsome. He looked like a movie star. And in that moment, he became the first modern media superstar.

Third, and perhaps most important, this was a moment in which the entire world was all on one team. Everybody in the world loved Lindbergh. Nobody had a disagreement about Charles Lindbergh in 1927. This surpassed nationality. It surpassed any beliefs anybody had about anything.

The entire human race, for the first and maybe the last time unless and until we're attacked by Mars, was interested, was rooting for this one man. As one, people on earth looked hopefully at the sky.

DR: Five years later, he's married, has a child, Charles Lindbergh Jr. That child is kidnapped and murdered. They caught the person they said did it — Bruno Richard Hauptmann, a German immigrant — and it became the trial of the century, before the O. J. Simpson trial. What happened? Was the right man caught and executed?

ASB: Not forgetting O. J. Simpson, I think it is still the trial of the century — for several reasons. First of all, the Lindbergh baby was the most famous baby since Jesus Christ. Everybody in the world knew about the most beautiful baby of the most beautiful pilot, the most famous man alive.

Lindbergh was, in fact, the most celebrated living person who ever walked the earth. Now, his baby was kidnapped and killed, almost certainly as the kidnapper was descending the ladder [at the Lindbergh home] in Hopewell, New Jersey. The ladder broke, the baby fell two stories to the concrete and died.

320

The crime was solved a few years later. The trial of the century occurred, trying the man for the crime of the century.

There is no doubt in my mind that this man received an unfair trial. There is also no doubt in my mind that they got the right man — Bruno Richard Hauptmann.

DR: Lindbergh was very, very popular. But before World War II, he was seen by some as a Nazi sympathizer and an anti-Semite. Was he either of those?

ASB: Everyone knows two and a half things — or should know at least two and a half things — about Charles Lindbergh: the flight, the kidnapping, and his political position. In the last twenty years especially, a couple of things have been conflated.

Here's the thing: Charles Lindbergh was not a Nazi sympathizer.

He did spend time in Nazi Germany between 1936 and 1938. What most people didn't realize then, and what most people don't realize now, is that he was there doing reconnaissance for the United States government.

He had been asked by the air attaché at the American Embassy in Berlin, an army colonel named Truman Smith. Colonel Smith had been there throughout the thirties, and he saw the Luftwaffe building up, and he

"One of the greatest of crimes!" Cartoonist Clifford Kennedy Berryman pictured the scene in the Lindbergh baby's nursery after the kidnapping.

thought, "But they're being very secretive. We don't know how big the German air force is, how powerful it is. If there were just some way we could learn."

He had read that the Lindberghs were then living in England. And he thought, "If I were able to reach Charles Lindbergh and bring him over here to Germany, they would be so happy to have Charles Lindbergh, the greatest, the most celebrated living human being on the planet, the greatest pilot who ever

322

lived. If we could get him to Germany, they will show off everything they have."

And that's exactly what happened. Lindbergh came, and the Germans guided him through their factories and showed him their airfields. And Lindbergh was sending detailed reports to the White House and to Whitehall in London as well. This was really the extent of his connection to Germany.

Now, that said, he had seen the entire world undergoing an incredible depression, mostly financial. He saw every country was really teetering — except Germany. They were really succeeding. And this fascinated him.

He even thought of living there for a moment — until November of 1938 and the Night of Shattered Glass, Kristallnacht [November 9–10, 1938, when the Nazi Party set off violent riots that destroyed Jewish businesses and homes in Germany].

The next morning, he said to his wife, "We're not moving to Germany. We're going home because there's a problem, and I must warn Americans." Almost like Paul Revere, he said, "I must tell the Americans that Germany is building an air force that can wipe out any country, and we've got to start defending America first."

DR: He did come back, and he did defend the idea of not going to war. When war did break out, when the Japanese bombed Pearl

Harbor on December 7, 1941, what did Lindbergh want to do, and why did President Roosevelt prevent him from doing it?

ASB: There's a little backstory. Charles Lindbergh and FDR had squabbled in the earliest days of the New Deal over the U.S. Air Mail. Lindbergh lived for aviation. His first job, really, was delivering the airmail.

FDR, when he came into office, rather arbitrarily canceled all the airmail contracts with the major aviation companies. Lindbergh thought this was a huge mistake and got into a huge public fight with Roosevelt. After Roosevelt assigned airmail delivery to the army, there was one plane crash after another delivering the mail.

Once again, Lindbergh emerged a great hero in the public eye. And this made FDR crazy. So there's been bad blood simmering on the back burner for several years.

Now, after war has broken out in Europe, FDR every day wants to get us into this war, moving us closer. And Charles Lindbergh became the leading spokesman for what became known as the America First movement. He was giving speeches on the radio and participating in large rallies. Every time Lindbergh spoke, the majority of the country embraced his point of view.

The next week FDR would give a fireside chat, trying to move the people back. But as late as September of 1941 — three months before Pearl Harbor — the United States backed Charles Lindbergh most decidedly.

The day after Pearl Harbor, Charles Lindbergh volunteered. He was in his early forties at that point, so he was a little old; but he was still America's greatest pilot. And when he asked to serve, FDR said that he could not, that he would not let him, thus keeping him from becoming a hero all over again.

DR: Let's go back to the beginning of Lindbergh's life. His father was a member of Congress for ten years.

ASB: Charles Lindbergh was born in 1902 in Detroit, Michigan. His mother was a schoolteacher.

Lindbergh's father was an attorney in Little Falls, Minnesota, then Minnesota's Sixth, now Eighth, Congressional District. He became a congressman — elected in 1906 and serving until 1917. He was a very progressive and, I would say, eccentric Republican.

So that's Lindbergh's background, except to say this: his parents were a badly matched pair. It was a deeply unhappy marriage.

[Lindbergh split his childhood between Little Falls and Washington, D.C., where he briefly attended the private Sidwell Friends School and worked as a congressional page.

He also spent a year at Redondo Union High School when his mother briefly moved them to California.]

DR: He ultimately applies to the University of Wisconsin in Madison. He goes there to be an engineering student. Is he a good student?

ASB: He's a terrible student. I cut him a little slack, because he's one of the few college students I've ever heard of who left home, went to college . . . and his mother went with him. And they shared an apartment.

I once asked Anne Lindbergh about Charles's mother, and Mrs. Lindbergh said to me, "Well, why do you think he flew to Paris? It was to get away from that mother."

DR: So he flunks out of the University of Wisconsin and decides to get involved in flying. How did he decide to get involved in flying?

ASB: This was a lonely boy, an only child, with two half sisters from his father's first marriage. When he flunked out of college, the dean sent a letter to his roommate — his mother — and essentially said, "Your son Charles is very immature." He was not socialized at all.

DR: He'd never had a date.

ASB: Never had a date, not even a friend. He was moving all the time. So there was really never anybody in his life. This is a boy who lived in his thoughts, head in the clouds. He was mechanically minded, and he began to read about aviation, became intrigued, and went out to Nebraska, where he learned how to fly.

DR: He turned out to be a reasonably good flyer.

ASB: Reasonably good.

DR: But he almost killed himself four different times, is that right?

ASB: Four different times. He became a barnstormer for several years, working throughout the South and the Midwest. Then, looking for a steadier job, he became one of the first airmail pilots in this country in 1926 and 1927. He flew the airmail between St. Louis and Chicago. It's one of the worst places to fly in the country because the weather is so changeable, so fickle. And he became a highly skilled pilot.

DR: But he was a barnstormer, which meant he would show off in flying. He would do things like stand on the wings.

ASB: He was a wing walker. He did all sorts of crazy stuff.

DR: How do they actually walk on the wings without falling off?

ASB: Well, somebody else is flying the plane while you're walking on the wing. But even so, it's still risky business.
While flying the mail — and performing stunts — he did jump from an airplane with a parachute four times and lived. [In addition to his barnstorming experience, Lindbergh trained as a pilot with the U.S. Army Air Service, the precursor of the U.S. Air Force, in 1924–25. When he graduated, he earned a commission as a second lieutenant in the Air Service Reserve Corps.]

DR: So he was a pretty accomplished pilot.

ASB: Accomplished, fearless, and really knew the plane. He knew the machinery.

DR: Somebody came up with the idea that if you flew across the Atlantic either way, you would get $25,000, which was a lot of money then. Whose idea was it, and how did Lindbergh decide he should be involved in that?

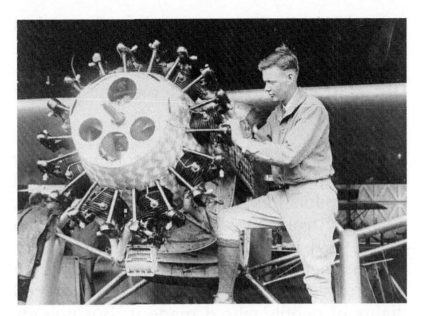

An experienced barnstormer and airmail pilot, Lindbergh was well acquainted with the machines he flew. In this 1927 photograph, he examines the cylinder of the Spirit of St. Louis.

ASB: A Frenchman named Raymond Orteig, who owned hotels in New York City and in Paris. Now, you have to remember, this is just a few years after World War I had ended.

Orteig was so filled with pride about Franco-American friendship, he said, "We are going to make the world a little smaller. We're going to unite these countries. And I will offer $25,000" — $25,000, that was a lot of money — "to the first person or persons who can fly nonstop in either direction between New York and Paris."

So here's this prize that's been sitting there

since 1919. Several men vied for it and lost their lives.

DR: Had anybody flown across the Atlantic between lesser cities?

ASB: Some people had done the Atlantic incrementally. Famously, Alcock and Brown [British pilots John Alcock and Arthur Brown, who flew from Newfoundland to Ireland in June 1919] had flown from the northern tip of Europe to the northern tip of North America. So there were some asterisked flights of people who'd made it. But nobody had flown nonstop from New York to Paris.

DR: There were many people trying to win this $25,000 prize, but they were much better known than Lindbergh, and they were thinking of doing it as a tandem, two people in a bigger plane. What made Lindbergh think that he could do this by himself, and why would he want to do it by himself?

ASB: There were teams with big, expensive planes, big $100,000 luxury planes with leather seats and three motors. They all went down or failed for one reason or another. And they were all famous pilots. And don't forget, Lindbergh is a twenty-five-year-old airmail pilot. He so understands the machinery, so understands the capabilities of an airplane and of himself at age twenty-five, that he came up with an idea: that the key to this is the number one. "I want a monoplane, one set of wings, one engine, one pilot. That's the way to do it. I don't have to worry about anybody else. I'll be responsible for everything."

DR: He designs this plane, gets somebody in San Diego to help build it. Where does he get the money for it, and how much did it cost?

ASB: Because he was then flying the airmail in and out of St. Louis, he went to the civic leaders of St. Louis — the half dozen men who ran the Chamber of Commerce, who ran the newspaper, who ran a bank — he went to them all and said, "I think I can win this Orteig prize. What do you think?"

And the civic leaders of St. Louis thought, "Oh, this is a wonderful commercial for our city. Yes, we can help you with that money if you put our name on the plane," basically. And that's what he did. And so, for $10,580, six or seven guys chipped in. Lindbergh himself put in $1,000. And then he found somebody who would build the plane for him.

There were a few people in New York who would sell him a plane, but they insisted somebody else would have to be the pilot, somebody famous and somebody with more experience. Lindbergh said, "No. One pilot . . . and I'm the one." He went out and found a manufacturer in San Diego, Ryan Aircraft, and they built the plane according to the specifications he had envisioned to make the flight.

DR: He gets the plane, takes it from San Diego to St. Louis. And then from St. Louis he goes to New York. Where does he decide to take off from?

ASB: He arrives in New York after he's done this great transcontinental flight, which was magnificent in its own right. Meantime, that very week that he's flying to the East Coast in May 1927, two Frenchmen — Charles Nungesser and François Coli, veterans of the French air force — have left Paris. It looks as though they are going to collect the prize. Lindbergh has got to get to New York City in time to start the race.

And Nungesser and Coli, these two Frenchmen — well, we're still waiting to hear from them. Their plane still hasn't come in.

Lindbergh lands, in the middle of May, in Long Island, where there are three airfields, including Roosevelt Field, all adjacent to each other. And Lindbergh and two other planes sit on the runway and wait to take off.

The two others are bigger planes with seasoned teams of pilots, and here's our little *Spirit of St. Louis*. You wouldn't enter this

The Spirit of St. Louis *was built in San Diego to Lindbergh's specifications. From there he flew the plane to New York, the jumping-off point for his successful solo transatlantic flight.*

plane in the Soap Box Derby. This plane was built out of aluminum tubing, canvas, and piano wire.

DR: And was there any window to look out? How did Lindbergh see where he was going?

ASB: There is no forward outlook on the plane because Lindbergh realized, "What I need most of all to make it to Paris is gasoline. I need enough fuel." So every inch that he could fill with gasoline, he did. That included a huge tank in front of the instrument panel.

The only way Charles Lindbergh could see where he was going — well, he had two options. He was sitting in a porch chair —

DR: It wasn't an airplane seat?

ASB: It was a wicker chair from somebody's porch. And if he wanted to see ahead, he could do two things from that chair. He could go like *this* out this side or he could do *this* out that side. That's it.

DR: To look out, he has to have windows. Did he have glass there to look out?

ASB: It was Plexiglas, actually, a new product that was coming out of DuPont Chemical. And he could pull these windows out. He always went to the left window. And there was a sunroof.

DR: Let's go to the night he takes off.

ASB: Bad weather descended upon New York and its environs for ten days. There was just fog that nobody could get through.

And on the night of May 19, 1927, Lindbergh and his mechanics went into the city just to kill time. They were going to see a Broadway musical called *Rio Rita.* I could sing its title song for you, but I won't.

Before proceeding to the theater, Lindbergh said, "You know what? There's the Weather

Bureau. Let's just pop in and get the latest report."

And a guy at the Weather Bureau said, "The weather's terrible for the next few days, except tomorrow morning between about 7 and 9 a.m. there's going to be a break in the fog and the clouds. It's still going to be rough flying for the first hour or two, but maybe a good airmail pilot could get through."

Lindbergh went back to the hotel hoping to grab five or six hours of sleep before he was going to begin what would be thirty-three and a half hours in flight. But he got back and found chaos at the Garden City Hotel on Long Island, where he was staying, what with reporters' typewriters clattering down below and people knocking on his door. He got no sleep.

And now it's four or five in the morning and he thinks, "You know what, the window of decent weather is coming pretty soon. I'd better get down to the plane. We'd better gas this thing up. We'd better see if we can make it."

And that's what he did. He went out to Roosevelt Field.

DR: He gets out in the field. Is it clear that he can take off? Is the runway long enough? Is it concrete or is it grass or what?

ASB: The runway is mud because it's been

335

raining for ten days. It would have been grass if the summer grass had grown in yet, but it hadn't. It's just mud.

And it's still foggy. It's still wet. The plane is sweating with precipitation. There's a mile-long runway, and at the end of that runway are some telegraph poles with wires. Lindbergh has one mile to get five thousand pounds of airplane, fully loaded with fuel, off the ground. He's never flown the plane with that much fuel because he's never had to go 3,500 miles. He starts the plane.

The film footage is breathtaking, because you see this plane go down this muddy runway, and it's glue. The plane just can't lift off. And the air is so thick. You see the plane start to get off, and it bounces down. And then it bounces down again. And it bounces down again. And Lindbergh is just pulling back on the stick, and finally he clears the telegraph wires by twenty feet.

DR: What did he take with him? Did he have a lot of food?

ASB: Lindbergh understood this flight was largely a problem about weight. First of all, he benefited from the fact that his nickname was Slim. He was six feet, two and a half inches, and he didn't weigh 170 pounds. That helped.

He trimmed the maps he traveled with, cutting their quarter-inch borders off every map. Everything got shaved down to its minimum. He took a canteen of water and a half dozen sandwiches. And that was it.

There was no radio on the plane because the radio would have weighed too much. Somebody asked what he'd do if he found himself in trouble. He said, "If I'm in trouble over the Atlantic and I get on my radio, who am I talking to? Nobody can hear me, and nobody can rescue me. So what's the difference?" And that was that.

DR: When he did later meet King George V of England, the king says to him, "By the way, how did you pee?" What's the answer to that?

ASB: The regal question. Nobody knew how Lindbergh peed during the flight. It wasn't until I went through the flight checklist, where he had checked everything three times on what he had brought on this trip, that I realized — and remember that he's counting every half ounce — he had packed a paper cup. And I thought, "There's only one reason for a paper cup." It's not as if he was pouring from his canteen into a cup — cheers! So he used the paper cup to pee in and then — *shweet!* — out the left side window.

DR: He takes off. He clears the telegraph lines. How does he navigate? He's got instruments, or is he doing it just by looking at the stars?

ASB: He has rudimentary instruments. Did he have certain gifts? He certainly had a good sense of direction. He had a compass, but he did navigate by the stars.

When you consider how rudimentary all this was in 1927 — you know, when he charted his trip back in San Diego in the spring of 1927, the people building the plane said, "How far is it exactly?" And he said, "I don't know exactly. I'd better find out." And he went to the library in San Diego, where there was a gigantic globe, and he pulled out a piece of string and he measured his route on the globe.

Then he began to chart the flight, figuring how much gasoline was required for every hundred miles. That is how he navigated.

During the flight, he encountered every obstacle a pilot could imagine, including a magnetic storm that turned the plane around, he figured, at least three times. And the compass, the needle is just spinning around. And yet he pulls through all this and, some twenty-five or twenty-six hours later, he begins to recognize where he is, because the first bits of land are starting to appear.

DR: He saw a mirage — he thought he saw land, then he didn't see it.

ASB: Halfway across the ocean, around hour fifteen or sixteen, he started to hallucinate. He sees land where none existed. He later admitted, when he wrote his own book about the flight — *The Spirit of St. Louis,* a book that won the Pulitzer Prize — Lindbergh said that there was a moment where ghosts actually entered the plane. And the ghosts, he claimed, carried him through.

DR: At some point, he's falling asleep because he's been up for fifty-some hours. How does he keep awake?

ASB: He does everything he possibly can, including not eating, because he thought if he started to eat that would make him tired.

This is one of the most amazing things. There were times when to get over clouds and storms, he had to fly as high as ten thousand feet in this rickety plane. And there were times where he got so tired, he would fly ten feet above the Atlantic. He would pull out the window, and the spray of the ocean would come into the cockpit to wake him up. Because there were several times he really did nod off. We will never know how many times.

DR: He finally sees Ireland. He realizes he could land there and live. But he wouldn't get the $25,000 prize, so he keeps going.

How does he actually find Paris?

ASB: His sighting of Ireland is one of my favorite moments in the flight. He's now been flying for twenty-eight to twenty-nine hours, and he starts to see porpoises, he starts to see birds, and finally he looks out the window and he sees a fishing boat, and he sees a fisherman on the deck of the boat. This isn't a mirage. This is for real.

And now he circles the boat. He flies lower and lower and lower, pulls out the window, leans out, yells to the man on the boat, "Which way is Ireland?"

After all that, he was less than ten miles off the original course. And the next thing you know, there he is and there's Dingle Bay, just the way the map has it. And then it's just another hour to England and then another hour across the Channel.

And now he's over France. The French countryside is dark, but it starts to get brighter and brighter and brighter. And suddenly the lights of Paris come up. He can see the Eiffel Tower, and he's made it! It's fantastic! We're here!

Problem is he can't find where to put the plane down. He knows where Le Bourget Field is — the airfield where he's meant to land — but it's now ten-thirty at night in Paris, and the lights don't make sense. Here are all the lights of the great City of Lights, but then there's just one string of lights and then it goes black. And he can't figure it out.

He circles lower and lower and lower. And he realizes the one string of lights is the one road from Paris to Le Bourget Field. Every automobile that could fit on that street was out there with its headlamps on, creating a runway for Charles Lindbergh. And he landed at Le Bourget Field at ten-thirty-three that night.

He expected there might be a half dozen mechanics out there at the field. What he didn't realize was that the minute his plane had been sighted over Ireland, word spread through France.

Lindbergh brought it down, and 150,000 people were waiting for him. They rushed past the gendarmes and ran toward him — pulling at him, pulling his plane apart.

And that's the moment that Charles Lindbergh becomes the first modern media superstar. I have often said, "Twenty years ago now, there was an English princess who was chased through the streets of Paris and was killed. That car chase began the night Lindbergh landed in Paris."

DR: Lindbergh lands. He's pulled out by a number of people. The American ambassador ultimately gets possession of him and takes him to the American Embassy. Within the next day or two or three, he has a torrent of mail and calls. Could he believe what was happening to him?

ASB: Lindbergh, as I said, thought there would be six people at the airfield. He was going to spend the next couple of weeks flying around Europe, maybe go to Brussels, maybe go to Germany. He hadn't thought it through yet. But for the next few days, the next few weeks, the next few months, he became the property of the world.

And with his new modern-media superstardom, the city of Paris and the country of France spent the next three or four days heaping every honor they could on him. Wherever he went, hundreds of thousands, if not a million, people waited for him. Everywhere.

DR: How does the *Spirit of St. Louis* get back to the United States, and how does he get back?

ASB: After France, he went to England, where he met the aforementioned king with his urinary interest. And then he does come home. Lindbergh was planning some flights around Europe when he got a telegram from Calvin Coolidge, then president of the United States. It said, "It's time to come home, thank you very much."

And he thought, "Great, I'll fly home." Oh,

no, no, no, that is not going to happen. Calvin Coolidge sent a battleship. They took the plane apart and put it in two boxes; and with the plane, he sailed home. And then he came to Washington, D.C.

There never has been, there never will be a reception in this country like the one that fell upon Charles Lindbergh. The United States of America bestowed upon him every medal they could. They made up a new medal for him, in fact. And by the time he got to New York City a few days later, four million people turned out for the parade.

DR: Biggest crowd anybody had ever had.

ASB: Ever. They shut down the United States government. Wall Street closed that day. Every bank closed. Every school closed. Every business in the country closed — because Lindbergh came home.

He flew on a goodwill tour of the nation, at least flying over every state. He stopped in almost every state. An estimated quarter of the country saw Charles Lindbergh at some point during that tour.

DR: On one of his trips, he goes to Mexico, and the U.S. ambassador there, Dwight Morrow, is a former senior partner at J.P. Morgan. Morrow has several daughters, whom Lindbergh meets.

Lindbergh's dashing good looks helped cement his status as an international celebrity after his New York-to-Paris flight.

ASB: One daughter was very sophisticated, very elegant, and quite wonderful. Then there was a younger daughter who was a zippy little thing — kind of a sprite, fluttering all over the place.

And then there was the middle daughter, Anne, the shyest creature who ever lived. And wouldn't you know, the two shyest people on earth — because Lindbergh was also very shy — met and instantaneously fell in love. After the third date, he proposed marriage, and by the fourth, she accepted. They were — if I may say this in the Library of Congress —

both virgins on their wedding night.

They got married in a very secret wedding ceremony. You think you understand what the press is like now — what fame is like now. Lindbergh had become its first human quarry. He and Anne were chased everywhere they went, and not by a reporter or two, but by hordes, by armies. So they really had to pull off this wedding in intense secrecy, which they did.

DR: Anne Morrow Lindbergh had an extraordinary career herself as a writer. And putting up with him was not easy, right?

ASB: It was no picnic for all sorts of reasons. Sometimes Lindbergh would say to his wife, "I'm going out for a while," and then three weeks later a postcard would arrive, because he had gone to Samoa or someplace. He really marched to the beat of his own drum.

What was also difficult for Anne Morrow Lindbergh — who is one of the most celebrated American writers, one of the great diarists of the twentieth century, among other things, but also a novelist and an essayist — at a certain point in the late forties and early fifties, Charles decided to sit down and write a book, which he does. It became a huge best seller and won the Pulitzer Prize. [*The Spirit of St. Louis* won the 1954 Pulitzer Prize in Biography.]

And here's this poet, Anne, who's been writing beautifully all her life, and suddenly even literarily she is eclipsed by this pilot. It's one of the sad ironies. It was tough being married to Charles Lindbergh.

DR: After he died, and after you wrote your book, it came out publicly that he had seven children with three German women that his wife apparently didn't know about and that none of his legitimate children in the United States knew about. How did this come out and how did he hide it for so long?

ASB: None of this is in my book because the book prompted this story. It came out, and a German woman living in Paris read it and said, "I know I promised my mother I would never say a word about this, but I must now go public. I am Charles Lindbergh's daughter. And I will not rest until I meet Scott Berg and he looks me in the eye and says, 'Yes. You are Charles Lindbergh's daughter.'"

About a month after she had this epiphany, I heard from a reporter from a newspaper in Europe who said, "This woman would like to meet you. Can you verify this story? Because we're about to run it in the newspaper."

And I said, "Well, I've met so many 'Lindbergh babies' . . ."

"No, no, this isn't a Lindbergh baby. This isn't somebody claiming to be the dead baby."

This woman said she had letters from Charles Lindbergh to her mother, which she faxed to me. Remember fax machines? As soon as the letters came off the fax machine, I said, "Oh my God! These are real."

I flew over to meet her in Paris. And as she walked toward me, I said, "That's Reeve Lindbergh, Charles Lindbergh's youngest daughter, twenty years earlier." I didn't need the DNA. These were Lindberghs walking toward me. [The woman had also brought her brothers to the meeting.]

Reeve Lindbergh, Charles Lindbergh's youngest American child, used to say, "You know, there used to be signs all over America, 'George Washington slept here.' Well, there should be signs all over Europe, 'Charles Lindbergh slept here, and here, and here, oh, and there.' " Anne Morrow Lindbergh and the Lindbergh children in America had not a clue that any of this happened.

DR: After the famous flight and his marriage to Anne, and before World War II broke out, Lindbergh became an ardent America First person. What was that about?

ASB: This is an important subject that you should all know about — it's very timely now — and that's the movement called America First. It's a much-misunderstood movement.

In 1940, before Pearl Harbor, this country

was having one of the four or five great debates in its history, including what kind of constitution would we have, would there be a civil war, and Vietnam.

There was also a great debate about our entry into the Second World War. Most of this country, as late as September of '41, was against our entering the war, and Lindbergh was the great spokesman for that point of view.

Now, when I started this book, I believed, as I'm sure many of you do who had history teachers as bad as mine, that America First was a midwestern movement started by a bunch of old Republican senators. I learned that it was, in fact, a youth movement started by a half dozen college students, mostly at Yale University in 1940.

The guys who started it were named Gerald R. Ford, Sargent Shriver, Potter Stewart, Kingman Brewster — who, of course, became president of Yale and ambassador to the United Kingdom — and a man named Bob Stuart, who ran Quaker Oats for many years, as his family had before him. And these five or six students got this movement off the ground.

Lindbergh had come back from Europe, where he had seen the Luftwaffe building up, and he came back to warn the country, giving up his privacy in order to give speeches. One day these five guys from Yale got in touch

348

with Lindbergh and said, "Would you give speeches for our little group?" which he did.

Overnight this group mushroomed. We talk in politics about a big tent. This was a big tent. America First included the American Bund movement [the German American Bund or German American Federation] but it also included Norman Thomas, the great Socialist. It covered the entire waterfront of people who weren't isolationists, as Lindbergh always said he was not.

He was a noninterventionist. And he felt, until Pearl Harbor, that World War II was the continuation of a European war that had been fought for a thousand years among Russia, France, and Great Britain, and they were just going to keep fighting and fighting and fighting, and it had nothing to do with us.

DR: After Pearl Harbor, he wasn't allowed by FDR to get back into the army and to be a pilot in the war. How did he manage during World War II to be of service to the country?

ASB: The enmity that FDR felt toward Lindbergh was so intense that when on December 8, 1941, Charles Lindbergh volunteered, FDR said to Secretary of the Interior Harold Ickes, "I'm not going to let him become a hero again." And that was that. He basically said, "He cannot enlist anywhere."

So, said Lindbergh, "I can still be of use in

private industry. There are a lot of aircraft companies, a lot of motor companies. I can help the war effort by working for them."

He had meetings everywhere. Every company in America wanted to hire Charles Lindbergh. But the callbacks never came, because FDR had sent a message: "Any company that hires Lindbergh does not get a government contract."

So nobody would hire Lindbergh. There was one exception. Henry Ford said, "Oh, Ford's not going to get any contracts? I don't think so." He hired Charles Lindbergh as an advisor and a test pilot. Increasingly, Lindbergh got hired by other companies who let him work quietly on the side.

Lindbergh finally said, "I want to be where the action is." And they all said, "But you have no uniform. You're not a member of any of the armed services." So Lindbergh said, "I'll just fly there as a private citizen, as a pilot."

Lindbergh flew to the South Pacific, where he island-hopped. He would go to airfields and he would teach pilots how to fly more efficiently. People had noticed that Lindbergh would go out on these sorties, and he would come back with much more gasoline than any of the other pilots. The brass would say, "Can you teach our pilots to fly the way you do?" And that's what he did.

Finally Douglas MacArthur heard about

this, summoned Lindbergh, and said, "Listen, you go anywhere you want. You are under my protection. And if anybody questions you, say, 'Douglas MacArthur sent me.' "

Lindbergh went on fifty bombing missions without a uniform. This means if he is downed anywhere, he is a man without a country. He's just dead meat because nobody can claim him. He did it anyway.

DR: After World War II, his reputation was restored a bit as a result. And he got involved in civil aviation, helped start a number of airlines in the United States, but he also got involved in conservation. Can you explain how that became the latest love of his life?

ASB: This became the great passion of Lindbergh's life starting in the late fifties and really in the sixties.

Lindbergh spent his life working for aviation. He took no real money. He was offered $10 million after his solo transatlantic flight to endorse products. But he took none of those offers.

Instead, he accepted jobs working for budding aviation companies, which became TWA and Pan American. And he worked for United also. He got a lot of stock.

He spent the rest of his life flying on behalf of aviation. If any of you has ever been in an airplane and flown from one city to another in this world, chances are the person who first navigated that flight was Charles Lindbergh — not just in America, not just in the Western Hemisphere, but anywhere in the world. As late as the 1970s he was still flying on TWA, taking notes on everything — the service, the quality of the food, the service of the hostesses, of the pilot.

In making all these flights and independent flights of his own, especially in the fifties, he began to see from ten, twenty, thirty thousand feet how the physiognomy of the earth had changed. He had seen how civilization was encroaching upon wilderness, and this disturbed him, mostly because he felt responsible. He thought, "It is because I helped glamorize aviation that aviation took off as it did," and he decided to spend the rest of his life trying to fight that.

Without saying we should fight progress, because he never wanted to do that, he spent the last decade of his life doing everything he could for the preservation of the air, the land, the water, and also indigenous peoples all over the world, whose territories were being encroached upon. He became the first really famous international figure to become a tree hugger, one who totally embraced the environment.

DR: Part of his tree-hugging was he loved to have houses in exotic places close to nature.

The last house he built was a desolate place in Maui, Hawaii. Can you describe the end of his life and where he's buried?

ASB: You've got to remember that he was human quarry all his life — running from people and running from the press. He just wanted to be alone. He wanted to be as isolated as he could.

When he learned that he was going to die, he selected as his burial ground a churchyard near his home in Maui, a plot at the edge of a cliff at the edge of the community of Hana. The Hawaiian Islands are as far from anywhere on earth as you can get, and here he is at the edge of a cliff. [Lindbergh died of lymphoma in August 1974, at the age of 72.]

About three weeks before he died, he had gone to a hospital in New York to have his bloodwork done. He was feeling ill. And the doctor had said, "Charles, I'm afraid this is it. It's really the end, and we should make arrangements now for your death."

Lindbergh said, "That's fine, but I don't want to die here in the hospital. I want to go home. I want to be buried in Hawaii. That's where I want to die."

The doctor said, "That's impossible. Simply can't be done. No airline will fly you there." And Lindbergh said, "No airline will fly me? Get me a phone. Let me make a phone call."

He called a very good friend at Pan Am,

and they put him on a plane. They took the first-class section and decked it out as a hospital room. Lindbergh was able to fly with his wife and with his three sons — his three American sons, I hasten to add — and they flew to Hawaii.

I mentioned that he made checklists. That's what got him to Paris. In a similar manner, he had a whole routine of how he wanted to be buried, in what clothes he wanted to be dressed, what he wanted the casket to look like, where it was to be. He even designed the drainage in the burial ground at the end of this churchyard where he was going to be buried.

This gets biblical at a certain point. He asked his three sons to dig the grave. And he hands everybody the checklists and says, "You must do everything exactly like this."

And they did everything. They dug the grave. They put the rocks just the way he said he wanted them — everything done, done, and done . . . and not until then did he die.

Before that, he had said, "You will have a few hours. Do not wait a second. As soon as I'm gone, put me in the burial clothes, make this phone call, drive me down this road, do this —"

DR: Because he didn't want a media circus.

ASB: They didn't know what he was talking

354

about. But they followed his specifications precisely. They hastily performed a short service in a little church there that seats twenty people. They buried him, they lowered the coffin, they covered him up.

The Lindbergh family is driving away from Hana, Maui; and as they are driving down the one road, three television trucks are driving up the other way. Lindbergh knew they had two hours to "clear the wires."

DR: After all these years you spent studying him, do you admire him the way you did before you started, and do you have the view that he was a great man or a flawed man?

ASB: It's now really twenty years since I wrote the book, and my feelings have only intensified on each side. He makes me crazier than ever in some ways. He was incredibly willful, incredibly stubborn. He was a cold, cold man and — I say this with great love for his children, but I would not have wanted to be one of his children.

As one of them said to me, "There were two ways of doing things. There was Father's way and the wrong way." That's a tough thing to grow up with or around.

That said, I can't think of another human being who has packed as much life into a single lifetime as Charles Lindbergh. And

make no mistake about it, this man changed
the way we all live to this very day.

9
Jay Winik

ON FRANKLIN DELANO ROOSEVELT

"At Yalta, he had this image of two things that drove him. One was that he wanted to see the war to a close, and he needed to make sure Stalin was in the fight to the bitter end. And he wanted to create something called the United Nations. That was his great dream. And so he was willing to do anything to make that happen."

*1944: FDR and the Year That Changed
History* (Simon & Schuster, 2015)

In recent years, Jay Winik has become one of
the country's most respected historians. His
best-known book, *April 1865: The Month That
Saved America,* has become a classic on that
tumultuous month in American history.

Winik initially had a career in public service, focusing on international affairs, but he
recognized that his real passion is writing (he
had been an editor of the *Yale Daily News*)
and history. I was quite pleased that a few
years ago he became the inaugural historian-
in-residence of the Council on Foreign Relations, for I helped to create that position out
of a view that a real understanding of foreign
policy requires a knowledge of history.

This interview covers a book that Winik
wrote not about a historic month but a
historic year — 1944. Perhaps the two most
momentous events of 1944 were the epic
D-Day invasion of France by the Allied
forces, which led to the eventual Allied victory the following year, and the abject failure
to take action against the dreaded death
camp at Auschwitz — all this while there was
the reelection of FDR to an unprecedented
fourth term, in spite of health challenges so
severe that he would die three months after
his inauguration.

Winik discusses these episodes in the interview, but he also addresses a number of questions about key events related to World War II that occurred before and after 1944. For instance, how did Hitler manage to go from being an out-of-work artist and jailed leader of a failed coup attempt — the Beer Hall Putsch — to chancellor of Germany and leader of the Third Reich? Why was the United States unwilling to enter the war against Hitler in Europe, despite the entreaties of Britain's Winston Churchill, until it was attacked at Pearl Harbor by the Japanese? What led the leaders of the Third Reich to agree to a Final Solution for the Jews of Germany (and ultimately for the Jews of other European countries), and how was this hidden from the Allies for so many years? Why did FDR, beloved as a well-respected humanitarian, not override his military and diplomatic advisors and pursue efforts to stem the ongoing Final Solution murders? Was FDR so impaired physically and mentally in his last twelve months that he was unable to serve effectively as president, particularly in representing the United States' interests at the conference with Churchill and the Soviet Union's Joseph Stalin at Yalta?

Jay Winik answers each of these questions frankly in the interview. He's particularly frank in discussing the near-total failure of FDR and the U.S. government to do anything to thwart the Holocaust, despite their clear capabilities to do so toward the end of the war.

MR. DAVID M. RUBENSTEIN (DR): *1944* is an extraordinary book, but before we get into it, I wanted to ask you: Why do you pick years for your titles?

MR. JAY WINIK (JW): I could say it's a good marketing technique and marketing tool. If I have a talent or skill, it's isolating turning points in time that have been gone over by other people dozens or hundreds of times, and I find something new and different about them and I try to say why those turning points are important.

DR: In my view, there are five key parts of *1944:* the rise of Hitler; the Allied response to Hitler; Roosevelt's health, which was an important issue; the Final Solution; and the American and Western response to the Final Solution. The best thing I've ever read about that part of our history is in this book.

Let's talk about the first part. How did Hitler, a man who was a corporal in World War I — and not particularly brilliant, people would say — manage to rise so high in German politics?

JW: It's a fascinating question. He was really a ne'er-do-well. He was a failed artist, hawking his sketches to whoever would buy them. He was so down-and-out that he was shoveling snow for money, carrying people's bags at the train station, and yet this was the man who would come to dominate one of the most cultured states in the entirety of the world.

DR: He didn't found the Nazi Party, is that correct? He took it over when it was small?

JW: He was sent as an army corporal to monitor this party called the National Socialists, and he didn't know much about it. [The German Workers' Party became the National Socialist German Workers' Party, commonly called the Nazi Party, in 1920.] Rather than monitor it and report back to the state, he actually jumped up on the stage and he gave a speech. Somebody who was there, a member of the party at the time, said, "Good God, this man has talent." And Hitler quickly joined the party. He was party member 555, and the rest is history.

DR: What's with that mustache?

JW: I think that was his look. The great columnist Walter Lippmann said, when he heard Hitler speak, "We have heard the authentic voice of a great statesman." Whereas *Time* magazine compared him to a Charlie Chaplinesque character. Boy, did they get it wrong.

DR: In 1923, Hitler openly tried to take over the government. He staged a takeover in Munich that failed, and he was thrown in jail.

JW: It was almost pathetic. It was called the Beer Hall Putsch.

He went into this beer hall with about twenty compatriots. They fired their pistols in the sky, and about seven of them were killed. Hitler was injured, and he was sent to jail.

Interestingly enough, though, when he was sent to jail for this, he was not your average prisoner. He was actually regarded as a great celebrity. He was given a beautiful room, a nice desk, a lovely view of the yard.

Rudolf Hess, who would go on to infamy and notoriety, became a secretary to Hitler, and it was there in jail that this ne'er-do-well, this celebrity, wrote this book called *Mein Kampf.*

DR: Where did his virulent anti-Semitism come from? And was there any truth to the story his grandfather was actually Jewish?

JW: It's one of those questions that we can never fully answer. Suffice it to say that wherever that virulent anti-Semitism came from — and I think part of it came from kicking around in his younger days in Austria, where it really was quite prevalent, and all

the ills of the world were blamed on the Jews
— well, what Hitler did was he refined it to
an art.

DR: He was elected to the German parliament, but how did he actually become the
chancellor of Germany in 1933?

JW: At first his party got 2 percent of the vote,
and then 12 percent of the vote, and before
everybody knew it, it was 33 percent of the
vote.

What he did, which was very clever, is
Hitler spoke the language of democracy while
planning to subvert democracy. Interestingly
enough, when he was made chancellor, Goeb-
bels said this was like a fairy tale. A camera
actually captured a view of Hitler when he
was made chancellor, and they said it was
one of pure ecstasy and bliss, the look on his
face.

DR: During World War II, what was Hitler's
mental and physical state? He had some
physical issues and mental issues. What were
the principal problems that he had?

JW: After the Soviet Union entered the war
on the side of the Allies and America entered
the war, it was clear the war was not going
well for Germany. It was also clear to the
professional generals, who knew better, that

Hitler wouldn't win.

His physical and mental state sharply deteriorated. His eyes were cloudy. His hands had tremors. He walked with a stoop. He almost certainly had Parkinson's disease.

He would assemble all his inner circle, a coterie of quacks and yes-men and lackeys, and, of course, his doctor, and he would go into these dull, rambling monologues for hours. But he was really deeply sick. He couldn't sleep. He was depressed. He took twenty-eight pills a day. It didn't work.

DR: Let's talk about the Allied response to Hitler's rise. In 1938 Hitler gets the Sudetenland, part of what was then Czechoslovakia. Then, on September 1, 1939, he invades Poland. Then he invades the Benelux countries — Belgium, the Netherlands, and Luxembourg. Then he invades France. And then he is on his way to England. What stopped him from actually taking over England? In other words, why did he not just continue the bombing of England and invade?

JW: It's a fascinating question and an important question in terms of understanding this whole drama. What took place was the Battle of Britain, which was largely fought in the skies. It wreaked a great deal of damage on Britain. But the British people are made of stern stuff, and they fought back.

Of course, they were led by Winston Churchill, who gave that famous speech that "we'll fight them on the beaches, we'll fight them in the air." They were willing to do anything and everything, and it became clear with time that this set of invasion plans, Operation Sea Lion, would not succeed.

It was then that Hitler conceived of this idea — what he thought was his boldest and most brilliant idea, and it proved to be his most prophetic mistake — which was that he would invade the Soviet Union. As he told the generals, "All we have to do is kick the door down and the whole edifice will collapse." It did not.

DR: Had he not invaded the Soviet Union, with whom Germany had a nonaggression pact, and had he actually tried to invade England, do you think he could have succeeded, given all the military might he had?

JW: It's not easy to make that cross-channel invasion. We would do it with the D-Day invasion of Normandy in 1944, but we were a much larger country with a much larger population base. I'm not so sure he could have subjugated Britain.

DR: Let's talk about the American response. When the Sudetenland was taken over, when Poland was invaded, when France was invaded, when the Netherlands was invaded, when Belgium was invaded, the Americans said, "We're not doing anything." Churchill spent so much time trying to get us to help. Why were we so reluctant to go into the war?

JW: We were still exhausted and worn out from the memories of World War I. The images and the visions of the dead and dying were still very fresh in America.

And there was the America First movement, a movement with Charles Lindbergh as its spokesman. He was trim. He was handsome. He was articulate. And he said, "We must stay out of Europe's wars." He made the case for it over and over again. And America didn't have much of an appetite for intervening.

Roosevelt, interestingly enough, as charismatic as he was, with his fireside chats and with his speeches, you would think he could have gotten the American people to follow him to the edge of the universe. But he was careful never to get too far out ahead of public opinion, and public opinion was not at the point where we were ready to invade or join the fight against the Nazis.

DR: When Pearl Harbor is bombed on December 7, 1941, we declare war against Japan. Would we ever have gone to war in Europe had we not been bombed by the

Japanese?

JW: I think we would have gone to war, but much too late in the game. The longer it took, the stronger Hitler got, and as we waited, he took, and as we waited, he took.

DR: Why did Hitler declare war against the United States? The Japanese had bombed us. We didn't have a fight with him.

JW: As I said, he made two profound mistakes. One was trying to subjugate and take over the Soviet Union, and the other was declaring war on the United States. After Pearl Harbor, he said, "The Japanese haven't been defeated in a thousand years," and he was convinced that the Japanese would win again. That was when he made the mistake of declaring war against the United States.

DR: When the United States came into the war, why didn't the Allies just get all their militaries together and invade France or the Continent from England and do what later became the D-Day invasion? The bombing of Pearl Harbor occurred in 1941. D-Day didn't occur until June 6, 1944. What were we doing for those three years?

JW: The problem was that we had the seventeenth most powerful military in the world.

Wrap your heads around that for a second — not first, not second, not third, but the seventeenth. We were drilling our soldiers with broomsticks. That's how ill-prepared we were.

And while our generals, including Dwight D. Eisenhower and George Marshall, wanted one great, grand tank battle over the European plains against the Germans, Churchill, who had fresh memories of the disaster with the invasion at Gallipoli [World War I's Gallipoli Campaign of 1915–16 was a major defeat for the Allies], said to Roosevelt, "You're simply not ready."

Roosevelt thought about that and he thought about that, and it was then that he devised, along with Churchill, the North African Campaign. [The Anglo-American invasion of North Africa began with Operation Torch in November 1942; the subsequent military campaigns led to the defeat in 1943 of the German forces in North Africa under Field Marshal Erwin Rommel.] That got the American soldiers into the fight, it got America engaged, and it did something very important — it boosted the morale of the American people.

DR: Eventually, after we had a victory in Northern Africa and in Italy, the invasion of France occurred on June 6, 1944. Was it clear from the beginning that the invasion was a success? How dangerous was it? Could we have actually lost on D-Day?

JW: D-Day was a massive effort, but there really was no plan B. In the beginning, the battles went very well on Sword and Juno and the two other beaches in Normandy.

But on Omaha Beach, it was terrible, the pounding the Americans were taking. American soldiers were being cut down, mowed down like wheat. They were bleeding into the water. They had lost many of their senior military men. And it really looked like they could be losing at Omaha.

DR: Suppose the Germans had actually anticipated a Normandy landing. Would we have had a chance of winning then? Because they didn't anticipate it, is that right?

JW: No, they didn't anticipate it. They anticipated that the invasion would take place at a place called Pas-de-Calais. [The Allies' Operation Fortitude involved making the Germans believe this in order to distract them from Normandy.] But I think it was inevitable, given this vast armada of men and machines and battleships, that we would have won eventually.

DR: What about Hitler? Were they afraid to wake him up when it happened?

"Taxis to Hell-and-Back." Under enemy fire, troops from the U.S. Army's 1st Infantry Division wade ashore at Omaha Beach on June 6, 1944: D-Day.

JW: It's amazing, if you think about it. The great Erwin Rommel, the famed Desert Fox and one of the best generals of the Nazis — he was off buying shoes for his wife. Meanwhile, Hitler was asleep — he was taking sleeping pills then — and everybody was afraid of waking the Führer. That was so important because they had the panzer tanks ready and waiting. It was the one weapon in the arsenal of the Germans that could have repelled the Americans. But the panzers waited and waited and waited. And Hitler slept.

DR: June 6, 1944, we invade. Finally, we

capture France. But the war didn't end in Europe until April 1945. What was going on for almost a year? The Battle of the Bulge, what was that about?

JW: The thing about Hitler was he was willing to expend his men at almost any cost. He was conducting and overseeing battles with imaginary armies. But his motto also became, for what he saw as his cowardly generals — not a good way of leading his men — he said to his generals, "You must stand and die."

He conceived of one last-ditch effort, which was the Battle of the Bulge, where he threw everything he could at the Americans. He was hoping that if he could get the Americans to pull out of the war, then he could make a separate peace with the Soviet Union.

DR: Eventually Berlin was being bombed. Virtually every major city in Germany was being bombed by the Americans. Why did the Germans not just say, "Let's get rid of Hitler"? Why did they put up with this decimation of their country?

JW: Remember that the Germans were a great society. They had great culture. They had great arts. They had great government. They were really just a remarkable state. But something happened under Hitler where the country was in the grips of what I can only say was a form of national psychosis. They stuck with him until the bitter end, even knowing the terrible things he was doing to the Jews, even seeing the concentration camps, the knifing of their own people.

DR: There was an effort to kill him with a bomb. How did he survive that attempt?

JW: There were actually eleven efforts to kill him. But I don't want that to suggest that there was great mass resistance, because there wasn't.

Colonel Claus von Stauffenberg, an aristocrat in the army, came to despise Hitler. He offered to bring a bomb in a suitcase into the Hitler bunker. It went off, and a lot of people were killed and injured.

But like a cat with nine lives, somehow Hitler survived. And of course he thought this was destiny — that he was fated to win the war after all.

DR: Let's go to the third subject I wanted to cover, which is Roosevelt's health. Everyone knows that he contracted polio at Campobello, the island in Passamaquoddy Bay where he spent his childhood summers and that he often visited as an adult. He didn't really think he had a career in politics after that. He had run as vice president in 1920 on James Cox's ticket, but he was out of politics. How, as a polio victim, did he get elected governor of New York in 1928 when, in those days, people who had disabilities weren't treated the way they are today?

JW: He got elected because he had the hubris and the drive to get elected. He believed he was fated for high office. He actually thought that he could become president just like Teddy Roosevelt, his distant cousin, did. And while he couldn't use his legs, he could use other parts of his body. He could use his arms. There was the famous tilt of his head. He liked to do things that were physical. He liked to drive, to play cards.

DR: How did he drive without the use of his legs?

JW: He had a special car that was made for him. Driving was one of his favorite sports. But he thought he was fated and destined for greatness, and indeed he was.

DR: Why did reporters agree to not photograph him in his wheelchair or being carried? Very frequently he was being carried from his car to someplace else. Why did reporters never photograph that?

JW: It would be unthinkable to have something like this happen today. The press had a gentlemen's agreement that was rigorously adhered to never to show photos of him in his wheelchair, and never to discuss it in articles. And so he was able to do whatever he wanted.

DR: He ran for reelection in '36 and won. He ran for reelection in '40 and won — the first time somebody had served a third term. Then in '44 he ran again. What was his health like in 1944?

JW: This is what really struck me when I set out to write *1944* — his health was disastrous. He had congestive heart failure. He was a dying man. He had chills that wouldn't quit, a hacking cough that wouldn't quit.

People would walk into the Oval Office, and the Secret Service was stunned to see that sometimes he had fallen on the ground and was sprawled out. His mouth was hanging open. His eyes were cloudy. He could barely even sign his name on letters.

It was so bad that when he came back from the Tehran Conference [in 1943, when he, Churchill, and Stalin convened to talk wartime strategy], his daughter said, "He has to have a full workup, otherwise there will be hell to pay."

When he went to Bethesda Naval Hospital for the checkup, he was told that if he didn't have significant rest, he'd be dead within a

375

Joseph Stalin, Franklin D. Roosevelt, and Winston Churchill at the Tehran Conference in late 1943.

year. Those words were prophetic.

DR: In 1944, how did he manage to get the nomination of his party? Didn't he have to go to the convention and make a speech?

JW: He didn't make a speech at the convention. This charade continued in which he wasn't photographed.

By this point, there was talk that something was amiss with him. He would sometimes go in front of the press and he would put on a dog-and-pony show. He would pat himself and they would say, "Mr. President, how are you feeling?" And he would say, "I'm feeling pretty good." And then Fala, his little dog, would jump up in his lap, and he would say, "I'm a little tired today, a little sleepy, but otherwise all is good."

And they all fell for it. They loved him.

DR: When he was inaugurated in 1945, was the ceremony held in the Capitol?

JW: Rather than having a full-scale inauguration, they had a small little affair of five thousand people at the White House. Again, his health was really bad. There was a very touching moment where he went out there, it was freezing cold, and his son offered him a cape and he turned it down. He was a gutsy guy.

DR: But subsequent to the inauguration, he did go to Yalta in 1945 for his second big conference with Churchill and Stalin. How did he manage to fly there? He didn't like flying. Didn't the planes he traveled on have to fly very low because he couldn't breathe well above ten thousand feet?

JW: They flew low because that's what he liked, and because flying was hard for him because of his physical infirmity.

At Yalta, he had this image of two things that drove him. One was that he wanted to see the war to a close, and he needed to make sure Stalin was in the fight to the bitter end. And he wanted to create something called the United Nations. That was his great dream. And so he was willing to do anything to make that happen.

DR: When he gets to Yalta, was he able to really do a good job of representing the United States, given the mental state and physical state he was in?

JW: His mental state, I think, was still fairly sharp — but he was clearly circumscribed by his limited physical abilities and by his ill health. Where this really came into play at Yalta was in the treatment of what to do about Poland. [At Yalta, the leaders left Poland under the control of the Soviet Union, helping set the stage for the Cold War.]

DR: He died how long after Yalta?

JW: A few months later he was dead — April 1945.

DR: Let's skip for a moment to the question of the Final Solution — the Nazis' plan to exterminate the Jews. Early in the war, the idea wasn't to kill all the Jews, it was to get them out of Germany. Why did Hitler and the others decide to kill them instead?

JW: There's no absolute certainty about why they decided to do that. What happened with the Final Solution is that over time, it evolved. It began with just getting rid of the Jews, putting them in Siberia and relocating them to points east.

Eventually they started these mobile killing squads in the Soviet Union that would line up the Jews, thousands of them at a time, and would just — *boom* — point-blank shoot them, shoot them, shoot them, and they would fall into a pit. And then, if you can believe it, David, the Nazi doctors were saying, "This is causing problems for the mental health of the German soldiers operating in the Soviet Union."

That's when they convened a conference in 1942 at Wannsee [a suburb of Berlin] where all the great heads of the departments of the German Third Reich assembled with sun streaming in through the windows in this beautiful villa, they devised this policy in which they would destroy every living Jew — every man, every woman, every child.

I want to say one other thing about this. After devising this policy of the Final Solution, these extermination camps in Auschwitz and elsewhere, they retired to a beautiful library not unlike this, and they drank brandy and they toasted themselves for a job well done.

DR: Why did they decide to use gassing as part of the Final Solution?

JW: They realized that shooting was inefficient as well as causing these problems for the morale and the health of the German soldiers. They had done some experiments on mentally challenged people in which they used gas, and they realized they could use this.

They refined it to an art form. And it was dastardly.

People would arrive at Birkenau [the killing center that was part of the Auschwitz camp complex], and they would smell this smell like nothing they had ever smelled before. It was broiled flesh. Little did they know that, within an hour, they themselves would be nothing but ashes and dust.

DR: When you arrived at Auschwitz — there were many places like Auschwitz — when you arrived, they took the younger people who could do some work and they would tell them to go one place, and older people, or people who didn't seem like they could do any work, would be exterminated right away. They were just told to go into the gas chambers? What would the Nazis tell them?

JW: They told them that they would be showered. There was this fiction that they weren't actually going to kill them.

The Germans were terrified that the Jews would fight back. So, until the bitter end, until the moment that they walked into the gas chambers, they thought they were going for nothing but a shower. Somebody might say, "Oh, I want to be with my child afterward." And the guards would say, "Okay. Together afterward." Or somebody might say, "I want to be with my wife afterward." They would say, "Together afterward."

DR: They would tell these people, "Take your clothes off, women and men together," and they would put them in a gas chamber. Death occurred in two or three minutes?

JW: No, no, no. It was a little more horrific than that.

It took about fifteen minutes, seventeen minutes. In the beginning there would be a mass rush for the doors, because people were trying to get away from the gas. And then there would be shouting, and that shouting would become a death rattle, and eventually the death rattle would be a squeak.

Then all two thousand people — let me give you a sense of what two thousand represents: that's nearly as many men as died during Pickett's Charge [the failed Confederate military assault that was the turning point of the Battle of Gettysburg in the American Civil War] — everyone would be dead. And then the process would be repeated an hour later.

DR: What did they do with the bodies?

JW: The Germans were nothing if not meticulous. They would shave off the hair and use it for mattresses. They would take out the dental fillings — they would take out the gold. They would take all the victims' possessions.

Everything was saved. Everything was catalogued in a place that was called Canada, because Canada was deemed a rich country, and everything was to be used and to be disseminated throughout other parts of the Third Reich to help out the German people.

DR: Why were the Germans so obsessed with hiding the bodies? Why were they so obsessed with making sure that the Allies didn't know that they were doing this?

JW: I think it's safe to say that there were two reasons. The first reason is that they didn't want the Jews to fight back. That was reason number one. The second reason is Hitler understood that the German people were willing to follow him in almost everything, but he thought perhaps they were still too cultured to countenance this.

The West was uncertain in the beginning

about what was taking place, but as time went on, very quickly there were those in the West who pieced together what was happening.

DR: How many Jews were killed in the gas chambers?

JW: Nobody has an exact figure, but the best figure is six million.

DR: The Germans also exterminated others who were not Jewish.

JW: That's right. What was unique about the targeting of the Jews is it was a systematic attempt to exterminate an entire race. That's what separated them [from the Nazis' other victims].

DR: Did anybody ever escape from Auschwitz?

JW: That's a great question. It's worthy of a Hollywood movie. I actually have an agent who's trying to make one from my book.

There were two men, Rudi Vrba and Fred Wetzler, who were young and healthy, and they weren't gassed. They were rare people in Auschwitz because they were administrators, and they knew everything that was taking place.

When they saw that there was going to be

the worst mass murder in history, the killing of 750,000 to a million Jews from Hungary [and Poland, among other origin countries of Auschwitz's prisoners], they were determined to tell the truth to the world and especially to Roosevelt. They hid in a woodpile for three days, and they waited to be discovered.

They never were. Eventually while there was darkness, they turned around, they pushed the top of the woodpile open, and they looked toward Auschwitz, and they saw these flames going high into the sky, because the gas chambers were still going.

Then they ran like hell for seventeen days, escaping the SS, escaping German soldiers, escaping anti-Semites. Eventually they got to Slovakia, where they told a few remaining Jewish elders everything that was taking place. They had a photographic memory, these two men, and so there was unimpeachable evidence about what was taking place.

It would eventually wind its way to Washington and land on FDR's desk. But still nothing was done.

DR: That's the fifth subject I wanted to cover, the American and Allied response. Once these two men escaped from Auschwitz and people began to know what was actually happening — people weren't sure what was happening before — when Roosevelt found out, why did he not say, "Let's do something to prevent this"?

JW: This is one of the great puzzles in history. Roosevelt was considered one of the great humanitarians. He's the man who uplifted hearts with his fireside chats on the radio, who pulled us out of the Great Depression. And if he was such a great humanitarian, why, in the face of this, would he not want to do something?

Churchill, interestingly enough, when he got word of what was taking place in Auschwitz, he said, "This is the greatest crime in all of human history." And he told his air force, "Bomb Auschwitz. Use my name. Get everything you can out of it." Roosevelt did only the minimal amount of what he could do.

DR: Roosevelt had a secretary of the treasury who was a lifelong friend, Henry Morgenthau Jr., who was Jewish. Did Morgenthau lobby Roosevelt on this issue?

JW: For Morgenthau, Roosevelt was his best friend, they had a weekly luncheon meeting, and he owed everything to Roosevelt — for him to take on Roosevelt was not an easy thing. But he was so aghast at the failure of the American Allies to do anything to help out the Jews that eventually he had his department write a thirty-page memo.

This memo had to be the hardest-hitting memo ever given to a president — and not just any president, to the humanitarian Franklin Roosevelt. It was first titled *Report [to the Secretary] on This Government's Acquiescence in the Murder of the Jews.* [Written by Morgenthau's assistant Josiah E. DuBois Jr. and dated January 1944, the report was retitled *Personal Report to the President.*]

When Roosevelt got this, even though he was sick and ailing and not feeling well, he immediately called Morgenthau into a meeting in the second-floor Oval Office and he said, "What do you want?" It was at that point they set up the War Refugee Board, whose sole intent was to do nothing but save the Jews. But it was too little and way too late.

DR: The Pentagon's view was that if we divert efforts from the war, it might slow down victory. What was their reasoning?

JW: The man who was running point from the Pentagon was John J. McCloy, one of the great wise men and statesmen of American foreign policy. He came up with reason after reason as to why they couldn't bomb Auschwitz.

He said that we didn't have enough planes,

when we actually did have enough planes. He said they couldn't fly that distance, when in fact American planes had been flying around Auschwitz — three, four, or five miles away — for months, as part of the oil war to degrade the Nazi war machine. [Allied planes bombed oil refineries and a synthetic oil plant in the vicinity of the Auschwitz complex.]

Reason after reason was given, and the irony is that, in the end, Auschwitz was bombed, but it was bombed by mistake.

The great humanitarian and now departed conscience of mankind Elie Wiesel was in Auschwitz as a boy at that time, and he said, "We may have feared death, but we did not fear that kind of death." When they bombed Auschwitz by mistake, the inmates, who could barely stand, barely walk, barely talk, they rose up on their feet and they cheered.

DR: What about the State Department? What was their attitude about doing something?

JW: The State Department mirrored, in many ways, the Pentagon. A man named Breckinridge Long was the head of the visa policy section. At this point, when Jews were cramming American consulates to get visas, because it meant life and death for them, Long sent out a really dastardly memo in which he said to all the consulates, "By various administrative devices, we can postpone and postpone and postpone the giving of visas to the Jews." He said it not once but three times.

All he had to do was say yes, and two hundred thousand people would have been saved. That's two Super Bowls' worth of people. And it never happened.

DR: There was a refugee ship that came and tried to dock in Miami. What happened to that ship?

JW: That was the ship *St. Louis.* It had a couple hundred Jews on board, and they were escaping Nazi Germany.

They came so close to Miami that they could actually see the shores and the buildings. They had people coming out in little dinghies and little ships waving to them and giving them food. And yet, when they sent a telegram to Roosevelt — "Help us" — all they got was a nonreply. [The *St. Louis* was forced to return to Europe, where many of its passengers died in the Holocaust.]

DR: When the war was very much near the end, did the Nazis abandon the concentration camps, or did they still try to kill the Jews even though they knew they were going to lose the war?

JW: The very tragic thing, the pathos in all of

this, is that even as the war machine was winding down because the Germans were clearly losing the war, the empire of death, the killing of the Jews by any means possible, continued.

The Germans were afraid the Soviets would find out what they did at Auschwitz, so they tried to cover up their crimes as quickly as they could. They took the remaining Jews — there were some fifty thousand of them still in the camps — on a death march during which if anyone strayed, they shot them. If anyone halted, they shot them. And these were the remnants of the Jews. There were six million dead.

DR: When the war was over, the American generals and military went to see the remains of the concentration camps. What was the reaction, for example, of General Patton?

JW: Patton, who had seen more than his share of war and bloodshed, was so horrified by what he saw that he couldn't walk into the camp itself. From what he did see, he vomited.

DR: What about Eisenhower? What was his reaction?

JW: Eisenhower was infuriated. He mirrored Churchill in thinking this was one of the greatest crimes ever committed.

As one of the troops around him said, "Now, finally, more than anything else, we know what we've been fighting for." Eisenhower made sure that as many people as he could get — he got every congressman he knew to come to Germany and see what happened.

DR: If you had to summarize the main reason the American government didn't do more to solve the problem — to let refugees in and/or keep them from being exterminated — what would you say?

JW: I think it was the attitude of Franklin Roosevelt, who, despite his humanitarian impulses, was hardheaded and tough-nosed, and he didn't want anything to compromise the winning of the war. There was never a moment like Abraham Lincoln had with the Emancipation Proclamation.

In Lincoln's case, he made the war about the Union, about keeping the Union together, until the Battle of Antietam. And then he promulgated the Emancipation Proclamation and made the war a great humanitarian gesture as well. Roosevelt never gave World War II that higher sense of purpose.

DR: Who is the hero of your book *1944* — or heroes?

Photographed here during an impromptu meeting at an airfield in Germany with three top Allied generals — George Patton, Omar Bradley, and Courtney Hodges — General Dwight D. Eisenhower was among the military officers appalled by the Nazis' crimes against humanity.

JW: The heroes are those who escaped from Auschwitz. I certainly think Henry Morgenthau was a hero. There's a German named Eduard Schulte who was horrified by what was taking place and, at great risk to his own life, he got word out about the Final Solution. There were people who put their lives or their careers on the line, who had a moment where they said, "Enough is enough. We have to do something."

DR: What was Adolf Eichmann's role in the Final Solution?

JW: Eichmann was just dastardly. He oversaw the complete extermination of the Jews. Later, of course, he was captured by the Israelis. [Israeli agents caught Eichmann in Argentina in 1960 and brought him to stand trial in Israel, where he was convicted of war crimes and executed in 1962.]

Hannah Arendt talked about the "banality of evil," and she saw in him a soulless bureaucrat. But I don't buy that they were soulless bureaucrats who were carrying out the Final Solution. I think they knew what they were doing, and I think they did it with hate in their hearts.

10
Jean Edward Smith
ON DWIGHT D. EISENHOWER

"Eisenhower was always able to make the decisions that you expected a commander to make. He never waffled. He was never hesitant."

BOOK DISCUSSED:
Eisenhower in War and Peace (Random House, 2012)

Jean Edward Smith has an interesting twist

on what has been the conventional wisdom about Dwight D. Eisenhower: gifted and experienced general, and not a gifted or successful president.

Eisenhower has been seen as an extraordinary military leader who was the mastermind of D-Day, which led to the Allies ultimately defeating Germany. And there is no doubt that Eisenhower was the Supreme Allied Commander in charge of the invasion.

But Smith points out that Eisenhower had missed combat in World War I; spent much of his military career in office or staff positions (he was a longtime aide to Douglas MacArthur); was much less qualified to lead a large combat mission than Omar Bradley, George Patton, or George Marshall, who had long been expected to lead the invasion of Europe; and late in his career was given combat military leadership positions in Italy and in Africa, in large part to give him the experience he would need to later lead the D-Day invasion.

Eisenhower's strength, Smith notes in the interview, was not combat experience as much as the ability to get along with political leaders. Churchill really liked him, as did FDR, who ultimately made the decision on D-Day leadership.

Interestingly, Eisenhower was not sure that the D-Day plan would work, and prepared communications acknowledging defeat and accepting responsibility for a failed invasion. And it might well have failed. Smith points out that Hitler's best panzer troops were available to repel the invading Allies, and probably could have done so. But Hitler had to give the orders to use those troops, and no one dared wake him while he slept during the initial hours of D-Day.

As the Supreme Allied Commander who devised the successful D-Day invasion of Europe, which ultimately led to the demise of the Nazi regime, Dwight Eisenhower was a living legend, admired by all Americans. Not surprisingly, both the Democratic and Republican Parties wanted Eisenhower as their presidential nominee. Seven years after World War II, Eisenhower revealed that he was a Republican, accepted the party's nomination, and was easily elected in 1952 and reelected in 1956.

As president, Eisenhower was seen as passive or even dull, and the period of his presidency was considered relatively tranquil, certainly when compared to the period of the 1960s with the civil rights movement, the Kennedy and King assassinations, the Vietnam War, the student protests, and the musical and sexual revolutions brought about by, respectively, the Beatles and the pill.

The result was a view that the Eisenhower presidency, occurring during quiet times, did not accomplish all that much. Many scholars and historians considered that it made less of an impact on history than his war service did.

In recent years, the relative tranquility, not to mention the peace and prosperity, of the Eisenhower years has had scholars reassessing this presidency. That is perhaps because of the challenging presidencies that followed Eisenhower's, and also because his low-key, steady-as-she-goes leadership style is now much better appreciated.

Jean Edward Smith is among the scholars leading this reassessment of the Eisenhower presidency. A political science and history professor, Smith has also written very well-regarded biographies of Supreme Court Justice John Marshall, General Ulysses S. Grant, and General Lucius Clay, the American military governor of occupied Germany after World War II.

According to the conventional wisdom, Eisenhower was not very strong or effective as a government leader, and he left behind a record of little presidential accomplishment. But Smith points out that this traditional view has not been very accurate or very fair.

Smith notes that President Eisenhower kept the peace for eight years (no American soldier was killed in combat during his presidency); ended the military conflict in Korea; thwarted the rise of McCarthyism; proposed and built the Interstate Highway System, without impacting the federal budget; enforced the law on desegregation of public schools in the South by sending federal troops to Little Rock, Arkansas; and, with Canada, built the Saint Lawrence Seaway.

Smith's exhaustive research also led him to confirm some interesting facts about Eisenhower:

- He did seek permission during World War II from his senior military leader, George Marshall, to divorce Mamie Eisenhower in order to marry his "driver," Kay Summersby. Permission was strongly denied, and that seemed to end the subject.
- He selected Richard Nixon as his running mate without even talking to him. (He had met Nixon once.) Eisenhower relied completely on his political advisors, who surprised him by saying the vice-presidential selection was actually his choice and not the Republican Convention's.
- He wanted Nixon to remove himself from the ticket in 1952 after a controversy arose about the political fund Nixon used to pay his expenses. Eisenhower also wanted Nixon to take another position, such as secretary of defense, during a presumed second term. In both situations, Nixon resisted strongly, and Eisenhower simply did not

use his authority to force his preferences. He apparently felt more comfortable exercising the military power he once held than the political power he later came to hold.

How would history have changed if Eisenhower had been allowed to divorce his wife, or if Nixon was forced from the ticket in 1952 or in 1956? We will never know.

Our conversation made me appreciate the extraordinary depth of Professor Smith's research and storytelling abilities, and I made certain to read his other biographies shortly afterward. Professor Jean Edward Smith passed away in the summer of 2019. I am grateful for his devoted and singular contributions to the study of American history.

MR. DAVID M. RUBENSTEIN (DR): Let me start with this question. To be honest, many people do not rate Dwight Eisenhower as one of our greatest presidents. If you ask great historians to rank presidents, they wouldn't say he was one of the best. Yet at the beginning of your book, you say that, with the exception of Franklin D. Roosevelt, he was the most successful president of the twentieth century. How would you explain that?

MR. JEAN EDWARD SMITH (JES): I might even place him ahead of Franklin Roosevelt. If you consider international relations, Eisenhower immediately, after taking office, made peace in Korea. Truman had not been able to do that. Eisenhower did it. Not one American was killed in combat for the remaining eight years of his term.

Eisenhower also thawed the Cold War. At the Geneva Summit of 1955, he was friendly with the Soviet premier and defense minister Nikolai Bulganin and with Nikita Khrushchev. [Khrushchev was then first secretary of the Communist Party of the Soviet Union, later Soviet premier. The 1955 summit brought together Eisenhower, Bulganin, Prime Minister Anthony Eden of Britain, and Prime Minister Edgar Faure of France.]

He invited Khrushchev to the United States. Khrushchev spent three nights at Camp David. He went to the Eisenhowers' farm in Gettysburg.

Eisenhower knew the Soviet Union. He had been a guest of Stalin immediately after the war was over. On the flight from Berlin to Moscow, Eisenhower saw that there wasn't a house still standing. That convinced him that the Russians didn't want war, and he proceeded on that basis. Eisenhower also singlehandedly forced Great Britain, France, and Israel to withdraw from Egypt after they had seized the Suez Canal in 1956, one week before the American presidential election.

And he overruled the members of the National Security Council and the Joint Chiefs about dropping an atomic weapon to protect the French garrison at Dien Bien Phu [site of the pivotal battle in 1953–54 between French and Viet Minh forces in the First Indochina War], and then to protect the Chinese islands of Quemoy and Matsu. [The islands were attacked during the Taiwan Strait Crisis of 1958 that pitted the People's Republic of China against the Republic of China in Taiwan.]

Eisenhower said, "You guys must be crazy. We aren't going to drop an atomic weapon on Asiatic peoples twice in ten years."

That's in foreign policy. Domestically, Eisenhower punctured the bubble of McCarthyism. He built the Interstate Highway System, which we take for granted, and he built it without impacting the federal budget by simply raising the tax on gasoline. The Interstate Highway System cost more than was spent on the entire New Deal from 1933 to 1940, but without impacting the federal budget. He built the Saint Lawrence Seaway together with Canada, opening the Great Lakes to ocean traffic.

And — I think most importantly — he brought desegregation to the South. He ended segregation in the United States when he sent the 101st Airborne Division to Little Rock. [In 1957, three years after the Supreme Court's *Brown v. Board of Education* decision found segregated schools to be unconstitutional, the paratroopers escorted a group of African American students to Little Rock Central High School and kept white protestors under control.]

That's eight major achievements just off the top of my head.

DR: Those are pretty good things. But let me ask you this. Eisenhower rose up because, as you write in your book, he was a very good writer, very disciplined, a hard worker, very articulate, knew how to get things done. Yet as a president he seemed to be a little lazy, some people might say, and he was not very articulate in press conferences. Why did that image take hold, and is it unfair?

JES: Let me dispute his inarticulateness in

401

press conferences. Whenever Ike misspoke, he was misspeaking deliberately.

DR: Many people would say that about themselves. I'd say that about myself too.

JES: For example, on the question of whether he would use an atomic weapon to defend Formosa, he told his press secretary, Jim Hagerty, "Jim, don't worry about it. I'll confuse them in the press conference." At the press conference, he goes on for about three minutes around the topic, totally confusing everyone. Eisenhower wasn't that concerned about cultivating the press.

DR: If you were to ask Eisenhower, "What would you consider the greatest accomplishment of your life?" would it be the D-Day invasion or being president of the United States for eight years? Which do you think he was prouder of?

JES: One of the things I've learned writing biography is that you really don't want to guess what your subject is going to say. But it would seem to me it would be his eight years as the president. D-Day was a one-shot deal.

DR: Let's talk about Ike as a young man. He came from a religious family. You point out in the book that his military career was — I won't say a fluke, but it wasn't predictable. He lied about his age, and that helped him get into the military academy. While there, he injured his knee and probably shouldn't have been commissioned. Early in his career, he was almost court-martialed. Was his military career based on having a little bit of luck?

JES: Eisenhower was always lucky, yes. But let me go back to his military career.

Eisenhower took a competitive exam for the academy, did very well, and was appointed by Senator Joseph Bristow from Kansas. In his initial correspondence with Bristow, he lied about his age, because he thought he might get into the Naval Academy, which had a lower age limit. When he got to West Point, he found out that he was the proper age and didn't lie about it.

As for the knee injury, and later with the court-martial, Eisenhower was very fortunate in many respects. In the 1920s, his career was forwarded enormously by General Fox Conner. The court-martial arose because Eisenhower had claimed his son on his housing allowance — the sum involved was $250 — when the son was not living with the Eisenhowers but with relatives back in Iowa.

Eisenhower was caught. I don't think he intentionally did it — it was a routine matter. Conner, who had been the chief operations officer for General John J. Pershing in World

War I and later became deputy chief of staff, was going to Panama. He wanted to take Ike with him.

Pershing had just become army chief of staff. Conner saw Pershing, and the court-martial charges against Eisenhower were dropped before they were brought, really. The army's inspector general simply wrote a letter of reprimand.

Four additional times during the 1920s, Conner intervened on Eisenhower's behalf. After serving three years in Panama, Eisenhower came back and wanted to go to the Command and General Staff College at Fort Leavenworth — a normal stopping point for career officers. The chief of infantry had passed him over. Conner had him transferred to the Adjutant General's Corps. He attended Leavenworth as part of the adjutant general's quota of students and finished first in his class.

After a miserable stint at Fort Benning, Conner had him transferred to Pershing's staff in Washington, where he wrote a book on the battles of World War I. Conner intervened again after two years and sent him to the Army War College in Washington, D.C., for a year.

After that, Eisenhower rejoined Pershing in Paris. He spent fourteen months there on the American Battle Monuments Commission. [The commission oversees American war memorials and military cemeteries overseas.] After fourteen months, he felt that he was out of the mainstream of the army.

Conner intervened for the fifth time, and Eisenhower was assigned to be the military assistant to the assistant secretary of war in the War Department, which was in the old State, War, and Navy Building — what is now the Eisenhower Executive Office Building in Washington. So Fox Conner really was behind Eisenhower's career in the 1920s, and five times worked to his advantage.

DR: Eisenhower had an ability to have people promote him and help him. One of those was General Douglas MacArthur. What was the relationship between MacArthur and Eisenhower initially, and then later, when they went to the Philippines?

JES: Eisenhower was working in the State, War, and Navy Building for the assistant secretary of war when MacArthur became army chief of staff. His office was just down the hall. He saw Eisenhower and installed him as his military assistant. That was in 1931.

For the next four years, Eisenhower was MacArthur's military assistant in Washington. He wrote virtually everything that MacArthur signed, including the defense of the attack on the "Bonus Army" marchers. [The Bonus

405

Army comprised World War I veterans who marched on Washington, D.C., in 1932 to ask the government to cash out bonus certificates they had been given during their military service. Troops under MacArthur's command destroyed the marchers' encampment.]

When MacArthur went to the Philippines in 1935, he took Ike with him. They did not command the American Army in the Philippines. They commanded the Philippine Army, although they were still on active duty in the U.S. Army. They were paid additionally by the Philippine government. That continued until 1939.

Eisenhower's view of MacArthur began as hero worship in 1931. By 1938 and '39, it had eroded. In the Philippines, MacArthur spent most of his time in his elegant apartment in the Manila Hotel and left the day-to-day operations to Eisenhower.

The members of the Philippine legislature decided to introduce legislation abolishing MacArthur's job and giving it to Eisenhower. Eisenhower found out about it and said, "Gosh, don't do that." He then came back to the U.S. on a mission to purchase equipment. While he was gone, MacArthur found out about this piece of legislation. MacArthur believed that Eisenhower was behind it, which he was not. But from that point on, the relationship between the two was poisonous.

DR: Eisenhower missed World War I. He didn't get over there, to his regret. There's been no other chance for him to gain combat experience. When World War II breaks out, we're not in the war initially. How did Eisenhower manage to go from never having been in combat to leading the D-Day invasion? What qualified him to do that?

JES: Eisenhower was at Fort Sam Houston as the chief of staff of the Fourth Army when the Japanese bombed Pearl Harbor. Immediately afterward, General Marshall ordered him to Washington. When Marshall reorganized the War Department in March of '42, Eisenhower became head of the Operations Division in the department.

The United States decided to enter the war, and Marshall and Roosevelt wanted to invade the Continent from Great Britain in November 1942. Eisenhower then, in June of '42, was sent by Marshall to England to become the head of the American forces in Europe. He was going there simply to get things in order for Marshall to come over and take command in November when the invasion took place.

Well, the idea of invading Europe in November of '42 was wishful thinking. The British wanted no part of it. Eventually it was decided that the Americans and the British would invade North Africa in November of 1942.

General Marshall didn't want any part of commanding an invasion of North Africa. But Eisenhower was there. He was commanding the European theater, and so it just fell into his lap. He bypassed 250 generals more senior.

DR: The people who were military-commander types — George Patton, Bernard Montgomery — these were people who actually had combat experience. They were in effect working for Eisenhower during the North African invasion and later during the invasion of Italy. What did they think of Eisenhower as a leader, as a commander?

JES: Eisenhower was always able to make the decisions that you expected a commander to make. He never waffled. He was never hesitant. Don't forget, General Marshall had never been in combat either, so I don't think in the military chain of command that's all that unusual.

DR: After the invasion of North Africa more or less works and then the invasion of Italy more or less works, the Allied commanders go back to England and say, "Okay, let's plan for the D-Day invasion." Marshall is thought to be the person who is going to do it. How did Eisenhower manage to maneuver so that he actually led the invasion? How did Marshall get outmaneuvered?

JES: Eisenhower didn't maneuver it, nor did Marshall. Roosevelt made the decision.

And you're quite right. General Marshall believed that he was going to command the invasion when it took place in 1944. Mrs. Marshall was moving their furniture out of Quarters 1 at Fort Myer to their home in Leesburg. He had his desk shipped over to Europe.

On the way to the Tehran Conference in late 1943, Roosevelt stopped in North Africa to take a judgment of Eisenhower. He was going to spend one day there but really spent three days there and liked what he saw.

Stalin, at the Tehran Conference, pressed Roosevelt to name a commander. Roosevelt said he would think about it.

Marshall's problem was that he was not popular with the British. They did not want Marshall to command the invasion. Churchill did not want Marshall to command the invasion. Roosevelt knew that. He had looked at Eisenhower and felt that Eisenhower, having experienced the North African Campaign and the Sicily Campaign and the landing in Italy, had good credentials as a military commander.

And so, on the way back from Tehran, Roosevelt met with Marshall in Cairo and asked him if he wanted to command the invasion. General Marshall, to his credit, said, "It's not my decision to make. It's your decision." The president said, "In that case, it will be Eisenhower."

DR: So the D-Day invasion is being planned. It takes many months to do it. Did Eisenhower ever think we might not win? Did he prepare for that?

JES: Oh, I think he was prepared for it. Whenever you do something like that, you realize that it's a very risky business. Eisenhower wrote a letter taking full responsibility for the failure, if it failed. He had it in his pocket and was ready to issue it.

But let me go back to North Africa just for a moment. Eisenhower learned in North Africa. He did not know anything about command in warfare until the North African Campaign. It was really a school for Eisenhower in which he learned how to command.

His three deputy commanders — air, ground, and navy — were British, and Eisenhower learned from them. He learned in Sicily, and he learned in Italy as well. And he had accumulated the lessons from those campaigns, which were not pretty.

DR: And D-Day succeeded, as we all know.

"General Dwight D. Eisenhower gives the orders of the day . . ." Ike speaks to U.S. paratroopers in England on D-Day, June 6, 1944.

But suppose the Germans had their troops in a different position or Hitler had been more alert to what was going on. Do you think we would not have prevailed?

JES: It would certainly have been much closer. The German commander, Marshal Gerd von Rundstedt, had five panzer divisions in reserve in the general area, and his orders were that he couldn't mobilize them until Hitler agreed to do so. It took them twenty-four hours to get Hitler to agree and put the panzers in place, and by that time the beachheads were secure.

411

There were also nineteen divisions north of the Seine. Hitler did not believe that the invasion that took place on D-Day was a real invasion. He thought it was a fake and that the real invasion would come north of the Seine across the English Channel. And so these nineteen divisions were unavailable to the Germans fighting the landings for the first two weeks of the campaign.

DR: Let's talk about Eisenhower's personal life for a moment. As a young man, Eisenhower married a woman named Mamie Doud. She was from a wealthy family. How was their life together when he was moving around so much?

JES: Ike met Mamie in November of 1915, just after he graduated from West Point. He was twenty-five. Mamie was nineteen. They were married July 1 the next year. He was stationed at Fort Sam Houston in Texas. Mamie came down and lived with him there. World War I came very quickly after that, and they were transferred out to Fort Meade.

They did not have quarters at Fort Meade initially, and that became a problem. But during the war itself, that was not a problem.

It was a much greater problem for them when Ike was sent to Panama after the war. Mamie did not like Panama at all. She came back from Panama to join her parents in

Portrait of Mamie Eisenhower. She and Ike married the year after he graduated from West Point. Their marriage survived his wartime attachment to his driver Kay Summersby.

Denver. John, their second son, was born in Denver. So the time in Panama was a difficult time for them in the marriage.

After that they were in Washington and Paris, and that was fine. But when Eisenhower went to the Philippines in 1935, Mamie did not go with him for the first year. Mamie stayed in Washington. They lived at the Wyoming apartment building, which you may know is down at the corner of Connecticut Avenue and Columbia Road. They had a very large apartment there. Mamie stayed there for an additional year before she came to the Philippines. Panama and the Philippines were difficult times.

DR: Now, when he was in England, he had a driver named Kay Summersby. He developed a relationship with her. It was later reported by President Harry S. Truman that Eisenhower had written a letter to George Marshall saying, "I want to leave my wife and marry Kay Summersby." How did Marshall respond to that?

JES: Marshall said if he did that, he would relieve him of command, a threat that Eisenhower took literally. Let me go into that a little bit.

Kay Summersby was Ike's driver in London in 1942 from the end of June until he went to North Africa in November. From that point on, Kay was no longer his driver. She was his executive assistant. In order to get to Eisenhower's office, you had to go through Kay's office.

Kay lived with Ike in the same quarters both in North Africa and outside of London in the country. The Eisenhower family always tried to disguise this by calling Kay his driver. That really insulted Sergeant Leonard Dry, who was actually his driver and who remained his driver for many, many years, even into the presidency.

Kay was very close to Eisenhower, and Eisenhower did write to General Marshall telling him that he wanted to divorce Mamie, and General Marshall did threaten to relieve him if he did so. Eisenhower at that point simply turned on a dime, and never mentioned it again.

When he left Germany to come back to the United States in November 1945, Kay, who was still with him, was due to come back with him. The day they were to come back, her orders were changed. She was assigned to General Clay in Berlin and did not come back to the United States until a year later. She called on Eisenhower at the Pentagon. She was in the American Army at the time. And the next day she was ordered to California.

DR: He was not the only general who may have had a driver. Is that right?

JES: I believe everyone did except General Omar Bradley.

DR: Wow, okay. Let's talk about what happens after the war is won. Eisenhower comes back and replaces George Marshall as army chief of staff. Truman says, "I don't want to run for reelection in 1948. Why don't you come and run as a Democrat?" What does

The prime minister and the future president: Winston Churchill and Ike share a pint at the Raleigh Tavern in Williamsburg, Virginia, circa 1948.

Eisenhower say?

JES: It happened before that, at the Potsdam Conference right outside Berlin, in 1945. Truman and Eisenhower and Bradley went for a tour around Berlin to look at the ruins from the war. It was during that ride around Berlin that Truman said, "If you would like the Democratic nomination in 1948, I will step back and become vice president again." Bradley couldn't believe it at the time. Eisenhower mumbled and said he really wasn't interested. Later on, Truman offered it to him once more, and Eisenhower again said no, he didn't want it.

DR: He didn't take the job. But he later leaves the military and takes a job as president of Columbia University.

JES: Columbia had offered him the presidency, to succeed Nicholas Murray Butler, who had been president for forty years. Eisenhower saw President Truman, who urged him to take it and said he would relieve him as chief of staff in late 1947, which he did.

Before reporting to Columbia he wrote his book *Crusade in Europe*. And then after *Crusade in Europe* was completed, he became the president of Columbia.

DR: He did that job for a few years and then rejoined the military. He went back to Europe?

JES: Yes. In late 1950, after NATO had been established, President Truman asked him to go back to organize the ground forces for NATO, and Eisenhower agreed to do that. He left Columbia in January of 1951 to become the first commanding officer of the NATO military forces, in order to organize them and get them together. Field Marshal Montgomery was his deputy. It was sort of a repeat of World War II. Eisenhower was still president of Columbia but was on leave.

DR: It's hard to imagine today somebody being on leave from an Ivy League university and going over and being in the military. But that's a separate issue.

JES: That's true. But let me say a word about Eisenhower as president of Columbia, because Eisenhower did an excellent job and he's not generally given credit for it. Nicholas Murray Butler, who had been president for forty years, hadn't raised any money for the last ten. In the 1940s, Columbia was the only major university whose endowment went down, because Butler was living on it.

Eisenhower not only balanced the budget, he organized the first fund drive that Columbia had ever had. He raised $3 million for Columbia in 1947. Multiply that by twelve to put it into today's dollars.

And Eisenhower as president of Columbia defended academic freedom. He defended the right of Communists to speak on campus. "We're not going to erect an intellectual iron curtain," he said. He defended the faculty and the faculty's right to hire whom they wanted and did an excellent job as president.

DR: When he goes back to Europe to be the NATO commander, his friend Lucius Clay, who had worked under him as a general in World War II, had gone into investment banking. Clay said, "Why don't you consider running for the Republican nomination?" instead of the Democratic nomination. What was Eisenhower's response?

JES: The crucial point is that Tom Dewey lost the election in '48. If Dewey had won the election in 1948, Eisenhower would simply have remained as president of Columbia. But having run twice, Dewey was not going to get the nomination in '52, which meant that the Republican nomination was open. Eisenhower was aware of that.

Clay and Governor Thomas Dewey and Herbert Brownell in New York were really behind the campaign to get Eisenhower to announce that he was willing to become a candidate for the Republican Party. And that was very difficult.

In November of 1951, President Truman offered him the Democratic nomination once again, for the 1952 election. Eisenhower again said no, he really didn't want it.

It was at that point that Clay and Dewey and Brownell began to work for Eisenhower, but they could not get him to say that he wanted to be a candidate. The problem was that Senator Robert Taft was running now, having run in 1940, 1944, and 1948. He was running for the fourth time in the Republican primary and was amassing a very significant number of votes. And Clay and Dewey and

Brownell could not get Eisenhower to announce.

DR: He decided to give his assent if somebody wanted to move his nomination forward. Is that how it happened?

JES: At the time of the New Hampshire primary, in order to enter a candidate, the candidate had to be a member of that party. Eisenhower would not announce that he wanted to be a candidate. General Clay told Henry Cabot Lodge Jr. to go ahead and file for Eisenhower, announce that he's a Republican. Lodge thought that Clay had talked to Eisenhower and cleared it, which he had not.

After it was done, Clay wrote to Eisenhower, and Eisenhower said, "That's okay." He didn't object to it — which, again, was one of those indications that it was okay with Ike.

But they really couldn't get Eisenhower to announce. He carried all sixteen delegates in New Hampshire in the primary, but Taft was still rolling up delegates throughout the Middle West and was really on his way to the nomination, and still they could not get Eisenhower to announce.

Finally, the Republican National Committee announced that General MacArthur was going to give the keynote address at the Republican Convention. Clay told Dewey,

"Write to Eisenhower. Tell him that Mac-Arthur is going to give the keynote and that we are afraid that he will mesmerize the delegates and he will be nominated by acclamation." Dewey's letter was hand-carried over to Paris, where Eisenhower was, by a TWA airline pilot. That's the way they communicated.

The day after Eisenhower received Dewey's letter, he announced that he was leaving NATO, coming back, and would announce his candidacy for the Republican nomination. It was his animosity toward MacArthur, which Clay of course knew about, that did it.

DR: When he announced, Taft was still way ahead, but Eisenhower obviously got the nomination. How did he decide who would be his vice president?

JES: Let me say a word about the nomination. When the roll call was called, Eisenhower was not over the top. He was leading Taft, but he was not over the top.

Minnesota had voted for Harold Stassen, its favorite son. Warren Burger, *the* Warren Burger [who went on to become chief justice of the U.S. Supreme Court], was waving the Minnesota standard. Joe Martin, presiding officer of the convention, recognized Minnesota. Governor Edward Thye of Minnesota then switched from Stassen to Eisenhower

Ike turned down a chance to run for president in 1948 but was persuaded to stand as the Republican nominee four years later.

and put him over the top in the first ballot.

That evening in Eisenhower's suite at the Blackstone Hotel, Ike was having dinner with Herbert Brownell and Clay. Brownell asked him, "General, have you given any thought to whom you would like to be your vice-presidential candidate?" Eisenhower said, "Isn't that up to the convention?" Brownell and Clay looked at each other and rolled their eyes, and Brownell said, "Yes, yes, that's up to the convention, but I'm sure they will look to you for guidance."

Eisenhower nodded and nodded and he said, "Well, I think C. R. Smith, the head of American Airlines, is a terrific executive; and Charles Wilson of General Electric, General Electric Wilson is a good executive. They'd both make good vice presidents."

Brownell and Clay are looking at each other again, and Brownell said, "Yes, General, they're all good, but we really need a candidate whose name would be recognizable to the delegates on the floor. If you haven't thought about it any, General Clay and I believe that we should go with Richard Nixon. Nixon is young, he's from California. He was in the navy. He's had good public relations lately."

Eisenhower said, "Well, I think I've met him. Clear it with the Taft people, and if they say okay, that's fine." That's how Nixon got the nomination. I might add that it was Herbert Brownell who told me that story.

DR: Then Nixon ran into a problem: he had a political fund paying some of his expenses. Eisenhower was nervous that they wouldn't win, and he wanted Nixon to resign from the ticket. How did Nixon outmaneuver Eisenhower on that?

JES: Just before Nixon was to go on television

that evening, Governor Dewey called Nixon and said, "Eisenhower wants you, at the end of your speech, to take yourself off the ticket — to resign." Nixon hemmed and hawed. Eisenhower legitimately thought that Nixon was going to take himself off the ticket that night. They had brought Senator William Knowland back from Hawaii to make him the replacement if they took Nixon off the ticket.

Eisenhower was watching the speech with a yellow pad and a pencil, and when it got to the end and Nixon didn't take himself off the ticket, Eisenhower broke his pencil on the pad. He was really annoyed at that point that Nixon hadn't taken himself off the ticket.

You may recall that Nixon said, "I'll leave it up to the Republican National Committee. If you think I should withdraw from the ticket or stay on the ticket, contact the Republican National Committee." He was going over Ike's head, he thought, by saying that. Eisenhower was really annoyed at him at that point and stayed annoyed at him for a long time.

DR: He stays on the ticket, and they get elected in a landslide over Adlai Stevenson. As president, Eisenhower puts together a cabinet known as "eight millionaires and a plumber." Who were they, and how did they get picked?

JES: On Election Day, Herbert Brownell came to see Eisenhower, who was still at Morningside Heights in New York City being the president of Columbia. During the conversation with Brownell, Eisenhower asked him if he wanted to be attorney general. Brownell said yes. Eisenhower went down to Augusta, Georgia, to the golf course and left it up to Clay and Brownell to pick the rest of the cabinet.

Clay wanted John McCloy to be secretary of state, but Dewey and Brownell argued that they really owed John Foster Dulles, so Dulles was made secretary of state. But all the other cabinet officers were picked by Brownell and Clay, and Eisenhower went along with them. At the end, they realized they didn't have a Democrat in the cabinet, and so they got Martin P. Durkin, who was head of the plumbers' union, to become secretary of labor.

DR: Eisenhower played a lot of golf and was criticized at the time for it. Today, we wouldn't criticize a president for that. Was he a good golfer?

JES: Eisenhower had a thirty-six-hole workweek at one point. He wasn't a great golfer, but he was a good golfer and he was very consistent.

DR: Let's talk about the Interstate Highway System for a moment. Eisenhower's idea for this may have come to him when he was a young man. Where did he get the experience that made him think that an interstate highway system was necessary?

JES: Immediately after World War I, the army decided to send a convoy from the Ellipse in Washington, D.C., to San Francisco, across country. It had never been done before. Eisenhower was one of six officers who volunteered for the convoy.

It took them sixty-two days — sixty-two days, think about it — to go from the Ellipse here in Washington to San Francisco. Eisenhower was aware of the need for public transportation, for a highway system.

In Germany, Eisenhower saw the autobahns that Hitler had built and recognized the need for something similar in the U.S. After the Korean War, the economy turned down, and Eisenhower also needed something to spur the economy on. He appointed Lucius Clay — Lucius Clay again — who put together a committee of five people. They devised the Interstate Highway System. At the end of the process, Clay recommended that they pay for it by simply raising the tax on gasoline, which they did.

DR: Let's talk about the U-2. The U.S. had a

special spy plane, the U-2, and Eisenhower personally approved the missions every time. The last one that he approved turned out to be the one that was shot down. Can you go through the importance of that mission?

JES: The U-2 came in in the mid-fifties and did an excellent job. I'll give you an example. At the time of the Suez Crisis, U-2 flights determined that the Russians were not moving any troops into that area. So it served a useful purpose, but it kept on and on and on and it had outlived its usefulness, and Soviet antiaircraft fire improved in the process.

Finally, in 1960, just prior to the Paris Summit between Eisenhower and Khrushchev, the CIA recommended sending one final U-2 flight across the Soviet Union — this is on the eve of the summit — and Eisenhower approved it.

It was a serious mistake. The U-2 was shot down. Its pilot, Francis Gary Powers, was captured alive. The episode really aborted the Paris Summit, which would have been very successful had it not been for that.

Khrushchev and the Russians throughout gave Eisenhower lots of slack so that he could blame CIA director Allen Dulles and the CIA for this. Eisenhower, in some ways to his credit, declined to do that, and took personal responsibility for it. He had plenty of opportunity to simply say that this was something that they didn't need to know anything about. But he did not do that.

DR: Eisenhower had some health problems in his first term. He had a heart attack. He had some intestinal issues. Did he ever consider not running for reelection? Did he ever consider not keeping Nixon on the ticket?

JES: He considered not running for reelection in 1955 when he had a very serious heart attack out in Denver. He recovered satisfactorily from the heart attack and concluded that there was no one else suitable for the Republican nomination.

He believed that Lucius Clay and George Humphrey, the secretary of the treasury, were both capable but had no political support. All the other Republican candidates, he felt, were not up to it, and so he decided to run for reelection.

DR: Did he want to keep Nixon as vice president?

JES: He tried to drop Nixon. He had a conference with Nixon and told him he thought he really ought to become secretary of defense or secretary of the treasury, so he would get some administrative experience. Nixon did not do that, and Eisenhower was not ready to formally drop Nixon.

DR: Nixon runs for president in 1960 against John Kennedy. At a press conference, Eisenhower is asked: "Can you name some great things that Nixon did during his term as vice president for eight years?" What does Eisenhower say?

JES: Eisenhower says, "Well, give me a week and I will think about it and I'll let you know." That was not a mistake.

DR: When Eisenhower retires, he decides he doesn't want to be called "Mr. President" the rest of his life. He wants to be called something else. What?

JES: He wanted to be called "General of the Army." It's one of those permanent ranks that you never retire from. If you're made general of the army, a five-star rank, you stay a general of the army until you die. And Eisenhower, after he left the presidency, wanted to become general of the army again. He had resigned when he announced his candidacy for the presidency. President Kennedy was a little surprised at that, but the Democrats passed the appropriate legislation to reinstall Eisenhower as general of the army.

DR: Golfers are sometimes known to pray for

their shots. Was Eisenhower known for being a religious person?

JES: Eisenhower's family was very religious. He had five brothers who lived past infancy. Their parents were fundamentalists. They were originally River Brethren, a fundamentalist sect from Germany that settled on the Susquehanna River, then moved out to Kansas.

His parents were extremely religious. His father read the Bible at mealtimes, and in the evening the children were required to do so. Interestingly, none of the children carried those religious beliefs into their adult lives.

Eisenhower is the only person ever elected president of the United States who did not belong to a church at the time. MacArthur once asked Eisenhower, "Ike, why don't you go to church on Sunday?" Eisenhower said, "Because when I was a cadet at West Point, they made me go every Sunday, and I'm not going back."

And Eisenhower did not go back. He did not belong to a church, and he did not go to church.

After he was elected and during the election campaign, many in the Republican Party suggested that he join the church. Eisenhower declined to do so. But finally, Clare Boothe Luce, after he was elected, talked Ike into joining the church, and he joined the Presbyterian Church. [Luce was an author, journalist, and political figure who became U.S. ambassador to Italy during Eisenhower's presidency.]

Now, I don't mean that Ike was an atheist or antireligion. He just didn't want to belong to a church.

DR: When Nixon ran in '68, was Eisenhower reconciled to him at that point? Did he support him?

JES: Eisenhower was in the hospital at the time. Yes, he supported Nixon. His grandson had married Nixon's daughter. The animosity had passed. But Eisenhower was never really a fan of Richard Nixon.

11
RICHARD REEVES
ON JOHN F. KENNEDY

"A great test of a president, it seems to me, is whether he brings out the best or the worst in the American people. Kennedy brought out the best."

BOOK DISCUSSED:
President Kennedy: Profile of Power
(Simon & Schuster, 1993)

I believe that I have read at least one biography of each of our forty-five U.S. presidents, but I think I have read every single biography written about President John F. Kennedy.

Perhaps that is because he was the president on whom I first focused some real attention. He gave his inaugural address while I was in the sixth grade. My teacher went through that compelling speech with my class, line for line and word for word. I realized that it was truly poetry in prose form, and a call to public service.

The speech inspired my own interest in public service and in becoming a lawyer — which I thought would be a helpful prerequisite to public service — and in also working someday at the White House as an advisor. (To the good fortune of the American people, I never saw myself as a candidate for public office.)

Toward that end of being an advisor, I thought some of the Kennedy eloquence and commitment to public service would rub off on me if I initially practiced law at the firm where Ted Sorensen, Kennedy's counsel and speechwriter, was a partner. None of the eloquence rubbed off, but my ability to perform public service was no doubt aided by Sorensen's support, as I moved to Washington to work first in the Senate and then in the White House for President Jimmy Carter.

In recent years, my fond early memories of President Kennedy — and his inaugural address — have remained with me and may account in some ways for my decision to be supportive of the John F. Kennedy Presidential Library and Museum in Boston, the Kennedy School of Government at Harvard, and the John F. Kennedy Center for the Performing Arts in Washington, where I serve as chairman of the board of trustees.

So, what author of a book about President Kennedy would share my deep interest in him and would be best to interview for the Congressional Dialogues series?

Unfortunately, many of President Kennedy's best-known biographers have passed away, including Sorensen and Arthur M. Schlesinger Jr., author of *A Thousand Days: John F. Kennedy in the White House.* However, there remain a number of talented Kennedy biographers.

One of them is Richard Reeves, a well-respected newspaper journalist and biographer. He published his book on President Kennedy in 1993, and thus had the benefit of writing it after information about the White House recordings of the president's conversations and about his health problems had come into the public domain. (That was not the case with many of the earlier biographies.)

For many in my generation, President Kennedy still holds a fascination, a magical allure that transcends the actual legislative or foreign policy achievements of an administration that lasted less than three years. And that allure — the Camelot factor, perhaps — exists despite the revelations in recent years of the precarious nature of the president's health and, at times, the incautious nature of his personal behavior.

In Reeves's view, that allure is due in part to Kennedy's ability to bring out and to appeal to the best in our human instincts, and in part to the tragic nature of Kennedy's death as a young man, with so much of his promising future ahead of him. There is no doubt that when charismatic young leaders in any field die young, they tend to be remembered forever as young and vibrant. There will never be pictures of these individuals with gray hair or wrinkles, with physical ailments or in wheelchairs.

Perhaps the perpetual image of a young President Kennedy, sailing or throwing a football or playing with his very young children, is part of his continuing appeal. But Reeves does justice in the interview to Kennedy's more tangible accomplishments, the most significant of which is the brilliant negotiation that led to the peaceful ending of the Cuban Missile Crisis.

Those who lived through that crisis no doubt remember thinking a nuclear war was imminent. (My ninth-grade teacher, I remember vividly, said there was no point in assigning homework that week, for we would not likely be around in a few days.)

Kennedy's youth, vigor, charm, and tragic assassination are what those in that era most vividly recall about our thirty-fifth president. But they, and future generations, should most remember the skill he used to peacefully end a thirteen-day stalemate with the Soviet Union that had brought the world closer to a nuclear confrontation than it had ever been before.

MR. DAVID M. RUBENSTEIN (DR): Why is it that, fifty years later, so many people remember President Kennedy's death — where they were when it happened — and why do we have such a high view of his presidency? He passed not a single major bill as president of the United States. He had the Bay of Pigs invasion, had problems in Laos and Vietnam. Why is President Kennedy still so idealized and so popular?

MR. RICHARD REEVES (RR): He was an athlete dying young, not unlike James Dean, and Marilyn Monroe. That's why, I think. The whole future was ahead of us, we thought.

A great test of a president, it seems to me, is whether he brings out the best or the worst in the American people. Kennedy brought out the best. That's part of it.

DR: How long did it take you to write your book?

RR: Ten years. You can do it in five years now with Google.

DR: All right, but it took you ten years. After ten years of research and writing, did you admire him more or less than when you started?

RR: Much more.

DR: Why?

RR: In the first place, I didn't pick Kennedy because I was a Kennedy-phile. Congressman Steve Solarz gave me a copy of a book called *The Emperor* by the Polish journalist Ryszard Kapuściński. He said, "You should read this. It's really good." [Published in 1983, *The Emperor: Downfall of an Autocrat* chronicles the final years of Ethiopian emperor Haile Selassie, drawing on accounts by his servants and courtiers.]

What we often do in journalism is study the men near the center of power — in this case, in Addis Ababa rather than Washington. I read *The Emperor* and admired it greatly. Then I thought, "I could do this about an American president."

With a president, everything — almost everything — is on paper. There are always witnesses. Meeting or working for the president was the high point of anyone's life. I thought I could reconstruct Kennedy's presidency based on that.

Historians write knowing the ending, but I thought I could write it forward as narrative history — write about what Kennedy knew and when he knew it, and what was on his desk when he made decisions.

DR: You never met President Kennedy?

RR: No. I was in school.

DR: If you had the chance to meet him now and you could ask him one or two questions, what would you ask him after having studied him for ten years?

RR: I would ask him first to show me the paper trails to two incidents in his presidency. One was the Berlin Wall, which he knew about in advance and for which he was practically a co-contractor. [Built by the Communist German Democratic Republic with Soviet backing in August 1961, the Wall shut democratic West Berlin off from Communist East Berlin.]

It was a desperate time, really, in human history. Soviet premier Nikita Khrushchev had a problem. More than two thousand people a day were leaving East Germany through East Berlin, and they were the best. They were the doctors, the lawyers. The elite were running, and Khrushchev had to do something about that.

On the other hand, from Kennedy's viewpoint, we had fifteen thousand men in Berlin at that time, surrounded by hundreds of thousands of Russian soldiers in East Germany and Eastern Europe. If it came to a military action, they could have driven us out of Germany in two weeks and probably out of Europe in a month. The only thing that Kennedy could have done was use nuclear weapons, which was the thing he and other presidents have least wanted to do.

DR: So one thing you'd like to know is whether he in effect consented to the building of the Berlin Wall?

RR: I'd like to see it on paper. I think I showed pretty well that he did, but I never found documents.

DR: What else would you like to ask him?

RR: I wouldn't ask him about his personal life. We didn't do that so much in those days.

I'd like to get him to admit that he was behind assassination attempts on Cuban president Fidel Castro and the assassination of Rafael Trujillo. [Trujillo was the dictator who ran the Dominican Republic from 1930 until his death in 1961.]

I've done books on three presidents — Ronald Reagan, Richard M. Nixon, and Kennedy — and my conclusion from all of that is the president knew. The president always knows.

DR: But he had deniability.

RR: Right. He's protected by, in this case, his brother Robert Kennedy. [He served as JFK's attorney general and close advisor.]

DR: Your book was published in 1993, but many of the books written about President Kennedy were written in the sixties and seventies and eighties. So when you were writing your book, you had the advantage of knowing two things about Kennedy that the world didn't really know when the other books were written. One was about his health. How ill was he? Did he really have Addison's disease? Would he have lived through a second term?

RR: He probably would have lived through a second term. He was in pain every day of his life because of his back. He was a very, very sick man.

One of the things that helped me in writing the book was that, if people remember who Max Jacobson was, "Dr. Feelgood" — he supplied the Kennedys with amphetamines and cocaine — he kept a journal, and his wife gave it to me.

In the first place, Kennedy never took a physical to go into the navy. His sense was that you would not be able to succeed in this country if you weren't part of the war. The Civil War was like that.

All our presidents for decades were Civil

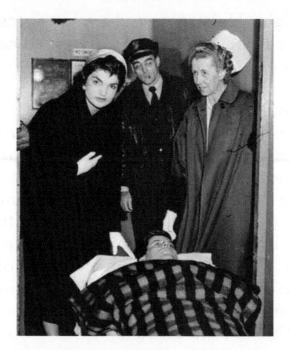

A bad back left Kennedy in pain much of the time. Here he leaves the hospital with his wife, Jackie, following spinal surgery on December 21, 1954.

War officers. So Kennedy wanted that uniform. His father had friends and enough influence to get his son in the military without a medical.

DR: He also had Addison's disease but denied he had it, is that right?

RR: It was denied again and again, including on election eve in 1960.

DR: But the medication for that was cortisone, which made his face and his hair thicker. What other side effects does cortisone have?

RR: Well, it increases your sex drive. You feel pretty good about most things.

Kennedy collapsed in a hotel room in London while he was with Pamela Harriman, then Pamela Churchill. He collapsed. Pamela called her father-in-law, Winston Churchill, and his doctor came to the hotel, the Connaught, and did an examination.

The doctor asked Pamela to come outside. He said, "Your young friend has only a year to live. He has Addison's." A fatal disease at that time.

But in Chicago, an American doctor in the public health service — a guy making maybe $25,000 a year — figured out how to make synthetic cortisone. Before that, the only available (and expensive) cortisone came from live sheep. Kennedy's father had put cortisone in safety deposit boxes around the world.

Three times his son got the last rites of the Catholic Church. One time he was saved while traveling in the Pacific with his brother, because they got the cortisone in time.

It was a terminal disease he had and knew that he had. It is no longer a terminal disease.

DR: The back pain that he often suffered

from, to the point that he couldn't walk, came from the cortisone weakening his bones more than from a war injury?

RR: I don't think a war injury had anything to do with it at all. It was from birth. The amount of drugs he was taking every day, and the fact that his doctor, Janet Travell, was a total fool, almost killed him.

DR: He had three doctors, in effect, when he was president. He had the navy doctor, who was a regular doctor. He had Janet Travell for his back. And then Dr. Jacobson — Dr. Feelgood — would come down and give him shots.

RR: And would travel with him. He shot him up before the summit in Vienna with Khrushchev.

I want to say something about Travell and what she did. All she was doing was shooting him up with novocaine. So he felt better but his back was getting worse and worse and worse. Ironically, at the time of his death, with exercise replacing novocaine, John Kennedy was probably in the best health of his life.

DR: The other thing that's come out in the last few years is more information about his personal life. Without going through all the details of it, was he not worried that it would be discovered? And why did the press corps never comment on it?

RR: A lot of people exaggerate now what they knew then. To make a long story short, rich people have long driveways. You don't know who comes in, who goes out, how long they're there.

Then there's the fact that Kennedy was a great generational figure. The symbolism of going from having the supreme commander of the Allied forces, Dwight D. Eisenhower, as president, to a lieutenant in the navy — Kennedy's first political slogan was "The new generation offers a leader." The press was part of that new generation. Men related to each other at that time by what they had done in the war.

In those days, men bragged to each other, often without any substance, about what they were doing and whatnot. With the combination of that and the fact that he had hundreds of paid liars working for him, he got away with it.

I had lunch with one of the presidents of the United States who succeeded him. He had read the book. When his wife left the table to go on to greater things, as soon as she left he said, "How did he get away with it?"

DR: He didn't have a physical, but he served in World War II. His *PT-109* boat was split by a collision with a Japanese destroyer. He heroically saved his crew, and they were rescued. He came back and was in the hospital for a while.

His brother Joseph P. Kennedy Jr. was killed in the war. Joseph was more outgoing and was the one many people thought would be running for office. After he was killed, did their father pressure John Kennedy to run?

RR: He did pressure him. But in the end, I think history would have been the same even if he hadn't. John Kennedy, who always thought he would die young because of all the illnesses he had, lived life as a race against boredom. He was a man who would not wait his turn. He invented the idea of a self-selected presidency because he thought he would be a dead man before he was fifty.

DR: He was elected to the House of Representatives in 1946, the same year as Richard Nixon. Why, after just a few years in the House, did Kennedy think he was qualified to run for the Senate against a Republican incumbent, Henry Cabot Lodge Jr., in 1952? Eisenhower was probably going to run for election as the Republican presidential candidate and win that year. Why did Kennedy take that chance?

RR: One of his great friends was Charles Bartlett, who was the Washington correspondent for the *Chattanooga Times*. They'd served together in the war. Bartlett said, "Why don't you wait to run?" Kennedy said, "I can't wait. They won't remember me."

In 1956, in a very short campaign, he tried unsuccessfully to be Adlai Stevenson's vice-presidential nominee, and he was surprised by how easy it was to get national recognition and credibility. He had always planned to run for vice president first. Janet Travell asked him, "Are you sad about this?" He said, "No. I've learned I have to be a complete politician, and I will run from this day to the day I'm elected or die."

DR: When he was elected to the U.S. Senate in 1952, he had a back injury. He was in the hospital awhile to have surgery, and wrote a book called *Profiles in Courage* then. How did he, when he was in the hospital, manage to write a book that won the Pulitzer Prize?

RR: Well, it didn't deserve a Pulitzer Prize. It's really a fairly simple little book. It was his idea and his notes, which then went to Ted Sorensen. [Sorensen was the senator's chief legislative aide at the time.] Ted did a draft, and then Kennedy, who could write and had been a journalist briefly, edited it. Sorensen rewrote it, Kennedy edited it again. But Ted

447

Sorensen wasn't the author of that book; John Kennedy was.

DR: In those years he was in the Senate, there was a resolution against Joe McCarthy to condemn him for some of the things he had said and done during his hunt for suspected Communists. Senator Kennedy did not vote for that resolution. Why not?

RR: One, he was in the hospital after his back operation. Two, McCarthy was a friend, particularly of his father's. Kennedy stayed in the hospital to avoid that vote.

When we talk about Kennedy's health, by the way, journalism wasn't as good in those days. Neither was negative research. Anything anyone wanted to know about John Kennedy's health, including the fact that he had a terminal disease, was in the *Journal of the American Medical Association,* because he was the first Addisonian ever to survive major surgery.

Because of that, the AMA covered this in depth — although his name was never used. He was referred to as the "thirty-seven-year-old man." Any journalist today would have figured it out.

DR: So he was in the Senate and didn't vote against McCarthy. He didn't actually pass a lot of legislation. Why did he think he was

Then senator John F. Kennedy, shown campaigning in Yonkers, decided to seek the Democratic presidential nomination in 1960.

qualified to be president of the United States?

RR: Every president I've ever talked to — and I've talked to a lot — would point to whoever was in the field at the moment and say, "If they can, why not me?"

DR: He decided to run in 1960. How many primaries did he run?

RR: Three.

DR: There were only three primaries?

RR: Right. He totally changed American

politics. He was the first self-selected president.

During the four years that Kennedy was never around the Senate, Lyndon Johnson thought he was going to be the Democratic nominee. Kennedy was either campaigning all the time or in the hospital.

But the press had become his constituency, and he had that nomination won before the 1960 convention. He used the primaries as leverage. Again, it was generational. The convention was over before he got there.

DR: The 1960 convention was held in Los Angeles. Johnson went out there and thought he had a chance of getting the nomination, but you say he didn't really. In the end, he was offered, by John Kennedy, the vice-presidential nomination. Then Robert Kennedy went to take it back. Did John Kennedy authorize that? Why did they offer it to Johnson in the first place?

RR: They offered it because it was the only way they could win. [The Democrats needed the southern money and votes that Johnson, with his deep Texas ties, could deliver.] John Kennedy knew, months before that convention, where he would go with the vice presidency, and so he lied to his brother — a thing he did more than once.

His brother was against it all the time, even

*Youthful, charismatic, and adept at deal-
ing with the press, Kennedy represented
a generational shift in American politics.*

at the last moment in Los Angeles, in the
hotel, where Bobby went down and tried to
talk Johnson into withdrawing. But John Kennedy would not have been president if he had
a different vice-presidential candidate.

DR: Now, there had never been presidential
debates before the election of 1960. The
famous Lincoln–Douglas debates of 1858

were actually Senate debates. Why did Nixon agree to have debates in 1960, and how did John Kennedy prepare for those debates?

RR: He had a group of very smart people throwing questions at him, as did Nixon.

As for why Nixon agreed, there are a couple of things we know. One is that the incumbent is always in trouble in a debate.

As Jerry Brown once said to me — I asked him what was the difference between his governorship and his father's, and he said, "Everyone's the same size on television. Some housewife in Ventura is just as big as I am on television." They didn't know that then.

Nixon thought he could destroy Kennedy in debate, and he thought he could end the campaign right there.

DR: What about the famous makeup issue? Kennedy was asked if he wanted makeup. He said no, and Nixon then said no. But Kennedy already had a tan and had makeup on.

RR: He had pancake makeup. Going back to another point, I want to say one thing about the two of them.

Most of us, if we're old enough, probably remember the picture of Lieutenant John F. Kennedy, bare-chested, a fatigue cap on, sunglasses, sitting in the cockpit of his *PT-*

109 boat. That was his official picture at that time.

Richard Nixon, who was also a lieutenant in the navy — a supply officer and a senior-grade lieutenant — his campaign picture was standing at attention in dress blues on a beach. And you didn't have to be Marshall McLuhan to figure out who's going to win that contest.

DR: The election was held and Kennedy won, with the help of a few friends in certain states, you might say. Who wrote his enormously successful inaugural address, which is only fourteen minutes long? Why was it so special?

RR: It was so special because the country was ready to fall in love. Kennedy had succeeded a much older man, and there was a generational change coming across. He wrote it. Sorensen did drafts.

In the text that Kennedy approved, there was not a single mention of domestic policy. Harris Wofford, a white man who was his civil rights advisor, said, "There are things going on in this country. You've got to put something in this speech." And Kennedy said okay. He added that people are crying for freedom, both abroad — and then the three words "and at home." Meaning African Americans.

DR: But that was the only reference to domestic policy in the entire speech.

RR: That's the only reference. We were a Cold War nation, and we thought we were at war. He was a Cold Warrior.

DR: At the beginning of his administration, President Kennedy authorized the Bay of Pigs invasion in Cuba. [The 1961 invasion involved a group of Cuban exiles who planned to overthrow Fidel Castro's government, with U.S. backing. The invasion, which took place on April 17, 1961, was a military and diplomatic disaster.] Why did he make such a big mistake?

RR: He was stupid and inexperienced. He believed that Eisenhower had okayed the operation. He later found out that was not true.

The CIA, which did plan the operation, lied to him, and thought that no American president would ever let an American invasion fail. They just assumed the president would call in the marines — that if things went bad on the beaches with these Cuban rich kids, he'd call in the marines.

Well, Kennedy refused to do that. Finally he agreed with the CIA and the air force that he would allow three old B-26 bombers to fly over the beaches of Cuba, so they could evacuate these kids, these invaders, but first the planes were painted over gray. There were no American insignia visible on them.

There also were no Cubans, because the people who planned the raid did not take into account that Cuba is in the Central time zone. The CIA made the whole plan based on Eastern Standard Time, and the planes flew over and nothing happened.

DR: President Kennedy did something that other people like to do today, which is to take responsibility for what happened. When he took responsibility, his poll numbers went up. When he said, "I take responsibility," did he expect to be more popular?

RR: No. He thought he was finished. He literally said, "Can you believe this? The worse you do, the better they like you." His approval rate went up into the eighties after the Bay of Pigs.

He was no fool. I actually am not old enough to remember this, but he had this whole series of patriotic meetings, beginning with Eisenhower and Nixon, saying, "We're with him all the way" — although in private Eisenhower told him he thought he was a goddamn fool. He said, "Did you have anybody in your office who was arguing against this?" Kennedy said no, and Eisenhower said, "Well, you better try next time."

But there was this great feeling of national redemption with every Republican coming to say, "The president is fine."

DR: Part of the problem in Cuba was that the Soviet Union was supportive of the Castro regime, so Kennedy really wanted to meet with Khrushchev. He had never met him before. They scheduled a meeting in Vienna in June 1961. What happened at that meeting?

RR: What happened in that meeting tells you more than you want to know about John Kennedy. One, Dr. Jacobson was there, injecting him with amphetamines — speedballs — when he went in.

Second — there are a couple of other politicians who have done this over time — Kennedy's résumé was faked. It said that he had studied under Harold Laski at the London School of Economics and therefore was an expert on Marxism. [Laski was a famous political theorist, socialist, and Labour Party leader.]

The truth was he enrolled there but never went to England, never met Harold Laski. But all the people around him, who bought into the résumé, thought their president, their boss, was an expert on the Marxist dialectic. He walked into the meeting with Khrushchev, who was an expert in it, and Khrushchev

456

walked all over him.

DR: Kennedy recognized he had been beaten up during the two-day meeting. Khrushchev then felt, "This man I can really take advantage of." Is that what led to his putting Soviet missiles in Cuba?

RR: It certainly was part of it, although their relationship was a little different by then. Khrushchev's motivation — Kennedy later said if he were Khrushchev, he would have done exactly the same thing — was that the Soviets did not have any long-range missiles capable of hitting a target in the United States, while we had picket fences of missiles surrounding the Soviet Union and had submarines that could fire missiles that could reach Russia within minutes.

DR: Kennedy had said during the campaign that there was a missile gap. There was no gap, right?

RR: It was a lie. There was a missile gap of a hundred to one in our favor. The Soviets only had sixteen. We had thousands.

Khrushchev had medium-range ballistic missiles. We had long-range, medium-range, and short-range missiles. But if the Soviet leader could get launching sites in Cuba, those medium-range missiles could reach as far north as Washington. It was a gamble. We caught it. I want to repeat that Kennedy said, "If I were Khrushchev, I would do the same thing."

DR: How did we catch it? Were we surprised that they were getting ready to have the nuclear missiles so close to here?

RR: The Republicans weren't surprised. Kenneth Keating was not surprised. [Keating, a Republican who served as a senator for New York from 1959 to 1965, suspected the Soviets had nuclear intentions in Cuba.] Keating and other Republicans and the defense intellectuals were saying, "This is really trouble." And the White House was denying it.

To bring another figure into it, one of the clues that led to Kennedy realizing it was true was that he had a young sometime foreign affairs advisor named Henry Kissinger. Our spying was nowhere near as comprehensive as it is today, and Cuba, during this two-month-long period, was mostly clouded over.

We used the U-2 spy plane to get photographs when the clouds broke, and Kissinger noted that there were new soccer fields in Cuba. The Cubans played baseball. They didn't play soccer. They do now. They didn't then. Kissinger, who was a soccer fanatic, said, "There must be Russians there. Russians play soccer."

DR: Kissinger was then a thirty-seven-year-old consultant to McGeorge Bundy, who was Kennedy's national security advisor. So they discovered these missile sites. What did they decide to do? The military wanted to go in and invade and bomb? Why did they decide to use a quarantine strategy — a naval blockade — instead?

RR: The military, particularly Curtis LeMay, the U.S. Air Force chief of staff, wanted to destroy the island. And the rest of the world too, if it took that.

It was an interesting thing about Kennedy and the military. He hated LeMay. After one session, in which LeMay talked about eliminating the Soviet Union, he said, "Never let that man near me again." But six months later, he appointed him chief of staff. His brother said, "How could you do that?" He said, "Look, the man is like Babe Ruth. He's a bum, but the people love him."

DR: He also didn't want him out there saying bad things.

RR: Right.

DR: After they discovered that missiles were in Cuba, they ultimately decided to go for the quarantine approach. Why did Khrushchev send the Soviet ships back and agree to take the missiles out?

RR: Because, from the experience in Vienna — the summit at which he was humiliated — John Kennedy came to understand, as many of his people, say, Secretary of Defense Robert McNamara, did not understand, that Khrushchev was just another politician in a different system. Kennedy didn't want to start World War III, and he knew Khrushchev didn't either.

Then there was a back-and-forth of ghostwritten military memos. It was Bobby actually who suggested, "Ignore this one, answer this one," and when he answered this one, what came back from Khrushchev was: "We can work this out." There was a secret codicil, of course, which was that Kennedy — no one knew this at the time — promised we would never invade Cuba.

DR: We also agreed to take our missiles out of Turkey, more or less in a secret deal.

RR: Yeah. But those missiles were worthless anyway.

DR: Let's talk about civil rights for a moment. When he was running for president, Kennedy famously called Coretta Scott King when her husband, Martin Luther King Jr., was arrested. Why did he make that call, and why was Bobby Kennedy upset about it?

RR: They thought it was a disaster. They didn't want Kennedy to be seen as the candidate of black people. It was his brother-in-law Sargent Shriver, a true liberal, who convinced Kennedy to make that call.

Bobby didn't know about it. Bobby was furious when he found out about it, because the last thing in the world the Kennedys wanted was to be heroes of the civil rights movement. It was only when George Wallace barred the door at the University of Alabama and it was on national television that Kennedy decided he had to make a stand. [In June 1963, Wallace, then the governor of Alabama, physically stood in the way of African American students attempting to enroll at the segregated state university.]

He asked Wofford, "Why are these black people" — he wasn't a racist or anything — "why are they doing this? Who are they listening to?" And Wofford said, "They listened to you. You were talking about individual action and freedom."

It was Wofford and Lyndon Johnson and Johnson's press secretary, George Reedy, who had been a Communist as a young man, who told him, "You've gotten this far in politics by being a northerner. The southerners controlling Congress think you're only doing this for politics. They think you're secretly like your father — that you're secretly on their side." And the young black activists believed JFK was on their side. Events forced Kennedy to choose.

On the other hand, Kennedy couldn't get anything done without the southerners. He didn't want to rile them up. But he then made one of the great speeches in American history — not all of it on paper, working from notes — saying, "This is not a political question. This is not a regional question. This is a moral question. It is a question of what kind of people we are." One of the great moments in American history.

DR: Why did Kennedy oppose the 1963 March on Washington? He opposed it, and he refused to speak at it.

RR: Absolutely. And his brother had someone stationed in the bowels of the Lincoln Memorial with the switches to turn off the microphones.

DR: If the speeches weren't appropriate?

RR: Yeah. If they thought they had to do it. What happened next was that Kennedy, who knew a star when he saw one, watched Martin Luther King Jr. deliver the "I Have a

A president for the television age: Kennedy at a TV taping, July 3, 1963.

Dream" speech on television, and called Bobby and said, "I want him to come to the White House."

It took King twenty minutes to get there because Kennedy had never allowed his picture to be taken with Martin Luther King Jr. or any black person. Sammy Davis Jr., the black song-and-dance man — and Kennedy friend — was thrown out of the White House because he had a white wife.

In the twenty minutes it took them to get there, Kennedy had a meeting with the National Security Council — these were big days, dense with events — at which he signed off on overthrowing President Ngo Dinh Diem in South Vietnam, which is what, in the end, got us involved there. [Diem was

463

overthrown in a military coup on November 1, 1963, after the United States indicated it would not interfere. That strengthened the position of the Communist North Vietnamese government.]

DR: Let's get to that right now. Many people associate President Johnson and President Nixon with the Vietnam War, but when Kennedy came into office, we had a few hundred military advisors in Vietnam. When he died, we had about sixteen thousand or so there. Many people who support President Kennedy and like him say that he would have definitely, in a second term, gotten us out of Vietnam. What is your view on that?

RR: My view is he would not have done what Lyndon Johnson did. Diem was a Catholic. That was very important to the Kennedys. It was a minority religion, hated in Vietnam. I have no doubt in my mind that Kennedy would have pursued that war for a while, but nowhere to the extent that Johnson did.

DR: But Kennedy wanted to be reelected, obviously. He began campaigning, and took his wife, Jackie, with him. The first time she went on a political trip with him — the first time she went west of the Mississippi as first lady — was when she went to Texas in

Enduring glamor: John F. Kennedy and Jacqueline Bouvier Kennedy at their wedding reception, September 12, 1953, in Newport, Rhode Island.

November 1963. Why did they need to go to Texas?

RR: She decided to go. He was going to Texas because the state's two senators at that time were at each other's throats. One was a liberal, one was a conservative, both were Democrats. Johnson was supposed to take care of that. There's money in Texas, and Kennedy wanted that money and wanted the votes. That's why he went.

It was the first time Jackie agreed to go with him. It wasn't him saying, "I want you to go with me." It was her saying, "I want to come with you." He was dazzled by the way she was received.

12
TAYLOR BRANCH

ON MARTIN LUTHER KING JR. AND THE CIVIL RIGHTS MOVEMENT

"The longer I studied him, the deeper and more profound for me was his understanding of ecumenical, spiritual, and political movements."

BOOKS DISCUSSED:
The America in the King Years trilogy
Parting the Waters, 1954–63 (Simon & Schuster, 1988)
Pillar of Fire, 1963–65 (Simon & Schuster, 1998)
At Canaan's Edge, 1965–68 (Simon & Schuster, 2006)

One of the most significant social, political, legal, and cultural occurrences in my lifetime has been the civil rights movement of the late 1960s. It spawned the 1964 Civil Rights Act, among other epic legislation, and subsequent movements for equal rights for other disenfranchised elements of American society.

So I thought that an interview on the civil rights movement, with a focus on the most visible leader of that movement — Dr. Martin Luther King Jr. — would be an interesting subject for one of the Congressional Dialogues. Fortunately, the ideal person for the interview — Taylor Branch — was available. His 2,912-page trilogy on this subject, the first volume of which won the Pulitzer Prize, is the well-recognized gold standard for coverage of this subject.

Branch has an eclectic background: journalist, editor, college lecturer, political organizer, and biographer. These activities have been recognized with the MacArthur "genius" Fellowship and the National Humanities Medal.

Branch lives in my hometown of Baltimore, and we have many friends in common from there and in Washington. But we had not met before the interview.

I wish we could have had more time to cover this important subject, but the interview does touch a good amount on the important highlights of the author's epic work, which took him twenty-four years to complete.

It is no doubt difficult to recognize the full impact of a social movement when you are living through it, especially if the movement spans two to three decades. I know I did not recognize the full impact of the civil rights movement as it was unfolding.

With hindsight, it is now clear that the civil rights movement, transcendental in its impact in the United States, also spawned a number of other transformative social, legal, and political movements over the past several decades: the movement for equal opportunity and protection for all minority groups; the movement for equal rights for women; the social and political protest movements, ranging from the Vietnam War to LGBTQ rights; the voting registration drives among underrepresented voters; and the use of federal courts to protect rights guaranteed by the Constitution and by related laws.

With each of these movements, there were many leaders. No one person can be said to be the sole person responsible for the movement. Branch makes clear that this is the case with the civil rights movement. Dr. Martin Luther King Jr. was, for much of the 1960s, the most visible African American civil rights leader. But the movement began in the early 1950s, and became widely visible to the white population with the Supreme Court's unanimous *Brown v. Board of Education of Topeka* decision in 1954; and it continued in the courts, in Congress, and in society well after Dr. King's assassination in April of 1968.

But, all that said, Dr. King personified the movement, to whites and to blacks, in the 1960s. He was the visible and spiritual leader (though not initially of his own choosing) of the Birmingham campaign of 1963, the March on Washington for Jobs and Freedom of 1963 (where he gave his memorable "I Have a Dream" speech), the Selma to Montgomery marches of 1965, the Chicago Freedom Movement of 1965–67, and the Memphis sanitation strike of 1968, which led to his assassination by James Earl Ray.

And, of course, outside the United States, Dr. King was widely seen as the most important leader of the civil rights movement. He was the sole recipient of the Nobel Peace Prize in 1964 for his civil rights efforts.

In the interview, Branch discusses the challenges that Dr. King constantly faced as the visible leader of the movement: he sparred with more-senior civil rights leaders, who often disagreed with his tactics and resented his visibility; many in the African American community questioned the effectiveness of Dr. King's commitment to nonviolent protest, especially when they were confronted with violence by their opponents; he and his family were constantly subjected to death threats; he was accused of being supported and advised by Communists (and the FBI, with Attorney General Robert Kennedy's approval, wiretapped his conversations, and also disseminated salacious details about King's personal life to his wife, among others).

Today, for those who may not have lived through the 1950s and 1960s, Dr. King may be best remembered for the memorial to him in Washington and for the national holiday honoring his birthday (both of which his widow, Coretta Scott King, sought as appropriate commemorations of Dr. King's epic civil rights leadership).

But for others, he may be best remembered for the extraordinary speech he gave at the March on Washington. In the interview, Branch points out some interesting facts about that speech:

- Dr. King was assigned the final speaking position that day by the organizers. Because of Dr. King's well-known rhetorical skills, the other speakers did not want to follow what they expected would be a barn burner of a speech.
- Dr. King had assistance with writing the speech late into the night before it was given, but he strayed from the prepared text and gave his now iconic "I Have a Dream" remarks extemporaneously. But these were remarks he had previously

given and felt quite comfortable delivering, preacher-style, without notes.

- The next day, newspaper coverage did not really focus on Dr. King's remarks, now so well known (a situation that reminds one of the next-day coverage of Lincoln's Gettysburg Address).
- President Kennedy chose not to speak at the march. The federal government was worried about violence at the event, and Kennedy did not want to be visibly identified with it and its purpose. But he did greet Dr. King afterward at the White House with the line "I have a dream," signaling his admiration for the speech's rhetoric, if not its substance.

MR. DAVID M. RUBENSTEIN (DR): You spent how many years working on these several thousand pages of books that you wrote on the civil rights movement and Martin Luther King Jr. in particular?

MR. TAYLOR BRANCH (TB): Twenty-four years — 1982 to 2006.

DR: Did you ever think maybe you were giving too much time to this project?

TB: No, I was enthralled. It was supposed to take three years, which was two years longer than any other book I had done. But I knew it was a big topic, and the more I got into it — I didn't want it *never* to end, but I never regretted how long it took.

DR: How many total pages are the three books?

TB: It depends on whether you count the footnotes. But there are 2,200 pages of book and about 700 pages of notes.

DR: After all of the time you spent on this, what would you like to convey to people about the civil rights movement? Could you summarize, in just one or two sentences, the main point you wanted to convey in these 2,200 pages?

TB: That it was the essence of patriotism. It was modern founders doing what the original Founders had done, confronting systems of hierarchy and oppression and moving toward equal citizenship. And in that sense, I think the civil rights movement is still a shining example of patriotism.

DR: Martin Luther King Jr. is not the only person in the books, but he's the main person featured. After all your research, what thing or things most surprised you about him?

TB: The surprises begin with his name and never stop. He wasn't born Martin; he was born Michael. His father went to Germany and saw the birthplace of Martin Luther, and got so carried away with himself that he changed his own name to Martin Luther King and his son's name to Martin Luther King Jr. This embarrassed his son, who was reluctant to use the new name.

Black men, in those days, didn't want to use their first names anyway, because it would allow white people to diminish them by being familiar. So he went by M. L. until the end of the Montgomery bus boycott, when *Time* magazine put him on the cover.

They asked him what his name was, and he said it was M. L. King, and they said, "No, we can't do that." Sheepishly, he said he was Martin Luther King Jr. After that, his revised name was public.

DR: Did you come away respecting him and admiring him more or less after you did the research?

TB: Much more after I did the research. At the beginning I was a fellow Southern Baptist who thought maybe he got carried away by turning the other cheek and stumbled into a historic movement. The longer I studied him, the deeper and more profound for me was his understanding of ecumenical, spiritual, and political movements. He was a much more profound figure than I was prepared to believe at the beginning.

DR: If you could have dinner with him tonight and could ask him one or two questions, what would you like to ask the man that you spent twenty-some years researching?

TB: If I had one question, it may not make much sense to most people. To me, the turning point of his career — and a turning point in American history that pushed the civil rights movement into momentum that lasted — was in Birmingham on May 1, 1963, when the movement was about to fail and he was getting run out of town.

He was under tremendous pressure to let

children march, and *not* to let them march, when adults became too afraid or discouraged to demonstrate anymore. It was the biggest crisis of his life so far, and angry black parents came to him and said, "You are absolutely insane. You are not going to skulk out of here leaving our children with criminal records, spoiling what little chance they have to have a decent life."

He decided to go for broke and to let the children march. On Friday they had 13 adults march, on Saturday they had 600 children march, and on Sunday they had over 1,500 march.

It was "D-Day." The photographs of dogs and fire hoses turned on young children, I think, melted emotional resistance in the United States to the civil rights movement. It was a turning point.

It's amazing to me that there's never been a PhD dissertation analyzing why America turned on the witness of schoolchildren as young as six years old, but it happened, and it was a tremendous risk for him. He had to go in and face those parents and say, "Don't worry about your children."

DR: What would you want to ask him?

TB: I would want to ask him, how did he make that decision? How did he decide to let two thousand small children march into Bull

Connor's jail in early May 1963? Because that was a turning point for American history. [Bull Connor was the commissioner for public safety in Birmingham who led the savage attacks on the marchers.]

DR: Your books feature the period from 1954 to 1968 — a fourteen-year period of time. Between the Thirteenth, Fourteenth, and Fifteenth Amendments after the Civil War — when slavery was outlawed, African Americans could be citizens, and they could have the right to vote — between that time and 1954, virtually no progress was made in civil rights for almost a hundred years. Why, in the fourteen-year period you write about, did so much happen when so little had happened in the one hundred years before?

TB: For a lot of those one hundred years, we were busily misremembering everything that had produced the Thirteenth, Fourteenth, and Fifteenth Amendments. We more or less buried them. They didn't apply the Fifteenth Amendment at all. In retrospect, it's amazing that you had a Fifteenth Amendment there, guaranteeing the right to vote, but black people couldn't vote, and nobody seemed to notice.

Even the Fourteenth Amendment — giving equal citizenship and due process to freedmen, that's what it was for — was nullified within ten years by the Supreme Court. Thereafter, those rights really applied more to corporations than they did to African Americans.

American history can go backwards in race relations, and we were doing that busily. What turned us was in part World War II, in part the Depression, and in part ceaseless agitation that finally confronted, in the 1950s, how we could live up to the ideology that we had extolled when we were fighting Hitler and Japan.

DR: In 1954, we had the Supreme Court's unanimous decision in *Brown v. Board of Education,* ruling that school segregation was unconstitutional. Was it a shock to the country that the decision went that way and that it was unanimous?

TB: It was absolutely a shock that nine white men would say that the central institution of southern segregation violated the Constitution. Everybody was in shock, including a lot of black people who said, "This is a hallelujah day," but then in the next breath said, "What's going to happen to our black schools and our black principals? Are they all going to get fired?"

DR: When the decision came down, the Supreme Court said that with all deliberate

478

speed we should implement this, but things didn't happen that quickly. Why was it in Little Rock, Arkansas, that there was a confrontation, and did Eisenhower really want to send troops into Little Rock? I thought he was not really in favor of that decision.

TB: He wasn't so much in favor of the decision. But the more I have studied it, the more I give Eisenhower credit, because once he decided that the honor and the legality of the federal government was at stake in enforcing the court's orders against open resistance by the state powers, he said, "I want to do this effectively," and he sent in paratroopers.

He sent in the 101st Airborne. He said, "If I'm going to intervene militarily, I want to do it decisively." And he did.

DR: Why Little Rock and not some other city?

TB: Little Rock had two things. It had a committed small group of children willing to take upon themselves the burden of being guinea pigs to march into this very large school. They had a lot of support in the local NAACP, and they had a state governor who was very ambitious — not particularly a segregationist, but when push came to shove, he felt that he had to stand up against the federal government and against the power of the courts. He got himself trapped so that he had his state troopers and his National Guard preventing the children from entering.

It was unlike anything since the Civil War. You had the powers of the state resisting the powers of the federal government over the issue of race.

DR: In 1955, Rosa Parks refused to give up her seat to somebody who was white and move to the back of the bus in Montgomery, Alabama. Was that the first time that had ever happened in the South?

TB: No. A large handful of people were arrested for violating the segregation laws for one reason or another. Many of them were not considered suitable to become a test case because the people involved were drunk, or pregnant out of wedlock, or didn't have an exemplary record.

Rosa Parks was respected by everybody. She was a unique person in that she was a seamstress who spoke perfect English and was the secretary of the NAACP, so that middle-class black folks respected her, and the working-class black folks respected her because she never looked down on them. She had this cross-class admiration, so that when it happened to her, people said, "It happened to Rosa, so we've got to stand up for her."

DR: When she was arrested, there were protests. How did Martin Luther King Jr. get in the middle of this? He was a preacher in that city then, but he was not that heavily involved in civil rights before that, was he?

TB: No. He was fresh out of grad school, and he had just come to Montgomery. He was a brand-new preacher in town, and that's arguably the reason that he became the leader of the bus boycott. All the established preachers thought it was a ticket to get run out of town, a ticket to certain failure. So they voted him in to head the bus boycott that many felt was going to go down the tubes.

Fortunately, some blessed person recorded the speech he gave on the first night of the bus boycott, December 5, 1955. I spent a week trying to capture the dynamics in his first public address, talking about what the bus boycott meant.

It was full of theology but also full of the Constitution, and what it meant to protest, and why they should protest, and how much discipline it took to protest, and how they were going to make each other proud and stand together.

He was fishing around for an applause line, and finally he said, "There comes a time when people get tired of being trampled over by the iron feet of oppression." He went on to the next line, and then all of a sudden in

481

the tape you can hear the thunder of applause come rolling through. He gets the rhythm of that, and you can see the public person being born in that speech.

DR: Did he want to be a preacher? When he was growing up, his father was a preacher in Atlanta. Did Martin Luther King Jr. say, "I want to be like my father"?

TB: No. He said he wanted to be *unlike* his father, because his father was bombastic and selfish and wanted to drive a big car. King always used to say that in the black South of that era, if you were an idealist you wanted to be a lawyer, and if you wanted to be rich you wanted to be a preacher, which was the reverse of white culture.

So it was a big struggle for him to want to become a preacher. He knew he had been groomed for it and that he loved speaking, but for a long time he wanted to be a lawyer, and it was hard for him to reconcile himself to idealism in the ministry for which he was born.

DR: What was the outcome of the Montgomery bus boycott?

TB: The outcome was that those people who loved Rosa Parks marched for a year and proved that they could do it and made an enormous and inspirational story, but the Supreme Court basically ordered bus segregation to end. It didn't have that much effect on bus segregation elsewhere. Nothing was ever solved all at once.

But it did become a victory. And it became a victory that the NAACP associated with a legal strategy and winning a court case, and that King associated with people standing up for their rights to make them real, because if you don't stand up for those rights, it doesn't matter what the court says.

DR: Not too long after the bus boycott, there was a sit-in at a Woolworth's counter in Greensboro, North Carolina. What was that about?

TB: That was a spontaneous protest by students who were frustrated that, six years after the Brown decision, not much had changed. Segregation was still there, and the blacks-only and whites-only signs were still everywhere.

The students went and sat down at the whites-only lunch counter and were amazed that they weren't arrested. So they decided to do it again the next day, and it spread. It spread like wildfire, so that ten weeks later, students from all over the South came to form a student coordinating committee because there were protests going on in so many different places.

Now, King became important then because he was the only adult civil rights leader who instantly said, "This is a breakthrough, because these students have found a way to amplify their words with sacrifice. They're willing to go to jail. You can't boycott someplace that won't let you in."

King, coincidentally, had been frustrated in the late 1950s because he thought he could preach America out of segregation, like Billy Graham. He traveled hundreds of thousands of miles doing it and failed. He was the first one to say, "This is a breakthrough. My words aren't enough. I'm a gifted preacher, but if you're going to be a citizen, you've got to be willing to make sacrifices and go beyond just telling everybody what to do."

DR: There were hundreds of these sit-ins. John Lewis, the future congressman, was involved in one in Nashville, Tennessee. What happened there?

TB: John Lewis is famous for saying, "We're going to march through the Yellow Pages of Nashville," because they would march against the theaters, which were segregated, the lunch counters, the hotels, everywhere. Even the airport. They went everywhere that was segregated, and they had a lot of victories.

The message was that every city in the

South needed to have sit-ins, because there were no public officials who were openly against the segregation laws. You pretty much couldn't get elected if you opposed those laws, and so the civil rights protestors marched and marched and marched.

Meanwhile, the people defending segregation mobilized, to the point that King said, in 1962, "The defenders of segregation are mobilizing more rapidly than these isolated movements that I keep getting called to like a fireman for support. We're losing our moment, our window in history, if we don't establish a foothold pretty quick."

That's why he went to Birmingham and made his supreme gamble there: "We have to make a breakthrough. I have to risk more."

DR: The segregation that existed in housing and elsewhere — was that only in the South? What about the nation's capital? What about the North?

TB: There was segregation everywhere. There were segregation laws in the South, but there were segregation policies everywhere. America's neighborhoods were segregated as a result. We like to tell ourselves that it's all the result of private decisions, but it's Federal Housing Administration loans, it's bank loans, it's government policy, city after city, in decisions that determine where the highways go, where the public housing is built, and those patterns. We're still living with decisions that were made at every level of government in every region of the country a long time ago.

DR: King came up with a theory that his supporters should use nonviolent response. Why was that so novel? Where did he get that idea from?

TB: At the beginning, I thought it was from Jesus. After all, that's what Jesus says: "Turn the other cheek, resist not evil." The cross is the ultimate symbol of nonviolence.

DR: Was King influenced by Mahatma Gandhi?

TB: He was influenced by Gandhi, but then he went over to India in 1959 to study the Gandhians and came back saying, "They fast all the time. We can never do that in America. Those Indians haven't eaten barbecue." Jawaharlal Nehru, the preeminent nonviolent Gandhian, is building nuclear bombs in India, and other Gandhians are fighting over whether they should step on insects, or do this, that, or the other.

He said, "We need our own nonviolence in the United States for black people, because we're a tiny minority and the only thing we have is our faith and our commitment to democratic principles." Then he said, "Most Americans think nonviolence is exotic and strange, but American democracy is built on votes, and a vote is nothing but a piece of nonviolence. So if you believe in democracy, you believe in nonviolence, whether you know it or not."

DR: Was nonviolence a very popular approach at the time?

TB: No. It was not popular. First of all, it was scary, because it meant you're willing to accept violence.

But King said, after the Freedom Rides of 1961, "If you look at the basis of American democracy after the Revolution, it was self-government — Madison said all our political experiments rest on the capacity of mankind for self-government — and public trust. Without virtue in the people, no form of government can secure liberty."

King said, "Nobody exemplifies that better than a disciplined Freedom Rider looking at somebody who's about to hit him in the face, and saying, 'We may not make a connection, but our children will, because of what we're doing here today.'"

King thought that this kind of nonviolence was the essence of patriotism in the American tradition from the Revolution forward, and that our successes are the advances of non-violence to make votes count, and that we take them too much for granted and get seduced into measuring democracy by lapses into violence.

DR: At the time all this was going on, King was a rising leader in the African American community. Who were the established leaders? What did they think of him? Did they think he was somebody they didn't have to pay attention to? At what point did they realize that he was one of them?

TB: Some of them never realized he was. Black critics said they were like crabs in a barrel, some of these leaders — that when there's not a lot of prestige and money to go around, you squabble over it harder.

Thurgood Marshall called King "a man on a boy's errand" who didn't understand the law. Roy Wilkins of the NAACP thought that King was trying to steal his members. Whitney Young Jr. of the National Urban League admired King, but his constituency and business were so different. And James Farmer Jr. thought that King was stealing his thunder in nonviolence, because Farmer was more of an overt Gandhian, whereas King was saying, "I respect Gandhi, but we have to develop our own form of nonviolence." [Farmer was a main organizer of the Freedom Rides of

Freedom Riders outside a burning bus, May 14, 1961.

1961, in which activists defied segregation on interstate buses.]

So there were a lot of different factions. Then there were these students whom King supported and said had made these breakthroughs, but they resented him later because he got all the publicity. They felt that they were the shock troops and they were always going to jail, but the reporters only wanted to talk to Martin Luther King Jr. And that made some of those students revolt against him.

DR: There was a Student Nonviolent Coordinating Committee. Who headed that?

TB: John Lewis headed it for a while. Marion Barry headed it for a while. Stokely Car-michael took it over from John Lewis in the summer of 1966 and instantly launched Black Power. But by that time, the Student Nonviolent Coordinating Committee was no longer students, not so nonviolent, didn't coordinate much, and wasn't much of a committee. Stokely became kind of a shooting star.

DR: Going back to 1960 and the presidential election that year — King is put in jail in Atlanta. Republican presidential nominee Richard Nixon doesn't call him or call Coretta Scott King, but John F. Kennedy does. Why and how did that call occur, and why was Robert Kennedy upset about it?

TB: Robert Kennedy was upset about it because he thought that the staff aides, Harris Wofford and Sargent Shriver, who tricked Jack Kennedy into making this quick courtesy call from the Chicago airport, had lost the election. The Kennedy campaign was utterly dependent on the solid South of segregationist Democrats. If Kennedy associated himself with a black leader, Democrats feared that Nixon was going to make inroads in the South. So Bobby Kennedy was furious.

Then, typically, he felt guilty about being furious. Kennedy wondered how in the world a court of law could put King on the chain gang, for four months, for not getting his driver's license transferred from Alabama to Georgia quickly enough. When Kennedy's aides told him, "Democrats run everything down there, they can do whatever they want," he felt bad and called the judge. So Robert Kennedy's education on race went round and round.

But the fact of the matter is that Daddy King [Martin Luther King Sr.] and most of his generation were all Republicans in 1960. This was the party of Lincoln. Black people voted Republican. Democrats had been the party of solid South segregation for a hundred years. It was a different world than the one we live in.

DR: Kennedy wins the election in 1960. Does he say, "I want to propose civil rights legislation right away"?

TB: He said he wanted to change some of the federal laws and regulatory practices that fostered segregation in housing. The FHA would not approve any integration in FHA-supported housing development.

Kennedy promised that he could change that with the stroke of a pen. Two years later, civil rights activists mailed him thousands of pens, saying, "Here's a pen. Sign."

It was easy to say he was going to do it, but he was always nervous about what the effect was going to be in the South. He didn't think he could get reelected if he lost any more southern states.

DR: The March on Washington occurred in August of 1963. Why did John Kennedy not speak at it? Was it controversial to have the march? What was the big fear about it?

TB: The march occurred after those kids that I mentioned marched in Birmingham in May of '63. Because that event broke emotional resistance, demonstrations spread. There were seven hundred demonstrations in a hundred-something cities within the next few weeks. It was that firestorm that made King call a march on Washington.

Kennedy was not ready to introduce legislation, and the standing presumption was that a black march for freedom in the nation's capital in 1963 would inevitably produce a bloodbath. The Pentagon stationed paratroopers all around Washington. Public employees were sent home. The city canceled liquor sales. Hospitals stockpiled plasma. Major League Baseball canceled two Washington Senators baseball games, the day of the march and also the day after, in advance, because they assumed we would be cleaning up from violent disorder.

So it was a terrifying event. No aide would recommend that the president go to such an event if that's what people were expecting.

One reason that it has such a sunny reputation now, the March on Washington — " 'I have a dream,' this is nice, who could be against that?" — was the stark relief from what people publicly expected.

DR: King was the final major speaker there. Why was he last?

TB: Nobody wanted to go after him. With good reason.

He was a really accomplished speaker. He was great at reading an audience, a skill he used at the march, because the famous parts of his speech were extemporaneous. They weren't what he wrote. He went off on a riff like a good jazz musician, which is what Baptist preachers were.

A lot of people think that he stayed up all night and wrote a really great speech, but he discarded his written text in the middle of delivering it and went off on two or three of his familiar riffs: "With this faith." "Let freedom ring." "I have a dream."

DR: That speech was one that he had given before. White people had not heard it, but many black people who were there had heard it before, is that right?

TB: Black people in the audience probably hadn't heard it, but those who traveled with

Dr. Martin Luther King Jr. delivers his "I Have a Dream" speech at the Lincoln Memorial during the March on Washington, August 28, 1963.

him had heard it. Crowds had heard it in Chicago and Detroit not that long before, or at least themes from it. Riffs — we call them riffs.

DR: After the march, the leaders went to the White House. What did President Kennedy say to Dr. King?

TB: He said, "I have a dream." Kennedy recognized a good line. He kind of teased him.

DR: Did the speech instantly become famous? Did it make the front page of the *New York Times* and the *Washington Post* the next day?

TB: The press reaction mostly was astonishment that there wasn't any bloodbath. The *Washington Post* didn't have many stories at all. The *New York Times* had seven stories on the front page about what a phenomenon the march was, but it didn't isolate the speech initially as a great thing, in part because it was so late, they probably had their deadlines coming up and wrote other stuff.

DR: J. Edgar Hoover, the director of the FBI, didn't seem to like King. How did he persuade President Kennedy and Robert Kennedy to let him wiretap him?

TB: That is still a historical conundrum. I wish more historians were writing about it.

Hoover asked Bobby Kennedy to wiretap King in the summer of '63, right after Birmingham, when all the demonstrations were going on. Kennedy turned him down. After that, King gave the "I Have a Dream" speech and the administration submitted its civil rights bill, with King as a prime supporter, so they kind of married each other in politics. Yet Kennedy approved the wiretap afterwards, in the fall of 1963. He was under tremendous pressure.

It's one of the great wrestling matches in American history, why he approved that. Bobby Kennedy knew he was handing his rear end to J. Edgar Hoover by putting his signature on that document. Hoover would have that secret over him for the rest of his life.

DR: Did John Kennedy get the results of the wiretaps? Did he ever talk to King about it?

TB: He didn't talk to King about the wiretaps. He wouldn't have disclosed that he had them.

But even before the wiretaps, Kennedy felt so exposed politically when he had to submit that civil rights bill in the summer of '63 after Birmingham and all those demonstrations. JFK said, "We can't fight all these fires one by one. We've got to put a bill out there to stop them."

He had King to the White House in June of 1963 because he felt that he needed to control him. He took him out into the Rose Garden for privacy, astonishing King.

It seemed to King that President Kennedy thought Hoover was bugging the Oval Office. Kennedy took him outside to escape it and whispered, "They're after you. If they shoot you down, they'll shoot me down too. We have to be really careful. You've got to get rid of some of your supporters because they're Communists."

Kennedy named some, and King said he was astonished. He kept saying, "What's the evidence? I love these people. They're volunteers. They don't work for me." He said, "I don't believe in shunning people."

They went round and round. King went home and put this case before his aides, Harry Belafonte, and a bunch of others. Some of them said, "This is how a witch hunt starts." Some of them said, "Is this the price of the civil rights bill?" It's that kind of politics going on behind the scenes.

DR: Kennedy is assassinated a few months later, in November of '63. Lyndon Johnson becomes president. He pushes Kennedy's legislation through. Why did a southern senator, a senator from Texas, who had been so close to the segregationists in the Senate, push civil rights legislation, and how did he get that through?

TB: For one thing, the death of President Kennedy had a cathartic effect on the whole country. People thought hatred and division had something to do with it, and the civil rights bill was about addressing and trying to overcome hatred, so that helped.

But Johnson doesn't get enough credit for his inner drive, and what he really wanted to do as president, and where he came from in life. To me, the biggest proof of that is that within a month of passing the Voting Rights Act, he passed the Immigration and Nationality Act of '65, which opened legal immigration to the whole world that had been previously excluded.

He said, "Never again will freedom's gate be shadowed by the twin barriers of prejudice and privilege." I think he was speaking from his heart there, and he risked a lot for the civil rights legislation.

DR: The Voting Rights Act came about in part, I assume, because of the 1965 marches in Selma and other places. Can you describe what the Selma march was about and why voting rights had not really spread to the South? How many black voters were there in some of the southern states and southern congressional districts?

TB: Practically none. The march from Selma to Montgomery went through Lowndes County. No black person was known to have tried to register to vote there in the entire twentieth century into 1965, even though Lowndes County was 70 percent black. It was almost medieval.

The Fifteenth Amendment said everybody should have the right to vote, that it should not be abridged on account of race, but we had turned a blind eye to that for a century. It took these marches to wake people up to that fact. In a way, this was the crescendo of a movement that had been building for a long time.

The events of Bloody Sunday — March 7,

1965, when the marchers were attacked, those famous pictures of John Lewis being beaten on the bridge — occurred on a Sunday morning, and it was not until that night that footage of it made television. In those days you had to take your film, run to an airport, get on a prop plane, fly to New York, get the film developed, take it in, and figure out how to put it on the air. It went on that night.

King sent out a telegram that same night, Sunday night, saying to all of his contacts in the church mostly, "Come to Selma." He didn't say, "Discuss this at your next meeting," or "Vote for a new candidate," or "Ask Congress to do something." He said, "Please come to Selma to march with me on Tuesday from the same spot where these people were beaten."

On Tuesday, there were a thousand people — nuns and priests and everybody, from all over the country — who figured out, before Expedia, how to get there in less than thirty-six hours. It was a stunning mobilization.

DR: During the march, he gets to the end of the bridge and the troopers say, "Go ahead." Why did he turn around?

TB: That's one of the great studies in politics. The federal court had ordered him not to march until they could hold a hearing on whose fault it was that there had been beatings in the first place. John Doar, an assistant attorney general trusted by the civil rights leaders, went down and told Dr. King, "You've never defied the federal courts. You can't afford to do it now because it'll throw us against you."

King was negotiating at the same time with members of Congress about whether they would introduce a voting rights bill. He's secretly negotiating also with Alabama governor George Wallace's people about what they're going to do, thinking that they may be laying a trap by asking him to march and defy the federal court order and then get out into Lowndes County where the Ku Klux Klan is very strong. Nobody thought they would march more than five miles.

He was battered by some people saying, "This is a breakthrough. We can march right through there. You're a coward if you don't march," and by other people saying, "You're a fool if you do." It was a very, very critical moment.

In that moment, Dr. King decided to put his faith in the promise of the federal government to deliver a voting rights act. He said, "We are half-marching. We're keeping the movement going, but we're turning around. Let's go back to the church. We're not willing to defy this federal order."

As Johnson later told him, "It's the best thing that ever happened in American his-

President Lyndon B. Johnson hands Dr. King the pen he used to sign the Voting Rights Act of 1965.

tory. You mobilized that public opinion that allowed me to go before the joint session of Congress and propose the voting rights bill. That's the way it's supposed to work: active citizens and responsive government."

DR: King won the Nobel Peace Prize in 1964. Was he surprised? And was it controversial in the United States at the time that he won?

TB: It was controversial to J. Edgar Hoover, who said that he was the most notorious liar in the country, and that they really had to drag the bottom of the barrel for that prize.

But of course, Hoover was a unique person.

He thought that *he* should get the Nobel Peace Prize

It was a surprise, but it went over pretty well. It marked a turning point for King, because he had been trying to build the influence of his movement. He gets to a pinnacle in Oslo, and Andy Young says, "We're going to celebrate this for ten years. We've finally gotten an antisegregation bill through, and you've got the Nobel Prize."

King says, "No. We're going to Selma. Not next year but next week." And within a month he's in jail in Selma.

He had been very reluctant to take personal risk. He resisted being in the sit-ins of 1960. He didn't go on the Freedom Rides in 1961. He resisted the kind of sacrifice that the students were making. But from the Nobel Prize on, he dragged his staff to Selma, then he dragged them north, saying, "We have to prove that the race issue is not now and never has been purely a southern issue."

DR: He said, "I care about poverty as well as racism, and there's poverty in the North," and he went to Chicago. Why did he pick Chicago?

TB: He knew Chicago pretty well. It was kind of the center of black culture in the North. But he also went to Boston. He tried out six cities as the best laboratory to demonstrate

Lives on the line: Dr. King displays a photo of three murdered civil rights activists, December 4, 1964.

that there was racial conflict and ghettoization in northern cities.

He went to Boston, he went to Rochester, he went to Philadelphia, and he went to Cleveland, in addition to Chicago. Ultimately he picked Chicago, and was subjected to what he said was the worst violence that he ever saw in trying to march for integrated housing in Chicago.

But he said, "At least we proved two things. We proved that there's a lot of racial feeling in the North, and we also proved that the northern press will not cover civil rights demonstrations as sympathetically in Chicago as they did in Selma." The press turned on him. He said, "That's a price we will willingly pay."

DR: Later, in 1968, he gets involved in a sanitation workers' dispute in Memphis. Why did he get in the middle of that?

TB: By that time, he was in his poor people's campaign. The end of King's career is a series of witnesses — bearing witness to things that he knew he had already lost the momentum to change in his lifetime. He came out against the Vietnam War very publicly.

Then he said he wanted to leave behind a witness on poverty — that the government could be a positive force to relieve poverty. His model, believe it or not, was the Bonus Army marchers of World War I, who came to Washington in 1932 during the Great Depression and got run out of town. [Many of the marchers were desperate out-of-work veterans who wanted the government to redeem bonus certificates it had issued for their wartime service.]

That was part of the gestation of the G.I. Bill. King said, "If we come to Washington, we'll be run out of town too, but maybe the equivalent of the G.I. Bill will come out of this in the future." That's what he was doing.

Memphis laws at that time did not allow sanitation workers, all of whom were black, to seek shelter during rainstorms, because it offended the white residents. During a particularly terrible storm, the "tub men," the ones who carried the tubs of garbage, wouldn't fit in the cab of one truck, and two of them had to get in the back, and their broom hit the compact lever and they were compacted with the garbage.

That precipitated the strike in February of 1968. When you see these signs that say, "I am a man," that's the origin of that slogan. It was not just "I am a man." It means "I am a man, not a piece of garbage to be compacted in the back of this garbage truck because we can't seek shelter and we have no rights."

King felt that he couldn't resist that. He went to support those people, and that's what he was doing when he was killed.

DR: Do you have any doubt that James Earl Ray killed Martin Luther King Jr. alone?

TB: No. It's virtually certain that he had aides and accomplices, but more or less at his own level, which was a petty-criminal truck-stop type thing. Not SMERSH, or a helicopter company from Texas, or Russians, and God knows who else fits in a conspiracy theory.

I don't believe in the conspiracy theories, and neither did King when he was alive. He said, "Conspiracy theories are belief in the devil, and they relieve people from the obligation of confronting the problem as it is."

DR: King was almost stabbed to death in 1958 in Harlem. Had the knife gone a half inch another way, he would have been dead. Had he been killed, would the civil rights movement have occurred much differently? How would history be different had he not lived in the sixties?

TB: Wow. You are really tough. The civil rights movement would have been different. It was percolating, and there would have been more protests. But King was the effective public voice.

The best way I know to talk about how he did it was that he consistently put one foot in the Scriptures and one foot in the Constitution and the Declaration of Independence, in a balanced way that invited people to understand the mission for equal citizenship, either in secular terms or spiritual terms. They could take their choice. He didn't try to subdue one with the other. It was the gift of his rhetoric that made it seem both religiously and spiritually inspiring, and patriotic in a way that people couldn't resist.

It's that patriotism that we've really lost today. It made him a leader for all of us, not just for black people trying to get rights about quaint things that no longer apply. It's about the future, not about the past.

13
Robert A. Caro
ON LYNDON B. JOHNSON

"I never had the slightest interest in writing a book just to tell the story of a famous man. I was interested in political power."

BOOKS DISCUSSED:
The Power Broker: Robert Moses and the Fall of New York (Knopf, 1974)

The Years of Lyndon Johnson, Volumes 1 to 4
The Path to Power (Knopf, 1982)
Means of Ascent (Knopf, 1990)
Master of the Senate (Knopf, 2002)
The Passage of Power (Knopf, 2012)

Robert Caro is as legendary and respected a biographer as is alive today — and not just because of his epic, Pulitzer Prize–winning biography of Robert Moses, *The Power Broker.* That biography, the result of seven years of research and writing, was so detailed, dramatic, and interesting in its description of the unelected official who built much of New York's infrastructure during the 1950s and 1960s that *Time* magazine named it one of the one hundred best nonfiction books ever written.

It might fairly be asked how one could top that achievement. Some authors (e.g., Margaret Mitchell, Ralph Ellison, and Harper Lee) published first books that made such an impact that they found it almost impossible to publish a second book.

Fortunately, that was not the case with Robert Caro. After *The Power Broker,* Caro embarked on a mission, now forty-five years in the making, to produce the definitive biography of President Lyndon B. Johnson.

To date, four volumes have been researched, written, and published — all by an author who does his own painstaking research, along with his wife and longtime research partner, Ina Caro; and who writes on a no-longer-manufactured (and thus difficult to repair) Smith-Corona typewriter. These four volumes — *The Path to Power, Means of Ascent, Master of the Senate,* and *The Passage of Power* — have each received awards (including a Pulitzer Prize for *Master of the Senate*) and highly favorable critical commentary.

In our interview, Robert Caro discusses why he became interested in Robert Moses and, later, in Lyndon Johnson. Both were studies in how to obtain, consolidate, and use power. For Moses, it was local power. Caro, in seeking his next subject, wanted to see how power was mastered at a national level. Little did he realize at the outset that mastering Lyndon B. Johnson would take more than four decades.

Caro describes in the interview a young Johnson interested in power almost for power's sake. He got elected to the House of Representatives and quickly became a protégé of the Speaker of the House, Sam Rayburn, and, to some extent, a favored congressional supporter of the president of the United States, Franklin D. Roosevelt.

That his mentors' views were somewhat different did not bother Johnson. They had power, and some of it could rub off on him.

When he was elected to the Senate in 1948

by 87 votes (made possible, Caro points out, by getting 200 of 202 votes in one precinct where the voters apparently voted in alphabetical order), he quickly figured out that the power there was held by Senator Richard Russell. So Johnson quickly became Russell's protégé and best friend, despite Russell's ardent segregationist views.

Within six years of becoming a senator, Johnson became the Senate majority leader — an unrivaled ascent in the modern era. And he became the most powerful majority leader in anyone's memory.

The only way for him to get more power, Caro relates, was to become president. Johnson thought this would happen in 1960, for his rival for the Democratic nomination was an often absent, frequently ill, and ineffective figure in the Senate — John F. Kennedy.

But, as Caro notes, Kennedy did master the nomination process, and Johnson had to settle for the vice-presidential nomination. Although his Texas base helped Kennedy to hold the South in 1960, Johnson became a vice president with little to do and with far less power than he had wielded in decades.

That changed, of course, when he became president and once again had real power. Johnson was back in his element, often subjecting those from whom he needed something to the famous "Johnson treatment."

Despite the humiliations he suffered during the Kennedy presidency, Johnson resolved to use his power to push the Kennedy agenda through Congress. He succeeded in doing so most visibly with the civil rights legislation that seemed so inimical to Johnson's roots and to the views of his closest supporters in the Senate.

Caro observes that Johnson did not just do this to honor the Kennedy legacy — though that was a factor — but because he had resolved as a young man that if he ever had the power to help the poor and disenfranchised, he would do so. "What is the point of having power if one does not use it?" Johnson would regularly say to his closest advisors.

In the interview, Caro did not discuss Vietnam very much, for he had not yet finished the volume dealing with the subject that ultimately drove Johnson from office and damaged his legacy as president. Caro's definitive conclusion about Johnson and about Vietnam will presumably come in the long-awaited fifth volume.

Caro is now researching and writing that volume, presumably the final book in this epic series on our thirty-sixth president. The publication date has not been announced, but Caro is now eighty-three, and intent on publishing this much-anticipated work on the

Johnson presidency in the near future. (To the surprise of many hoping that he would complete the fifth volume soon, he published a different book this year — *Working: Researching, Interviewing, Writing,* an informal memoir. He expects to write a full memoir at some point.)

The difficulty in interviewing Robert Caro is trying to get him to distill forty years of work in about forty-five minutes. That was the mission when I interviewed him on November 3, 2015.

Caro clearly has an uncommon command of the details of his subject's life, and that comes through in the interview. What also comes through is the biographer's admiration for Johnson's highly developed political and legislative skills, though he fully recognizes that Johnson was not without his flaws and failings.

What does not come through is the respect, indeed awe, that the members of Congress who attended the interview have for Robert Caro. That was evident from the number who brought their dog-eared copies of his books in order to get them autographed. None of them knew Johnson, but all of them were familiar with (and admiring of) the kinds of legislative skills that he used to work his way in Congress.

Unlike many of the authors interviewed for the Dialogues, I really did not know Robert

Caro well beforehand. But like the members, I greatly admired and had read all of his books. I particularly admired his commitment to mastering details through laborious, first-person research, and his persistence in writing without the aid of modern technology.

MR. DAVID M. RUBENSTEIN (DR): When you decided you wanted to do a book on Robert Moses, did your publisher say, "That's going to be a great-selling book"?

MR. ROBERT CARO (RC): My publisher said, "Nobody's going to read a book on Robert Moses."

DR: It's still in print forty-five years later. Did you know instantly after Robert Moses that you wanted to do Lyndon Johnson?

RC: I never thought really that I was doing a biography of Robert Moses. I never had the slightest interest in writing a book just to tell the story of a famous man. I was interested in political power. And I looked at *The Power Broker* as being about a man who was never elected to anything.

In a democracy, of course, we think power comes from the ballot box, from being elected. Yet Robert Moses had more power than anyone who was elected — more than any mayor or any governor, more than really any mayor and governor combined. And he had it for forty-four years.

I wrote that book to try to figure out and explain how he got that power, what the power was. After that, I wanted to do national power, so I wanted to pick Lyndon Johnson.

DR: When you started on Lyndon Johnson, did you expect to spend thirty-nine years of your life so far on it?

RC: No.

DR: And did you expect initially it would be one volume?

RC: I wanted it to be three volumes. The reason is that, as long as *The Power Broker* is, the book as you read it is 700,000 words. The finished manuscript that I wrote — not a rough draft, but the finished book — was 1,050,000. I had to cut out one-third of the book. A lot of stuff was cut out that I've always regretted. When my publisher wanted me to do a book on Lyndon Johnson, I said, "I'll only do it if I can do it in volumes."

DR: Now that you've spent thirty-nine years so far on Lyndon Johnson, do you admire him more than you did before, or do you admire him less than you did before?

RC: When I think about Lyndon Johnson, I don't think in terms of "admire," or liking or disliking. I'm sort of in awe of him.

Because the books are really about political power. So when you see Johnson, how he gets political power and how he uses it in the House of Representatives and the Senate, even before he becomes president, you're just in awe of him. Over and over again, you say to yourself, "Look what he's doing now."

DR: You never met Lyndon Johnson, is that correct?

RC: I shook his hand once when I was in the press corps.

DR: If you had a chance to have dinner with him, what one or two questions would you actually ask him after now spending forty years of your life reading about him?

RC: "What I really want to know is [what] you felt, President Johnson, when your father failed."

His father, Texas businessman and rancher Samuel Ealy Johnson Jr., was his idol. He was a member of the Texas House of Representatives and a very successful politician. Then he made one mistake financially and became the laughingstock of the Hill Country. And Lyndon Johnson's life changed with that. The rest of their life they were very poor.

DR: You write these books on an old Smith-Corona typewriter. Since there are no more Smith-Corona typewriter manufacturers anymore, what happens when your typewriter breaks down?

RC: I try to collect as many typewriters as I can because if a key breaks or something, they don't make spare parts anymore, so you have to cannibalize another typewriter.

Whenever a book of mine comes out, profiles on me all mention that I use this Smith-Corona Electra 210, so people write me letters and say, "I have one in my garage. I'd like you to have it. I'm sending it to you." Some of them write me letters and say, "I have one in my garage. I'll sell it to you for $14,000."

DR: Let's go back to Lyndon Johnson's beginnings. He came from a family that had some prominence, but they lost their money. Was it clear as a young man he wanted to run for Congress or get involved in politics?

RC: He would follow his father around campaigning. He would stand in the back of the Texas State Capitol in the House of Representatives and watch his father. When his father would finish for the day, Lyndon never wanted to go home. What he wanted to do was watch how the Texas House worked.

DR: He runs for Congress in 1937, and he gets elected. So he goes to the House. How does he become so close to Sam Rayburn, then the forty-third Speaker of the U.S. House of Representatives, and also so close to President Franklin D. Roosevelt as a freshman congressman?

RC: Lyndon Johnson always had an instinct for power.

We can't even imagine today someone like Sam Rayburn. He once lost a vote that he was interested in, and he simply said, "We'll have another vote tomorrow." He called twenty freshmen representatives to his office and said, "You will all vote for this bill tomorrow." They all voted for it.

If someone rose and said, "Point of order, Mr. Speaker," he would say, "I'm not interested in the point of order."

Sam Rayburn was a fascinating figure. He was a very feared figure. He was a huge, massive man, with a tremendous bald head — very fierce, never smiled. He believed that he was socially inept. He once said, "I went to a party once and I tried to make a joke and I was the joke." So he wouldn't visit people.

Lyndon Johnson comes to Washington, and Rayburn had served in the Texas House with his father. Using that as an excuse, Lyndon Johnson invites Rayburn to dinner. Rayburn goes once. But — this was his fashion — he would never go again to someone's house.

But he took pity on LBJ's wife, Lady Bird Johnson. Sam Rayburn was a very shy man, and he saw in Lady Bird a very young woman who was as shy as he was. So when the

Johnsons would invite him back, he would come. Lady Bird took to making his favorite foods — homemade peach ice cream, very hot Texas chili — and Rayburn started to come every Sunday to Lyndon Johnson's home.

Lyndon Johnson develops pneumonia in 1938, his second year in Washington, and he's really quite ill. Rayburn comes to the hospital and sits all night in a straight-backed chair next to Johnson's bed.

When Johnson wakes up in the morning, he sees that Rayburn was so afraid that he would move and disturb him when he was sleeping that his vest is covered with cigarette ashes from the cigarettes he had smoked during the night, because he didn't want to get up to brush it off. Johnson wakes up and Rayburn, who's never shown any emotion for him at all, leans over him and says, as Johnson recalls, "Lyndon, never worry about anything. If you need anything, call on me." That was the start of Lyndon Johnson's rise in the House.

DR: They're both from Texas. I can see some maybe simpatico feelings. Why would FDR have been close to Lyndon Johnson?

RC: James H. Rowe — a name which I'm afraid is getting forgotten in Washington — was a very close advisor to both Franklin

Roosevelt and Lyndon Johnson. I asked him the very question you asked me.

He said, "You know, Franklin Roosevelt was a political genius. Most people didn't understand what he was talking about when he started to talk to them about government and politics. But he saw that Lyndon Johnson understood it all from the beginning." These were two political geniuses.

DR: When World War II breaks out, Lyndon Johnson says he wants to go in. [A lieutenant commander in the U.S. Naval Reserve, LBJ signed up for active duty immediately after Pearl Harbor and was stationed in Australia and New Zealand until July 1942.] How did he manage to stay in the House of Representatives while he was in the military?

RC: Well, at that time, congressmen could stay in the House and serve in the military. That's the easiest answer.

When he's out in Australia, the senior senator from Texas dies — a man named Morris Sheppard. It's 1942. Johnson has to decide whether to run again for the House of Representatives or whether to run for the Senate. And President Roosevelt has told him that he can call the White House if he needs any help with anything.

We know what Johnson decides. He decides to stay in the House.

Lyndon B. Johnson (right), shown shaking hands with President Franklin D. Roosevelt, circa 1936–37, shared the older man's political acumen.

DR: He finally decides to run for the Senate in 1948. Why is he called Landslide Lyndon after the '48 election?

RC: Six days after the election, he's still behind the governor of Texas, Coke Stevenson. And suddenly another ballot box is found, a ballot box for Precinct 13. They open it and, if I remember this correctly, two hundred ballots were cast for Johnson. They were all cast by someone using the same handwriting and the same pen, and these people actually voted in alphabetical order.

DR: Technically, he won by how many votes?

521

RC: Eighty-seven votes.

DR: Eighty-seven votes. So he comes to Washington and he becomes a senator. How does he get so close to Richard Russell? [Richard Russell Jr. was a conservative Democratic senator from Georgia who served from 1933 to 1971.]

RC: He gets close to Russell in sort of the same way he got close to Rayburn. Russell and Rayburn shared a number of characteristics. They were both bachelors. They were both lonely men.

When Johnson is elected to the Senate, the first interview he has is with the secretary of the Senate then, Bobby Baker. Baker said, "All the young senators came to me and they would ask, 'What's the best committee to be on? What's the best place to have an office?' Lyndon Johnson didn't ask me any of those questions. He only asked one question. He said, 'Who has the power in the Senate?' I said, 'There's only one power in the Senate — Richard Russell.' "

Johnson was to recall that he realized the only way he could be close to Russell was to be on his committee, which was Armed Services. That was not one of the major committees. Foreign Relations, Appropriations, etc., were the major committees then.

But Johnson asks for Russell's committee,

and he starts to work late. Russell worked late every night because he had no one to go home to.

Often Russell would go to a hamburger place near the Capitol to get a hamburger, and Johnson would happen to be going to the same place to get a hamburger at the same time. And they start to sit next to each other at the counter.

Johnson is just wonderful with older men. And he says to Russell, as he said to Rayburn, "Come by the house for dinner tonight." Russell also was a man who didn't go out to dinner very much. Johnson would say to him, "You know, you have to eat somewhere. You might as well come and eat."

And when Russell starts to go to Johnson's home, Johnson and Lady Bird and their two daughters make Russell feel like an uncle in the family. That's part of the reason Johnson became close to Russell.

The other reason is that Lyndon Johnson makes Richard Russell believe that he thinks the same way on segregation and civil rights as Russell did. Russell was the most ardent segregationist. He was the most racist of senators.

He was also a great senator in the area of foreign relations. But in domestic affairs, he really had a very low opinion of people who were not white. Johnson makes Russell, makes all the southern senators believe —

there are twenty-two southern senators — that he feels the same way about blacks that they do.

I went to Atlanta to interview Senator Herman Talmadge in his retirement. So you drive down Herman Talmadge Highway and you get off at the Herman Talmadge exit and Herman Talmadge Boulevard, and you drive to Lake Talmadge, and you go to this house with a lot of pillars in front, and a servant in a waistcoat opens the door and says, "The senator is waiting for you in the library."

I asked the senator, "What was Lyndon Johnson's belief about the relationship of blacks and whites?" And Talmadge said to me — this is what Lyndon Johnson had made him believe — Talmadge said, "Servant and master."

So Johnson had convinced the southerners that he was on their side. Russell really anoints him as his successor in the Senate.

DR: Two years after he's elected to the Senate, he becomes the Senate majority whip. Two years after that, he becomes the minority leader. And two years after that — six years into the Senate — he's the majority leader. How did he rise up that quickly?

RC: No one wanted to be leader then. Alben Barkley, who had been the Senate leader during the 1940s, had this quote which was famous around Washington. Barkley said, "Nobody can lead the Senate. I have nothing to promise them. I have nothing to threaten them with."

That was the belief. The Senate was sort of in a mess at that time, had been in a mess for a long time. And nobody wants the leadership jobs. So when Johnson says to Russell, "I'd like to be assistant leader," Russell just gives him the job.

Of course, Johnson made something out of every job. He becomes majority leader two years later. And he does something which is really worth discussing. No one ever picks this out of my book.

Johnson was a genius at political power. He saw things that nobody else saw. Up until then, seniority had governed everything in the Senate. It was a very rigid rule. It's not seniority as we think of it today. You got whatever committee assignment your seniority made you eligible for. You got whatever office space your seniority dictated.

The *Washington Post,* the week before Lyndon Johnson became leader, has the sentence — if I remember it correctly — "The Senate would no more change the seniority system than it would change its name."

Johnson says he wants to be leader, and he's going to be leader. Russell has made sure of that.

If we look at Washington in January 1953, Dwight D. Eisenhower has just been elected president. The inauguration stands are being hammered into place. All the bunting is going up. That's the transfer of power from the Democrats in the White House to a Republican in the White House.

But there's another transfer of power going on, which nobody writes about, which nobody understands, and it's going on in Lyndon Johnson's office, behind the closed door of his private office.

He's in there all alone. But he's talking on the telephone, and we know that because there are four buttons for his four lines on the desk of his assistant, Walter Jenkins. And one or another of those buttons is always lit hour after hour. Because over that telephone, Lyndon Johnson is trying to change the seniority system. And he does it with a lot of arguments.

The Democrats have controlled Congress for so long, and many of the Democrats have been chairmen of their committees for so long. But Eisenhower brought a Republican majority into the Senate with him, so all of a sudden, these senators are not chairmen anymore.

And Johnson is telling them that if they want to become chairmen again, they have to make a legislative record against Eisenhower strong enough to have a chance to take the

Senate back in two years. He says, "We can't do that by putting our best young senators on the worst committees. We have people like Hubert Humphrey [the Democratic senator from Minnesota] and Paul Douglas [the Democratic senator from Illinois] and Mike Mansfield [a Democratic senator from Montana who previously represented the state in the House]. We have to use them."

As an example, I'll take one thing that he does. He sees that Ohio senator Robert Taft, who is not only the Republican majority leader but a great debater and a great speaker, is moving to the Foreign Relations Committee so he can attack the Marshall Plan, our policy on China, all the Roosevelt–Truman initiatives in foreign policy.

We have two young senators. Mike Mansfield was a professor of Far Eastern history before he became a senator, before he became a representative. And Hubert Humphrey is, of course, the great orator.

Johnson says, "We have to put Humphrey and Mansfield on Foreign Relations." He says, "Hubert can out-talk Taft and Mansfield can out-know him."

There are two vacancies at the bottom of that committee. But there are senior senators — one is Harry Byrd, the Democratic senator from Virginia — who are entitled by seniority to those places.

Johnson goes to Byrd and makes this argument to him. Byrd wants his chairmanship of the Finance Committee back, so he agrees not to take his seat on Foreign Relations. Johnson does this with another senator, and all of a sudden you have two strong new Democratic voices on Foreign Relations.

He says to Humphrey, "I'll put you on Foreign Relations" — which Humphrey wants because it's the most prestigious committee — "I'll put you on Foreign Relations if you give up both your seats on Agriculture and Labor." Humphrey agrees to do that, and all of a sudden there is now a vacancy on Agriculture.

Earle Clements, the senator from Kentucky, has always wanted to go on Agriculture. Johnson says to Clements, "I'll put you on Agriculture if you give up your seats on Public Works and Rules."

Johnson looked at this as if it was a giant chessboard. There are 203 spaces on it — 203 committee slots. And he uses those spaces, moving senators around on them, to create power — power for *him.* Because all of a sudden, he is making the decisions about who's going where. It's no longer seniority, it's not just saying, "You automatically do this"; it's who the leader says is going to be on the committee, and he is the leader.

At one stroke, Johnson does a lot to change power in Washington. He changes the nature of legislature power in Washington forever.

DR: One famous thing written about is the "Johnson treatment," where Johnson basically persuades members to do what he wants. And I always had thought it meant he would curse at people and yell and scream at them. But when you listen to the Johnson tapes from his time in the White House, there are no curse words. What was the Johnson treatment?

RC: Johnson was not foul-mouthed in this respect. He didn't get what he wanted many times. He often did.

But he would read a person. Lyndon Johnson did not like to read books. But he was a great reader of men, and he had rules for reading men.

When young staffers would come to work for him, one thing he would say to them was, "Read their eyes. Read their hands. What they're telling you with their hands is more important than what they're telling you with their lips."

He would say, "Never let a conversation end. There's always something that someone doesn't want to tell you. And the longer the conversation goes on, the more likely you are to find out what that is."

DR: While Johnson is the majority leader of the Senate, he has a heart attack in 1955. Did that incapacitate him?

LBJ and Lady Bird Johnson on their ranch in Stonewall, Texas, January 3, 1958.

RC: Yes, because it was a major heart attack. He was only given a fifty-fifty chance of living, although he was only forty-eight at the time. He went back to Texas for some months to recuperate.

DR: He decides in the latter part of the fifties that he would like to be president of the United States. He's done the Senate, wants to be president — a not uncommon thing for some people in the Senate.

But there's a young senator named John Kennedy. How did Lyndon Johnson view John Kennedy in those days?

RC: With absolute contempt. He used to say, "Kennedy doesn't even know how to make a motion. He doesn't know how to address the chair."

DR: What was Johnson's strategy to become the Democratic nominee in 1960? How did he think he was going to be nominated?

RC: I should say he also viewed Kennedy with contempt because Kennedy, of course, at this time was still very sick. He had Addison's disease, and they had just discovered that cortisone might work for it. Kennedy was so thin and scrawny, and Johnson used to say, when Kennedy said he was going to run for president, "Look at his ankles. They're only this big around. And he's yellow all the time." Kennedy had a yellow cast to his complexion then because of his illness.
So Johnson did not regard Kennedy as a serious opponent. Johnson thinks he doesn't have to campaign. He's the most powerful Democrat, and he expects to get the nomination.

DR: When it turns out that Kennedy does get the nomination, he calls Johnson and says, "Would you like to be vice president?" How did that come about, since Lyndon Johnson was not close to John Kennedy?

RC: John Kennedy was very good at not telling anybody what he was really thinking, including his brother Bobby Kennedy, who hated Lyndon Johnson. Nobody has any clue that Jack Kennedy is even considering Lyndon Johnson until the morning after he wins the nomination.

Jack Kennedy calls his brother Robert early in the morning — Robert is actually in the bathtub — and says, "Count up the electoral votes of all the northern states plus Texas." And Robert Kennedy says, "You're not thinking of nominating Lyndon Johnson, are you?" And Jack Kennedy says, "Yes."

So he comes down to Johnson's room. They're both staying in the Biltmore Hotel in Los Angeles [the site of the 1960 Democratic Convention]. Kennedy's on the ninth floor. Johnson's on the seventh floor. They both have corner suites, and there's a back staircase between them. At ten o'clock in the morning, Jack Kennedy comes down and offers Johnson the vice presidency.

Johnson calls his closest advisors, Rayburn and John Connally and Bobby Baker. It's decided he's going to accept the nomination. And he does accept it. He thinks he's accepted it.

That afternoon, Robert Kennedy comes down those back stairs three times to Johnson's suite to ask him to withdraw from the ticket. When people would say he did this without his brother knowing, Robert Kennedy would say, basically, "What are you, crazy? You think my brother took a nap, so I went down to get his vice president to withdraw?"

However, he comes down three times. At one point he comes down and Lady Bird says, "Don't let the two of them meet, because Lyndon Johnson and Robert Kennedy really hate each other."

The first time, Rayburn sees Robert Kennedy, and Robert Kennedy comes in and says they want Lyndon Johnson to withdraw from the ticket, and Rayburn, this mighty figure — I wrote in the book he was old and he was blind, but he didn't seem old or blind when he said to Robert Kennedy, "Are you authorized to speak for your brother?" Robert Kennedy says, "No." And Rayburn says, "Come back and see the Speaker of the House of Representatives when you are."

Robert Kennedy retreats back up the stairs. A little while later he comes down, and Lady Bird is still trying to keep them from meeting. John Connally sees them. And this time Robert Kennedy makes a firm offer. He says that if Johnson withdraws, the Kennedys will make him chairman of the Democratic National Committee. Goes back upstairs, and finally he comes down and the two of them meet alone in the room.

We don't really know what happened in that room. Robert Kennedy says Lyndon Johnson started to cry. We don't know if that's true or not.

But we do know that Johnson was terribly upset until somebody says to him, "Call Jack Kennedy yourself." He calls Jack Kennedy, who says, "No. I want you to be vice president. I'm announcing it. I'm going out this minute to announce."

DR: So it happened. They get elected in 1960. Probably Texas helped. When Lyndon Johnson becomes vice president, what does he try to do with the Senate?

RC: Johnson thinks, at the beginning, that he's going to continue to run the Senate as if he were still majority leader. It's a total miscalculation because, of course, when he goes to the first caucus, they make clear to him that "you're not in the Senate anymore and we're not going to listen to you."

DR: He wanted to run the Democratic caucus still.

RC: In fact, he tries to take the chairman's chair at the first caucus.

DR: So that doesn't work. What jobs did John Kennedy actually give Lyndon Johnson to do as vice president?

RC: Johnson is given nothing to do. He's never consulted on legislation. This is the greatest legislator in American history, and the Kennedy legislative program has trouble from the very beginning.

In fact, when Kennedy is assassinated, none of his major legislation — civil rights, various other bills, his tax-cut bill — none of them were going to be passed. But nobody comes and asks Lyndon Johnson about legislation. No one asks for his help.

DR: John Kennedy took a trip to Texas in November of 1963. Why did he need to go to Texas when he had Lyndon Johnson as vice president? Why did he need to shore up Texas?

RC: The situation in Texas was that Lyndon Johnson's protégé and long-time administrative aide, John Connally, had become governor. I spent several days with Governor Connally down on his ranch. He was a very conservative man. He really was philosophically opposed to Lyndon Johnson's liberal philosophy. And he had taken over not only the Democratic political machine in Texas but the money-raising.

Texas was the major source of financing for the Democratic Party as a whole. Connally had brought that under his control, and he and Johnson were in a very tense situation.

Eisenhower had actually carried Texas in 1952 and 1956. And Jack Kennedy knows that he has to have Texas, the money and the vote, in 1964.

Was he planning to drop Lyndon Johnson from the ticket? If you talk to anyone who was close to Lyndon Johnson, it's very important to them to say that Kennedy was not planning to drop him from the ticket, and of course Jack Kennedy would say in public, "No, of course I'm not going to do that."

In fact, Kennedy said different things to other people. There's enough reason to believe that Johnson might have been dropped.

DR: So President Kennedy is assassinated. Where is Lyndon Johnson at the time of the assassination?

RC: He's three cars behind Kennedy's car in the presidential motorcade in Dallas. In the motorcade there is, first, the open limousine with Jack Kennedy and Jackie. In front of them on the jump seats were John Connally, this tall, very handsome man with a leonine head of white hair, and his wife, Nellie Connally, who was once Sweetheart of the University at the University of Texas, still a very beautiful woman.

Behind them was the Secret Service car known as the Queen Mary because it was so heavily armored. In that car, there were four agents standing on the running boards, and inside there were four agents in the back with their automatic rifles concealed on the floor of the car.

Then there's a seventy-five-foot space between the cars, because the Secret Service wants the president and vice president to be separated. And then comes Lyndon Johnson's car. He's sitting in the back seat on the right-hand side. Lady Bird's in the center. On the left is the senator from Texas, Ralph Yarborough, and in the front seat next to the driver is a Secret Service agent named Rufus W. Youngblood, a tall, lanky Georgian.

They hear a sharp, cracking noise. Nobody knows what it is. It sounds like the backfire from a policeman's motorcycle or someone popping a balloon. But when I interviewed John Connally, he said to me, "You know, Bob, I was a hunter. I knew the moment I heard it that it was the sound of a hunting rifle."

Nobody quite knows what's happening. Youngblood, in the front seat of Johnson's car, hears this sound. He doesn't know what it is.

Youngblood recalls, "I saw the president leaning to the left. All of a sudden, I saw the Secret Service agents in the Queen Mary jumping to their feet. One of them has a rifle in his hand and was looking around."

And then they realize what's happening, and Youngblood whirls around. Lady Bird Johnson, who recalled this very vividly, says, "He shouted in a voice I had never heard him use before, 'Get down! Get down!' " And he grabs Lyndon by the right shoulder and pulls him down onto the floor of the back seat and jumps over the back of the front seat and lies on top of Lyndon Johnson to protect him with his own body.

Because it wasn't just the president who was hit by a shot; so was the governor of Texas. Who knew if there were going to be more shots, if the vice president would be a target?

The Secret Service agents then all had radios, which they wore like a shoulder holster. As Youngblood is lying on top of Johnson, his radio is near Johnson's ear, and Johnson hears all this jumble of voices and he hears someone saying, "He's hit! He's hit!"

Someone says, "Get out of here! Let's get out of here!" Then he hears the word "hospital."

Youngblood realizes that the place where he'll have the most protection for Johnson is to be as close as possible to the Secret Service car. He tells the driver, a Texas highway patrolman named Herschel Jacks, "Close it up."

If you look at films of this, Jacks puts the vice president's car almost against the bumper of the Queen Mary. And the three cars squeal up onto the expressway, race along the expressway, squeal off the expressway and into the emergency bay at Parkland Hospital.

DR: Johnson is then put in a separate room and guarded by Youngblood and others. When they're told that President Kennedy has died, what happens?

RC: Johnson is not told that President Kennedy is dead for forty-five minutes. He's standing in this room. No one will give him any information. Twice he sends somebody out to try and find out, and both times that person comes back with the word, "The doctors say they're still working on the president."

So Lady Bird writes in her memoirs about one of Kennedy's closest aides who had worked for him all his life, a man named Kenny O'Donnell. Lady Bird says, "Then Kenny O'Donnell came through the door and, seeing the stricken face of Kenny, who loved him, we knew."

A moment later, another Kennedy aide comes in, goes over to Johnson, and addresses him as "Mr. President." That's the first Johnson knows that he's president.

No one knows what Johnson is thinking during these forty-five minutes. I certainly don't know. But when this word finally comes and the Secret Service starts to try to give him orders, he knows what he wants to do.

Remember, it's the height of the Cold War, and they don't know if the attack is part of a conspiracy. And they say, "The place we can protect you best is Washington. We have to get to Air Force One and get off the ground and get back to Washington."

Johnson says, "I'm not leaving without Mrs. Kennedy." They say, "Mrs. Kennedy won't leave without her husband's body." He says, "Then we'll go to the plane and wait for her there."

DR: So they go to the plane. But the local police say, "We're not giving you the body. We have to do an autopsy. A murder has been committed in the state." But Kennedy's aides got the casket to the plane. Mrs. Kennedy is on the plane and they're getting ready to go, and Lyndon Johnson wants to be sworn in. How did that come about?

RC: He makes a call to Robert Kennedy. It's a very sad scene. As I say, these two men really hated each other.

You want to know how historians get information? Robert Morgenthau was for many decades the U.S. attorney for New York, a very respected figure and a friend of mine. We always go to the same Hanukkah party every year, and he always comes over to me to tell me some wonderful story.

While I was writing this last book, he says to me, "Bob, I have something I really want to tell you now." I said, "Let's wait till after the service." He says, "No. I really want to tell you this right away." So we go into another room. And he says, "I was there when Lyndon Johnson called Robert Kennedy."

Robert Kennedy was at Hickory Hill, the Kennedy family home in McLean, Virginia. J. Edgar Hoover calls him to tell him his brother's dead. And ten minutes later, the man he truly hates, Lyndon Johnson, calls to ask the exact procedure by which he can take over his brother's presidency.

He didn't have to do that. The information on that happens to be in the Constitution.

DR: Nicholas Katzenbach, the deputy attorney general, calls back and says, "The oath of office is in the Constitution." Lyndon Johnson wants to get a judge that he likes, Sarah Hughes. She comes out [to Love Field]. She swears him in. Why does Lyndon Johnson insist that Mrs. Kennedy get in the picture of the swearing-in?

RC: What I'm saying now is what the Kennedy people believe. They believe that he was using Mrs. Kennedy, that he wanted to convey the feeling that the Kennedys were behind him in his new presidency. I do not

541

know if that's true or not.

DR: The plane ultimately takes off. It comes back to Washington. Lyndon Johnson is president. Does he go to the Oval Office right away?

RC: He goes to the Oval Office the next morning, and one of Kennedy's secretaries is there and runs and gets Robert Kennedy and says, "He's going into the Oval Office." When Johnson sees the reaction, he goes back and he works out of his office in the Executive Office Building for the next four days.

DR: How did he decide to have a report on the Kennedy assassination, and how did he persuade Earl Warren and Richard Russell to be on the Warren Commission that prepared that report?

RC: These are two of the strongest-willed men in Washington. Earl Warren is the chief justice of the Supreme Court, and he has said to people, "I will never serve on any commission like this. The Supreme Court should stay aloof from things like this."

Johnson comes in and says to him, "You were a private in World War I." He says, "You put on our uniform for your country. Now your president is asking you to serve as head of this commission." And Warren agreed.

With Richard Russell, he called Russell, who's back in Winder, Georgia, his hometown. Johnson calls, and Russell says, "I will not be on this commission." Among other things, Warren passed the *Brown v. Board of Education* decision that declared school segregation unconstitutional, so Russell truly hates Earl Warren and he doesn't want to be on this commission anyway. He says, "No. I won't do it."

Johnson calls back a few hours later and says, "I want to read you the press release that I've just announced." Russell says, "I'm on it?" And Johnson says, "Yes." Russell says, "Take my name off." Johnson says, "You know, we passed the deadline for the *New York Times* about ten minutes ago."

DR: We've largely covered the four volumes of *The Years of Lyndon Johnson* that you've written. With the beginning of the Johnson administration, you end the fourth volume. When is volume five coming out? Is it going to be one volume or two volumes?

RC: Well, you're ruining this terrific interview. I'm about halfway through.

DR: You do all your research and then you write — or type — on your Smith-Corona?

RC: That's in theory true, but when you get into each chapter, you suddenly realize that some file that you had thought wasn't important at the Johnson Presidential Library is key. So you have to go back and look into it.

I want the last book to be in one volume. I'll tell you why: because the arc of Lyndon Johnson's presidency is one arc. He starts with the greatest victory in the history of American politics — to this day, still. Sixty-one-point-one percent over Barry Goldwater, his Republican opponent in the 1964 presidential election.

So he starts with the greatest triumph you can imagine. By the end of it, Vietnam has consumed his presidency, and he has to leave office and go back to his ranch. I want that all to be in one book because I see it as one story.

DR: One question that I've always wondered about is this. John Kennedy proposed belated civil rights legislation but didn't get any of it anywhere. Lyndon Johnson bonded with members of Congress who were segregationists.

Why does Lyndon Johnson decide to be Mr. Civil Rights? Was it to prove that he could do something better than Kennedy, or did he really believe in the end that civil rights legislation was necessary?

The Vietnam War challenged Johnson's legacy. LBJ with Secretary of Defense Robert McNamara (right) and Secretary of State Dean Rusk (left), July 21, 1965.

RC: Lyndon Johnson really believed. How do I feel, anyway, that I know this?

He was very poor when he went to college, and between his sophomore and junior years, he has to take a year off from college to make enough money to go on. What he does for that year is he teaches in a little town called Cotulla, Texas. He teaches in what was called the Mexican School, for the children of migrant workers.

Some of the students later gave oral histories, and as I wrote, "No teacher had ever cared if these children learned or not. This teacher cared."

He thought it was desperately important that they learned to speak English. So he insisted they speak English, and if at recess he heard some boy shouting something in Spanish outside the window, he would run out and spank him. If it was a girl, he would yell at her.

You could say, if you want to be hard on him, that this was just an example of Lyndon Johnson doing the best job he could at whatever job he had, which was a characteristic of his. But I felt, I knew that he really believed in this because he didn't just teach the children, he taught the janitor.

The janitor's name was Tomas Gomez, and he said Johnson wanted him to learn English, so Johnson bought him a textbook. Before and after school each day, they would sit on the steps of the school and, if I remember the janitor's words correctly, he would say, "Johnson would pronounce, I would repeat. Johnson would spell, I would repeat."

So when Johnson becomes president and he's given these great civil rights speeches to deliver, one of Kennedy's speechwriters who was still working for him, Richard Goodwin, asked that question: "Do you really believe?" He asks it in a more polite way, although not much more polite. "Do you really believe in this?"

And Johnson said, "I swore when I was teaching those kids that if I ever had the power, I would help them. And now I have the power and I mean to use it."

DR: Lyndon Johnson died of a heart attack at the age of sixty-four, relatively young. Would he have been able to survive with modern medical technology?

RC: I asked his cardiologist that very question. He said, "We could have fixed him in a half-hour angioplasty."

14
Bob Woodward

ON RICHARD M. NIXON AND EXECUTIVE POWER

"He had the idea that he was untouchable. He was president of the United States. He thought no one would ever find out about these tapes, let alone get access to them."

BOOKS DISCUSSED OR MENTIONED:
All the President's Men (with Carl Bernstein; Simon & Schuster, 1974)
The Final Days (with Carl Bernstein; Simon

& Schuster, 1976)

The Secret Man: The Story of Watergate's Deep Throat (Simon & Schuster, 2005)

The Last of the President's Men (Simon & Schuster, 2015)

Fear: Trump in the White House (Simon & Schuster, 2018)

Shadow: Five Presidents and the Legacy of Watergate (Simon & Schuster, 1999)

The Brethren: Inside the Supreme Court (with Scott Armstrong; Simon & Schuster, 1979)

The Commanders (Simon & Schuster, 1991)

Bush at War (Simon & Schuster, 2002)

Plan of Attack (Simon & Schuster, 2004)

Obama's Wars (Simon & Schuster, 2010)

Bob Woodward is without doubt the best-known, most respected, and most prolific journalist/author of the past half century.

He first came to the public's attention as the partner with Carl Bernstein in breaking and pursuing the Watergate story for the *Washington Post,* reporting for which the paper won the Pulitzer Prize.

These two young journalists (Woodward was twenty-nine and Bernstein was twenty-eight) demonstrated the power of persistent, focused, and investigative journalism. They had a major role in the disclosures that ultimately forced President Richard M.

Nixon to resign. Bob and Carl subsequently wrote two *New York Times* number-one best sellers about Watergate: *All the President's Men* and *The Final Days.*

With the publication of those books behind him, Bob Woodward has continued, for the ensuing four decades, a dual-track career — as a journalist and editor at the *Post* and as a best-selling book author.

Last year, he wrote *Fear: Trump in the White House,* a best-selling account of the Trump tenure. That was Bob Woodward's nineteenth book.

Every single one of Woodward's books has been a *New York Times* best seller — thirteen of them at number one, a record matched by no other nonfiction writer.

I have known Bob since my days working in the Carter White House in the late 1970s. He managed to obtain and write about one of my memos (written with Stu Eizenstat, then my boss) to President Carter. That was not an especially pleasant experience for me at that time. But I came to know — and greatly admire — Bob after the Carter administration ended and have interviewed him on other occasions.

His careful research, persistence, focus, hard work, and fairness are legendary. For journalists and writers about government, he is the gold standard.

In this interview, I tried to cover many of

Bob's books, though there are too many of them to do any one justice in an hourlong interview. The principal focus was on Nixon, for Bob's work there is what launched his unrivaled career.

In the conversation, Bob Woodward recounts how, by sheer happenstance, he was in the right place at the right time. He had been working at the *Washington Post* for only nine months when the Watergate break-in occurred, and his editor assigned coverage of the story (thought at first to be about a normal burglary) to him and to another young reporter, Carl Bernstein.

Bob describes how he and Bernstein doggedly pursued the story — when others thought there was little real interest to it — and how they made mistakes that could have been career-ending. And their perseverance paid off. The *Washington Post* won a Pulitzer Prize for their work; the criminal activities surrounding the Watergate break-in (most especially the presidential cover-up) were exposed; and a president was forced to resign for the first (and so far only) time in the country's history.

While Bob Woodward wrote best-selling books about all of Nixon's successors — and gives his views on them in this interview — he will forever be linked with Nixon.

And he reveals that at no point did he ever

meet Richard Nixon. One wonders how such a meeting might have gone.

MR. DAVID M. RUBENSTEIN (DR): I think it's fair to say, Bob, that in the lifetime of everybody in this room, you're the most famous journalist our country's ever produced. You didn't go to journalism school, and you weren't really a journalist when you were in college. Your father was a lawyer and a judge, and I think expected you to go to law school. How did you wind up as a journalist rather than a lawyer?

MR. BOB WOODWARD (BW): Good luck, I think, is the best answer. I was in the navy. I was going to go to law school after five years in the navy. It was during the Vietnam era, and I was, quite frankly, unhappy with myself that I couldn't do something about the Vietnam War.

I worked here in Washington in the Pentagon for the last year. I was reading this newspaper called the *Washington Post,* and they said there's a guy named Bradlee there who's called "the rocket thruster."

I went and asked for a job. I had no experience. They gave me a two-week tryout and I failed. I went to the *Montgomery County Sentinel* for a year, and the *Post* hired me back.

DR: When you went back, were you on probation?

BW: In a sense. It's like being in Congress.

553

You're always on probation.

DR: So one weekend in June 1972 there's a break-in at the Democratic National Committee headquarters at the Watergate. How did you and Carl Bernstein happen to be assigned to cover that?

BW: I'd been at the *Post* nine months and really enjoyed the work. I was covering the night police beat from 6:30 at night till 2:30 a.m., and I would come in during the day and work on follow-up stories.

The morning of the Watergate burglary — June 17, 1972 — was a Saturday morning. It was one of the most beautiful days in Washington. The editors had this strange burglary to cover, and they thought, "Who would be dumb enough to come in and work today?"

My name immediately came to the lips of a number of people. So I got called in.

DR: They said you should cover this with Carl Bernstein?

BW: No. The first day there were a group of people covering it, and then on Sunday there were only two people who came to work — Carl and myself.

DR: As you began to investigate it, at what point did you realize it was more than just a break-in by some average citizen? When did you realize there might be a connection to the White House?

BW: It was immediately obvious that there was a connection to the White House, but of course they denied everything. The reporting was incremental over two years. Sometimes each piece or story advanced it in a significant way, sometimes the stories were marginal.

DR: There are stories about how when you'd written about Watergate, and the famous movie about it came out [the 1976 movie *All the President's Men,* starring Robert Redford as Bob Woodward and Dustin Hoffman as Carl Bernstein], you would go knock on people's doors, and sometimes they'd let you in and sometimes they'd shut the door. How complicated was it to knock on somebody's door and get them to let you in?

BW: It's hard, rejection. I'm sure it's like when you knock on someone's door and say, "I'd like to invest in your business," they're reluctant to let you in. In this case they were sometimes reluctant, but significantly it was the look on their faces of anguish and pain and "Don't bother me." It was clear the lid was on from the White House.

DR: One time you and Carl Bernstein wrote

an article that wasn't quite accurate, and the White House went after you. Did the *Washington Post* support you? What was the inaccuracy?

BW: It was a misattribution involving Nixon's chief of staff, Bob Haldeman. It was a very serious error, because we said somebody had testified about something involving Haldeman to the grand jury — and they had not.

The substance was true. It was a very interesting moment because Ben Bradlee, the *Post*'s executive editor, looked at this and said, "We stand behind the boys."

We didn't actually deserve that support. We'd made a serious mistake. We couldn't prove a lot of this.

I'm sure everyone in their life has had somebody — a boss, a friend, a spouse — stand by you in a way that maybe you knew you didn't deserve. But it accelerates your devotion to the cause and to the person. In this case, it was a very generous act on the part of Ben Bradlee.

DR: As you and Bernstein were writing these articles, where was the *New York Times*? They're a pretty good newspaper. How come you managed to outmaneuver them so much?

BW: I don't think we outmaneuvered them. We were young. If you look back at the clues, so much of it was obvious. The *New York Times* had people on it and did some very good stories. But, you know, it consumed us.

And, again, this is a leadership question. Bradlee and the *Post*'s editors were very much of the mind-set "What's going on with Watergate? Let's get to the bottom of this." They were saying that and demanding answers.

DR: Your articles were criticized by some for using unnamed sources. Was that a common technique before you began doing it, or was it relatively new?

BW: It was common in diplomatic reporting and political reporting, but this was necessity. Our sources were not going to allow their names to be used. And the editors of the *Post* understood that.

DR: One of your famous sources was somebody who was known as Deep Throat. Did Deep Throat call you up and say, "I'd like to see you in a garage"? How did that come about?

BW: No. He was somebody I had met as a courier at the White House — Mark Felt, who was number two in the FBI later. He was not a volunteer source. I was a pest. I had his phone number, and he helped on one initial story on the White House connection involving Howard Hunt, who was one of the supervisors of the Watergate burglary.

Because I was such a nag, Felt said, "Let's meet in this garage and set up these very complicated signals." Again, I was starting out, and I thought this was kind of common practice.

DR: Washington is not famous for keeping secrets, I think it's fair to say. But you and Carl Bernstein managed to keep the secret of who Deep Throat was for thirty-some years. How did you manage to do that? What was it like when everybody came up to you and said, "I think it's X" or "I think it's Y"? How did you respond?

BW: I said, "We're not going to talk about it." It was part of the rules of engagement. I did tell my wife, Elsa, who is here. I told her on about our fourth date.

DR: Wow, okay. You kept that secret for a while. Why ultimately did you decide to write a book about it and expose Deep Throat's name?

BW: He came out and identified himself, Mark Felt did.

DR: Let's talk about the Nixon tapes for a

NIXON'S THE ONE!

"He had the idea that he was untouchable."

moment. Why did Richard Nixon tape so many of his White House conversations?

BW: There are two elements. He wanted to write the best memoirs a president had ever written. He knew that the process of getting people to take notes at meetings was insufficient.

But most importantly, I think, he had the idea that he was untouchable. He was president of the United States. He thought no one would ever find out about these tapes, let alone get access to them.

So he kind of cruised along. If you listen to any of these tapes, it is a shocking story. In fact, in the end, Nixon resigned not because of the media or the Democrats. It was the Republicans.

DR: When it was exposed publicly for the first time that he had the tapes, why didn't he just burn them?

BW: I think part of it is that he was so deluded, he thought they would exonerate him.

DR: The man who exposed the tapes was a man named Alex Butterfield, an aide to President Nixon. He testified before the Senate Watergate Committee and he said, yes, there was a taping system. Recently you wrote a book about him, and he shared with you that he'd been holding a lot of documents for thirty-plus years. Why did he call you, and what did you learn from his documents?

BW: He didn't call me, I called him. There's this idea that reporters sit around and wait for Daniel Ellsberg to come in with a grocery cart of documents. [Ellsberg was an analyst for the RAND Corporation who, in 1971, leaked the Pentagon Papers, a secret government report on the Vietnam War, to the *New York Times*.]

I'd been waiting a long time for that to happen. You have to go out and find sources. These people are not volunteers.

DR: What did Butterfield tell you all these years later that you didn't already know?

BW: All kinds of things. He told me stories that were almost not credible until you saw the documents.

For instance, he said that Nixon threw a fit because some staff members had pictures of John F. Kennedy in their offices. There actually is a memo where Butterfield reports to Nixon that he got these pictures out. The subject of the memo is "Sanitization of the Executive Office Building."

Nixon thought these pictures, somehow, were disloyal. It's almost unthinkable. Suppose you're gone and somebody else comes along and runs the Carlyle Group and someone has a picture of you in their office. Do you think your successor would say, "We have to sanitize"?

DR: I'm not sure.

BW: Hopefully not. Hopefully there would be enough self-confidence and comfort to say,

561

you know, "That's the old guy."

DR: What did it feel like to have a movie written about this and to be played by Robert Redford? What was that like?

BW: You have no idea how many women I have disappointed. Universally, they thought there would be some resemblance and were horrified rather than disappointed to discover that there was no resemblance.

DR: You wrote a book about the final days of Nixon. Who was really running the White House in that final year and a half or so? Was the president really in control of things, or was it Alexander Haig?

BW: Al Haig was the chief of staff. He was running lots of things. But it's a sad story about the disintegration of power and the disintegration of Nixon.

In a blizzard of self-knowledge, the day he resigned — if you've seen the video of it, Nixon was there, his daughters, his sons-in-law, his wife — and he gave a speech with no text. It was Nixon raw. He talked about his mother and his father and was very maudlin.

Then, near the end, he kind of waves his hand like, "This is why I called everyone here. This is the message I have to say." Then he said, "Always remember, others may hate you, but those who hate you don't win unless you hate them, and then you destroy yourself."

Now, the wisdom in that could not be larger, because Nixon did destroy himself. At that moment, he said, the hating was the poison that did him in.

We've had lots of presidents, and we've had lots of disagreements, and there's a lot going on. I tried to write about and understand some of the other presidents, but none of them were haters like Nixon. He just could not get over the fact that people would cross him or disagree with him. He had no sense of the wonderful feelings of goodwill that people had, even Democrats.

DR: He resigned in August 1974. In all the years after he left office, did you ever meet him?

BW: No.

DR: He never called you and said, "Let's talk about old times," or something like that?

BW: When we were doing reporting for our books, we tried to talk to him, and it was always no. We did not even get on his Christmas card list.

But when he gave his famous interviews to TV host David Frost, at one point Frost asked him about Carl and myself. Nixon said, "That's Washington. That's politics. That's the *Washington Post.* They're liberals, and what they write is trash, and they are trash."

I called my mother to get some comfort. I said, "What did you think about Nixon calling us trash?" She said, "That's Washington. That's politics." Pause. "What's this about being a liberal?" Mother could always figure out what the problem might be.

DR: Before he got on the plane the day he resigned, do you think he had a feeling that President Gerald Ford was going to pardon him? Was there a deal cut before he left office?

BW: There actually was not a deal. There was suspicion that there was a deal. I did a book twenty-five years after this called *Shadow* and spent lots of time investigating this.

It was a Sunday morning, Nixon had been out of office for a month. Ford was president. Ford went on television on Sunday morning announcing a full pardon for Nixon.

I was asleep. My colleague Carl Bernstein called me up and woke me and said, "Have you heard?" Carl — who then had and still has the ability to say what occurred in the fewest words with the most drama — said, "The son of a bitch pardoned the son of a bitch." And I even got it.

In October 1974, President Gerald Ford testified in front of the House Judiciary Subcommittee about pardoning Nixon — a decision that helped push the Watergate story off the front page.

I thought this was the most corrupt thing, you know, perfect. Nixon, who led all of this, gets off, and all these other people go to jail. Then I looked at it twenty-five years later and, when you really dig into it, you realize that what Ford did was quite a courageous thing, in the country's national interest, to get rid of Nixon and Watergate, to get them off the front page.

I interviewed Ford many, many times, and I will never forget him saying, "I had to get rid of Nixon. I had to preempt the process." He said, in this plaintive tone, "I needed my own presidency."

DR: Did Ford tell you that, had he not done

the pardon, he would have been reelected? Did he believe that?

BW: No. What he did tell me is that Al Haig, who was Nixon's chief of staff, came and offered him a deal. And Ford said — convincingly — that he rejected the deal.

DR: After Watergate, you wrote another book on a different branch of government, and that's the judiciary. You wrote a book on the Supreme Court called *The Brethren.* In it, you have a very interesting passage about a case involving Muhammad Ali. You might describe that. [Ali died on June 3, 2016, a few days before this conversation took place.]

BW: If you read the stories in the last week about Ali, it said the Supreme Court overturned his conviction for draft-dodging. He had been convicted. It was in the court system.

What I find most interesting about this is how it illustrates the large theme: we don't really know what goes on. There's a behind-the-scenes that is always much richer and real.

In the case of Ali, we were able to talk to 140 law clerks and five of the justices and get lots of documents. It turns out that, yes, Ali got off at the end, 8 to 0, but it started out where they were going to send Ali to jail.

The first vote at conference was 5 to 3. Justice Thurgood Marshall, because he'd been solicitor general, was out of the case, so there were eight justices voting. Chief Justice Warren Burger gave the assignment of writing the opinion to Justice John Marshall Harlan II, a very conservative justice, and everything seemed to be fine.

Then a clerk read the literature that Ali cited as to why he was a conscientious objector — that it was part of the Black Muslim religion. The clerk said, "Ali is a legitimate conscientious objector." He gave this material to Harlan, who at this point was nearly blind and could not read.

Harlan took all this stuff home and, under this intense light he had, read it and came in and said, "Ali is a legitimate conscientious objector. I'm switching my vote." So instead of 5 to 3, it's 4 to 4. As we know and are reminded now, when the Supreme Court is split 4 to 4, it upholds the lower court opinion, which was to send Ali to jail.

But [in that situation] there's no written opinion from the Supreme Court. Justice Potter Stewart said, "This isn't right. We need to find some way to explain what we've done." He found a technicality and switched his vote.

So now it was 5 to 3 the other way. Two of the other justices quickly got on board, so it was going to be 7 to 1 to free Ali. Chief

Justice Burger said, "People are going to think I'm a racist. So I'll join the 7," making it 8 to 0.

The day it was announced, Ali said, "I thank Allah and the Supreme Court of the United States." He had no idea that he was heading to jail.

The reversal of his conviction brought him back. Everything he did in the seventies was made possible because of that.

DR: In *The Brethren,* you also talk about the *Roe v. Wade* case. When that was decided, Justice Harry Blackmun wrote the opinion. Did that vote switch back and forth as well?

BW: It was immensely complicated. The *Roe v. Wade* opinion is not a legal opinion, it's a kind of doctor's opinion.

Harry Blackmun was very close with doctors — people at the Mayo Clinic — and wanted to make sure that doctors had the right to practice what they thought was correct. That is really the root of the abortion decision.

DR: You began writing books about the Nixon administration, and subsequently you wrote a number of books about other administrations. You also wrote a book about the CIA under Ronald Reagan. Do you think Reagan knew about Iran-Contra or not? [In the Iran-

Contra affair, the administration arranged for covert arms sales to Iran, which was under an arms embargo, and used the proceeds to support the U.S.-backed Contra rebels in Nicaragua.]

BW: I think he did not know, or he did not remember. Casey [William Casey, director of the CIA] was one of the truly most interesting characters, somebody who was very elusive but agreed to let me talk to him. He would scream and yell at me and run away from me, and then have me over to his house for dinner.

DR: And he mumbled all the time. How did you understand what he was saying?

BW: You could just say, "Could you repeat that, please?" And then he would repeat it.

DR: You wrote a book, *The Commanders,* about what happened in the Kuwait war — the Gulf War of 1990–91. Why did that war seem to work so well, in the sense that it got done the way it was supposed to get done, relatively few Americans were killed, and the mission was more or less accomplished? Was the administration's team working together so well?

BW: This was George Bush Senior's war, and

the team did work well together. The theory of the case, held by Colin Powell, who was chairman of the Joint Chiefs of Staff, was that we had to send a force that was absolutely decisive. So we sent nearly five hundred thousand troops and airmen and navy men over to the Persian Gulf, and the war lasted, what, forty-two days?

DR: How did we get people to pay for it? The Saudis and others paid for the war?

BW: Most of it, yes. Jim Baker used to say we "tin-cupped" it. He was Bush's secretary of state, and he went around the world with his tin cup and the Saudis and others filled it up.

DR: When the September 11 attacks occurred, you wrote a book about that. Do you think that U.S. intelligence capability today is such that we could have pieced together the intelligence and prevented that from occurring? Or are we still as vulnerable as we were before 9/11?

BW: It's a great question, and the answer is, I don't know. Let me just skip ahead to President Barack Obama, because I think this is important. I was thinking about this.

When I interviewed Obama for *Obama's Wars,* the focus was really his decision-making in the war in Afghanistan. But out of the blue, not in response to a question — this is a question I should have asked, stupid me — he said, "You know what I worry about at night? What I worry about the most is a nuclear weapon going off in an American city."

He said that would be a game-changer. He then went further and said that a significant number of our intelligence operations are geared to keep that from happening.

DR: Staying on Obama for a moment, how obsessed was he about getting Osama bin Laden, the al-Qaeda leader behind the 9/11 attacks? Was it really a matter of luck? Was it a courageous decision to go after bin Laden in light of the intelligence Obama had?

BW: A lot's been written about that. Again, like Ali or Nixon or any of these things: the full story has not been written.

My curiosity about the bin Laden raid is that they learned that bin Laden was probably at this place in August 2010, and the raid was not until May 2011. [A team of Navy Seals killed bin Laden in Pakistan during a covert operation on May 2, 2011.] Why would it take so long if you could be sure where he was?

They said, "Well, we weren't really sure," but they had satellite photos. They called him "the pacer." He was visible on satellite photos

571

pacing back and forth in the compound. It was pretty clear it was him. So I think there are things we don't know about that, quite frankly.

DR: Okay. Back to 9/11. When President George W. Bush was informed about the attacks, he was reading to these young children at a school in Florida. After he was informed by his White House chief of staff, Andy Card, he didn't get up and rush out. He stayed there frozen for a while.

His explanation was he didn't want to scare anybody. Do you accept that explanation, or do you think he wasn't really prepared to deal with it?

BW: I'm sure he, like most people, didn't know what it meant, whether it was true. It was incomprehensible in many ways.

DR: Later, the Bush administration's strategy was to go into Afghanistan. That worked, but it didn't get Osama bin Laden. Was Bush obsessed with getting bin Laden?

BW: No. It was symbolic but probably not strategically that significant to take out Osama bin Laden.

DR: You wrote another book, *Plan of Attack,* about Bush's decision to invade Iraq in 2003.

Why did the intelligence community make such a big mistake in thinking that there were weapons of mass destruction in Iraq?

BW: Because they knew that Saddam Hussein had had weapons of mass destruction. It seemed logical. [Hussein, the strongman president of Iraq from 1979 to 2003, was toppled by the U.S. invasion.] They did not look at alternative explanations seriously.

And there was a momentum to war. George Tenet, the CIA director, memorably told the president that the intelligence was a slam dunk. You notice that when people are talking about politics now and they're sure about things, they don't use that term anymore.

DR: Do you think President Bush would have invaded had he known there were no weapons of mass destruction there?

BW: In hours of interviews with him, I asked him about that. His answer was, "We're better off with Saddam not in power."

If you really look at it — and I looked at the war plans and interviewed people and interviewed Bush for, as I said, hours on that — the explanation for the Iraq War is momentum, that the military told Bush at the beginning, "Oh, it's going to take a year, it's going to be complicated." Then they said it would be faster and much easier.

Each time the top-secret war plan was presented to President Bush — the code word, interestingly enough, was Polo Step — each time the Polo Step plan came to him, it looked easier and easier. I chart in detail in the book what happened each day, what Bush thought, what his reactions were.

There was no one in there saying, "What about an alternative explanation?" And I quite frankly think, in our politics today or anything else, you have to go for that alternative explanation.

DR: Was Bush ever briefed on the difference between Shiite and Sunni Muslims? Was that ever included when he was briefed about the possible problems of invading?

BW: The focus was, for him, Saddam Hussein. He became obsessed with this.

DR: The surge strategy was later used. Who do you think deserves the credit for the surge more or less working? Had it not worked, what would have been the result?

BW: To a certain extent, we know now, the surge actually didn't work. The drop-off in violence in Iraq was attributable not to the addition of these twenty to thirty thousand troops but to top-secret intelligence operations to locate the leaders, and to the Sunni

Awakening movement and some other things that happened. If you really look at that, the surge as something that put us on a better track in Iraq is a myth.

DR: You've met with many presidents, interviewed them. Could you give us your impressions of the great features and the weaknesses of the presidents that you have met or interviewed?

Let's go over Nixon first. You didn't meet him, but what would you say his greatest strength was? What was his greatest failing?

BW: The hating was his greatest failing. It just doesn't work. It doesn't work in politics. It doesn't work in your personal life. There is a great lesson for everyone in studying Nixon.

DR: Any strengths you'd mention?

BW: Sure. He did some important things in foreign affairs. But he was a criminal, a provable criminal.

Barry Goldwater, of all people, had Carl Bernstein and myself up to his apartment here in Washington and read his personal diary about the last days of Nixon and what happened when he and other Republican leaders went to see Nixon.

It's an astonishing scene, because this is August 1974. Nixon knows he's going to be

The Watergate scandal overshadowed Nixon's foreign policy accomplishments. Here he is in 1973 with (left to right) Soviet leader Leonid Brezhnev, Soviet minister of foreign affairs Andrei Gromyko, and Secretary of State William P. Rogers, toasting the signing of U.S.-Soviet agreements on oceanography, transportation, and cultural exchange. June 19, 1973.

impeached in the House. The question is what the Senate will do, as is always the question.

Nixon said to Goldwater, "Barry, so what do I have in the Senate? Twenty votes?" He needed thirty-four to keep from being removed from office. Goldwater said, "I just counted. And, Mr. President, you have four votes. And one of them is not mine." The next day, Nixon announced he was resigning.

DR: What about Gerald Ford? Greatest strength?

BW: Courage. Democrats acknowledge this, with the pardon he made with the national interest in mind.

DR: What about Jimmy Carter?

BW: Whom you worked for when you were a very young aide who wrote, as I recall, a memo to the president suggesting a war on OPEC.

DR: Well, somebody leaked it to you, and you wrote about it. But yes.

BW: How old were you then?

DR: Twenty-seven or twenty-eight.

BW: Twenty-seven, twenty-eight — what an age to have that wonderful lesson of the cleansing power of a leak. Right? You didn't feel that way at the time.

DR: I thought I would lose my job, but that's another matter. Maybe a war on OPEC would have worked, but that's a separate issue. So, your impression of Carter?

BW: Carter gets a bad and unfair rap on lots of things — and, you could argue, correctly on a number of things.

But the Camp David Accords of 1978,

where he invited Menachem Begin, the Israeli prime minister, and Anwar Sadat, the Egyptian president, to Washington — they went up to Camp David for two weeks, and came up with, effectively, a peace treaty between the two countries. A big step forward.

I remember asking Hamilton Jordan — your boss, the chief of staff, who had a side of him that could be very candid — I said, "How did Carter pull this off?"

He said, "Look, if you'd been locked away at Camp David for thirteen days with Jimmy Carter, you too would have signed anything."

Now, there's a lot of truth in that. What I think is the lesson, and very much to Carter's credit, is he was able to set a priority. He was able to say, "It's worth spending two weeks to really do this."

If you look at their schedules, presidents will spend maybe a half a day on something — fifteen minutes there, some calls here. It is a pressure cooker, to say the least. Presidents more often should say, "This is really the most important thing going on. Let's try to fix it. Let's spend time on the problem."

DR: What about Reagan?

BW: Can I ask a question? How many people here have been involved in a negotiation at one time in your life? Raise your hands. How many people are married? It's the same question.

And what do you learn in a negotiation? That you have to spend time, you have to listen. It gets down to one for you, one for me, one for you, one for me. That's how you solve things.

What Reagan did is he attacked Soviet president Mikhail Gorbachev verbally: "The Soviet Union is the evil empire." Then he negotiated with him. He attacked the Democrats, and then he negotiated with Tip O'Neill, the Speaker of the House. As he said, the purpose of a negotiation is to reach an agreement. And that seems to be a new idea.

DR: What about your impression of George Herbert Walker Bush? Did you spend much time with him?

BW: He would never be interviewed by me. He had been the Republican National Committee chairman during Watergate and spent a lot of time going around defending Nixon. That was his duty, and I think that had an effect.

What he did in the First Gulf War was a model for how to go to war: keep it short. I think he bungled the economy, or appeared to bungle the economy, and that's why Bill Clinton beat him.

DR: What was your impression of Clinton?

BW: Can I use the line "easier to describe the creation of the universe"? What's so interesting about him is that his eight years as president were peace and prosperity, by and large. But the Monica Lewinsky business is going to be in the first paragraph of his obituary. [Clinton's relationship in 1995–97 with Lewinsky, then a White House intern, caused a major scandal and contributed to impeachment proceedings against the president in 1998.]

Somebody was asking me today what I think the ratings are going to be for the presidential debate between Hillary Clinton and Donald Trump. It's going to make the Super Bowl look like an afternoon soap opera.

Trump is going to attack her, presumably: "Crooked Hillary" and "Look at all the things your husband did" and so on and so forth.

Somebody was saying, "How can Hillary Clinton deal with that?" Somebody said, "Let Trump go on and Hillary could say, 'I forgave Bill, and that was very hard, but I forgave him.' " That would maybe end that issue.

DR: Two final ones. George W. Bush — what is your impression of him?

BW: He was the most open person when I

wanted to talk to him. He made a mistake in Iraq, and a significant one, and we still have that problem.

DR: And your impression of Barack Obama?

BW: As one of his aides says, "Obama has the armor of a good heart." I think he really does. If you look at his first inaugural address, where he says that "we're going to be known for our good deeds and the justness of our cause and our sense of restraint" — it's not the way the world works.

I remember, a couple of years ago, having breakfast with one of the world leaders who is one of our best allies. I said, "What do you think of Obama?" He said, "I really like him. He's really smart. But no one's afraid of him."

There's a lot of truth in that — the message in this world we learn as parents: sometimes you have to be tough and you want your kids to be afraid of you.

15
H. W. Brands
ON RONALD REAGAN

"Reagan was a conservative and his philosophy was 100 percent Barry Goldwater's, but he was also an optimist. He had as much faith in the American future as anybody in American politics."

BOOK DISCUSSED:
Reagan: The Life (Doubleday, 2015)

In the view of some scholars, Reagan was the most consequential president since Franklin Delano Roosevelt. That was not widely thought to be a credible possibility early in Reagan's career (he was a B-level motion picture actor); at the time he entered politics (he was first elected governor of California in 1966); or during any of the three times he sought the presidency, finally getting elected in 1980 at the age of sixty-nine, then the oldest age at which anyone had been elected to that office.

There are, of course, more than a fair number of excellent Reagan biographies, many of which were written by those who worked with or had direct access to Reagan while they were writing. H. W. Brands brings an academic's perspective to his subject, for he did not know or ever interview Ronald Reagan. That said, as a result of his research, Brands came to admire Reagan and his presidency. That admiration, tempered with appropriate academic evenhandedness, comes through in the interview.

Bill Brands began his academic career as a high school math teacher, but quickly realized his real passion is history, his undergraduate major at Stanford. After obtaining his PhD in history at the University of Texas, Brands began a dual career — teaching history (at Texas A&M and the University of Texas) and writing books. He has now written an eye-popping twenty-eight books, many of which are critically acclaimed biographies. Two were Pulitzer Prize finalists. His subjects have included Benjamin Franklin, Andrew Jackson, Ulysses S. Grant, Theodore Roosevelt, and Woodrow Wilson as well as Ronald Reagan.

As Brands points out in the interview, Reagan was frequently underestimated throughout his career. I know I was among those who underestimated him.

When I worked in the Carter White House as a young domestic policy staffer, my colleagues and I hoped that Reagan would be our Republican opponent in 1980. I thought that Reagan knew little about policy, and thus would stumble in a debate with a policy-focused Carter; that he was far too conservative and war-prone to capture a majority of the electoral votes; and, most important, that he was far too old at sixty-nine to campaign strenuously or to serve effectively. (I was then thirty-one but am sixty-nine as I write this; it seems closer to the prime of life than it did thirty-eight years ago.)

We were told in 1980 by Reagan's gubernatorial opponent in 1970, Jesse Unruh, that Reagan was smarter than we thought, a more compelling speaker and debater than we thought, and more vigorous than we thought. He said that we should not underestimate Reagan. At our peril, we dismissed his view.

But he was right.

Brands indicates in the interview that Reagan was underestimated throughout his life for a number of reasons: he was outwardly friendly and easygoing (hiding well any large career ambitions); he had an inner reserve that tended to keep him from developing close relationships (even with his four children); he did not seem to focus on details; and he tended to repeat his basic views over and over, and the views seemed simplistic to many. (In brief, Reagan thought that government should be smaller and Communism had to be defeated.)

And, of course, as president he may have been initially underestimated by the Democrats in Congress, who were surprised that Reagan was able to develop the support needed to get his epic tax-cut legislation passed in 1981; by the Soviet leaders, especially Mikhail Gorbachev, who felt Reagan could not be serious about his "Star Wars" missile program; and by those (in both parties) who thought that he might be too old at the age of seventy-three to run effectively for reelection. (He won forty-nine states against the Democratic candidate, Walter Mondale, in 1984.)

In the interview, Brands also discusses the issue that perplexed Reagan's authorized biographer, Edmund Morris: What really made Reagan tick? What really motivated him? How does one penetrate the invisible shield that no one, other than his wife, Nancy, seemed to penetrate? Morris famously inserted himself, as a literary device, into *Dutch,* the official biography, as one way to bring more color to the Reagan story.

Brands did not feel the need to do that to understand Reagan. He concluded that Reagan's emotional shield was the by-product of Reagan's youth (where he had to deal with the complications of a seriously alcoholic father). And he felt that Reagan was secure in who he was; knew his strengths and his weaknesses; and was able to use his charm and sense of humor, often self-deprecating, in ways that less secure leaders or political figures could not.

MR. DAVID M. RUBENSTEIN (DR): Before I start the discussion, how many members here actually served with Ronald Reagan? Anybody? How many were appointed to jobs by Ronald Reagan?

MR. H. W. BRANDS (HWB): How quickly time flies.

DR: So let's have a good conversation about Ronald Reagan. You spent five years researching him and working on this book. Is that right?

HWB: Yes. But I have to say that because I teach American history, I've been thinking about Reagan and lecturing about him since he was president. So I had a long head start on writing the book.

DR: In the latter part of the Reagan administration, a great historian, Edmund Morris, was appointed as Reagan's official biographer. He traveled with him and stayed with him for two years or so.

Then he wrote a book, *Dutch,* that was criticized because he inserted himself into the book as a character in Reagan's life, when he obviously wasn't. He said he did that because he just needed to liven up the book. He couldn't really get his hands around the Reagan personality.

Did you have that same problem? What was the difference between your assessment of Reagan and Morris's?

HWB: The first thing I have to say is that I have the greatest admiration for Edmund Morris as a historian, as a writer. He's a brilliant writer.

I found his book to be very useful. But a lot of people didn't.

I found it useful as a source because I was willing to take the time to tease through the stuff that he writes and the notes to figure out what was true and what was not. It was a fictionalized memoir. I have heard Edmund Morris confess — or admit — that he finds politics boring.

Morris got the job of being Reagan's authorized biographer on the strength of a book that he wrote about young Theodore Roosevelt, who is a compelling character for a biographer. Morris wrote a great book called *The Rise of Theodore Roosevelt.* It won the Pulitzer Prize and was a best seller. On the strength of that, he was brought on board to do the authorized Reagan biography. But the difference is — and I think Morris figured this out in doing the research — that Theodore Roosevelt was a compelling character separate from his political career.

I spent a lot of time on Ronald Reagan, but I will say that if he had not been president of the United States, nobody would have written a biography of him. The importance of Reagan and the interest in him lies with his political career. If you don't find politics interesting, then you're probably going to find Ronald Reagan kind of boring.

I think what happened is that Morris found himself in this cul-de-sac, and that Reagan was an enigma to Morris. To me, the enigma of Ronald Reagan is not what made him tick, but what made him successful. Those are two separate things. I don't think Reagan as an individual was any more puzzling than any of us are.

DR: You start your book with a very interesting part of Reagan's life. In 1964, Barry Goldwater is running for president on the Republican ticket. He isn't doing that well. The campaign decides to put Reagan on TV, and that speech launched his political career. For those who aren't familiar with that speech, what did he say? Why was it so significant that you started your book with it?

HWB: This was the turning point in Reagan's life. He was fifty-three years old. He had had a film career that fizzled out. He couldn't get any roles on the big screen. He had become a TV host, which wasn't really much when TV was really the small screen.

He had earlier developed a certain interest

in politics, but he had no visibility. People in Southern California were aware that for a couple of years Reagan had been speaking on behalf of political candidates. If you weren't from Southern California, you would never have connected him to politics. But the people who saw him saw that this guy had potential, and they wanted to get him before the American public.

Reagan's political philosophy in 1964 was essentially interchangeable with Barry Goldwater's. What Reagan's supporters saw in him that they didn't see in Goldwater was an attractive personality.

Goldwater was a staunch conservative, but he was stern. He was off-putting, even scary, and he was trailing badly in the polls. There was a week left before the election. It was clear he was going to lose badly. So the campaign was willing to throw a Hail Mary pass — not that they really expected he would win, but they were hoping to close the gap a little. So they were willing to put Ronald Reagan on TV.

It wasn't a national show. They recorded a speech of Reagan's in Southern California and aired it in various markets around the country.

It's a striking moment, because Reagan realizes that his career is on the line. His career as an actor has essentially ended, and he doesn't know what he is going to do next. He is in his early fifties. He is not sure if he's going to have a job.

In some ways, this speech was Reagan's second screen test. He'd gone to Hollywood in 1937 and had a screen test there.

He gives the speech, and he knocks it out of the park. Republicans all over the country were smacking themselves in the forehead afterward saying, "We nominated the wrong guy."

By the next morning, there were Ronald Reagan for President committees being formed in various states around the country. It would take him another sixteen years to actually get the nomination, but that speech was the beginning of his political career.

DR: Some people say that if he hadn't been married to Nancy Reagan, he would never have been president, because she was very interested in his running for that office. Do you think that's fair or unfair?

HWB: I would take issue with that. Nancy Reagan was interested in the success of her husband. She had no particular political agenda, and no real interest in politics.

When he became governor and when he became president, she would promote whatever seemed to promote whatever he was promoting. But when he was president, for instance, Nancy had no particular notion of

Acting the part: California Governor-Elect Ronald Reagan riding a horse, 1966.

what the top marginal rate on personal income taxes should be. She had no particular idea of how American relations with the Soviet Union should unfold. What she wanted to do was to make sure that her husband was successful.

She was ambitious for him. But if he had chosen a career in the business sector, I think she would have been just as energetic in promoting his career.

I will say this for Nancy. She was a better judge of character than he was. She was a better judge of who could get in his way.

He was a notorious softy when it came to administration and management. He would let people hang around in his administration long after they had stopped doing any positive good — in fact, even when they became a hindrance to what he was trying to accomplish. Nancy was often the one who would have to work behind the scenes to get them fired.

DR: After five years of researching and working on Reagan, do you admire him more or less now?

HWB: I was a college student in California when Reagan was governor. Then I was teaching American history to high school students by the time he became president. Like a lot of other people, I was wondering where this Hollywood actor got whatever he got to make him as successful as he became.

Some of it was natural. Okay, he's an actor, and he knows how to read lines, and he knows how to give speeches. That was the facile explanation for Reagan's success.

But I realized eventually that I had really underestimated Ronald Reagan. You think of an actor as somebody who reads somebody else's lines. Reagan wrote more of his own lines probably than any president since Woodrow Wilson, who wrote all of his own speeches. Reagan was intimately involved in the development of every important speech that he gave.

Partly that was easy, because he gave essentially the same speech again and again. From that first speech in 1964 right up until the end of his political career and his farewell address in 1989, it's the same message: The government is too big. It needs to be reduced in size. Communism is evil. It needs to be defeated. The rest was details. But the thing that I came to appreciate about Reagan was that he really did change the world.

The Reagan book that I wrote was in some ways a sequel to a biography that I'd written of Franklin Roosevelt. I concluded, in the course of doing the research on Reagan, that these were the two most important presidents of the twentieth century. What Franklin Roosevelt was in the first half of the twentieth century, Ronald Reagan was in the second half of the twentieth century.

In certain respects, each one tried to correct what he saw as an imbalance between the private sector and the public sector. When Roosevelt became president, the private sector amid the Great Depression was on life support, and it needed an injection of government energy. By the time Reagan became president, most American voters — at least the voters who first elected him and the 60 percent of the American electorate who reelected him in 1984 — concluded that the government had gotten too big.

I teach undergraduates at the University of Texas. I boil things down for them. I say, "In American politics, if you think that government is the solution, you're a liberal. If you think that government is the problem, you're a conservative."

DR: Let's go back to Reagan's beginnings. He grows up in Illinois. His father is an alcoholic — not a very good provider, you would say. His mother is the bulwark of the family. He has an older brother, Neil. How did Reagan go from a small town — Dixon, Illinois — to Hollywood? What was his career path?

HWB: When he was very young, Reagan discovered that applause, the laughter of audiences, could alleviate the anxieties of being the son of an alcoholic father, of being someone who didn't know whether his father on one day was going to be his best friend and the next day was going to be utterly unreliable.

His mother became the rock of the family. His mother, who was active in her church, Disciples of Christ, took the younger child in the family, Ronald — Dutch, as they called him — along with her to church.

DR: Where did the nickname Dutch come from?

HWB: The family didn't have any money, so his mother would cut his hair by putting a bowl over his head and just trimming what the bowl didn't cover. So he looked like a little Dutch boy. That's the origin of the name.

Reagan trailed along with his mother to these church events. Among the various events that his mother undertook at the church were plays and musicals and skits. He was a cute kid. He was a good-looking kid. Something inspired her to put him onstage when he was four or five years old. He got up there and he did what cute kids do, and the audience applauded and they laughed.

Reagan, writing his memoirs at the age of eighty, looks back and remembers how it felt. He said he could still remember the music of the applause.

The reason Reagan went into acting was very similar to the reason he went into politics. He reflected on this again in his memoirs. He said the reason a lot of people go into acting is precisely because when they're onstage, people will laugh and applaud. As uncertain as their personal lives might be, their lives onstage are very satisfactory because they get these positive strokes.

He goes from Eureka College into radio.

He intended to go to Hollywood from the time he was in college, but thought that was going to be a step too far. He said he wasn't willing to admit to his college classmates that he wanted to become a Hollywood star. To say instead that he wanted to go into radio, that was more acceptable.

He's always looking for a bigger audience: first at these church performances, then his high school, then his college, then in radio. Then, after a few years in radio, he does a screen test and goes to Hollywood, and he's got a new audience.

DR: He's on the radio in Des Moines, broadcasting Chicago Cubs games. He isn't able to watch them, but he reads the ticker tape, broadcasts the games, and then goes with the team to California. He gets a screen test and gets hired. He's a handsome guy, a nice guy. Why did he not become Clark Gable or Errol Flynn? Why did he not make it to the top?

HWB: Reagan interpreted it as a case of bad timing. He did okay. He did what B actors do. These were the days of B films. He did his introductory work — played in the farm league, so to speak. Just when he was going to hit the big time, just when he was going to make the major leagues, World War II breaks out. That interrupts his career.

In fact, that wasn't it, really. The thing was

that Reagan — I'll backtrack a little bit to his childhood — grows up with this alcoholic father. The person on whom a son is most apt to rely, the one that he's likely to look to for modeling what kind of person to be, is someone who's utterly unreliable.

When I was writing the book, I was on tour for a previous book, and I did an interview with a radio host in Chicago. At the end of the interview he asked a question that often comes up in these kind of things: What's your next book? I said, "I'm working on Ronald Reagan." He put his hand over the microphone and said, "As soon as we get off the air, there's something I need to tell you."

I'm all ears. We get off the air, and he says, "If you want to understand Ronald Reagan, you need to keep in mind that his father was an alcoholic." I didn't know exactly how to react to this bit of intelligence, because I knew perfectly well that his father was an alcoholic. Reagan writes about it in his memoir. Was I supposed to be surprised? I didn't say anything, and I let him continue.

And he continued, "I speak as the son of an alcoholic father." He said, "I will tell you that when you grow up in that kind of environment, you develop a kind of emotional shield around yourself, because this person that you want to look to for guidance, the person you want to lean on, the person you want to model yourself after, is quite unreliable. One day he is your best friend and he's telling you funny stories and throwing the ball around in the backyard, and the next day he's beating the living daylights out of you."

Now, this is not Ronald Reagan exactly, but you'll see where I'm going with this. I'd done a lot of research on Reagan by that point, and I thought, "I'm not going to take this guy's word for it that this explains Reagan." But I was on the lookout for various manifestations of this mind-set.

One of them came from the memoir of Nancy Reagan. It's a wonderful memoir, in part because it is so candid. It is one of the most open and revealing memoirs of somebody in American public life in the last fifty years.

Nancy Reagan was Reagan's closest — I'm tempted to say only really close — friend. She was almost the sum of his emotional universe. But she acknowledges in her memoir that there were times when even she didn't know what was going through his head and his heart — that this wall would come up and she just had to wait for it to come down again.

She realized this was something deep within him. So this is part of the story.

Another bit of evidence comes from Ronald Reagan's own memoir, describing a moment when he's walking home from an after-school activity at the YMCA in Dixon. It's in the winter. The temperature's below freezing. There's snow on the ground. It's starting to get dark.

He turns in to the walkway leading up to the house, and sees his father passed out in the snow. He says, "And I stood there for a moment and I asked myself, 'What should I do? Should I simply walk on by and go into the house and leave him there?' "

He doesn't spell this out, but the obvious conclusion is that he is thinking, "Okay, I'll just leave him there. He'll die in the snow." Reagan is writing this from a distance of nearly seventy years, and he still remembers this moment when he was eleven years old.

In the next sentence, he says, "I decided to pick him up and drag him." But for a kid that age to entertain the thought that his life might be better if his father were dead — that's a pretty heavy thing. This is what Reagan is trying to get away from by going into acting.

DR: He goes into acting. He's a B actor, doesn't get to be Errol Flynn or John Wayne. World War II breaks out. He does training films, later becomes the head of the Screen Actors Guild. Why was he so involved in that?

HWB: I didn't quite answer your question about why Reagan didn't become Clark Gable. This is my inference, and you'll have to take it for what it's worth. It's because Reagan was so reluctant to let down this emotional wall.

If you're going to convey deep emotion as an actor, you have to have someplace in yourself where you can go to feel that deep emotion. Reagan never let himself go there.

So Reagan, by the mid-1940s, had reluctantly come to the conclusion that he was not going to make the top of the marquee. When Reagan announces he's going to run for governor of California, Jack Warner of Warner Brothers hears about it and says, "No, no. Jimmy Stewart for governor. Ronald Reagan for best friend."

That was the kind of role that Reagan was good at. The leading roles, the ones where you really have to dig deep, those were the ones he wasn't good at. He couldn't quite go there.

He realizes that he's not going to make it as a top-level actor, so what else can he do in Hollywood? He discovered an interest in politics. First he goes into the politics of the film business, which is how he gets involved in the Screen Actors Guild.

DR: He becomes the head of SAG for a while. In those days, he's an active, visible Democrat. He campaigns for FDR. He campaigns for Harry Truman. What converted him to being a Republican?

HWB: One of the most difficult questions that I had to answer in writing the book, and I'm not sure that I quite got it, is how exactly to explain this. Reagan was a Democrat from his youth. I think of him as a legacy Democrat.

He was a Democrat because his father was a Democrat. His father got a job as a low-level functionary in the New Deal at a time when the family really needed for his father to have that job. Like very many people who benefited from the New Deal, Reagan developed a certain feeling of gratitude toward Franklin Roosevelt.

But there was more than that. Reagan grew up in the age of radio. His first job was in radio. He was learning how to become a radio personality when Franklin Roosevelt was using radio to connect with the American people.

I'm sure that at this time Reagan had no notion that one day he would want to connect to American voters the way Roosevelt was connecting in the 1930s. But he developed a respect and admiration for Roosevelt's ability to be president. Like a whole lot of people who inherit their political philosophy, Reagan hadn't thought seriously about the essence of it.

He admitted — boasted sometimes — that he had voted for Franklin Roosevelt four times. But he never independently concluded that he agreed with Roosevelt's politics. It was Roosevelt's style of leadership he liked.

That's part of it. The other part is that Reagan says he shifted from being a Roosevelt Democrat to being a Republican in the mid- and late 1940s, when the threat of Communism was becoming more apparent.

He felt it in a personal way as head of the Screen Actors Guild. There were bitter union disputes in Hollywood, and some of the unions were very clearly Communist-oriented, if not outright Communist-dominated.

Reagan, in making various decisions on behalf of the actors — that they would cross picket lines in these strikes — came under personal threat. He got a threat one day that said, "We're going to end your career if you persist in this." He didn't know exactly what this meant, but when he told the police about it, they said, "What they do is they throw acid in your face and you're never going to get an acting job again."

Reagan claims that was the beginning of his turn from a Democrat to a Republican. That doesn't entirely wash, because in the 1940s and 1950s the Democrats were fully as vigorous in opposing Communism as the Republicans were. The Cold War was originally a Democratic project. Conservatives like Robert Taft of Ohio were the ones who were laggards.

The other thing was — and I don't know exactly how much credit to give this — Reagan was making a good salary at a time when the top marginal tax rate on personal income was 90 percent. You don't have to be a raving reactionary to think that ninety cents of every dollar being taxed away is a bit much.

DR: His agent, Lew Wasserman, gets him a job as the host of *General Electric Theater*, which airs first on radio and then on TV. Does that make him a little bit more conservative? He goes and talks to GE employees all the time, and the head of GE was a very conservative Republican.

HWB: Reagan had had no particular interest or education in politics, and particularly in the policy side of politics, before he took this job with GE. He needed the job. He wasn't getting any film roles. He had played through his years as the president of the Screen Actors Guild.

He needs work, and GE's willing to hire him. This is an experiment in how to use television to market products, and the public face of GE is Reagan as the host of *GE Theater*. Every Sunday night, he spends two or three minutes introducing the made-for-TV play of the week.

But he spent the rest of the week traveling the country on behalf of the company. GE's writing his check, and while it doesn't exactly tell him what he's supposed to say, people get influenced by the incentives they have and the work they are conducting.

Sometimes he spoke to groups of GE employees. He's speaking on behalf of GE management and trying to convince the employees that they should avoid trade unions, they should accept what management offers.

Reagan is being educated in this by some of the folks who work at GE. There's a coincidence between what works for Reagan in terms of his job and this dawning notion that the larger government enacted by the New Deal is too big, and furthermore that these high tax rates are really hitting him in the pocketbook. It's a constellation of events that shifts Reagan in a rightward direction.

DR: His TV career ultimately goes away as well, and he's not sure what to do. He makes the speech in '64 that you talked about, and then all of a sudden people say, "You should run for governor," and he decides to run in '66. How did that campaign go?

HWB: Reagan ran for governor of California primarily because he needed to do something before he ran for president. It wasn't that he really wanted to be governor of California. He was thinking bigger than that.

In fact, when Reagan became governor, he

As governor of California, Reagan — photographed here with former pro football player Jack Kemp, circa 1967 — strategized on how to win the presidency.

had to educate himself on a lot of the issues that a governor of California has to deal with. But he was thinking beyond that. In those days, anyway, you had to demonstrate that you could win elections before you got to run for president.

DR: In '66 he runs and gets elected. He beats the incumbent governor, Pat Brown. Then, in '68, although he's only been governor for two years, he starts to run for president. Did he have a chance in '68?

HWB: This demonstrates that Reagan was thinking about the presidency all along. As I said earlier, on the morning after that speech supporting Goldwater, there were Reagan for President committees established around the country.

He runs for president in 1968. He later would claim that he just ran as a favorite son from California, a placeholder so the state delegation wouldn't be caught out when they couldn't decide which of the major candidates they should support.

In fact, Reagan hoped that he could get the nomination, but he was ahead of himself in two respects. One, he wasn't seasoned enough in politics to know what he was getting into. Two — and this is really important in understanding the Reagan phenomenon, and applies to the success of any individual president — has as much to do with the state of the country as with the character of the individual candidate.

In 1968, the Republican Party was not in a position to nominate someone like Ronald Reagan, and the country was not in a position to elect a Ronald Reagan. If he had somehow gotten the nomination in 1968, it might very well have ended his career.

But the fact is he couldn't get the nomination. He realized before going very far that he wasn't going to get very far, that the Republicans were going to nominate Richard

Nixon, who gets elected in 1968.

That demonstrated that as late as 1968, in fact as late as the 1970s, there was a substantial liberal wing in the Republican Party. Now, Republican liberals didn't call themselves liberals, they called themselves moderates. But if you look at the presidency of Richard Nixon, in many ways it tracks the presidency of Lyndon Johnson. The country was not ready for Ronald Reagan in '68 even if he had gotten the nomination.

DR: Reagan gets reelected as governor in 1970, and then his term is up in '74. He then decides to run for president against the incumbent, Gerald Ford. What chance did he really have then? Why did it go so badly at the beginning, and how did he turn it around?

HWB: That Reagan would challenge an incumbent president of his own party demonstrated that Reagan realized or thought in '76 this was his last chance.

DR: He was then sixty-five?

HWB: Yes. He was old by political standards. It was now or never.

Reagan, in various moments of his career, was able to convince himself that what he needed to believe was in fact right. He convinced himself that Ford was too moderate for the United States, that Ford was too squishy on détente, that he had never been elected president and therefore was vulnerable to challenge. [Ford became president when Richard Nixon resigned in August 1974.] I can't disagree with that, and it certainly is what Reagan believed.

But he must have understood that, in challenging Ford the way he did, he was taking a long shot on getting the nomination. Even if he did get it, he might have sufficiently divided the party that it wouldn't have been worth it, and that by challenging and weakening Ford, he might prevent him from getting elected in his own right in 1976, which is exactly what happened.

DR: Reagan lost all the early primaries, then wins in North Carolina, wins other primaries, and moves forward. He announces that Senator Richard Schweiker of Pennsylvania would be his vice president, thinking that would help win the Pennsylvania delegation. It didn't really help.

HWB: The lesson is that if you're running for president, don't announce ahead of the convention whom you're going to choose for your vice-presidential candidate.

DR: At the convention, Ford gets the nomination. Apparently Reagan had said to somebody, "I don't want to be vice president on that ticket." In your book, you point out that Jim Baker, who later worked for Reagan as his White House chief of staff, was told by him at one point that if they'd offered him the vice-presidential slot in '76, he would have taken it.

HWB: This is a case where memories differ, and the historian has to try to parse them. I don't think Reagan would have taken it.

He disagreed with most of Ford's policies, and he thought this was his last shot. When he didn't get the nomination in '76, he basically went home and sulked in his tent. This alienated Ford and caused a lot of Republicans to think that this guy, for all he talked about loyalty and solidarity of the Republican Party, was not a very loyal Republican. He challenges a Republican president, and then, when he loses, doesn't go out and campaign for him. Then Ford loses, and the Ford camp held this against Reagan.

DR: In 1980 he runs for president, and he loses the Iowa caucuses, to the surprise of many people. Then he turns it around in New Hampshire. What happened there that became so famous?

HWB: What Reagan demonstrated is that if you have stage presence, if you know how to cultivate television cameras, if you know how to deal with the media, you can go far.

Reagan seizes the stage in one of the New Hampshire debates and shows this commanding presence. This wasn't the first time, nor was it the last time, but he demonstrated that one-liners — sound bites — can take you a long way in politics.

Again and again, this would convince Americans that Reagan was the kind of guy they could identify with. Much of the support for him had very little to do with his policies per se. It had everything to do with Reagan's personality — the notion that "this is a guy that I would like, this is a guy who has a sense of humor."

I cannot overstate the importance of Reagan's sense of humor in his political success. He used to open nearly every speech with a joke.

The jokes ranged from kind of banal to silly. They were never particularly profound. They were mildly clever at times. But there would be a ripple of laughter that would run through the audience. And as people laughed, they would think, "Maybe this guy's not so bad after all."

DR: He ultimately does get the nomination in 1980. All of a sudden there's a discussion of making Gerald Ford the vice president, on the theory that Reagan isn't really qualified to be president, because he doesn't know enough. Why did that fall apart?

HWB: The idea that Jerry Ford might become the VP nominee was one of the worst ideas ever floated in modern American politics. It was also a demonstration of something that would become characteristic of Reagan's presidency. He allowed bad ideas to develop below his level of recognition and consciousness.

Reagan went out to Palm Springs to talk to Jerry Ford at his home in Rancho Mirage, basically to mend fences. Ford was still sore at Reagan for not campaigning for him more vigorously in '76. Ford and various people associated with him thought that Reagan's challenge and the fact that he had not campaigned for Ford had cost him the election.

Reagan was an easygoing guy, not a political strategist. He didn't think this stuff through. It's unclear who first suggested it, but the idea was that they were going to have this super ticket with Reagan as the presidential nominee and Ford as the vice-presidential nominee.

Somehow word got out to the press. Once the people who were — I'll call them the professionals in the campaign — started thinking it through, they realized there are some overwhelming stumbling blocks. For instance, we would have to address the presidential nominee as "Governor Reagan" and the vice-presidential nominee as "President Ford." The adults on the campaign came to Reagan and said, "Governor, this isn't going to work."

DR: The person he ultimately picked as his vice president was somebody who had criticized him for "voodoo economics," and who, in Reagan's view, had not done a very good job at that New Hampshire debate. Why did he pick George H. W. Bush?

HWB: In large part because they needed somebody really fast. They have to get rid of the story about Ford and, almost in the same news cycle, come up with a nominee. Reagan and the people around him are thinking, "Who's available and credible? Who's not going to cause us any trouble?" Bush was the name that came up and he was willing, so he gets the nomination.

DR: In the general election, there's one debate with Jimmy Carter, the Democratic nominee. Was Reagan a skilled debater? That famous line he came up with — "There you go again" — did he think of that in advance?

HWB: Reagan was a master of one-liners, and he had thought this one through. He was trying to figure out where he would drop it in.

He was not a particularly skilled debater, and understood that his strengths probably didn't show up particularly well in debates. He recognized that Jimmy Carter was a master of policy to a degree that he never was, and that Carter might very well best him in a debate.

I told you at the very beginning that the thing I had to figure out was not what made Reagan tick but what made him successful. One of the things he realized was that a president does not have to master all the details of every policy. He has to establish an atmosphere, a sense of leadership, some guiding principles.

Reagan also recognized that things were moving in his favor. He had been trying for the presidency since 1964, in a formal way since 1968, and he realized that by 1980 the country had shifted in his direction.

He's going to say in his first inaugural address that "in this present crisis" — and I have to stress the phrase "in this present crisis" — government is not the solution, it is the problem. The initial phrase is often ignored, with people saying that Reagan was the enemy of government forever and ever, which is not true. When I was interviewing people for the book, one of them said, "We were conservatives. We were not anarchists."

Anyway, so Reagan realized that things are moving in his direction. The 1960s and '70s

President Reagan in the Oval Office, 1986.

were a hard period for the American dream
— the idea that this country is getting better
all the time. The 1960s and '70s were decades
of riots in the cities, of Vietnam, and the
stumbling of the economy.

At the end of the 1970s, we had the American hostage crisis in Iran, and the perceived
notion that America was weak and unable to
deal with its problems around the world.
Jimmy Carter was in deep trouble, and Reagan knew that all he had to do was to present
an alternative, a notion that America is actually getting better.

I'm not going to say to this audience that
Reagan was the only American conservative
who was at the same time an optimist. But if
you think about it for a minute, conservatives
by nature tend to be pessimists. The reason

you're conservative is that you think change is usually for the worse.

Reagan was a conservative and his philosophy was 100 percent Barry Goldwater's, but he was also an optimist. He had as much faith in the American future as anybody in American politics. In some ways, what Reagan did was to marry the political philosophy of Barry Goldwater with the political style of Hubert Humphrey. It's a formula for victory, as Reagan won in 1980.

DR: He gets elected overwhelmingly. He then names, as his chief of staff, Jim Baker, the man who had been Bush's campaign manager and previously Ford's campaign manager. Where did that idea come from?

HWB: Reagan was not one who overthought personnel decisions, but at times he had good instincts. He observed that Jimmy Carter brought his "Georgia Mafia" with him to Washington, and they basically spurned the idea that they had to have any Washington expertise.

Reagan usually measured his presidency by what he perceived as the failure of the Carter presidency. Something in Reagan, and some of the advice that he got, said, "We need somebody who knows the ways of Washington, somebody who's not a true believer, somebody who will not accept what Reagan says simply because he says it." James Baker was somebody who fit that bill. In some ways Baker became the model of a White House chief of staff.

DR: Was it Nancy Reagan's idea?

HWB: It's not at all clear that Nancy chose Jim Baker. But she wanted someone who was more of a professional than the true believers from California.

DR: At the beginning of the Reagan administration, his highest priority is the tax-cut legislation. How did he get through a Democratic Congress a massive tax cut that was against what many Democrats wanted?

HWB: Reagan campaigned on and promoted the idea of tax cuts and spending cuts. When he became president, the litmus test for conservatives, especially Republican conservatives, was the balanced budget. The way you balance the budget, especially if you're a conservative, is you can cut taxes but you have to cut spending as well.

Reagan runs for office on this idea: we're going to shrink government and we're going to balance the budget. He pointed to the deficits that dated from the Great Society days of the 1960s as something that needed to be fixed.

But he made what I would call a tactical decision. He didn't think of it as a strategic decision in 1981.

He realized that the nature of politics was such that he could get the tax cuts through but he couldn't get all the spending cuts through, in part because he exempted defense, he exempted Social Security, he exempted the big-ticket items, so he really had to gouge the discretionary spending. Even that was a stretch, a tough haul.

What Reagan eventually got in 1981 was tax cuts written in stone and spending cuts to be determined. I still haven't figured out whether Reagan simply overestimated his persuasiveness or underestimated the stubbornness of Tip O'Neill and the Democrats on the spending side. For the rest of his presidency and indeed until the end of his life, Reagan said, "I'm still a balanced-budget guy. It was just those profligate Democrats who insisted on their big spending programs."

But any realist would have said, once you've gotten your tax cuts, a lot of the pressure on people to give you the spending cuts is gone. Tax cuts are comparatively easy. Spending cuts are harder.

Some of the big deficits of the 1980s and up until today date back to Reagan's presidency. The national debt doubled in real terms. The amount of debt that had been run up since George Washington's presidency to

1980 — that much again was accumulated during Reagan's presidency.

DR: There was an assassination attempt on Reagan in March of the first year of his administration. How close did he come to death?

HWB: If we measure it, probably half an inch or so. That's basically how far the bullet was from his heart. It might have been even closer than that, because Reagan didn't realize initially that he had been hit.

He heard the shots. He was shoved into the back of the presidential limousine and his Secret Service agent came in on top of him to shield him. Reagan felt this pain, and he thought that he had broken a rib by hitting it on the hump of the car.

They first head toward the White House to get him safe there, but he coughs up blood, so they turn and go to George Washington University Hospital. He still has no idea that he has been badly wounded. He insists on walking from the limousine into the hospital.

He gets inside the double door of the hospital and passes out. He nearly collapses on the floor, but he's surrounded by Secret Service and hospital personnel, so they prevent him from whacking his head on the floor. And they realize he has been hit.

It took the surgeons a while to figure out

exactly where the slug was. It took them even longer to figure out how they could get it out. They worried that they might actually cause more damage, because the bullet had ricocheted off the limousine and had flattened out, so it was this almost ninja-like disk with sharp edges. Every time it moved, it risked doing more damage to Reagan's internal organs.

The surgeons were finally able to get it out. But it was a very close call, a closer call than the public knew at the time.

DR: He survives, and later in his first term he tries to get other legislation through. What was the most significant thing he accomplished in his first term other than spending cuts?

HWB: That was the most important. The next thing, in terms of legislation, was the bolstering of Social Security in 1983.

DR: Some people say the assassination attempt on Reagan affected him mentally and that he never was quite as sharp afterward. Do you agree with that?

HWB: Perhaps out of delicacy, you declined to mention Bill O'Reilly's book *Killing Reagan*. Its basic thesis is that the shooting in 1981 eventually led to Reagan's death in

2004. My thinking on this is that if something happens to you when you are seventy years old that kills you over two decades later, that's a lethality we can all live with.

There are those who claim — O'Reilly is one, along with his coauthor — that somehow this triggered Reagan's failing memory. Now, his memory quite clearly did fail after he left the White House. The question of whether he was becoming forgetful while he was president was one that I had to deal with. Everybody who's looking at the Reagan presidency closely has to look at the possibility.

There were certain moments when it was an issue that became quite public. When Reagan was running for reelection in 1984, he had two debates with Walter Mondale, the Democratic candidate. In the first debate, Reagan was uncharacteristically clumsy and flummoxed.

This is a trained actor, a guy who knows how to memorize his lines. He tripped over his opening statement, which everybody memorizes. He tripped over his closing statement, repeated himself. People who watched this became kind of embarrassed for him.

The next day, the *Wall Street Journal* — the Reagan-friendly, Republican-friendly *Wall Street Journal* — had a masthead headline that asked, "Is Reagan Too Old to Be President?" This was the first time the issue was raised in a serious way.

The usually polished Reagan's clumsy performance in a 1984 debate with Democratic challenger Walter Mondale raised questions about his ability to be president.

Ron Reagan, Reagan's youngest child, said in a memoir he wrote after his father died that he watched this debate and became convinced this was the first public sign of what would eventually be diagnosed as Alzheimer's disease. Ron Reagan was pilloried for this, and he was sort of forced to retract it. But it's an issue that did come up.

Reagan didn't really address the issue at all. He just made people laugh about it. People could say, "He's got a sense of humor. If he's laughing it off, we can laugh it off too."

There were various people who observed Reagan during his second term and said that he was clearly slowing down. John Poindexter, who was his national security advisor at the time of the Iran-Contra scandal, told me in an interview that he thought Reagan's failing memory was part of the Iran-Contra stuff.

DR: What about Reagan's children? He had four children, but he seemed to have no relationship with them while he was president. What was that about?

HWB: This goes back to what I was saying earlier: that Reagan seemed to have an emotional universe that could encompass Nancy but almost no one else. Reagan was friendly but had no real friends.

I have thought that if he had not been politically important, if he hadn't been famous in that way, nobody would have come to his funeral. There was nobody outside of Nancy he confided in. He didn't reveal much of himself to anyone, and the kids often felt on the outside of this.

When they were young, sometimes they attributed it to the fact that their father and Reagan's first wife, Jane Wyman, the mother of his first two kids, were both Hollywood actors and they were busy. But it was more than that. Reagan just didn't have room in his emotional world for the kids.

There's a very telling moment when his son Michael is about to graduate from high school, except that he doesn't have enough credits and he's been bouncing from one school to another. The boarding school he's attending says, "We will allow you to graduate if you can get your father to give the commencement address."

Michael calls up his dad: "Dad, can you come down and give the commencement address?" Reagan is thrilled, because he was not sure that Mike was ever going to graduate from high school. He goes down there and he's in politician mode, working the room with the graduates. He says, "Hi, I'm Ronald Reagan. What's your name?" "Johnnie Smith." "Hi, I'm Ronald Reagan. What's your name?" "Mary Jones." "Hi, I'm Ronald Reagan. What's your name?" "Dad!!!"

He didn't even recognize his own son. Michael tells this story in his memoirs.

DR: One last question. Is that hair really his? No dye?

HWB: Was his hair really that black his whole life? Reagan claimed it was, and I never found evidence to the contrary. Being a responsible historian, if I don't have evidence, I can't say.

16
CHIEF JUSTICE JOHN G. ROBERTS JR.
ON THE U.S. SUPREME COURT

"I get to do the kind of work I enjoy, in service of the country that I love, with eight wonderful people. And I can do it for as long as I want. That's a pretty good combination."

The legal world has produced, in every generation, a few individuals who seem destined to rise to the top of the profession. John G. Roberts Jr. is one of those individuals: an honors graduate of Harvard College (he made it through in three years), an honors graduate of Harvard Law School (where he was the managing editor of the *Harvard Law Review*), a clerk for Judge Henry J. Friendly of the U.S. Court of Appeals for the Second Circuit, a clerk for Supreme Court Justice William H. Rehnquist, a special assistant to the attorney general of the United States, an associate White House counsel, the principal deputy solicitor general, and one of the finest Supreme Court advocates in recent decades.

But life rarely goes forward without setbacks. John Roberts had one in 1992 when he was nominated to be a judge on the U.S. Court of Appeals for the D.C. Circuit by President George H. W. Bush. The end of the first Bush presidency arrived before the U.S. Senate acted on the nomination, and Roberts remained in private practice for another eleven years.

He might well have stayed there for the rest of his career. A lawyer who wants to be a judge rarely gets a second bite at the apple.

But in 2001, President George W. Bush, recognizing the obvious legal talent of John Roberts, nominated him again to the Court of Appeals for the D.C. Circuit. The Senate confirmed him in 2003. Two years later, with Justice Sandra Day O'Connor's retirement, Bush nominated Roberts to be her successor.

However, before the Senate could consider the nomination, Chief Justice William Rehnquist passed away, and President Bush then nominated Roberts to be chief justice. He was confirmed in September 2005 by the Senate. With that he became, at the age of fifty, the youngest chief justice in two hundred years.

The new chief was not only young by the standard of his predecessors, he was young compared to me. (I am five years older.) Perhaps it is a sign of aging when you first realize that the high position of chief justice of the Supreme Court is held by someone younger than you.

The chief justice's main responsibilities obviously revolve around leadership of the Supreme Court and the federal judiciary. But one of his other duties is to serve as the chancellor of the Smithsonian Institution, the government-supported organization, created in 1846, that now operates nineteen museums and nine research centers. I was appointed to the Smithsonian's board of regents in 2012, and now serve as chair of the board's executive committee. In that capacity, I have worked with Chief Justice Roberts on Smithsonian matters and have come to know him reasonably well, and to admire him a great deal (because of his accomplishments, legal acumen, intellect, wit, and work ethic).

Although Chief Justice Roberts is not a

professional historian, I thought a departure in the Congressional Dialogues series from a historian interviewee would certainly be warranted if he would agree to let me interview him in this setting. To my delight, he did, and the result was a quite interesting look at his career and at the Supreme Court. The chief justice's self-deprecating humor and wit, perhaps not widely known, are apparent in the interview.

Of all of the interviews held in the Dialogues series, this one probably attracted the greatest number of members of Congress. While they work in buildings only a few hundred yards away from the Supreme Court, most have little regular contact with the justices. This was therefore an opportunity for them not only to meet the chief justice but to hear his views on so many matters relating to the court.

It is not considered appropriate to ask a sitting justice about the reasoning behind a particular decision or the possible outcomes of future cases. So the discussion does not include those kinds of subjects. But it does nonetheless offer interesting, even rare, insights into the court and its current (still quite young) chief justice.

Chief Justice Roberts provided an inside look at how the Supreme Court operates — how cases are selected to be considered, how oral arguments are used, how the cases are voted upon and assigned for opinion-writing, how the opinions are drafted and announced (without leaks — a Washington rarity), and how the collegiality among the justices is generally maintained, despite wide ideological differences in many areas.

The chief justice might never have had the chance to lead the court, he reveals in the interview, but for a chance encounter while he was an undergraduate at Harvard. He expected to be a historian, and was a history major. But during a cab ride in Boston, the driver mentioned that he too had gone to Harvard and majored in history. That prompted John Roberts to expand his academic interests and to pursue a career — the law — less likely to force him to be driving cabs after graduation.

MR. DAVID M. RUBENSTEIN (DR): We're very honored tonight to have the chief justice of the United States, John Roberts. Thank you very much for coming. We won't take it as a comment on anything he says if some people get up and leave between nine and nine-thirty, because we understand there might be a Senate vote.

CHIEF JUSTICE JOHN G. ROBERTS JR. (CJR): Or a World Series game, one or the other.

DR: You labor very hard on your opinions, obviously. But you got the most attention I've seen recently for a speech you gave at the ninth-grade commencement of your son. Why did that speech go viral? What did you say that got so much attention from everybody?

CJR: I didn't even know it was being filmed. What may have caught some eyes is that it was ninth grade, so it was different than most commencement speeches. You can't tell the students that they have reached a great milestone or that they are about to go out into the world. I had to think about what was suitable for them.

It occurred to me that the start of high school is an important time. For a lot of people, character is really shaped in high school. College will test your character, of course. But in high school you have to go through a few rough things, and it shapes what you're going to be like.

DR: You told the ninth-graders you hoped that they failed — that you hoped they weren't successful because they would learn more from that.

CJR: If you fail at things in high school, it is usually not that dramatic. I wished them bad luck — because if you experience that, you come to realize that chance plays an important role in life, and you can decide to be bitter about it or you can decide to understand that success is not entirely due to one's own efforts, and neither is failure.

DR: At least from the outside, it doesn't seem like there have been a lot of failures in your life. You were a superstar student. You're the chief justice of the United States. Let's talk about your background. You're from Indiana?

CJR: I was born in Buffalo but grew up in Indiana.

DR: Were you a good student in high school? I assume you were pretty good.

CJR: The eighth-grade class from my elementary school comes and visits the court every year, and one year they brought my permanent record. I mean, it is a *permanent* record.

To be honest, I expected it to be pretty good. It was mixed. There was one year when I had good grades except for one D from what I figure must have been a conduct issue.

DR: You must have done well in high school. You got into Harvard. When you got there, did you realize that either everybody there was smarter than you or that you were smarter than most of the other people there?

CJR: There were some very smart people there. People like Yo-Yo Ma were in my graduating class.

DR: Wow! Did you know him then?

CJR: No, no. Bill Gates was also in my entering class. He didn't graduate, of course. Think how well he could have done if he had stayed in school.

DR: You graduated in three years. How do you graduate from Harvard in three years?

CJR: It is not that dramatic. If you took enough Advanced Placement tests and did well enough on them, you could skip your first year.

DR: When you graduated, did you decide to do a gap year, or did you want to go right to law school?

CJR: I went straight to law school. The idea of gap years wasn't very common, and my father wasn't that sympathetic to it.

DR: Were there lawyers in your family?

CJR: No.

DR: What propelled you to go to law school? Did you know when you went to Harvard you wanted to go to law school?

CJR: No. I didn't want to go to law school. I wanted to be an historian. I enjoyed history and thought I could make a career out of it.

I was driving back to school from Logan Airport in Boston one day and I talked to the cabdriver. I said, "I'm a history major at Harvard." And he said, "I was a history major at Harvard."

DR: So you decided to go to law school.

CJR: I thought I would move to law.

DR: I went to law school. In the first year of law school — really in the first month or two — you realize certain people have the ability to quickly do legal reasoning. They have the knack of it, and some people don't. You must have realized that it wasn't as hard as you had thought it would be.

CJR: It *was* as hard as I thought it would be. It was pretty hard throughout.

DR: But you made the *Harvard Law Review,* which meant you were near the top of your class, and so you got a clerkship. Did you know when you were in law school that you wanted to be a judge?

CJR: I thought I would practice law. The idea of being a judge did not cross my mind.

DR: You clerked for a very famous judge named Judge Friendly, who was probably the most famous federal court of appeals judge. How was that experience?

CJR: It was transformational. It really was. Harvard Law School, at the time, the late seventies, was a pretty cynical place. I think it's changed somewhat. But then, it left students with the sense that the law was either the means by which the upper class oppressed the lower class, or it was a tool that could be manipulated to promote particular causes. So I left law school not thinking it was a particularly noble calling.

That changed with Judge Friendly. He was somebody who did think that the law had stature of its own, independent from the uses to which it could be put; that the law was something very noble, that laws were the wise restraints that make men free.

To see him not only believe that but also practice it at the highest level changed my view of the whole profession.

DR: After that you got a clerkship with Justice William Rehnquist. Was he the chief justice at the time?

CJR: No, no.

DR: What was it like clerking for him?

CJR: It was a very different experience. I was not close in age to Justice Rehnquist, but he was at most a generation removed from his law clerks, and Judge Friendly was a couple of generations removed.

It was very easy to clerk for Justice Rehnquist. We did not have to do bench memos. He did a lot of the work without the need for a law clerk. He was very crisp in logic and writing style. He had really a whole different style than Judge Friendly, but I was very fortunate to have both clerkships.

DR: When Rehnquist was chief justice later,

he was famous, I am told by some of his clerks, for having betting pools on everything. Did he do that when he was a younger justice?

CJR: Yes.

DR: Always betting on various sporting events?

CJR: It was worse than that. He would bet you when the first snowfall would be. Or how deep the snow was, and then you'd get outside with a ruler and measure it. The bets were usually shaped in such a way that he had a real advantage in terms of knowledge.

DR: After you finished your clerkship, you went to work at the Justice Department, and later you went to work in the Reagan White House. I'm told that the first day you showed up at the White House, the president of the United States was supposed to call you. What happened?

CJR: The phone rang, I picked it up, and the operator said, "Could you hold for the president?" I said, "Yes." I thought it was very nice that President Reagan would call someone on his first day just to say hello.

I was holding a little while, then holding longer, and then I started to think, "How long should I hold?" I thought, "Maybe he's

636

talking to the Soviets," or that he was held up by something else important going on. And so I waited on hold some more. I waited on hold a long time.

Then, all of a sudden, I heard laughter outside the door to my office. My new office-mates had a pool about how long I would just sit there and wait on hold. I don't know who in the pool had fifteen minutes, but he won.

DR: You did that for a while, and then you went to practice law in Washington. Then you became a litigator and a Supreme Court appellate lawyer?

CJR: There are some very good trial lawyers here, and I wasn't one of those. I liked to do appellate work, but it really was not a specialty then. You didn't say, "I do appeals."

Usually the lawyer who tried the case would handle the appeal, so I looked to develop a practice like that. I worked with a more senior lawyer, a fellow named Barrett Prettyman Jr., who did have that kind of practice. I hoped to emulate him.

DR: Then George Herbert Walker Bush becomes president, and you get a job in the Solicitor General's Office as deputy solicitor general of the United States and you're arguing before the Supreme Court regularly. Was that an intimidating experience?

CJR: Yes. It is absolutely terrifying. I remember the minute before ten o'clock, when the justices are about to come out on the bench, just thinking, "Why am I doing this?" But then as soon as you sit down, you wonder, "When can I do it again?" It is a very special opportunity.

DR: How long does it take to prepare for an argument in the Supreme Court? A week?

CJR: Oh, no, no. If you can arrange it, a couple of months, because there are nine justices. They can ask anything they want. They do. It was a very, very hot bench, as it is today. You just cannot anticipate every hypothetical, every factual question.

I started a fresh legal pad whenever I had a new case, and I would just write down every question that occurred to me. By the time of the argument, I would have five hundred questions I had prepared to answer. But I still realized they were going to ask some questions that were not on my list.

DR: So you did that for a while. Then the president of the United States said, "I'd like you to be a judge on the D.C. circuit." You were sent up to the Senate for confirmation. What happened?

CJR: The election of 1992 happened. I did not get a hearing before the election, and the president lost, so that was it.

DR: So you went back to practicing law. At that point, did you think your legal career as a jurist was never going to happen?

CJR: I did not think the bus would stop on my block again, no.

DR: So you practiced mostly Supreme Court law?

CJR: Yes. Having been in the Solicitor General's Office, I had experience, and so it was a little easier to do.

DR: Then you get an opportunity to get on the bench again. George W. Bush becomes president, and in 2001 he nominates you to be on the D.C. circuit. Did you get confirmed pretty readily?

CJR: Well, I wouldn't go that far.

DR: So you're on the bench for about two years. There's a Supreme Court vacancy in 2005 when Justice Sandra Day O'Connor decides to retire. President Bush has some interviews with potential nominees. You had an interview. What was that like?

Justice Sandra Day O'Connor, the first woman appointed to the U.S. Supreme Court.

CJR: I was very impressed by the president. It was a much more substantive discussion than I had expected. He had a very considered, educated view of the courts and their relationship with the other branches. I was just very, very impressed. After our conversation, we went out to the Truman Balcony of the White House. It was an uplifting moment. I felt proud to be an American.

But I was teaching a summer session in

"WELL, IT'S ABOUT TIME"

"Well, it's about time": July 8, 1981, newspaper cartoon by Herblock marking the
confirmation of Sandra Day O'Connor to
the Court.

London at the time, and when the interview
was over, I got on the plane and flew back to
London to finish the class, because I did not
expect to be chosen.

As soon as I got there, the White House
staff said, "You need to come back again."
But they were very careful. They said, "This
doesn't mean you're going to get the job." I
thought maybe they were still looking at a

couple of people.

It was a traumatic day because it was the day, in 2005, of the London subway bombing, and I was near the cordoned-off site of the attack.

I figured if I returned to Washington I was not going to come back to London again, so I got all my stuff. It was hard to get a cab. I got to Heathrow, and there was this very long line of people waiting for a plane.

I remember walking to my flight thinking, "Oh, these poor people. They're stuck here." That was the line for my plane. The computers had all broken down.

I did not think I was going to get out in time. I knew that White House and that president. If the president's first-choice nominee was late, I thought he might well just nominate the next person on his list.

Eventually I got on the plane, but it was very late. I landed at Dulles Airport and made it home just in time to answer the phone call. It was Harriet Miers, the White House counsel. I was a little disappointed, because I assumed she was calling people who did not get the job. But then the president came on the line and offered me the nomination.

DR: You had a ceremony at the White House, and your son stole the show, as I remember it. He was about four or five?

CJR: Five.

DR: Five years old. You and the president were talking, and your son was running around in front of you. Was that distracting to you and the president?

CJR: To both of us, as I found out. Jane, my wife, was there with the kids, and I looked over and our daughter, Josie, was holding her hand — and Jack was not there. He was in front and he was dancing around. In retrospect, it is cute. At the time, it was not.

DR: Shortly thereafter, Chief Justice Rehnquist dies. The president called you and said, "How would you like to be more than just a justice — to be chief justice?" You didn't have to do another interview?

CJR: Yes. It was a very emotional time.
Chief Justice Rehnquist died on a Saturday. My hearings were set to begin on the Tuesday. I got the call that Chief Justice Rehnquist had passed away, and President Bush invited me to the White House to talk about it Sunday night. Monday morning my nomination to be chief justice was announced. And Tuesday I was walking up the steps to the court carrying Chief Justice Rehnquist's casket. So there was a lot going on in those few days.

DR: When you had your confirmation hearing, you famously said that you were going to be like an umpire. Is that because you like baseball? How did that metaphor or analogy come to you?

CJR: A lot of law professors have written articles about how ridiculous the analogy was. They said I did not sufficiently appreciate how difficult it was to be a judge. And I think they did not sufficiently appreciate how difficult it is to be an umpire.

I don't think it is a naïve analogy. Basically, you want to make sure you understand that an umpire doesn't make the rules. He applies them. The courts are not Congress. You are not on either team when a case is in front of you.

DR: So you are confirmed. You were the newest and youngest member of the court and also the chief justice. Was that a little awkward?

CJR: The scenario was worse than that. The court had been together for eleven years without any change, the longest time in modern Supreme Court history. The other justices were all older than I was. They all had vastly more judicial experience than my two years. And I had been arguing cases in front of them, so I literally had been beneath them looking up. To come in as the chief was a little daunting.

I will always be grateful for how they made me feel welcome and comfortable. In conference, the chief justice presents the case and says what he thinks ought to be done, but I did not know quite how it worked. So at my first conference, I called on "Justice Stevens" and then "Justice O'Connor." Then Justice Scalia said, "What is all this? That's John. That's Sandra. I'm Nino." And, he said, "You're the Chief."

It was a real gripping moment to realize I had the support of the court — not because they thought I was in any way superbly qualified for the position, but they realized that somebody had to occupy that role, and they were going to be supportive of me in doing that. And it meant a lot to me.

DR: Explain how the court decides what cases it's going to hear. What is a writ of certiorari?

CJR: It's an old law term. And that's all I know.

We get about 8,500 to 9,000 of these petitions every year from people who want us to hear their case, and we will hear fewer than 1 percent of those cases. There are some that we will almost surely take. If a lower court has held an act of Congress unconstitutional, we will decide that question as a matter of comity with the legislative branch across the street.

Typically, though, it is a conflict question. To take the simplest example, if the Court of Appeals for the Ninth Circuit in California says you can deduct these taxes on your federal return and the Court of Appeals for the Second Circuit in New York says you cannot do so — it has to be the same answer throughout the country, so we will take that case.

Which is why a lot of the cases on our docket are not terribly interesting. They are conflicts in interpretation of federal laws that need to be resolved. That is the easiest way to get a case brought to the court.

DR: You need four justices to agree to hear a case.

CJR: Right.

DR: Do you actually talk about the cases you're going to hear?

CJR: We review 150 cases a week. All the justices look at them, through whatever system each justice has, and we put on the "discuss list" all cases anyone wants to talk about. Of those 150 for each weekly conference, there might be a dozen that we will want to talk about, and we talk about each of those.

DR: Let's suppose you've agreed to hear a case and the case is argued. Before the argument, does every justice actually read all the briefs? Or do they skim them? They can't read all the amicus briefs, I assume.

CJR: Sometimes we can. In some cases, there will be six or seven amicus briefs, and we can read those. In one of the big marquee cases, there might be eighty amicus briefs. I do not read that many. I do read the summary of argument of each one.

And I will pick ones that I think are important. If it is a labor case, for example, I will likely read an amicus brief from a national labor union because of its perspective. Then my law clerks will read all eighty of the briefs, and they'll say, "You should read these seven or eight."

DR: Before the oral arguments, the justices do not talk about the cases other than when they granted the writ of certiorari?

CJR: Certainly not in any formal way — not at conference and not walking down the halls. People come to the arguments on their own.

DR: When an argument is being made in

front of the Supreme Court, the justices ask questions. Are they asking questions because they want the answers or because they want to influence other justices, or do they just want to make a public point?

CJR: We do not ask questions to make public points, but we ask questions for a number of different reasons. Sometimes you just have a question and you want to know the answer. Sometimes you have formulated in your mind a tentative view, and you think, "Well, it does depend on this," and you will ask that question.

If a justice asks a question and it reveals to me that the justice is focused on something in a particular way, and I see it differently, I might ask a follow-up question so that the lawyer can have an opportunity to make us all comfortable with an answer.

Sometimes it is like Wimbledon. I remember one exchange — I think it was between Justice Scalia and Justice O'Connor. Justice O'Connor says, "I don't think there's any jurisdiction here." And before the lawyer can answer, Justice Scalia jumps in and says, "Well, there's diversity between the corporations, isn't there?" And before the lawyer can answer, Justice O'Connor jumps in and says, "Well, but the corporation's principal place of business is here, isn't it?" The lawyer is standing there looking back and forth.

Finally it gets to the point where Justice O'Connor asks another question, and the lawyer turns to look at Justice Scalia. He leans over and says, "You're on your own."

DR: When a justice asks a question and the lawyer says, "I'll get to that later," that's a bad answer, right?

CJR: Yes. That does not usually work.

DR: Are justices' opinions really changed by oral argument, or does it really not affect the outcome?

CJR: Oral argument is a very important part of the process. I had been on the arguing side for twenty years, so I would have been very disappointed if that turned out not to be the case.

It is part of a process of winnowing down. You read the first brief, you think, "Well, that sounds right." You read the other side's brief: "Well, maybe that's right." The oral argument is part of the winnowing down until you get to a decision point.

You may have particular issues you want to talk about. You might have hypotheticals to illuminate them. You learn for the first time what your colleagues think. It is the first time you learn, for example, that Justice Neil Gorsuch might think there is a jurisdictional issue. You hadn't thought about it, so you react to that. And you might have thought you knew how one justice was going to proceed, but his questioning reveals a totally different perspective, so you look at that.

It is very, very hard for the advocates because they have to juggle all these different data points. But it is exhilarating. I enjoyed being on both sides.

DR: We have a Supreme Court Bar in the United States now. We had one at the beginning of the country's history. Do you ever feel sorry for the lawyer who has never argued in front of the Supreme Court and just doesn't know how to do it?

CJR: If they do not know how to do it, yes. But there is a sophisticated Supreme Court Bar. It is very, very good. We are very fortunate that we have lawyers who specialize in that practice, because it is not like arguing in a state court or even a court of appeals. In a half hour there will be a hundred questions and you have to know how to field them.

We all have a romantic image, a sort of *Mr. Smith Goes to Washington* image of the lawyer with the battered briefcase, and he's there alone. That happens sometimes.

I remember one occasion in which a lawyer said, "Well, that's pretty much all I have. I just want to say this has been the experience of my life." I do not remember if he won or not. But it takes an enormous amount of work, and for a sole practitioner to devote months to preparing — you just cannot do it.

DR: Can you tell when an experienced Supreme Court practitioner is making an argument only to win the vote of a justice who it's well known has a certain view? Is that apparent to the other justices?

CJR: Yes. An experienced Supreme Court advocate will not do that. You really do have to have an overarching concept of your case. If you say, "Oh, Justice So-and-So, you did this . . . ," that will annoy the other justices.

DR: How long after the oral argument do you have a conference about the case?

CJR: Two days. Cases we hear on Monday, we conference Wednesday afternoon. Tuesday and Wednesday cases, we conference on Friday morning.

DR: How long is a conference, typically?

CJR: On Friday morning, we also look at what cert petitions to take. So that takes up the whole morning. Wednesday afternoon, it is just two cases. When there is a big case, it can take several hours. On the other hand,

Left to right: Attorneys George E. C. Hayes, Thurgood Marshall (the future Justice), and James M. Nabrit on the steps of the Supreme Court following the 1954 decision declaring school segregation unconstitutional.

for a straightforward case, it might take a half hour.

DR: When you're in conference, nobody other than the justices is allowed in the room. Is that right?

CJR: Right.

DR: If somebody knocks on the door, who's

supposed to answer that?

CJR: Justice Gorsuch now. It is the most junior justice. For some time after Justice Gorsuch joined the court, Justice Kagan would instinctively get up, and we had to remind her to sit down.

DR: I understand that the most junior justice is also in charge of the Cafeteria Committee.

CJR: Right.

DR: And that's a very prestigious position?

CJR: No, no, it is part of the hazing ritual. There is the loftiness of being nominated to be a member of the Supreme Court and being confirmed, and then you go meet with the Cafeteria Committee. Somebody has to do it.

DR: As the chief, you start the conference discussion. Does everybody get asked their opinion in order of seniority?

CJR: Right. We just go around the table. The rule I apply is that no one speaks twice until everyone has spoken once. That is the tradition. Usually there needs to be a second round, or people will have other points they want to make in reaction to points they did not have a chance to respond to.

DR: After you hear everybody's arguments, if you're in the majority, you then assign the opinion to somebody?

CJR: At the end of the two-week session, because I need to know who is available for each case.

DR: And if you're in the minority, then the most senior justice in the majority assigns the opinion?

CJR: Right.

DR: When the opinions are being written, do people ever change their minds about how they're going to vote?

CJR: A number of things can change. One, the rationale might change. You might have thought that *this* was the basis for the decision, but maybe when you see the writing, you think, "That's not so good. I think it should be this." And sometimes people change their votes as well.

Sometimes the votes will be in, and one justice will say, "I'm very tentative about this." You try to take that into account in making assignments.

"Nine people acting collegially": The Justices of the Supreme Court, group portrait, May 20, 1957. Sitting, left to right: Justices Douglas, Black, Warren, Frankfurter, and Burton. Standing, left to right: Justices Brennan, Clark, Harlan, and Whittaker.

DR: Can one justice walk down the corridor to another justice's chambers and say, "I'd like to talk to you about this case," and try to lobby them?

CJR: I wouldn't use the word *lobby.*

DR: Convince?

CJR: It does not happen as often as you might think. There is kind of a general ethos that we are nine people acting collegially. We would like to have the discussions when everybody is there. We do that orally a couple of times, but the rest of it is in writing.

So if you have a particular idea that has not

been fleshed out, you would write a memo and send it around to everybody. That isn't to say that every now and then somebody won't walk down the hall. But it would be to talk over the merits of a particular issue.

DR: So if one member of the court wants to talk about the merits of a case and he wants to persuade someone, and he says, "I could maybe agree with you on this, but maybe you could agree with me on another case"? Do they ever do that?

CJR: They don't do it with me. I don't know what they do among themselves.

DR: All right. How does the Supreme Court avoid leaks? Never have I seen an opinion leaked in advance. What's the secret to that?

CJR: It is a source of considerable pride that we do run a tight ship. I meet with all the law clerks at the beginning of the term and that is one thing I emphasize to them.

The people in the building are an extraordinary workforce. They are dedicated to the institution, and I don't think they are going be the source of any leaks.

DR: How do you pick law clerks? Each justice has four clerks?

CJR: Four, right.

DR: What do the clerks do?

CJR: Whatever the justice wants them to do. They write memos. In many chambers they do bench memos: "Here's an outline of what the case is about." I inherited the practice from both Judge Friendly and Justice Rehnquist not to have those.

But I might request a memo on a particular jurisdictional issue that came up. I like to use my clerks as sounding boards. All of them will work on each case. One takes the lead on any particular case, but the others will help prepare it. I'll bounce ideas off of them to get some sense of areas where my thoughts might be weak or need some shoring up.

DR: You pick law school students who, I assume, are at the top of their class?

CJR: I talk to some professors that I know and they'll say, "This is a good person to look at." And I talk to judges, because clerks usually work on a lower court before coming up to the Supreme Court. They send me good recommendations.

DR: Have you ever picked one and said, "Oops, I made a mistake" afterward?

CJR: Well, some are better than others.

DR: All right. What is the biggest challenge of the federal judiciary? Is it the compensation level of judges? For example, your clerks, when they leave, their first day at a law firm they get paid more than you get paid.

CJR: Right.

DR: As I understand it, the starting salary in law firms is maybe $200,000 or $250,000, and the bonus for having been a Supreme Court clerk is $250,000.

CJR: They tell me it is up to $300,000.

DR: So they're making maybe $550,000 their first year, and the chief justice is making a lot less. What is the biggest challenge to getting judges compensation?

CJR: I worked hard for several years to try to get a judicial pay increase, and for a lot of reasons it is a tough sell.

One point that I think is worth noting with regard to judicial pay is that lower salaries make things especially difficult for lawyers who are supporting more than their immediate family. Minority lawyers are more likely to be the first member of their family to have a job as a lawyer. It can be very hard for them to take a dramatic pay cut, and they may be exactly the people you want to be taking the bench. That is worth considering.

DR: How hard was it making decisions when you had only eight justices on the court between the death of Justice Scalia in 2016 and the confirmation of Justice Gorsuch in 2017? Was that particularly difficult?

CJR: It was particularly difficult. We did work hard. I am very proud of the fact that we only had four cases that we were unable to break out of a four-four position — that is, we had only four that were affirmed by an equally divided court. There were two cases that we had reargued, but that is a small number given the situation.

We worked hard to see if we could find grounds on which enough of us could agree so that we could move the case along. Maybe not on the question we intended to decide, maybe not on the most momentous issue, but something where enough people could get on board so that the process could continue.

DR: What's the greatest pleasure of being chief justice of the United States, other than being able to do interviews like this?

CJR: I get to do the kind of work I enjoy, in

service of the country that I love, with eight wonderful people. And I can do it for as long as I want. That's a pretty good combination.

DR: What do you do for relaxation?

CJR: The way it works is you work full-out for ten months and then July and August are lighter. We are still on call. We still get emergencies. But we are away from each other.

Justice Louis Brandeis said he could do the twelve months' worth of work in ten months, but he could not do it in twelve months. I think there is a lot of wisdom to that. So I travel. I spend time with my wife and kids a little more than during the year.

DR: Do the justices socialize a lot with each other?

CJR: You know, we work very closely together all day for a long time.

DR: That's enough.

CJR: If you have interrelated interests, you will. Justice Ginsburg and Justice Scalia used to go to the opera. Maybe the other justices are socializing and I am just not invited. I don't know.

Ruth Bader Ginsburg during her nomination hearing, 1993.

DR: When you are the chief justice of the United States, can you go shopping in Washington or go to a restaurant without having people bother you or ask for selfies?

CJR: It is actually not that much of a problem. And sometimes as people recognize me, they just say hello. I would say in twelve years there have only been a half dozen cases where it wasn't pleasant.

I recall that once, a woman came up to me and was just so effusive about how grateful she was for a particular opinion. I just did not have the heart to tell her I was in dissent.

DR: Did your parents live to see you become

chief justice?

CJR: Yes.

DR: Wow. Did they say, "We never thought we'd live to see this"? Or did they say, "Well, maybe you could have done a little better"? You're chief justice of the United States. What do your parents say?

CJR: Well, it was better than when I got a clerkship on the Second Circuit. My grandmother was still alive. She called to congratulate me, and she said, "Don't feel bad that you didn't get the First Circuit."

ACKNOWLEDGMENTS

This book was the product of many people working together, and I want to acknowledge their help.

Two Librarians of Congress, Dr. Jim Billington and Dr. Carla Hayden, deserve enormous thanks from me for serving as the official hosts of the Dialogues. Both Jim and Carla assigned individuals to help recruit the authors whom I thought would work best for the series. Jim assigned the responsibility to his chief of staff, Liz Morrison. Carla asked Marie Arana, the former book editor of the *Washington Post* and a consultant to the Library, to undertake this task.

Both Liz and Marie did an outstanding job of contacting the authors and working out the schedule of their appearances. (Scheduling can be difficult, for we must always take into account the often changing congressional schedule.)

Many other people at the Library of Congress contributed to the success of the Dialogues and the making of this book. Helena Zinkham, director for Collections and Services and chief of the Prints and Photographs Division, and her staff were extremely helpful in tracking down images and related information, as were Becky Brasington Clark, head of the Library's publishing office, and her colleague Aimee Hess. Barbara Bair, a historian in the Manuscript Division, and many other curators at the Library did a wonderful job of preparing exhibits of manuscripts, photographs, and other objects from the Library's collections for each event. The Library's special events coordinators, most recently Kimberly McCullough, helped arrange the Congressional Dialogues dinners and tracked down interview transcripts. John Haskell, director of the John W. Kluge Center, program manager Travis Hensley, and other Kluge Center staff provided much-appreciated logistical support for the editing process. And Ryan Ramsey, Dr. Hayden's chief of staff, contributed invaluable coordination and feedback.

This book would not have been possible without the enthusiastic participation of so many distinguished authors. I would like to thank each of them for adjusting their schedules to appear at one of the Dialogues, to meet with the members of Congress at the pre-dinner reception, and to let me interview them in the Great Hall of the Library.

Bob Barnett, my law school friend of nearly forty years, was outstanding in his role representing me and working with Simon & Schuster.

Jonathan Karp, the president and publisher of Simon & Schuster and devoted supporter of history-related books, agreed to publish the book, and was very helpful with his ideas about organizing it and describing the whole Dialogues process.

One of Jonathan's best decisions was to assign the editorial role to Stuart Roberts, who also has a real interest in and knowledge of history. His editorial suggestions throughout the process were invaluable.

Among his best suggestions was the title. I proposed about two dozen possible titles. He proposed one that I instantly recognized was far better than anything I suggested.

To prepare the interviews for publication, I enlisted the help of Jennifer Howard, an accomplished editor and writer who shares my affection for the Library, for books, and for precise writing. Jennifer was highly recommended to me by Marie Arana, and I want to thank Marie again for that help with this undertaking.

I asked Jennifer to get the interview transcripts, to review them and edit them for accuracy, to get the authors to approve the edited versions of the transcripts, and to review and help edit the summary that I wrote about each author's background and interview. In all of these tasks, Jennifer did a spectacular job, for which I am very appreciative.

My personal staff was also extremely helpful with the Dialogues series and with this book.

My chief of staff, Mary Pat Decker, helped the Library of Congress to organize the events and helped to make certain that the congressional schedule, the authors' schedules, and my schedule could come together.

Laura Boring and Amanda Mangum were also indispensable in their work on the Dialogues series and on the preparation of the text of the book.

Robert Haben was quite helpful in preparing materials for me to review about each of the authors and their books. I made it a personal requirement to read every author's book (or books, when relevant). But Robert provided valuable research about what the authors had said in earlier interviews and what reviewers had already written about the books.

Finally, I would also like to acknowledge the support of so many members of Congress for the Dialogues series. Their attendance at the events, and inviting their spouses, staff, or constituents to attend, has certainly helped the Dialogues become an ongoing, bipartisan, and well-attended event in the unofficial congressional schedule.

Without each of the individuals described here, this book would not have come together. But to the extent that there are errors or omissions, they are undoubtedly my own responsibility.

ABOUT THE CONTRIBUTORS

A. Scott Berg is the author of five best-selling biographies. *Max Perkins: Editor of Genius* (1978) received the National Book Award; in writing *Goldwyn: A Biography* (1989), Berg was awarded a Guggenheim Fellowship; and his 1998 biography *Lindbergh* won the Pulitzer Prize. For twenty years, Berg was a friend and confidant of Katharine Hepburn, and his biographical memoir *Kate Remembered,* published upon her death in 2003, became the number-one *New York Times* best seller for most of that summer. *Wilson* (2013), his biography of Woodrow Wilson, received several history prizes. In 2018, he edited the Library of America's *World War I and America: Told by the Americans Who Lived It.* He is currently writing a biography of Thurgood Marshall.

Taylor Branch is an author and speaker known for his historical trilogy America in the King Years. The first book, *Parting the*

Waters: America in the King Years, 1954–63, won the Pulitzer Prize and other awards in 1989. Two successive volumes followed: *Pillar of Fire* (1998) and *At Canaan's Edge* (2006). Branch's 2009 memoir, *The Clinton Tapes: Wrestling History with the President,* chronicles a secret project to gather a sitting president's oral history. His 2011 cover story for the *Atlantic,* "The Shame of College Sports," touched off continuing national debate. Branch's latest book is *The King Years: Historic Moments in the Civil Rights Movement* (2013). He served as executive producer for the HBO documentary *King in the Wilderness* (2018). His career website is www.taylor branch.com.

H. W. Brands was born in Oregon, went to college in California, sold cutlery across the American West, and earned graduate degrees in mathematics and history in Oregon and Texas. He taught at Vanderbilt University and Texas A&M University before joining the faculty at the University of Texas at Austin, where he holds the Jack S. Blanton Sr. Chair in History. He writes on American history and politics, with books including *Heirs of the Founders, The General vs. the President, The Man Who Saved the Union, Traitor to His Class, Andrew Jackson, The Age of Gold, The First American,* and *TR.* Several of his books have been best sellers; two, *Traitor to His Class* and *The First American,* were finalists for the Pulitzer Prize.

Robert A. Caro has twice won the Pulitzer Prize, twice won the National Book Award, three times won the National Book Critics Circle Award, and also won virtually every other major literary honor for his biographies of Robert Moses and Lyndon Johnson, including the Gold Medal in Biography from the American Academy of Arts and Letters and the Francis Parkman Prize, awarded by the Society of American Historians to the book that best "exemplifies the union of the historian and the artist." In 2010, President Barack Obama awarded Caro the National Humanities Medal. Caro graduated from Princeton, was later a Nieman Fellow at Harvard, and worked for six years as an investigative reporter for *Newsday.* He lives with his wife, the writer Ina Caro, in New York City, where he is at work on the fifth and final volume of *The Years of Lyndon Johnson.*

Ron Chernow's best-selling books include *The House of Morgan,* winner of the National Book Award; *The Warburgs,* which won the George S. Eccles Prize; *The Death of the Banker; Titan: The Life of John D. Rockefeller, Sr.,* nominated for the National Book Critics Circle Award; *Washington: A Life,* which received the Pulitzer Prize for Biography; *Alexander Hamilton,* nominated for the National Book Critics Circle Award and adapted into the award-winning Broadway musical *Hamilton;* and *Grant,* which was named one of the ten best books of the year by the *New York Times.* Chernow has served as president of PEN America, has received eight honorary doctoral degrees, and was awarded the 2015 National Humanities Medal. He lives in Brooklyn, New York.

Doris Kearns Goodwin's interest in leadership began more than half a century ago when she was a professor at Harvard. Her experiences working for Lyndon B. Johnson in the White House and later assisting him on his memoirs led to her best-selling *Lyndon Johnson and the American Dream.* She followed up with the Pulitzer Prize–winning *No Ordinary Time: Franklin and Eleanor Roosevelt: The Home Front in World War II.* She earned the Lincoln Prize for the runaway best seller *Team of Rivals,* the basis for Steven Spielberg's Academy Award–winning film *Lincoln,* and the Andrew Carnegie Medal for *The Bully Pulpit,* the *New York Times* best-selling chronicle of the friendship between Theodore Roosevelt and William Howard Taft. She lives in Concord, Massachusetts.

Walter Isaacson is a professor of history at Tulane University and an advisory partner at the financial services firm Perella Weinberg. He is the past CEO of the Aspen Institute, where he is now a Distinguished Fellow, and has been the chairman of CNN and the editor of *Time* magazine. Isaacson's most recent biography is *Leonardo da Vinci.* He is also the author of *The Innovators: How a Group of Hackers, Geniuses, and Geeks Created the Digital Revolution; Steve Jobs; Einstein: His Life and Universe; Benjamin Franklin: An American Life;* and *Kissinger: A Biography.* A graduate of Harvard College and of Pembroke College of Oxford University, where he was a Rhodes Scholar, he is a member of the American Academy of Arts and Sciences, the Royal Society for the encouragement of Arts, and the American Philosophical Society.

David McCullough has twice received the Pulitzer Prize, for *Truman* and *John Adams,* and twice received the National Book Award, for *The Path Between the Seas* and *Mornings on Horseback.* His other acclaimed books include *The Johnstown Flood, The Great Bridge, Brave Companions, 1776, The Greater Journey,* and *The Wright Brothers.* His most recent book is *The Pioneers* (2019). He is the recipient of numerous honors and awards, including the Presidential Medal of Freedom, the nation's highest civilian award.

Jon Meacham is the author, most recently, of *The Soul of America: The Battle for Our Better Angels.* He received the Pulitzer Prize for *American Lion,* his 2008 biography of Andrew Jackson, and is also the author of *Thomas Jefferson: The Art of Power; Franklin and Winston: An Intimate Portrait of an Epic Friendship; Destiny and Power: The American Odyssey of George Herbert Walker Bush;* and *American Gospel: God, the Founding Fathers, and the Making of a Nation.* Meacham, a distinguished visiting professor who holds the Rogers Chair for the Study of the Presidency at Vanderbilt University, is a contributing writer to the *New York Times Book Review* and a contributing editor to *Time* magazine. He lives with his wife and three children in Nashville and in Sewanee.

Richard Reeves is the author of the Presidential Trilogy — *President Kennedy: Profile of Power, President Nixon: Alone in the White House,* and *President Reagan: The Triumph of Imagination* — and seventeen other books. A former chief political correspondent of the *New York Times* and chief correspondent of *Frontline* on PBS, he has made several award-winning documentary films. He is the senior lecturer of the Annenberg School for Communication and Journalism at the University of Southern California.

Cokie Roberts, who died on September 17, 2019, was a political commentator for ABC News and NPR. In her fifty years in broadcasting, she won countless awards, including three Emmys, and was inducted into the Broadcasting & Cable Hall of Fame. In addition to her reporting, Roberts wrote six *New York Times* best sellers, most dealing with the roles of women in U.S. history. Her books include the number-one best seller *We Are Our Mothers' Daughters,* an account of American women's roles and relationships over time; *Founding Mothers; Ladies of Liberty;* and *Capital Dames,* about women and Washington in the Civil War. Roberts and her husband, Steven V. Roberts, wrote a syndicated weekly newspaper column and wrote two books together: *Our Haggadah: Uniting Traditions for Interfaith Families* and *From This Day Forward.* In 2008, the Library of Congress named her a "Living Legend," one of the few Americans to have attained that honor. She was the mother of two and grandmother of six.

John G. Roberts Jr., chief justice of the United States, was born in Buffalo, New York. He married Jane Marie Sullivan in 1996 and they have two children, Josephine and Jack. He received an AB from Harvard College in 1976 and a JD from Harvard Law School in 1979. He served as a law clerk for Judge Henry J. Friendly of the United States Court of Appeals for the Second Circuit from 1979 to 1980 and as a law clerk for then associate justice William H. Rehnquist of the Supreme Court of the United States during the 1980 term. He was special assistant to the attorney general, U.S. Department of Justice (1981–82); associate counsel to President Ronald Reagan, White House Counsel's Office (1982–86); and principal deputy solicitor general, U.S. Department of Justice (1989–93). From 1986 to 1989 and 1993 to 2003, he practiced law in Washington, D.C. He was appointed to the United States Court of Appeals for the District of Columbia Circuit in 2003. President George W. Bush nominated him as chief justice of the United States, and he took his seat on September 29, 2005.

Jean Edward Smith was professor emeritus at the University of Toronto and Marshall University. He authored fourteen books, including *Lucius D. Clay: An American Life; John Marshall: Definer of a Nation; Grant; FDR; Eisenhower in War and Peace;* and *Bush.* His latest book, *The Liberation of Paris,* was published by Simon & Schuster in 2019, the seventy-fifth anniversary of the liberation.

Smith graduated magna cum laude from Princeton University in 1954, served seven years in the U.S. Army field artillery, and earned a PhD from Columbia University in 1964. He lived in Huntington, West Virginia, with his wife, Christine, whom he married in Berlin in 1959. Jean passed away in 2019.

Jack D. Warren Jr. is the executive director of the Society of the Cincinnati, the nation's oldest historical organization, founded in 1783 by George Washington and the officers of the Continental Army to perpetuate the memory of the American Revolution. He is also the founding director of the American Revolution Institute, created by the Society of the Cincinnati in 2012 to ensure public understanding and appreciation of the achievements of the Revolution. He is the author of *The Presidency of George Washington* (2000) as well as numerous essays on George Washington and other leaders of the American Revolution. He previously served as an editor of *The Washington Papers,* published by the University of Virginia Press. A native of Washington, D.C., he lives in Alexandria, Virginia, with his wife, Janet.

Jay Winik is one of the nation's leading public historians. He is the author of the *New York Times* best sellers *1944, The Great Up-*

heaval, and *April 1865,* which was a number-one best seller and is widely considered a classic. It was also turned into a TV special watched by more than fifty million people. Winik serves as the presidential historian for presidential inaugurations for Fox News, and was a historical advisor to the president of the National Geographic Networks. An elected Fellow of the Society of American Historians, he served on the governing council of the National Endowment for the Humanities, and was the inaugural historian-in-residence at the Council on Foreign Relations. He holds a BA from Yale, an MSc from the London School of Economics, and a PhD from Yale.

Bob Woodward is an associate editor of the *Washington Post,* where he has worked since 1971. He has shared in two Pulitzer Prizes, first in 1973 for the coverage of the Watergate scandal with Carl Bernstein, and second in 2003 as the lead reporter for coverage of the 9/11 terrorist attacks. He has authored or coauthored nineteen books, all of which have been national nonfiction best sellers. Thirteen have been number-one national best sellers. He has written books on nine presidents, from Nixon to Trump. *Fear: Trump in the White House,* which sold more than 1.1 million copies in its first week in the United States and broke the ninety-four-year-old first-week sales record of its publisher, Simon & Schuster, is the most detailed and penetrating portrait of a sitting president in the first years of an administration. More at www .bobwoodward.com.

IMAGE CREDITS

Endpapers

Front Endpaper: Universal History Archive/ Universal Images Group via Getty Images
Back Endpaper: George Rinhart/Corbis via Getty Images

1 Jack D. Warren Jr. on George Washington

Page 31: Portrait of Jack Warren by Jimmy Warren Photography
Page 31: Portrait of President George Washington. Library of Congress Prints and Photographs Division
Page 42: Painted and engraved by Charles Willson Peale, 1787. Library of Congress Prints and Photographs Division
Page 50: Lithograph published by E. Farrell, 1840–60. Library of Congress Prints and Photographs Division
Page 53: Photograph of an engraving by Amos Doolittle, 1790. Library of Congress

Prints and Photographs Division

Page 67: Lloyd J. Harriss Pies, Milwaukee, 1947. Library of Congress Prints and Photographs Division

Page 72: Lithograph by M. E. D. Brown, 1833, after a painting by Edward Savage. Library of Congress Prints and Photographs Division

2 David McCullough on John Adams

Page 75: Portrait of David McCullough by William B. McCullough

Page 75: Portrait of John Adams, lithograph by Pendleton's Lithography, c. 1828, after a painting by Gilbert Stuart. Library of Congress Prints and Photographs Division

Page 89: Henry Bowen's Chemical Print, Boston, 1850s. Library of Congress Rare Book and Special Collections Division

Page 103: "George Town and Federal City, or City of Washington." Aquatint by T. Cartwright from a painting by George Beck. Atkins & Nightingale, London and Philadelphia, 1801. Library of Congress Prints and Photographs Division

Page 104: Published by John Stockdale, London, 1798. Library of Congress Geography and Maps Division

3 Jon Meacham on Thomas Jefferson

Page 107: Portrait of Jon Meacham by Heidi Ross

Page 107: Portrait of President Thomas Jefferson. Library of Congress Prints and Photographs Division

Page 113: *Thomas Jefferson Papers.* Library of Congress Manuscript Division

Page 125: *Thomas Jefferson Papers.* Thomas Jefferson, drawn by his friend Tadeusz Kosciuszko, c. 1810. Aquatint by M. Sokolnicki. Library of Congress Prints and Photographs Division

Page 131: *Thomas Jefferson Papers.* Library of Congress Manuscript Division

Page 144: *Thomas Jefferson Papers.* Library of Congress Manuscript Division

4 Ron Chernow on Alexander Hamilton

Page 146: Portrait of Ron Chernow by Beowulf Sheehan

Page 146: Portrait of Alexander Hamilton, engraving by the Society of Iconophiles, 1902, reproducing the face from a 1792 John Trumbull portrait. Library of Congress Prints and Photographs Division

Page 154: Stereograph card published by the Keystone View Company, c. 1905. Library of Congress Prints and Photographs Division

Page 157: "A. Hamilton, drawn from life, Jan. 11, 1773." Photograph of a miniature watercolor and ink portrait, artist unknown. Library of Congress Prints and Photographs Division

Page 163: "Mrs. Alexander Hamilton." Engraving from a painting by Ralph Earl, 1780s. Library of Congress Prints and Photographs Division

Page 169: Title page of *The Federalist Papers,* printed in New York by John Tiebout, 1799. Library of Congress Rare Book and Special Collections Division

Page 187: Photograph by the Detroit Publishing Co., c. 1900–15. Library of Congress Prints and Photographs Division

5 Walter Isaacson on Benjamin Franklin

Page 189: Portrait of Walter Isaacson courtesy of the Aspen Institute

Page 189: "D. Benjamin Franklin." Mezzotint by Johann Elias Haid, 1780. Library of Congress Prints and Photographs Division

Page 197: Illustrated page from Benjamin Franklin's *Experiments and Observations on Electricity, Made at Philadelphia in America.* Engraving by Thomas Jefferys. Printed by E. Cave, London, 1751. Library of Congress Rare Book and Special Collections Division

Page 207: *Benjamin Franklin Papers.* Library

of Congress Manuscript Division

Page 211: "B. Franklin of Philadelphia." Mezzotint by Edward Fisher, 1763, after a painting by Mason Chamberlin, 1762. Library of Congress Prints and Photographs Division

Page 215: Woodcut published in the *Pennsylvania Gazette,* May 9, 1754. Library of Congress Serial and Government Publications Division

6 Cokie Roberts on Founding Mothers

Page 233: Portrait of Cokie Roberts courtesy of ABC News

Page 233: Portrait of Abigail Adams, engraving, c. 1850 after a portrait by Gilbert Stuart. Library of Congress Prints and Photographs Division

Page 249: National American Woman Suffrage Association Collection, Library of Congress Rare Book and Special Collections Division

Page 251: Lithograph by Dominique C. Fabronius, published by L. Prang & Co., Boston, c. 1864, after a 1796 portrait by Gilbert Stuart. Library of Congress Prints and Photographs Division

Page 260: Engraving by Charles Goodman and Robert Piggot, c. 1820, after a painting by Bass Otis. Library of Congress Prints and Photographs Division

Page 266: Carte de visite albumen photographic print by Mathew Brady, 1861. Library of Congress Prints and Photographs Division

Page 270: "Mrs. Franklin." Engraving by Joseph Andrews, 1840–45. Library of Congress Prints and Photographs Division

7 Doris Kearns Goodwin on Abraham Lincoln

Page 272: Portrait of Doris Kearns Goodwin by Annie Leibovitz

Page 272: Portrait of President Abraham Lincoln, carte de visite albumen photographic print by Alexander Gardner, Feb. 5, 1865. Library of Congress Prints and Photographs Division

Page 299: Albumen photographic print by Alexander Gardner, Oct. 3, 1862. Library of Congress Prints and Photographs Division

Page 304: Mezzotint print by Alexander Hay Ritchie, 1866, after a painting by Francis B. Carpenter. Library of Congress Prints and Photographs Division

Page 309: "Emancipation." Wood engraving by King & Baird Printers after a drawing by Thomas Nast, published by S. Bott, Philadelphia, 1865. Library of Congress Prints and Photographs Division

8 A. Scott Berg on Charles Lindbergh

Page 314: Portrait of A. Scott Berg by Aloma

Page 314: Portrait of Charles Lindbergh, photograph by Underwood & Underwood, 1927. Library of Congress Prints and Photographs Division

Page 322: Cartoon by Clifford K. Berryman, published in the *Washington Star,* March 1932. Library of Congress Prints and Photographs Division

Page 329: 1927 photograph of Charles Lindbergh, photographer unknown. Library of Congress Prints and Photographs Division

Page 333: Photograph by Martin J. Ford, 1927. Library of Congress Prints and Photographs Division

Page 344: Photograph by Hartsook, 1927. Library of Congress Prints and Photographs Division

9 Jay Winik on Franklin Delano Roosevelt

Page 357: Portrait of Jay Winik by Carl Caruso

Page 357: Portrait of President Franklin Delano Roosevelt, c. 1941. U.S. Farm Security Administration/Office of War Information Photograph Collection, Library of Congress Prints and Photographs Division

Page 371: U.S. Coast Guard photograph by Robert F. Sargent, June 6, 1944. Library of

Congress Prints and Photographs Division
Page 376: U.S. Army Signal Corps photograph, 1943. Library of Congress Prints
and Photographs Division
Page 391: U.S. Army Signal Corps photograph, March 1945. Library of Congress
Prints and Photographs Division

10 Jean Edward Smith on Dwight D. Eisenhower

Page 393: Portrait of Jean Edward Smith by
Rick Haye
Page 393: Portrait of President Dwight D.
Eisenhower, Oct. 14, 1957 — his sixty-
seventh birthday. MPI/Getty Images. Li-
brary of Congress Prints and Photographs
Division
Page 411: U.S. Army photograph, June 6,
1944. Library of Congress Prints and
Photographs Division
Page 413: Harris & Ewing photograph, mid-
to late 1950s. Library of Congress Prints
and Photographs Division
Page 416: Photograph by Colonial Studio,
Richmond, 1948. Library of Congress
Prints and Photographs Division
Page 422: "Vote for peace, vote for prosper-
ity, vote for Ike!" Campaign poster, 1952.
Library of Congress Prints and Photo-
graphs Division

11 Richard Reeves on John F. Kennedy

Page 432: Portrait of Richard Reeves by Patricia Williams

Page 432: Portrait of John F. Kennedy, 1961, White House Press Office photo. Library of Congress Prints and Photographs Division

Page 442: AP Photo/Anthony Camerano, Dec. 21, 1954

Page 449: AP Photo, Oct. 19, 1960. New York World-Telegram & Sun Newspaper Photograph Collection, Library of Congress Prints and Photographs Division

Page 451: "Kennedy for President: Leadership for the 60's." Campaign poster. Library of Congress Prints and Photographs Division

Page 463: AP Photo, July 3, 1963. New York World-Telegram & Sun Newspaper Photograph Collection, Library of Congress Prints and Photographs Division

Page 465: Photograph by Toni Frissell, September 12, 1953. Library of Congress Prints and Photographs Division

12 Taylor Branch on Martin Luther King Jr. and the Civil Rights Movement

Page 467: Portrait of Taylor Branch by Jean-Pierre Isbendjian

Page 467: Triptych portrait of Martin Luther King Jr., 1967, photographer unknown.

New York World-Telegram & Sun Newspaper Photograph Collection, Library of Congress Prints and Photographs Division

Page 489: Bettmann/Getty Images, May 14, 1961, United Press International photograph. Library of Congress Prints and Photographs Division

Page 494: Bettmann/Getty Images, August 28, 1963, United Press International photograph. New York World-Telegram & Sun Newspaper Photograph Collection, Library of Congress Prints and Photographs Division

Page 501: PhotoQuest/Getty Images, 1965, United Press International photograph. New York World-Telegram & Sun Newspaper Photograph Collection, Library of Congress Prints and Photographs Division

Page 503: AP Photo, December 4, 1964. New York World-Telegram & Sun Newspaper Photograph Collection, Library of Congress Prints and Photographs Division

13 Robert A. Caro on Lyndon B. Johnson

Page 507: Portrait of Robert Caro by Joyce Ravid

Page 507: Portrait of Lyndon B. Johnson, September 1955, photograph by Thomas J. O'Halloran. U.S. News & World Report Magazine Photograph Collection, Library of Congress Prints and Photographs Division

Page 521: LBJ and FDR, c. 1936–37, photographer unknown. Library of Congress Prints and Photographs Division

Page 530: Photograph by Bob Sandburg, January 3, 1958. *Look* Magazine Photograph Collection, Library of Congress Prints and Photographs Division Page

Page 545: Photograph by Warren K. Leffler, July 21, 1965. U.S. News & World Report Magazine Photograph Collection, Library of Congress Prints and Photographs Division

14 Bob Woodward on Richard M. Nixon and Executive Power

Page 548: Portrait of Bob Woodward by Lisa Berg

Page 548: Portrait of Richard Nixon, official White House photograph. Library of Congress Prints and Photographs Division

Page 559: "Nixon's the One!" Campaign poster, 1968. Yanker Poster Collection, Library of Congress Prints and Photographs Division

Page 565: Photograph by Thomas J. O'Halloran, October 1974. U.S. News & World Report Magazine Photograph Collection, Library of Congress Prints and Photographs Division

Page 576: Photograph by Warren K. Leffler, June 19, 1973. U.S. News & World Report Magazine Photograph Collection, Library of Congress Prints and Photographs Division

15 H. W. Brands on Ronald Reagan

Page 582: Portrait of H. W. Brands courtesy of the University of Texas

Page 582: Portrait of Governor Reagan at the White House, 1971, photograph by Marion S. Trikosko, 1971. U.S. News & World Report Magazine Photograph Collection, Library of Congress Prints and Photographs Division

Page 592: New York World-Telegram & Sun Newspaper Photograph Collection, Library of Congress Prints and Photographs Division

Page 606: *The Jack Kemp Papers.* Library of Congress Prints and Photographs Division

Page 615: Photograph by Carol M. Highsmith, 1986. Carol M. Highsmith Archive, Library of Congress Prints and Photographs Division

Page 622: "Bringing America Back!" Reagan-Bush campaign poster, 1984, by Dave Kilmer. Poster Collection, Library of Congress Prints and Photographs Division

Page 625: Portrait of Chief Justice John Roberts, courtesy of the Collection of the Supreme Court of the United States

Page 625: "The Chief Justices of the United States." Group portrait, c. 1894, lithograph by Kurz & Allison. Library of Congress Prints and Photographs Division

Page 640: Cartoon by Herb Block, cc. 1981, The Herb Block Foundation. Herbert L. Block Collection, Library of Congress Prints and Photographs Division

Page 641: U.S. Supreme Court photograph, 1981–83. Library of Congress Prints and Photographs Division

Page 652: AP Photo, May 17, 1954. New York World-Telegram & Sun Newspaper Photograph Collection, Library of Congress Prints and Photographs Division

Page 655: Photograph by Thomas J. O'Halloran, May 20, 1957. U.S. News & World Report Magazine Photograph Collection, Library of Congress Prints and Photographs Division

Page 661: Photograph by R. Michael Jenkins, 1993. Congressional Quarterly Photograph Collection, Library of Congress Prints and Photographs Division

ABOUT THE AUTHOR

David M. Rubenstein is a cofounder and coexecutive chairman of the Carlyle Group, one of the world's largest and most successful private investment firms.

Mr. Rubenstein is chairman of the boards of trustees of the John F. Kennedy Center for the Performing Arts, the Smithsonian Institution, and the Council on Foreign Relations; a fellow of the Harvard Corporation; a trustee of the National Gallery of Art, the University of Chicago, the Memorial Sloan-Kettering Cancer Center, Johns Hopkins Medicine, the Lincoln Center for the Performing Arts, the Institute for Advanced Study, and the World Economic Forum; a member of the American Academy of Arts and Sciences; and president of The Economic Club of Washington, D.C.

Mr. Rubenstein has served as chairman of the board of trustees of Duke University and cochairman of the board of the Brookings Institution.

Mr. Rubenstein is an original signer of the

Giving Pledge and a recipient of the Carnegie Medal of Philanthropy.

Mr. Rubenstein is the host of *The David Rubenstein Show: Peer-to-Peer Conversations* on Bloomberg Television and PBS.

Mr. Rubenstein, a native of Baltimore, is a 1970 magna cum laude graduate of Duke University, where he was elected Phi Beta Kappa. Following Duke, he graduated in 1973 from the University of Chicago Law School. Prior to cofounding Carlyle in 1987, Mr. Rubenstein practiced law in New York and in Washington, and during the Carter administration he was deputy assistant to the president for domestic policy.

President Franklin D. Roosevelt delivering his first inaugural address, March 4, 1933.

The employees of Thorndike Press hope you have enjoyed this Large Print book. All our Thorndike, Wheeler, and Kennebec Large Print titles are designed for easy reading, and all our books are made to last. Other Thorndike Press Large Print books are available at your library, through selected bookstores, or directly from us.

For information about titles, please call:
(800) 223-1244

or visit our website at:
gale.com/thorndike

To share your comments, please write:
Publisher
Thorndike Press
10 Water St., Suite 310
Waterville, ME 04901